Commercial
Leisure
Services

COMMERCIAL LEISURE SERVICES

Managing for Profit, Service, and Personal Satisfaction

John J. Bullaro
California State University, Northridge

Christopher R. Edginton
University of Oregon

Macmillan Publishing Company
New York

Copyright © 1986, Macmillan Publishing Company, a division of Macmillan, Inc.

Printed in the United States of America

Macmillan Publishing Company
866 Third Avenue, New York, New York 10022

Collier Macmillan Canada, Inc.

Library of Congress Cataloging in Publication Data

Bullaro, John J.
  Commercial leisure services.

  Bibliography: p.
  Includes index.
  1. Leisure industry—United States—Management.
I. Edginton, Christopher R. II. Title.
GV188.3.U6B85 1986   790'.01'35069   85-146
ISBN 0-02-316600-2

Printing: 1 2 3 4 5 6 7 8   Year: 6 7 8 9 0 1 2 3

ISBN 0-02-316600-2

PREFACE

The past several decades have witnessed an increasing interest in commercial leisure activities and an expansion of businesses such as health and fitness centers, game parlors, theme parks, home video sales and rental shops, and travel and tour bureaus. The implication of this dynamic growth is unmistakable: a fertile area of opportunity is opening up for those interested in new business ventures.

What is required to operate a commercial leisure business successfully? As William Demming, the famous industrial consultant who helped the Japanese develop their economic miracle, has often stated, no business can be run successfully without an adequate knowledge of the particular services and products it creates and distributes. Anyone with business expertise who lacks sufficient grounding in leisure concepts, practices, and philosophies may find it impossible to operate in this field. On the other hand, so may an individual who is firmly grounded in leisure theory but lacks business expertise. Ninety-five percent of all small businesses fail because the owner or manager or employees fail to understand thoroughly *all* aspects of their business.

This book was written to provide a basic understanding of the knowledge, skills, and values required for the successful management of commercial leisure service organizations. It blends conceptual, theoretical, and practical material and presents the steps necessary in establishing, marketing, and managing the human and financial resources in such a business. The book also offers guidelines for career development in the commercial leisure service industry and presents an overview of many different entrepreneurial opportunities in the field.

The book is divided into nine chapters and covers a diversity of topics such as:

- The relationship between the free enterprise system and the leisure service phenomenon
- The potential for career success within the field
- The preparation of feasibility studies, marketing analyses and strategy, and financial statements
- The particular language used in the leisure service business
- The most important legal aspects of the business
- The different kinds of ownership structure found in the business
- The different methods of generating and controlling revenue
- The ways computers may best be used in the business

Acknowledgments

A number of people contributed to the preparation, development, and completion of this textbook. First we wish to thank our editors at Macmillan, Ken Scott and Jim Anker, for their support. It was Ken's initial enthusiasm for the project that encouraged us to undertake it and Jim's continued support that enabled us to complete it. The authors would also like to acknowledge the contributions of their production supervisor, Hurd Hutchins, who became a major force in the development of this book. His commitment to the project, his thoroughness, and his editorial insight were greatly appreciated.

We would like to thank our two typists: Maarta Lawson in California, who typed the chapters written by the senior author, and Dawn Dougherty in Oregon, who typed the remaining ones. They did an outstanding job deciphering our rough drafts and retyping chapters promptly on short notice. We appreciate their support and commitment to our project.

We also wish to thank those who reviewed the manuscript prior to its publication and made many helpful suggestions: Dr. Joe Bannon, Dr. Craig Finney, Dr. Lynn Jamieson, and Dr. Jack Samuels. Their comments were an invaluable help in improving the organization of our material and the clarity of our writing. In addition we wish to acknowledge the many people who contributed ideas and inspiration to our project, including John Crompton, Arlin Epperson (who deserves special mention for his pioneering efforts in the area of commercial recreation), Craig Finney, Geoff Godbey, Dennis Howard, Jack Kelley, and Richard Kraus.

JJB
CRE

CONTENTS

6 Marketing for a Commercial Leisure Service Organization   207

7 Financial Management and Accounting   249

Commercial
Leisure
Services

Close-up: Northwest Whitewater Excursions

Galand E. Haas is the director and owner of Northwest Whitewater Excursions. This company, based in Eugene, Oregon, offers high adventure and outdoor recreation tours and services primarily focused on river rafting and fishing trips. Established in 1974, Northwest Whitewater Excursions attributes its success to "attention to quality and detail." Over the past decade, this organization has established and maintained an excellent reputation that has resulted in extensive return clientele.

Haas was graduated from the University of Oregon in 1974 with a degree in Park and Recreation Administration. An avid outdoorsman, he had supplemented his income through college by serving as a river guide and outfitter. Upon graduation, he had a strong desire to continue his involvement in the park and recreation field. Although he pursued job opportunities in the public park and recreation sector, his involvement in river guiding became increasingly profitable and began to command the majority of his attention and effort. Initially organized as a part-time venture, Northwest Whitewater Excursions today employs thirteen persons on a full-time and seasonal basis.

According to Haas, a key factor in the success of his organization has been the selection and recruitment of his personnel. "I try to hire persons who relate well to others, who are technically competent, and who present themselves well." He states that a second important factor is service. "Some people forget how important service is. People like to be treated as if they are important and that their business is not only desired, but also essential to the organization." Haas notes that many businesses neglect to personalize their services, which is a way that small businesses can compete successfully with larger businesses and organizations. In addition, Haas states that the comfort, safety, and character of the leisure experience are the factors that he and his staff key upon. They do not crowd participants into boats or otherwise scrimp on their excursions. They attempt to make participants feel that they are involved in a "quality" experience. Furthermore, participants are engaged in a full range of leisure activities, from volleyball games to nature hikes to fishing lessons. Haas also notes that much of the reason for the success of Northwest Whitewater Excursions is "our great love of the rivers. We take every opportunity to make the trip unforgettable, so that each participant will leave with an awareness and love of the environment, especially the wild rivers of the great Northwest."

Haas further maintains that a continuous positive rapport with his organization's clientele as well as his own personnel is essential to the successful operation of his business. Last, and perhaps most important, Haas suggests that living within the economic limits of the business is extremely crucial. "Economic reality was a difficult lesson to learn. I have learned that building a successful business is a gradual process; it must be done one step at a time." As one of the largest and fastest growing outfitter businesses in Oregon, Northwest Whitewater Excursions looks forward to another decade of prosperity and success.

1

Leisure: Prospects for Profit

During the past several decades, the individual and collective behavior of North Americans has changed dramatically. This change has affected both public and private organizations and institutions. The values concerned with work and leisure have undergone significant changes in our society. Work as a life focus has been coupled with a newer leisure ethic. We now live in a work hard/play hard society.

This new leisure ethic has directly influenced the type and amount of leisure products and services available to North Americans. In order to meet the increasing demands created by this new ethic, businesses, industry, and other commercial entities are vigorously entering the leisure market. A host of new enterprises have been established during the past several decades that cater to this rising demand for various leisure services and products.

This growth in the number and variety of commercial leisure service businesses has occurred at at time when public agencies providing leisure services have been forced to reduce their services as a result of tax referendums, inflation, and the public's general disillusionment with government. Increasingly, there is a need for people with the appropriate knowledge, skills, attitudes, and values to establish or operate commercial leisure service enterprises, but although there is an abundance of information about the organization and management of public park and recreation agencies, there are few resources available to those persons wishing to pursue a career in commercial leisure services.

This book focuses on the establishment, organization, management, and marketing of commercial leisure services. Its general purpose will be to help you understand the steps that are involved in establishing a small commercial leisure service enterprise, in organizing and managing its human and financial resources, and in marketing the service or product. There will also be a discussion of the legal aspects of such an enterprise. Furthermore, the book will explain the leisure experience and its relationship to the services provided by profit-oriented organizations. Finally, guidelines will be offered for individual career development and an overview presented of the status of programs and services, staffing, organizational patterns, and prospects for profit in a number of the settings in which commercial leisure service businesses operate.

Developing Your Career: What Are Your Motives?

In developing a career in the commercial leisure service area, you might first want to examine your motives. At first glance, it might appear that most people become involved in a business operation because of the financial opportunities. Certainly, commercial leisure service organizations have profit as a primary motive. However, there are other reasons for becoming involved in a commercial leisure venture that are equally important. From our perspective, there are three factors that can influence or motivate a person to pursue a career with a commercial leisure service organization. All three of these should be considered by those persons interested in pursuing a career in the commercial leisure services area. These are service to people, personal satisfaction, and financial remuneration (see Figure 1-1).

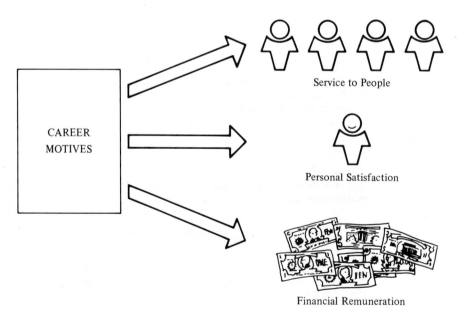

FIGURE 1–1. Motives for desiring a career in the commercial leisure area.

Service to People

Commercial leisure services invariably provide opportunities for consumers to participate in the activities and programs offered by the organization. A person who has a strong desire to work closely with other people to help them to meet their needs will be more likely to enjoy success in the commercial leisure service field than one who does not. Organizations that are wed to their consumers are, by and large, more successful than those organizations that are not. It is therefore essential that primary importance be placed upon serving people. This involves placing consumers first, ensuring that they are treated with respect, dignity, courtesy, and thoughtfulness, and ensuring that their welfare is upmost in the mind of the commercial leisure service professional.

A good exmple of a commercial leisure service organization that understands the importance of wedding itself to its consumers is Walt Disney Productions. For example, at Disneyland or Walt Disney World, participants are treated as "guests," not consumers. This philosophy of service to people can also be seen at McDonald's restaurants, where, as they themselves state, they "do it all for you." Whether a commercial leisure service organization is successful in wedding itself to its consumers can be determined from its ability to attract and retain its clientele. If people are attracted to a particular leisure experience offered by a commercial leisure service organization and they find that experience to be rewarding, satisfying, challenging, and worthwhile, there is a good probability that they will want to return and repeat their experience. They may also encourage others to "consume" the service or product. The ability to attract and retain consumers is the hallmark of a successful commercial leisure service organization. This is accomplished by having a philosophy of service to people.

What is the relationship between a commercial leisure service organization's philosophy regarding service to people and its profitability? Basically, people must perceive that a product or service has value to them and is of service to them or they will not purchase it. In other words, they must feel that they will derive some benefit from the service. If the commercial leisure service organization is able to cultivate this type of feeling in consumers, then with good management profitability will follow. As Konosuke Matsushita, founder of the Matsushita Electric Company, has noted, and we paraphrase, *profit is the reward for meeting people's needs.* In other words, there is a direct relationship between an organization's philosophy of service to people and its profitability.

Personal Satisfaction

Although many people start their own business with a view toward becoming wealthy, many small entrepreneurs own and operate their businesses because of the great personal satisfaction that they derive from the experience. Specifically, an owner or operator of a small business has a great deal of freedom in controlling the affairs of the business and, in addition, has opportunities for creativity, achievement, and status. Personal or life satisfaction therefore can be a major determinant in influencing a person to pursue a career in commercial leisure services.

Commercial leisure businesses also are often on the cutting edge of new developments in the leisure service field. Leisure can be very fad and trend oriented, and the service organizations must be able to respond very quickly to these changes. An environment often exists wherein a person has an opporunity to make greater use of his or her creative talents and abilities to respond to these changes. In addition, commercial leisure businesses may be more likely than public agencies to have the capital and other resources to explore and develop new and innovative programs, products, services, and facilities. This can be exciting and challenging to persons working in such enterprises.

Work in a commercial leisure service organization also provides opportunities for persons to take risks in making decisions that will affect their own well-being. This provides them with a sense of control and also enables them to develop a sense of self worth, dignity, and self respect. Persons who do not have an opportunity to "risk" may not have an opportunity to grow or to feel the exhilaration of risking and succeeding.

Another important motivating factor related to personal satisfaction is the idea that a person is doing something that is valued by others. Being appreciated by others, will, of course, increase self esteem. Having confidence in one's own abilities, in knowing that one can plan, organize, and implement a service that is seen as worthwhile by others and valuable enough to them to pay for it, is a very satisfying feeling. For example, the personal satisfaction may be greater for a person who successfully owns and runs a retail outlet specializing in sporting goods than will that of a person who runs the same type of sporting goods retail outlet but works for someone else.

Another factor that can influence a person's personal satisfaction is the power and influence that can be derived from involvement in commercial leisure service businesses, in particular ownership of such enterprises. Such persons are able to control the direction of the business and change or manipulate business operations if they feel it is warranted. They can use their skills and abilities to the maximum that they desire. In addition, they feel a greater sense of job permanency than persons whose job can be terminated by a "superior." It should be kept in mind, however, that small businesses of any type involve great risk, and their failure rate is high.

Financial Remuneration

Financial remuneration is, of course, a major factor motivating a person to purchase or develop a commercial leisure service enterprise. Financial remuneration, measured in terms of profit, also can be shared with successful and productive employees in an organization and thus serves as a motivating factor for those employees. In other words, the profit of an organization may be a major incentive for those who either own or have the opportunity to participate in the business.

Profit is an easily understood concept. It occurs when assets exceed liabilities. It is a measure of both the effectiveness and efficiency of the commercial leisure service organization in meeting the needs of its customers as well as its own goals. Efficiency involves the judicious use of organizational resources. For example, an organization's profit can be increased if a task can be completed with the same standards of quality but less resources. Effectiveness is the extent to which the organization identifies and reaches its financial objectives based upon a realistic assessment of meeting people's needs. The more effective an organization is, the more likely it will be to meet the needs of people and, in turn, its financial goals. Hence, the likelihood of profit is increased.

Profit is an important measure of an organization's success. As indicated previously, an organization's profitability and its relationship to serving people are tied to one another. A cost-efficient and effective organization serves the needs of people and does it in a profitable manner by ensuring that the individual consumer receives the type of service desired at the cost desired with profit to the organization. Profit, then, can be used as an evaluative tool and can indicate when an organization is operating effectively and efficiently and when it is not. For the owner of an organization or a person working within an organization and sharing in its profits, profit is a measure of the success of their individual and collective efforts.

As can be seen, profit as reflected in financial remuneration can be a powerful motivator. Some commercial leisure service organizations or individuals within such organizations may be motivated solely by the profit incentives inherent in such businesses. However, an organization that is motivated by a desire to be of service to people as well as by a desire for profit will be more likely to succeed financially and sustain profits over the long term than one that is not. Furthermore, profit or financial remuneration is thought of by some as a measure of personal achievement. Thus, a person's personal satisfaction, theoretically, can also be enhanced through the knowledge that financial objectives have been met or exceeded.

The three factors that motivate people to become involved in commercial leisure businesses are also the factors upon which the success of such organizations are based. The most successful commercial leisure service organizations are tied closely to their consumers and present their owners and employees with opportunities for individual achievement, recognition, status, and growth, and for financial remuneration based upon performance.

The Leisure Market

The leisure market is one of the largest and fastest growing sectors of the economies in the United States and Canada. Consider the growth of interest in professional sports, home entertainment, family-oriented theme and amusement parks, video arcades, and sporting and outdoor-related activities. Consider further the tremendous growth in industries that supply goods to this market. In 1982, Americans spent over $21.6 billion on radios, TV sets, records, and musical instruments, $15.8 billion on books, magazines, newspapers, and maps, $15.4 billion on sports and recreational equipment and durable toys, $14 billion on sports supplies and nondurable toys, $6.4 billion on movie theater and game tickets, $6.2 billion attending theme and amusement parks, and $4.5 billion on gardening supplies.[1]

The demand for leisure goods and services has grown consistently through the previous three decades. In 1965, Americans spent $58.3 billion for leisure goods and services. By 1972, this figure climbed to over $105 billion.[2] In 1982, spending for recreation and leisure in the United States exceeded $262 billion. In fact, leisure spending in 1982 exceeded the outlays for national defense or housing construction.[3] This is indeed a phenomenal growth rate, verifying the continued expansion and development of the leisure market. One out of every eight dollars spent by Americans today is spent for leisure goods or activities.

The leisure market is constantly changing and evolving. For example, in the past decade there has been a tremendous increase in opportunities for home entertainment. Cable television has played a major role in bringing more and varied options to people. This development has had a very dramatic impact on other segments of the leisure market. For example, in the late 1970s the sales of tapes and records declined drastically. The recording industry was given an immediate boost when audio was combined with video to produce a new dimension in home entertainment—videocassettes. An extension of this has been the tremendous success of MTV, which is a popular and sought after form of leisure entertainment among youths.

In fact, there has been a major transformation in the leisure market as a result of the evolution of electronic equipment. The quantum leap that is now being made in the processing of information via the computer and through audio and video systems will greatly alter the leisure market. In the future, audio, video, and the computer will be combined into an integrated home system. Such an integration of electronic media will provide a system that enables people to have their personal needs met more specifically. For example, the integrated home electronic system will provide people with greater access to information systems and more diverse forms of entertainment. The computer function of such a system could provide computer games, computer-controlled audio and video systems, and access to information, including schedules of activities and events, magazines, books, reviews, and so on. The audio component of an integrated system could provide instant communication with other persons or organizations via satellites or access to music and other forms of aural entertainment. The video function of an integrated electronic system could provide access to television, video tapes, video games, and home television production. Clearly, this sector of the leisure market will develop rapidly within the next several decades.

Another example of the rapid change that exists in the leisure market is the area of consumption of leisure goods. In the 1970s for example, tennis was a very popular and expanding sport. Participation in tennis rose nearly 400 percent between 1969 and 1971. The popularity of tennis affected the types of goods and services that people purchased. Today, over $340 million is spent on tennis and tennis-related goods and services annually. In fact, the entire fitness area has grown tremendously in the past several years. The physical fitness segment of the leisure market is a $30 billion a year business.[4] Over $1 billion is spent on running shoes, $5 billion on clothes, $3 billion on health clubs, $50 million on diet and exercise books, $1 billion on bicycles, $40 million on dance and exercise programs, $200 million on barbells and weights, and $2 billion on company fitness programs.[5]

Travel and tourism is another area of the leisure market. It has been estimated by the U.S. Travel Data Center that over $191 billion a year is spent by people traveling in the United States.[6] According to Jafari, in 1981 spending on travel generated 4.6 million jobs paying $40 billion in wages and salaries.[7] Jafari goes on to note that foreign tourists visiting the United States spent $12.2 billion and that international tourism receipts were $106 billion in 1981. He also points out that when the receipts for domestic tourism and international tourism of all nations are combined, the amount spent is $700 billion, or 6 percent of the total gross national product of the world.

There are numerous other examples of the development and expansion of the leisure market. Consider the significant impact that television as an entertainment form has had on North Americans. Americans today watch nearly seven hours of television per individual per day.[8] Spectator sports have also increased rather dramatically. As indicated in *U.S. News & World Report*, automobile racing attracted 51.0 million spectators; thoroughbred racing, 50.1 million; major league baseball, 43.7 million; college football, 35.5 million; college basketball, 30.7 million; harness racing, 27.4 million; greyhound racing, 20.8 million; NFL football, 13.4 million; minor league baseball, 12.6 million; NHL hockey, 11.5 million; soccer, 11.4 million; and NBA basketball, 10.7 million.[9]

All of these examples are indicative of the growth, diversity, and scope of the leisure market. It is a dynamic and constantly evolving market. There are many opportunities for individual initiative and risk in responding to leisure needs as they are created and as they develop. Because of its growth and rapid changes, the leisure market can be well served by commercial leisure service business ventures that have the capacity for flexibility and responsiveness.

Trends in the Leisure Market

Although it is very difficult to predict specific trends in the leisure market because of the constantly evolving attitudes of North Americans toward leisure, we feel that there are some trends that can be identified. Perhaps the most significant trend that is becoming evident is the expansion of the range of choices for leisure available to each person. We live in a society in which the expansion of information and its availability is increasing exponentially. We have moved from an industrial-based society contingent upon the mass production and consumption of goods and services to an information–based society where individual preferences and choices can be accommodated. We live in a society where people have instantaneous access to diverse forms of leisure, a society where personal choice is the controlling variable. Leisure trends and ideas will develop from the "bottom up" rather than the "top down." Thus, those commercial leisure service organizations that recognize the importance of individual choice will be successful. With the above in mind, the following trends have been identified:

High-Adventure and High-Risk Leisure Activities. Activities that provide opportunities for high-risk experiences are increasing. For example, in outdoor recreation, such activities as whitewater rafting, rappelling, spelunking, hang gliding, wind surfing, flying ultralight aircraft, and similar ventures will probably increase in popularity.

Self-Improvement and Self-Development Programs. Many individuals desire the benefits that can be obtained from participation in programs oriented toward intellectual and spiritual self improvement. The sales of books, periodicals, and products in this area have increased dramatically during the past decade.

Technological and Electronic Entertainment.   Integrated computer/audio/video systems are increasing dramatically the number and diversity of leisure and entertainment services available. This will most likely result in a host of new forms of entertainment related to technology, including further expansion of activities such as video games, cable TV, videocasettes, and so on.

Leisure Information and Related Services.   There has been an expansion of specialized leisure information sources and services made available to the public in recent years. We have moved from publications such as *Life*, *Look*, and the *Saturday Evening Post* to more specialized periodicals. For example, in the area of high-adventure, high-risk leisure activities, the following periodicals are representative of those currently available on the market: *Off Belay*, *Nordic Skiing*, *Backpacker*, and *Adventure Travel*. All of these publications have come into existence since 1976.

Continued Expansion and Distribution of Leisure Goods.   As personal choice increases, the scope and variety of leisure goods are increasing, as are retail outlets uniquely designed to distribute them by catering to specific niches within the marketplace. A good example of this has been the growth of goods related to personal fitness, especially those related to jogging.

Intense Personal Leisure.   People are increasingly looking for leisure experiences that provide a high degree of personal involvement or intimacy with others. This can be seen in the success of ventures such as Disneyland and Walt Disney World, where the consumer often becomes a part of the fantasy, not just an observer. It can also be seen in the growth of participation in sports events as well as the attempt by broadcasters of televised sports events to involve spectators in a more intimate way. For example, the United States Football League provides opportunities for ABC sports commentators to interview players on the sidelines during the game after crucial plays. The sports commentator is there to allow spectators to become intimately involved in the sports experience by drawing out the players' feelings, thoughts, and opinions of play at the height of the game. In this way, the spectator personally, yet vicariously, shares in the exhilaration felt by the players.

The Desire to Be with Others.   Related to the desire for intense personal leisure is the desire to engage in leisure activities with others. People want to be with other people. There are numerous examples of commercial leisure service organizations that provide opportunities for people to socialize with others. Entertainment and eating establishments provide the most obvious example of this growing trend in the leisure market. As previously indicated, the growth of spectator sports events is another example of this phenomenon.

Entertainment and Eating Establishments. It is likely that the fast food industry will continue to expand. In addition, a greater number of dining establishments are being developed that have leisure entertainment as a drawing card for consumers. Pizza Time Theaters in the San Francisco Bay area present an entire leisure experience via the use of audioanimatronics. The Magic Time Machine restaurant chain creates a physical and social environment focused on a "fantasy" dining experience.

Travel and Tourism. North Americans are traveling in record numbers. In 1983 alone, 4.2 million Americans visited Europe.[10] Not only are Americans traveling more internationally, but also in larger numbers domestically. This has direct implications for the hospitality industry and travel agencies as well as those locations (end destination points) visited by travelers.

Home Entertainment. Because of the increased availability of technological and electronic hardware and software, people increasingly have access to such equipment in their homes for entertainment purposes. Thus, the home will become a focal point for many leisure pursuits and interests. The television today is a "hearth" around which families tend to congregate. A large segment of the leisure home entertainment industry is centered on the sales of equipment that can be used in conjunction with television sets. Television has provided the basis for the use of videocassettes, video games, computers, and so on.

Fitness and Leisure. North Americans seem to be currently consumed with fitness and well-being. This leisure trend has tremendous implications not only for the delivery of services but also for the creation and distribution of goods. Running, jogging, aerobics, health clubs, squash, weightlifting, "health foods," and walking all are an increasing part of our popular culture. Information and services related to fitness, health, and well-being have increased dramatically and will probably continue to do so.

Wellness and Leisure. North Americans are becoming increasingly interested in a concept tied closely to the fitness movement known as "wellness." Wellness focuses on a person's total lifestyle. This would include nutrition, diet, preventative health, exercise, stress management, and leisure activity management. The wellness movement requires people to assume personal responsibility for their well-being. Because wellness can affect people's satisfaction with life, hence their productivity on the job, many businesses have successfully used wellness programs to increase the physical, mental, and emotional well-being of their employees. Such programs obviously benefit the business as well as its employees. Wellness and leisure programs often focus on finding a balance between a person's recreational pursuits and work.

Again, we are in a period of time where individual choices are becoming predominant in the marketplace. In society today, we acknowledge and accept diverse lifestyles, values, and attitudes. These, in turn, affect the leisure market. Discussing the lifestyle of the 1980s, the *U.S. News & World*

Report suggested that "people across the nation are mixing and matching, blending the traditional with the new, making things up as they go. In the process they are sometimes cautious, feeling their way, trying to find quality, to make things last. But once in a while, they will take a flyer because they've retained one thing Americans are most noted for—their sense of humor. The early 80's may be a time of anxiety, but it is also a time of fun."[11]

Commercial Leisure Services

Commercial leisure services are intangible. The person or organization involved in providing leisure services helps the consumer accomplish some desired end. A service is something that is provided by an organization that is perceived by a consumer to be useful, beneficial, or otherwise satisfying. Commercial leisure services not only involve the creation of activities, programs, and facilities (the "leisure experience" itself), but also may involve the wholesaling and retailing of leisure experiences and products. For example, the owner of a sporting goods store basically provides a service to consumers by arranging to have a selection of products available that can be purchased conveniently. The owner of a sporting goods store acts as a middleman between the manufacturer or wholesaler of the products and the consumer. Thus, we can think of a commercial leisure service as a process that helps individuals obtain products and attain leisure experiences that they perceive as being beneficial.

For the moment, let us focus on the creation of the leisure experience. Creating a leisure experience involves arranging for/or assisting people to be placed in a social, physical (man-made), or natural environment (see Figure 1-2). This may involve planning and organizing, assembling materials and supplies, arranging the use of facilities, providing leadership, or other actions that lead to the creation of opportunities for leisure. There are many ways in which services can be delivered. For example, the creation of a social environment may involve the planning and implementation of such activities as rock concerts, festivals, or fairs. These types of activities may provide such benefits as self awareness, fantasy, fun, enjoyment, excitement, and social contact. Physical environments might include golf courses, swimming pools, health spas, fitness centers, and racquetball courts. The use of these types of facilities might bring the consumer a sense of status, physical conditioning, acquisition of skill, and social contact. Last, natural environments might include ocean beaches, mountains, rivers, deserts and other such areas. A desire for physical challenge and a feeling of awe, beauty, spiritual awareness, and solitude are benefits that may be sought by consumers in the natural environment. A leisure experience created by a commercial leisure service organization may involve just one of these three environments or a combination of them.

Persons involved in providing leisure services must be able to deal effectively with people. The provision of commercial leisure services involves attracting consumers to various types of environments, ensuring that they have a beneficial experience, and motivating them to repeat their experience. In short, the provision of services involves "people processing."

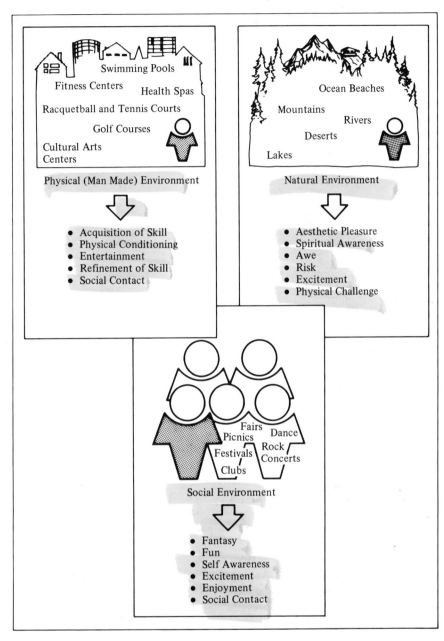

FIGURE 1–2. The leisure experience.

Even though a commercial leisure service organization may provide a product to a person, generally it will not be involved in the manufacturing of the product, but rather its distribution. The distribution efforts of a commercial leisure service organization may involve the sale of a product, the organization and implementation of an activity, the organization and implementation of a program, the provision and management of a facility, or a combination of these.

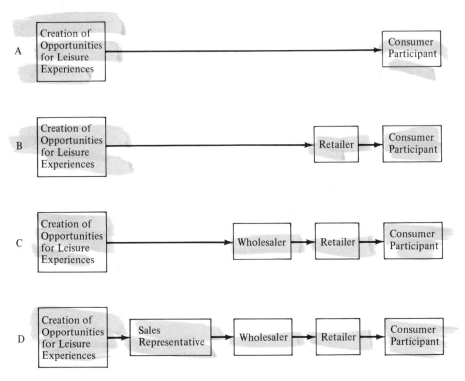

FIGURE 1–3. Channels of distribution for leisure experiences.

Channels of Distribution

As has been indicated, a commercial leisure service organization may provide the leisure experience and may also make arrangements that enable the consumer to become aware of the availability of the experience and participate in it. Or it can ask others to help in the distribution of the service. This is where wholesalers and retail agents may play a role. Figure 1-3 represents the four channels of distribution that can be used to provide leisure services to consumers.

In the first channel of distribution, channel A, the creator of the leisure experience or product sells directly to consumers. A commercial leisure service organization using this channel of distribution has direct influence over the manner in which its services are presented to its consumers. Selling directly to the consumer can, in some situations, be more profitable than selling through wholesalers, retailers, or other service agents. Many small commercial leisure service organizations use the direct approach in distributing their services to consumers. They attract consumers by using newspaper advertisements, direct mail advertisements, or personal presentations.

The second channel of distribution, channel B, involves the use of a middleman—the retailer. The organization creating the leisure service or product sells it to the retailer who, in turn, resells it to the consumer. The retailer may take the service on consignment. That is, the retail agent offers the service and receives a fixed fee or percentage upon sale. The retailer deals directly with the consumer. Retailing involves the sale of services, in small quantities at a time, directly to the consumer. Some of the functions provided by retailers include:

1. Selecting the leisure services and products that the consumer will buy. The retailer must carefully study sales trends, changes in taste, style, consumer attitudes, the actions of competitors, and so on.
2. Stocking leisure products so that they are readily available to consumers when required.
3. Making products and services available to consumers in quantities suitable for individual needs (as opposed to a wholesaler, who sells in bulk).
4. Packaging, promoting, and displaying products and services in ways consistent with consumer needs, interests, and desires.
5. Providing personal attention to consumers such as greeting them and helping them determine their needs.
6. At the discretion of the retailer, extending credit to consumers.
7. In some instances, delivering products or services for free or for a charge. This may include delivering the consumer to the service.[12]

Distribution channel C finds the addition of a wholesaler to the distribution process. A wholesaler acts as a middleman between the producer and the retailer. Wholesalers reduce the interaction that a producer would have to have with a large number of retailers. For example, if the activities of a commercial leisure service producer were sold through five hundred retail outlets, it would be easier to deal with ten wholesalers than with the retail outlets. Wholesalers provide the following services to producers:

1. Buying leisure products and services from the producer or selling them on behalf of the producer.
2. Informing the producer of the state of the market.
3. Storing leisure products on their way to the retailer.
4. Dividing and packaging leisure products into more convenient quantities.
5. Advising producers regarding promotional material and distributing it for them.
6. Visiting regularly with retailers.
7. Delivering products and services promptly to retailers where and when required.[13]

The wholesaler also provides services to retailers who distribute leisure products and services directly to the consumer. Some of the services provided by wholesalers to retailers include:

1. Taking orders for a great variety of leisure products and services in one visit of the wholesaler's salesman, thus providing the retailer with a saving of time.
2. Supplying leisure products and services in almost exactly the quantities or scope desired.
3. Delivering leisure products more quickly than would be possible from the producer.

4. Extending credit to retailers where possible because of better knowledge of local retailers and funds for financing than the producer.
5. Providing sales promotional aids (e.g., brochures and displays) and sales advice to retailers.[14]

The last distribution channel, channel D, finds the addition of a sales representative to the process. In this situation, the producer contracts with a sales organization to represent his or her products or services to a wholesaler. This additional middleman is employed so that a producer will not have to deal with a large network of wholesalers and retailers. It is economically more efficient to work through a sales representative. This person does not take title to the leisure goods and services but receives a commission for those services or products that are sold. Sales representatives are often employed because they have special knowledge of the market.

This distribution system provides an efficient way to deliver services and products to consumers. It provides a method that can cater to geographic preferences, lifestyle changes, and other consumer needs, interests, and desires. All of these channels for delivering leisure experiences and products are part of a "service." Therefore, when we refer to commercial leisure services, we are referring not only to the services themselves, but to the network used to distribute these services.

The travel and tourism area provides a good example of how a service can be distributed. Let us assume, for the purposes of this example, that

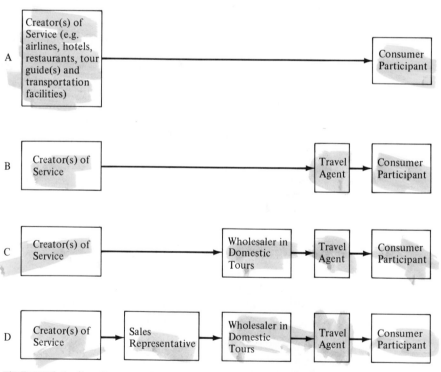

FIGURE 1–4. Channels of distribution for a tour to Hawaii.

a person traveling to and sightseeing in Hawaii will need a variety of services to make the leisure experience complete. Figure 1-4 presents the various channels of distribution that could be used to provide the consumer with the opportunity to experience leisure in Hawaii. The major tourist attraction would be the natural environment, the ocean, the beaches, the geological sites, and the horticultural displays and historical sites. An individual consumer wanting to experience this environment would need some means of transportation to Hawaii, as well as accommodations, meals, tour guides, and transportation at the end destination point.

In the first channel of distribution (A), the consumer would interact directly with each of the various businesses providing the services desired. For example, the consumer would contact the airline in order to purchase a ticket, would reserve his or her own hotel room, and would make provisions with local tour operators to travel to points of interest. As can be seen, this could be a very time-consuming and disorganized process if not properly coordinated by the consumer. The next channel of distribution (B) finds the travel agent purchasing airline tickets and accommodations on behalf of the consumer. The travel agent may accomplish this in two ways. First, the agent may arrange for services by directly contacting the producer of the service (e.g., the airline). On the other hand, the agent may solicit the services of a wholesaler who in turn makes the necessary arrangements with the various producers of services, as shown in the third channel of distribution (C). Travel agents and wholesalers are paid a commission by the producers for their services.

Distribution channel D would find a sales representative working with wholesalers on behalf of the producers. A producer interested solely in the production of a product or service and not in the marketing of the product or service would use the services of a sales representative to assume this function and sell the product or service to wholesalers. Major hotels, major airlines, and other large commercial leisure businesses often hire sales representatives to sell and promote their products or services to wholesalers.

Commercial Leisure Service Organizations

A commercial leisure service organization can be thought of as a business the primary purpose of which is to serve people while at the same time making a profit. A commercial leisure service organization has two basic characteristics. First, it creates and distributes leisure services; second, it has as its primary goal, profit. In this text, we have chosen to focus on business firms that provide "services" as opposed to those that are engaged in the manufacturing of products for sale. We will use the term *commercial leisure service organization* interchangeably with the term *commercial leisure service business*. We will also use the terms *consumer* and *participant* interchangeably. Furthermore, when referring to those persons who either own or manage a commercial leisure service enterprise, we will use the terms *owner*, *manager*, or *entrepreneur*.

We have focused our attention on the management of small commercial leisure service organizations. Nearly 60 percent of the people employed in the private sector of the economy according to the U.S. Department of Labor are employed in small businesses. Small businesses are those that employ 100 people or less. Businesses with 500 employees or more represent a very small fraction of the total number of private sector organizations. Less than 1 percent of the businesses that exist in the United States and Canada today have more than 500 employees. In terms of the total number of businesses, small ones make up 95 percent of the total.

Why have we focused on the management of small commercial leisure service organizations? There are three primary reasons. First and most obvious is the sheer number of small businesses compared with large businesses; as just noted, 95 percent of all businesses are small businesses. Second, employment opportunities will be greater with small businesses, as indicated by the distribution of the work force. Third, we feel very strongly that small businesses are uniquely suited to the types of changes that are now occurring in society. Specifically, we are moving from an industrial-based society to a postindustrial society. The postindustrial society, also known as the technological society or information-based society, reflects a shift in thinking that will place importance on self-initiating behavior, economies of scale, networking, decentralization, and an expansion of human rights acted out in an entrepreneurial environment.

As Naisbitt reported in his popular book *Megatrends*, there were approximately 93,000 new businesses started in the 1950s; in the 1980s there were over 600,000 new businesses started.[15] Obviously, we are going through a great period of change, a period of change that will be marked by an expansion and extension of entrepreneurial activity. As options within society have increased, there has been an expansion of the range of personal choices available to people. We live in a society that has diverse regional variances in taste, styles, and patterns of consumption. These factors suggest that there is a need for smaller commercial organizations to respond to these diverse lifestyles and cultural patterns. The action is clearly in the marketplace.

We can look back historically to the 1880s and 1890s in the United States and Canada for a similar flurry of entrepreneurship. As we moved from an agrarian society to an industrial one, there was a need to respond to the changes that were occurring. Small businesses provided the bulk of the innovations, new products, and management strategies used in responding to this change. Not only were there tremendous changes in the private sector but also in the public sector, as witnessed by the development of urban and regional park systems, playgrounds, community centers, and other social services.

Small commercial leisure service businesses are particularly suited to adapting and responding to change. They are very flexible in nature. A small business can be started with a relatively small amount of capital. They are further characterized by their closeness to their consumers or participants. The owner or manager often will have personal knowledge of the people served by the organization. Small commercial leisure service organizations can also specialize their services in such a way that they concentrate on a unique portion of the market. Thus, in a society where individual options are increasing and where economies of scale are important, small commercial leisure service organizations have the ability to respond to consumer needs in an effective manner.

Types of Commercial Leisure
Service Organizations

As mentioned previously, commercial leisure service organizations can be classified generically (in terms of producer, retailer, wholesaler, and so on). Commercial leisure service organizations can also be classified according to their functions. In other words, commercial leisure service organizations can be described in terms of the work that a person would do within these types of businesses. This classification system includes five different areas of business:

1. Travel and tourism
2. Entertainment services
3. Leisure services in the natural environment
4. Hospitality/food services
5. Retail outlets

We feel strongly that these five areas offer great opportunities for persons wishing to pursue a career in the commercial leisure service area.

Travel and Tourism. Commercial leisure service organizations providing travel and tourism services are basically responsible for transporting individuals to points of interest, tourist attractions, or end destination points. This could involve operating a tour and travel agency, serving as a tour guide, or providing transportation to and from attractions. Some of the positions that might be held in a commercial leisure service organization with a focus on travel and tourism are sales manager, travel agent, reservations clerk, host/guide, sales representative, or promotions director.

Hospitality Services. Hospitality services are provided by leisure service organizations that are involved in housing and feeding consumers. Organizations in the hotel management areas, including those that provide accommodations and food to people seeking leisure experiences, are involved in hospitality services. Resorts are a good example of commercial leisure service organizations that offer a hospitality service focusing on leisure. Food and beverage services are among the fastest growing services in the United States and Canada. This is especially true of the fast food industry and eating establishments where dining is considered a leisure experience.

Entertainment Services. There are a variety of entertainment services in the commercial leisure service sector. For example, professional athletics provides spectator entertainment as a leisure experience. Other commercial leisure service organizations providing entertainment include movie theaters, night clubs, bowling alleys, amusement parks, race tracks, circuses and carnivals, video arcades, tennis and racquet clubs, and fitness centers. There are diverse job opportunities for persons in these businesses—from manager of a facility to promotions director, sales manager, or booking agent. The entertainment industry is dynamic, often changing dramatically with new leisure trends.

Leisure Services in the Natural Environment. As previously mentioned, a variety of leisure services are dependent upon natural resources for their implementation. North Americans often seek out opportunities for adventure in the out-of-doors and increasingly are willing to pay for that opportunity, and there are a host of job opportunities that are emerging in this area. Primarily, persons are working as tour guides, hosts, instructors, and interpreters of the environment. Aquatic activities have also grown tremendously in popularity, providing many opportunities for persons to work in and around lakes, ocean fronts, and rivers.

Retail Outlets Focusing on the Sale of Leisure Goods. The growth in popularity of leisure goods and products in the past several decades has been enormous. There is a diversity of goods and products on the market today, ranging from recreation vehicles to sporting goods to toys and play equipment to clothing. Work opportunities in the retail area include serving as a salesperson, manager, district manager, or wholesaler. A good example of a commercial business that is involved with the sale of leisure goods and has seen tremendous growth is the Nike Corporation of Oregon. Established in 1975, this corporation today dominates the running shoe industry in America.

As can be seen, there are a number of different types of leisure service organizations. Such organizations exist in every community; however, some communities may have proportionately more of one type of leisure service organization, which is a reflection of the interest of the community. For example, some communities may have a large number of commercial leisure service organizations that cater to the entertainment needs of its citizens and other communities may have a larger number of commercial leisure organizations involved in hospitality services or retail sales. In other words, each community will have the needs and desires of its members and tourists reflected by its commercial leisure organizations.

The Spirit of Entrepreneurship

To be an entrepreneur means that you are willing to take risks, that you have vision, persistence and determination, creativity, and faith in yourself and your ideas. The entrepreneur of today is a person who is concerned with the needs of people and finding methods to meet those needs by creating unique services or by improving existing services. The task of the entrepreneur is not an easy one. It is challenging and at times frustrating. It requires a great deal of self discipline and self sacrifice. For those who succeed, however, the rewards can be great, both in terms of material gain and personal satisfaction.

Simply, an entrepreneur is a person who owns or invests in a business. This person takes a risk by investing time, talent, or financial resources to contribute to the operation of the business. An entrepreneur is a person who brings about innovation by creating new services that serve existing needs or help to create new markets. Entrepreneurial activity occurs when people are free to speculate or participate in ventures that result in products of utility or value to society.

By venturing into areas that entail risk, the entreprenuer must deal with uncertainty. Entrepreneurs often have to break with tradition to develop creative and innovative products and services, even though conventional wisdom might suggest a more cautious posture. Successful entrepreneurs are able to analyze and perceive things in new and bold ways. They are proactive rather than reactive in dealing with uncertainty. By listening to consumers and acting on the information received from them, entrepreneurs attempt to serve consumers in a way that will be mutually beneficial.

Entrepreneurs are not simply opportunists catering to and responding to market conditions; rather, they are pacesetters of opportunity. They do not merely consume fiscal, physical, human, and technological resources but rather define the value of our capital resources, create opportunities of employment for others, produce new technology, and define the worth of physical resources. As George Gilder has written in *The Spirit of Enterprise:*

> The capitalist is not merely dependent on capital, labor and land; he or she defines and creates capital, lends value to land, and offers his or her labor while giving effect to the otherwise amorphous labor of others. He or she is not chiefly the tool of markets but a developer of opportunity; not an optimizer of resources but an inventor of them; not a respondent to existing demands but an innovator who evokes demand; not chiefly a user of technology but a producer of it. . . . In their most inventive and beneficial role [entrepreneurs seek to start] a new fashion, create the unique product, the marketing breakthrough, the novel design.[16]

As can be seen, the work of an entrepreneur is dynamic, diverse, creative, and challenging. Although we often think of the entrepreneur as acting in his or her own self interest, clearly, being an entrepreneur involves giving of oneself in order to provide service to others. Because of the nature of the entrepreneurial role, persons are challenged to put forth their best effort and to maximize their potential to be resourceful and responsive to constantly changing environmental conditions.

The Free Enterprise System

In Canada and the United States, the system that results in the creation and distribution of products and services is known by various terms, including *the free enterprise system, the private enterprise system, a market system,* or *capitalism.* It is based on the idea that the welfare of the individual and society is best served when economic decisions are made on the basis of individual free choice. In contrast to socialistic countries, our free enterprise system operates without a predetermined centralized economic plan.

In our free enterprise system, the basis of decision making rests with the individual citizen. The individual decides what to produce, how much to produce, and what the cost will be. The individual consumer also decides what to consume, how much to consume, and what price he or she is willing to pay. In general, both business people and consumers are free to decide how they will go about earning their income and also how they will expend their financial resources. In Canada and the United States we have a free enterprise system with some government control, but the heart of the decision-making process remains with the individual members of the society.

The free enterprise system is a mechanism that helps society determine how it will make choices concerning the production and consumption of its resources. In any given society, at any time, there are never enough resources to meet all of the needs of all of the people all of the time. Therefore, decisions must be made about which resources will be used and consumed. The free enterprise system is based on the notion that individuals are in the best position to make the decision about which products or services best meet their needs.

Has the free enterprise system succeeded? By most standards, the answer to this question is yes. However, there have been times during the past several hundred years, since Adam Smith published his tenets on a free enterprise system in 1776 in a book entitled *An Inquiry into the Nature and Causes of the Wealth of Nations*, that our free enterprise system has been less than adequate. We have experienced depressions, recessions, periods of high unemployment, and inflation. But by and large the free enterprise system has produced one of the highest standards of living in the world today. It is interesting to note that social reform movements have throughout the years served to take the rough edges off of capitalism and have strengthened it as an economic and social process.

The free enterprise system has a number of distinctive characteristics (see Figure 1-5). These characteristics, again, focus on individual rights. Archer has suggested that there are six distinguishing characteristics of our free enterprise system. They include

1. The right to own property
2. The right to earn profit
3. The right to compete in business
4. The right as an employer to hire labor and other productive resources

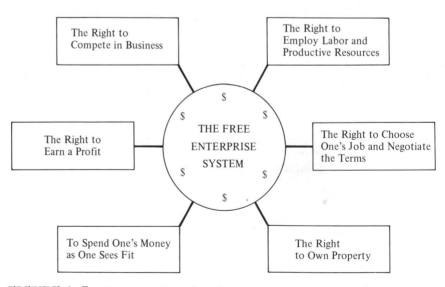

FIGURE 1-5. Characteristics of the free enterprise system.

5. The right as an employee to choose a job and negotiate the terms
6. The right as a consumer to spend money as one sees fit.[17]

The Right to Own Property.   The right to own property is a fundamental tenet of the free enterprise system. Ownership of property implies that individuals can control their own raw materials, equipment, and means of producing products and services. Ownership of property, both tangible and intangible, places the control of the use of such property at the disposal of the individual or the commercial leisure service organization. The right to hold and maintain property is protected in the United States and Canada by various laws and, with few exceptions, individuals are free to dispose of their property as they see fit.

The right to own property provides a person with the means of control and production. It provides an incentive for individuals to accumulate wealth. The accumulation of wealth or capital allows businesses to further develop and expand their enterprise, pay taxes, contribute to programs or projects that they feel are beneficial to society, as well as invest in other ventures. The ownership of property is criticized in that it promotes the individual's self interest. However, it also provides the incentive for individuals to assume the responsibility for their own welfare rather than depending upon a government for their security and well being. The ownership of property has created a faster rate of growth and, as such, a higher material standard of living than that in countries where the means of production are publicly rather than privately owned.

The Right to Earn a Profit.   The right to earn a profit is a fundamental aspect of free enterprise systems. It is a mechanism for rewarding the suc-

Most navigable rivers in the United States serve as operations bases for independently owned and operated white water rafting companies. These companies operate under a renewable permit issued by the U.S. Forest Service. Permits are frequently issued on a competitive basis. (Dave Miller)

cessful work of the individual or the organization in meeting the needs of people. A fundamental principle tied to the notion of the right to earn a profit is the idea that those who take a risk should benefit from the activity. For example, a person who invests $50,000 to establish a white water raft excursion company is taking a risk. At risk may be savings, a piece of property used as collateral to secure a loan, or other resources. Because the person has ventured personal effort, energy, and resources, the notion of profit suggests that he or she should be entitled to a reward if the business is successful.

What constitutes a fair profit? Some people would argue that there is no limit on the profit that a commercial leisure service organization could and should earn. They argue that the issue is not one of how much profit should be earned, but how much people are willing to pay for the service. We feel differently. All commercial leisure service organizations should have the opportunity to earn a profit. However, the profit earned should not be such that the consumer is exploited. A fair rate of return should be greater than the rate of interest charged for loans secured to run the business on a long-term basis. Competition, which we will discuss in the next section, is a mechanism that helps moderate the profit that an organization can earn.

The Role of Competition. The right to compete is an important factor in the free enterprise system. Because the free enterprise system allows individuals and organizations to pursue their own interests, the right to compete prevents abuse of power. For example, if a person purchased an item or consumed a service from a particular commercial leisure service organization and was dissatisfied with that product or service, what would be his or her alternative? In the free enterprise system, the individual consumer is free to choose another product, another service, or another supplier. The right to compete thus helps curb abuses that can occur when, in fact, individual needs are not met. The individual consumer can simply turn to another supplier or service. The same principle applies to the quality and value of services consumed by a person. If people are dissatisfied with the quality of a service or the cost, they, again, can turn to another supplier.

In a competitive economic system there is a greater probability that individual needs will be satisfied. In the late 1800s and early 1900s, there were a number of companies that had monopolies on the production of certain products. This period, known as the Progressive Era, found government intervening in order to break up these monopolies. This was known as *trust busting*. A good example of the efforts of government to ensure that competition exists within the telecommunications industry is the recent break-up of American Telephone and Telegraph. It is now possible, for example, to have competition in the area of long distance telephone calls.

Competition helps commercial leisure organizations remain responsive to the needs of the market. It prevents their offerings from becoming out of date, prohibitively priced, and of inferior quality. The pressure of rival organizations forces an organization to continuously engage in innovation of services and development of new management and production strategies.

It basically forces an organization to be on the alert for new ways of doing things in order to remain competitive and, in turn, earn a profit. It is a good system of checks and balances.

The Right to Employ Productive Resources.   In order for a commercial leisure service organization to produce its service, it often has to employ or use other resources. Basically, there are three types of resources to which a commercial leisure service organization must have access: labor, property, and capital. Most commercial leisure service organizations are labor intensive. That is, they require extensive numbers of persons to plan, organize, and implement the service or activity. Without the ability to employ such human resources, such organizations could not succeed. Furthermore, commercial leisure service organizations may need access to natural resources, power, or other man-made resources to implement their services or activities. Last, capital resources are the monies required to "run" the organization.

Again, using the example of a whitewater rafting company, all three types of productive resources—labor, property, and capital—could come into play. For example, the company would undoubtedly hire some people to serve as river rafting guides. It would also need access to a river in order to run its program and would need to purchase rafts and other relevant equipment, materials, and supplies. Last, the company might need to borrow money in order to purchase equipment, materials, and supplies, pay staff, and secure access to a river. Without all of these resources, the company would not be able to function effectively and succeed.

The Right to Choose One's Occupation.   The right to choose one's occupation and receive equitable compensation for one's skills is also a fundamental tenet of the free enterprise system. This means that there is competition for labor in the market place. For example, in certain occupations there is a surplus of trained individuals, whereas in other occupations there may be a lack of trained personnel. In the latter situation, individuals are able to command a salary or wage that they feel is appropriate, given the level and extent of their training or the demands of the occupation.

On the other hand, if one person asks for an apparently inappropriately high wage for his or her services, there may be others who would be willing to undertake similar tasks for lower wages. This self-regulating mechanism provides for a minimal amount of control and interference on the part of government. It allows businesses to compete for labor and, at the same time, it allows people to determine what they feel is their fair market value based on their skills, knowledge, and abilities. If persons feel that they are underpaid, they are free to seek out other employment opportunities that are consistent with what they feel is their value.

The freedom of individuals to choose their occupations offers them a large degree of control over their own destinies. People are free in our capitalistic system to create those opportunities that they feel will best satisfy their individual needs, wants, and interests. People may choose to be involved in an occupation for a variety of reasons. As indicated, a primary motive for some persons is that of serving people. On the other hand, there are people who are motivated by opportunities for financial remuneration. The freedom to choose one's occupation provides the opportunity for individuals to affect and directly control their future.

The Right of Consumers to Choose Services.   Certainly the ability of the consumer to choose freely among competing products and services is a central concept in the free enterprise system. In other words, in the free enterprise system consumers spend their income as they see fit. They have the ability to make decisions concerning the quality, value, and other characteristics of services based on what best meets their needs. The freedom to choose those services that meet one's needs has a very important effect on commercial leisure service organizations. It requires them to remain in tune with consumer needs, wants, and interests.

In the same way that people have the ability to choose the occupation they desire, consumer choice increases individual freedom and responsibility. It provides a way of directly empowering the consumer with the authority to control many of the decisions that affect his or her life. The right to choose those services that best meet one's needs is central to the leisure experience. When a person is free to choose, his or her sense of freedom is increased. In almost every definition of leisure, the notion of freely chosen experiences, activities, or services is central.

In countries that have free enterprise systems, consumer spending exceeds expenditures by businesses and government. Because of this factor, most resources—human, fiscal, physical, and technological—are focused on meeting consumer needs. The creation and distribution of consumer products and services has a priority over other uses of our resources. This regulating mechanism places at the disposal of consumers the majority of our productive resources. Without the freedom of consumers to choose the services they feel best meet their needs, these resources could be focused elsewhere. The right of the consumers to choose among services thus ensures that their needs are met and that services are not focused toward ends that have been predetermined by individuals holding authority within a government. Often it has been suggested that dollars in a free enterprise system are like votes. The person who expends his or her earnings is engaging in a process of selection of services and products. As long as people have equal opportunity and access to resources, the free enterprise system can operate effectively. When discrimination occurs and people are denied access to those resources that will enhance their ability to compete effectively in the market (i.e., education and capital), they are also being denied the freedom to earn an adequate wage, salary, or profit. This, in turn, reduces their freedom of choice between and among consumer goods and products. It could thus be said that creating equal and open opportunity is a key factor in enhancing freedom of choice.

Adam Smith felt that the free enterprise system would work as an invisible hand, regulating the affairs of humankind. The free enterprise system is a process where consumers and businesspeople meet in the marketplace to exchange tangible and intangible items of value. Smith argued that a system of production would develop that would foster individualism and social harmony. This, in turn, would promote economic growth and social progress. Certainly, the free enterprise system has provided more freedom, a greater opportunity for people to regulate their own affairs, and greater economic growth than any other economic system in existence.

Building and Maintaining Consumer Loyalty

As indicated previously, the objective of our free enterprise system is to identify and satisfy consumer needs. Thus, one of the major goals of a commercial leisure service organization is participant satisfaction. Although consumer satisfaction is loosely measured by organizational profit, it is important to develop a strategy to ensure consumer satisfaction. Since participant needs are constantly changing, building and maintaining consumer loyalty is a constant challenge (see Figure 1-6). Basically, it is our opinion that people will respond to an organization that is built on the following tenets.

Function. An essential element in building and maintaining consumer loyalty is ensuring that the product or service provided fulfills the function for which it has been developed. The function of a product or service can be thought of as the use or purpose, as perceived by the consumer, of the service or product. Simply, people desire things to operate smoothly and to fulfill their expectations. For example, if they pay for swimming lessons, their expectation will be that the service provided will enable them to acquire or further develop certain aquatic competencies or skills. When a service

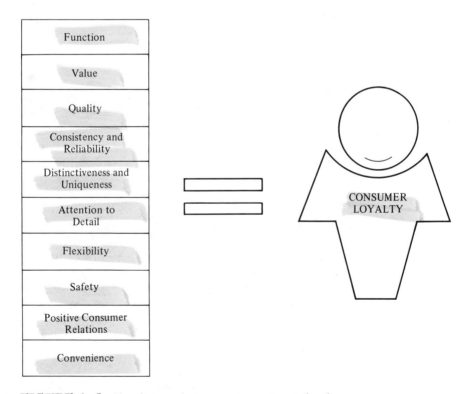

FIGURE 1–6. Ten factors that promote consumer loyalty.

or product is not functioning, it is not meeting the expectations of the individual and therefore will not serve to retain consumer loyalty.

Value.   Value is the evaluation on the part of consumers of whether the cost of a service is comparable with the estimated return. Consumers feel that they have received fair value when they perceive that the service they purchase is equal to or greater than the benefit they expected to receive. When consumers feel that they have received an adequate return on their dollar, they will feel that they were dealt with in an equitable, honest, and forthright manner. They will be more likely to repeat their business when this occurs.

Quality.   The quality of a service is the degree to which it is perceived as achieving excellence. Consumers desire services that are of exceptional merit. Commercial leisure service organizations that attempt to ensure that their services meet high standards of quality will, by and large, build and maintain consumer loyalty.

Consistency and Reliability.   Reliability and consistency suggest that the consumer can count on similarity of service each time it is purchased. The reliable and consistent organization is dependable in its operations and provision of services. For example, if a person is treated with courtesy and in a friendly manner when initially participating in a service, a measure of an organization's reliability would be its ability to reproduce that same atmosphere in future experiences. An organization's services should be organized and planned so that they are consistent, even when performed by different individuals within the organization. Consistency and reliability are heavily dependent upon adequate training of new organizational members.

Distinctiveness and Uniqueness.   Organizations that are distinctive or unique in some way may build consumer loyalty as a result of this factor. When an organization provides a service that is not offered by other agencies within the distribution area, consumers will seek it out and will return to it. This process involves the building of an organization's market niche, which is discussed in more detail in Chapter 8.

Attention to Detail.   Commercial leisure service organizations also effectively build and maintain participant loyalty by focusing on the details of their operations. Details can be thought of as the small components of an organization's service. These small components, when taken together, can have a large impact on the quality of the programs or services offered by a commercial leisure enterprise. Lack of attention to detail often results in repetitious mistakes that can be costly to an organization. Attention to detail can provide an edge over competitors and can give an organization an appearance of competence, superior organization, sophistication, and thoughtfulness. As a result, attention to detail can positively affect the experiences and loyalty of consumers.

Flexibility.   We live in a society dominated by change. In order to effectively meet individual needs and interests, it is important for an organization to remain flexible. Changing a program's format or structure may appear to be a relatively easy task; however, often it is difficult to change staff members' attitudes, habits, and work routines in order to meet changing conditions. Organizations that do not change may not retain their consumers. It is interesting to note that many amusement parks, such as Six Flags Over Texas, Magic Mountain, and Marriott's Great America are always in the process of renovation or replacement of their attractions. It is not unusual for such theme parks to introduce a new ride each year.

Safety. Although many recreation and leisure activities involve a degree of risk, consumers are also safety conscious. They are concerned with being free from danger or harm while at the same time engaging in adventurous activities that entail some risk. Most individuals will not consciously expose themselves to dangerous or hazardous conditions. When hazardous conditions are present, they can serve as a deterent to active participation of individuals. For example, a fitness program that has a poor record for safety resulting in injuries to participants might experience a decline in continued participation. Further, if such conditions were publicized through the media, there would be a serious impact upon the commercial leisure service business.

Positive Consumer Relations. The successful commercial leisure service organization attempts to build positive consumer relations. The organization should attempt to make consumers feel that they are welcome, important, and appreciated. Consumers should not be treated as if their business with the organization is unessential or unimportant. Each time an individual interacts with any member of the organization, the opportunity exists to establish positive consumer relations. Whether a consumer is simply requesting information or actually purchasing a service, the organization's goal should be to ensure that the consumer is dealt with in a courteous manner. There are countless instances within organizations where the discourteous behavior of an employee alienates one or more consumers. Courteous, helpful behavior on the part of an organization's employees can be taught and reinforced in training sessions or supervisory coaching conferences.

People like to be treated as individuals. They like the personal touch. Whenever possible, the organization should attempt to interact with consumers on an individual basis and tailor the service to the needs of each. For example, because of the availability of microcomputers, all correspondence can be individualized inexpensively. Personalized correspondence provides more intimate direct contact with the consumer than bulk mailings addressed to "occupant." Consumer relations is strongly tied to attention to detail. Flowers in a resort hotel room, jitney service to an activity, or the introduction of consumers participating in a service to one another are small details that can result in more positive consumer relations.

Convenience. Perhaps the major factor in retaining and attracting consumers is that of the convenience of the service. By convenience, we are referring to basically two dimensions: the location of the service and the time at which the service is actually delivered. The more convenient a service is in terms of these two factors, the more likely the organization will attract participants. Often little attention is given to determining what constitutes a convenient or acceptable time and location when providing commercial leisure services.

The establishment and maintenance of consumer loyalty requires constant attention on the part of the organization. It also requires that a long term perspective be taken toward consumers. If an organization's goal is not only to attract but also to hold participants, then it must focus its planning on both immediate financial objectives and long term ones. A long term orientation requires more thoughtful and careful planning, organization, and implementation of services. America's best run corporations are those that focus on long term goals for attracting and holding their customers.

Ethics for Commercial Leisure Service Organizations

Commercial leisure service organizations create and distribute products and goods with the expectation that they will make a profit. In doing so, they basically operate by consent of the public and with the broad goal of serving the needs of society. As such, it is important for persons and organizations providing leisure services for profit to recognize their responsibilities to their employers, i.e., the local community or constituency they serve and society as a whole. This calls for recognition of the ethical responsibilities of commercial leisure service organizations to these various constituencies.

Ethics are the standards of right or wrong in a society. To operate ethically implies that a person or an organization is in accordance with these generally accepted societal rules of right or wrong. This is difficult in a pluralistic society, where there is great diversity in our values, norms, and customs. This does not mean, however, that a person or organization should not establish and follow a code of ethics to guide behavior.

In general, there are three ethical areas that should be considered by a commercial leisure service organization: human social responsibilities, community responsibilities, and environmental responsibilities (see Figure 1-7). Human social responsibilities refer to the ethical standards that are

FIGURE 1–7. Ethical responsibilities of a commercial leisure service business.

California Parks and Recreation Society
Commercial Section
Code of Ethics

As we move into the 21st century, leisure time is becoming a major concern of educators, governmental leaders, social planners, and society as a whole. In response to this growing leisure interest, many diverse business interests have emerged to serve this market. This diversity of commercial enterprises has created a need for one professional organization to provide a forum for the interchange of ideas and the setting of professional standards for the delivery of products and services to the leisure market.

The life blood of Commercial Recreation is profit or self-sufficiency through the delivery of quality products and services to the consumer. To achieve this goal, the provider of these products and services should be committed to the highest level of professional excellence. Toward this end, I, as a member of this section, will endeavor to reflect this objective in the conduct of my professional affairs at all times under this code.

The Commercial Section/Private Recreation Section of the California Parks and Recreation Society is in concert with the Society Code of Ethics. In order to accomplish the goals and objectives of this section, the following criteria are held to represent standards by which we measure our performance and effectiveness. I shall support and preserve the highest standard of professional conduct in the field of the commercial section.

It is the responsibility of this section and membership to maintain honesty and integrity in all relationships with customers and to first emphasize quality and safety of products and services with accurate representation to the public. I recognize the basic marketing principle that there must be mutuality of benefit and profit to the buyer and seller in order to ensure true economic progress and thus to fulfill the inherent responsibility of marketing to advance our country's standard of living and quality of life.

I shall always strive for constructive and effective cooperation with all providers of leisure services in areas of appropriate interest, always with the objective of supporting and maintaining the free enterprise system. I will take an active role in the furthering of the growth and development of this Section.

---

established for dealing with consumers and the employees of an organization. For example, establishing ethical standards that require employees to deal forthrightly and honestly with consumers would be included in the area of human social responsibilities. Also included would be ensuring that consumers are informed of any risks associated with certain leisure activities, that activities are provided with concern for safety, and that consumers are dealt with fairly. In addition, human social responsibilities include the standards that are established within the organization itself in dealing with employees. For example, creation of a positive work environment that provides employees opportunities for growth, recognition, and status can be seen as a responsibility of an organization. Concern for the welfare of employees as reflected in fringe benefit packages, vacation time, wellness days, and other "perks" are ways that an organization can meet responsibilities to its employees. Organizations that place the welfare of their employees at a premium are often very successful.

Community responsibilities refer to the establishment of ethics that encourage positive, productive interaction between the commercial leisure service organization and the community within which it operates. The term *community* should be viewed in a broad sense. For example, not only does community refer to the geographic location or region served by the business, but also to those institutions that must be supported to ensure the welfare of the community as a whole. This means that a business has a responsibility to pay taxes to support health, social welfare, and educational institutions that maintain community stability and well-being and provide a trained productive work force. It also suggests that commercial leisure service organizations should provide leadership in the community to contribute to the community's growth, development, and enrichment. Businessmen often assume elected or appointed responsibilities in order to ensure that vital community functions are not only maintained, but also improved.

Environmental responsibilities refer to recognition of the need to protect and conserve our natural resources. Commercial leisure service organizations have an especially crucial role in this area, in that many leisure activities are dependent on the use of our natural environment. The protection and wise use of the environment will ensure that future generations have the same opportunities to participate in activities and view scenic wonders that have become a part of our heritage. Commercial leisure service organizations have a responsibility to promote the maintenance of a clean, healthy, safe, and ecologically balanced environment. Because the production of leisure services and products often requires the use of our natural resources, commercial leisure service organizations should be on guard to ensure that they do not abuse them.

The Commercial/Private sector of the California Park and Recreation Society is a newly formed professional body, the mission of which is to promote and maintain high standards of conduct for individuals and privately owned agencies providing leisure services and products for the purposes of profit or financial self sufficiency. This professional organization has set forth a Code of Ethics to assist individuals in their professional conduct. This concise and thought-provoking statement suggests a basic set of ethics for commercial leisure service operators (see page 31).

Summary

In this chapter, a broad overview has been presented of opportunities and prospects for profit in the leisure service area. A person should initially consider his or her basic motivation for entering the commercial leisure service area. Basically, there are three factors that influence or motivate a person to pursue a career in this area: service to people, personal satisfaction, and financial remuneration. All three of these factors may be interrelated.

The leisure market today is extremely large. It is estimated that over $260 billion is spent each year for leisure products and goods in the United States. Today, the leisure market exceeds expenditures for either national defense or housing construction. The leisure market is quite diverse and changes rapidly. It is being influenced dramatically as we move from an industrial-based society to an information-based society. An increase in personal choices and options has led to diverse leisure lifestyles.

Commercial leisure services are intangible. A service is something that is perceived as being useful or beneficial by the consumer. There are many different types of organizations providing leisure services, including those related to travel and tourism, hospitality, entertainment, the natural environment, and retail outlets. These organizations produce a variety of services and products to meet the diverse interests of consumers in our pluralistic society.

The production of services occurs primarily as a result of the organized efforts of people. This system is known as the free enterprise system. The free enterprise system is built on the assumption that individual consumer needs are the base for the creation and distribution of goods and services. Individual choice (to produce or to consume) is the factor that characterizes this system. The free enterprise system has a number of characteristics that focus on individual rights. These include the right to own property, the right to earn profit, the right to compete, the right to employ productive resources, the right to choose one's occupation, and the right of the consumer to choose those products and services that he or she desires to purchase.

Successful leisure service organizations have as their primary objective the identification and satisfaction of consumer needs. Organizations that establish principles focused on consumer satisfaction, as measured by organizational profit, are by and large more successful than those that operate in the reverse manner. A satisfied consumer remains loyal to the organization that meets his or her needs. Organizations that build on the following tenets are likely to be successful: quality, value, consistency and reliability, distinctiveness and uniqueness, attention to detail, flexibility, and consumer relations.

Commercial leisure service organizations are charged with operating in an ethical and responsible manner. They are responsible for establishing ethical standards for dealing with their consumers as well as their employees. Commercial leisure service organizations are also responsible for encouraging positive, productive interaction within the community that they serve. Last, such organizations have ethical responsibilities in the area of environmental concerns. They are charged with protecting and judiciously using our natural resources.

Study Questions

1. List those factors that you think motivate you to pursue a career in the commercial leisure service area. Discuss how these factors are interrelated.
2. Discuss the size and scope of the leisure market. What are some key indicators that could be followed during the next ten years to assist a person in determining where the leisure market is headed?
3. Identify ten trends in the leisure market. Cite specific examples.
4. Define commercial leisure services. Define commercial leisure service organizations.

6. Briefly describe five types of leisure service organizations.
7. What is the basis of the free enterprise system? What are its characteristics?
8. What is the relationship between consumer loyalty and organizational success?
9. Identify ten tenets upon which successful organizations are based. Seek out the philosophical statement or objectives of a commercial leisure service organization in your area and compare and contrast its basic philosophy with these tenets.
10. Identify ethical responsibilities of commercial leisure service organizations.

Experiential Exercise

Instructions: In this chapter we have outlined five different types of commercial leisure service organizations. These are businesses engaged in travel and tourism, hospitality services, entertainment services, leisure services in the natural environment, and retail outlets focusing on the sale of leisure goods. This profile can enable you to investigate those services that are of particular interest to you. The questions are straightforward and require that you investigate, independently, career opportunities that may be available and could be pursued.

Name of business _____
Location _____
Market orientation and philosophy _____
_____
_____
_____
_____

Organizational design: staffing _____
_____
_____
_____
_____
_____

Consumers served: numbers and general characteristics _____
_____
_____
_____
_____

Nature and scope of services _____
_____
_____
_____
_____

Facilities: size, design, unique features _____
_____
_____
_____
_____

General comments concerning the business _____

_____
_____
_____
_____

Critical evaluation and recommendations _____

_____
_____
_____
_____

Observation concerning opportunities, salary ranges, working conditions, employment possibilities and advancement_____

_____
_____
_____
_____

Notes

1. "Recreation: A $244 Billion Market," *U.S. News & World Report,* August 10, 1981, p. 63.
2. John J. Bullaro, "Career Potential in Commercial Recreation," *Leisure Today,* November/December, 1975, p. 36.
3. Michael Doan and Benjamin Cole, "$262 Billion Dogfight for Your Leisure Spending," *U.S. News & World Report,* July 26, 1982, p. 47.
4. J. D. Reed, "America Shapes Up," *Time,* November 2, 1982, p. 103.
5. Ibid.
6. Jafar Jafari, "Tourism Today," *Leisure Today,* April, 1983, p. 3.
7. Ibid.
8. Doan and Cole, p. 47.
9. "Recreation: A $244 Billion Market," p. 63.
10. Michael Demerest, "Americans Everywhere," *Time,* July 25, 1983, p. 40.
11. Susanna McBee, "Lifestyle of the '80s: Anything Goes!" *U.S. News & World Report,* August 1, 1983, p. 48.
12. Maurice Archer, *An Introduction to Canadian Business,* 2nd ed., Toronto: McGraw-Hill Ryerson Ltd., 1974, p. 205.
13. Ibid., p. 198.
14. Ibid., p. 199.
15. John Naisbitt, *Megatrends: Ten New Directions Transforming Our Lives,* New York: Warner Books, 1982, p. 16.
16. George Gilder, *The Spirit of Enterprise,* New York: Simon & Schuster, 1984, pp. 16–17.
17. Archer, p. 3.

Close-up: American Video

Randy and Shelagh Jansen own and operate American Video, a retail store specializing in the sale of video movies, video equipment, and related items. The video business has swept North America. This revolution has had a direct impact on the leisure market, fueling a growth in the use of audio and video systems, particularly in the home.

The Jansens have engaged in a number of business ventures. They felt that a business in this sector of the leisure market would succeed regardless of the economic climate in which it operated because of the low cost to the consumer for the rental service. They also feel that North America is on the verge of "a boom in the use of electronic equipment."

The basis of their philosophy as business people is "service." "We bend over backwards to try to at least let the customer know that we have done our best." They are very consumer oriented. They try to have a wide selection of merchandise and to stay abreast of the market trends. "We know our customers by name and they like that." "We have one customer who comes into the store and asks 'What shall I see today?' He knows that we are aware of his interests and he trusts our judgment."

The Jansens both feel that their success is due in part to their attention to detail. To take care of details, they make out a "to do" list every day of both short and long range plans. Attention to detail is what they look for in an employee as well. In addition, they seek employees who have a positive attitude. "As a small business, we have to have the right employees." They state that the "attitude of employees is everything in a retail store. If employees don't have the right attitude, it really comes across." They state that the attitudes of employees can affect the reputation of the store. Customers tend to talk to others of their bad experiences more than their good ones. Bad experiences with poor employees can affect the reputation of a store directly and swiftly.

The Jansens note "that they are people who like to make things work." They feel that it is very important for people to enjoy what they are doing. As Randy stated, "I'm not bored in this business. Some people just want to put in their time at work and retire, I want to enjoy what I'm doing. I don't want to work at a job just because it offers security. I feel I can do this by being self employed." This reflects their attitude toward their business, which they say takes considerable commitment. According to Shelagh, "your whole life can be consumed by the adventure of a new business. You should not expect to do anything else the first year of operation."

The Jansens also stress the importance of maintaining the excellence and atmosphere of their operation. They say that they would rather handle one or two stores well than extend themselves and risk the quality of the business slipping. They also like to promote a family atmosphere within their store. The employees within the store operate as a family and the store presents a wholesome family-oriented appearance.

2

Organizations Providing Leisure Services for Profit

The kaleidoscopic mix of leisure services offered by business and industry in North America is stunning. Capital investment in leisure service enterprises encompasses a wide range from small operations such as river-side campgrounds in which the investment is under $20,000 to spectacular theme parks such as Walt Disney World in which the capital investments exceed $300 million. Leisure service organizations also are diverse in terms of the services they offer and include such ventures as video arcades, mountaineering schools, circuses, hotels, marinas, wildlife parks, river rafting concessions, hobby shops, private hunting clubs, dude ranches, billiard parlors, nature guide services, and raceways, just to name a few. Table 2–1 gives a more complete sampling of the different types of commercial leisure service organizations.

In Chapter 1, we briefly identified and defined the different types of commercial leisure service organizations according to their functions, i.e., in terms of the work a person would do within one of these businesses. This classification system produced five general leisure service areas: travel and tourism services, entertainment services, leisure services in the natural environment, hospitality and food services, and retail outlet services (store and nonstore). The following is a more detailed description of these areas along with some typical line positions to be found in them.

1. *Travel and Tourism Domain.* Organizations in which persons holding line positions plan travel itineraries, transport people to points of interest,

TABLE 2-1. A Sampling of Commercial Leisure Services

Aquariums	Outfitters, outdoor guides
Art galleries	Performing arts centers
Boat rentals	Pool parlors
Bowling alleys	Private campgrounds
Camps: resident, day, sports, computer	Private schools of instruction (dance, gymnastics,
Carnivals	skiing, tennis)
Charter boats: sightseeing, fishing	Professional sports
Circuses	Raceways and dragstrips (automobile)
Convention centers	Racquetball centers
Country clubs	Resorts
Dude ranches	Rock concerts
Exhibits (e.g., the liner *Queen Elizabeth*, the airplane,	Rock hound shops, guides
the Spruce Goose)	Roller rinks
Fairs, expositions (World's fair)	Skateboard parks
Fitness centers	Ski areas
Guest houses (bed and breakfast inns)	Skin, SCUBA diving schools, guides, outfitters
Gun clubs	Spas
Hobby shops	Tennis clubs
Home video and entertainment centers	Theaters: live, outdoor
Horseracing tracks	Theme restaurants (e.g., Chucky Cheese)
Hotels, motels, and inns	Theme parks (e.g., Disney World)
Hunting preserves	Ticket agencies
Ice rinks	Tour bus lines
Marinas	Tour promoters
Movie theaters, drive-ins	Travel agencies
Museums, historical sites	Vacation farms
Night clubs	Zoos
Off-road vehicle sales and service	

or guide or lead travel groups belong to the travel and tourism domain. Examples include travel agencies, steamship lines, airlines, and tour bus lines.

2. *Hospitality and Food Services*. Businesses in which persons in line positions direct the lodging and feeding of consumers belong to the hospitality and food service domain. Examples of such businesses are hotels, restaurants, motels, resorts, and inns.

3. *Entertainment Services*. Commercial leisure service organizations in which persons holding line positions plan, supervise, and direct programs of interest (diverting, amusing) belong to the entertainment services domain. Examples include movie theaters, theme parks, night clubs, and professional athletic teams.

4. *Leisure Services in the Natural Environment*. Organizations which depend upon natural resources for the implementation of their services, and persons in line positions facilitate a pleasurable and safe outdoor recreation experience. Examples of these services include river rafting vendors; private, profit-oriented youth camps; hunting lodges; and recreational vehicle parks.

5. *Retail Outlets (Store and Nonstore)*. These provide goods and services in quantity to the consumer in a convenient way. Line personnel possess specialized knowledge and skills that support sales (either a product or service). Services are frequently taken to the customer. Examples of store-type retail outlets are bicycle, backpacking, and pro shops. Ex-

amples of nonstore retail outlets are mail order houses and leisure contracting services.

The above categories should not be viewed as inviolable. They primarily help to illustrate the vast array of commercial leisure services available today. Indeed, these separate areas are linked by the common denominators of competition for available leisure dollars, and, frequently, shared customers. These five commercial leisure service areas (domains) will now be discussed in terms of such topics as their history, the large service providers within them, their current status, their prospects for growth, and some of the jobs and functions of persons working within them.*

Travel and Tourism

Travel and tourism provide profit and economic diversity for many areas by supporting a variety of tourist-related enterprises, such as restaurants, hotels, resorts, wilderness outfitters, travel agencies, theme parks, museums, and small entertainment services (e.g., movie houses and night clubs).

The terms *travel* and *tourism* are difficult to define. Edginton and Ford define *travel* as the physical movement of persons from one place to another and *tourism* as those activities and services that often accompany travel, such as tours, lodging, food services, and visitor attractions.[1] Others consider travel to be within or a component of the tourism industry. For the purposes of our discussion, travel and tourism are separate components of the travel and tourism domain. A *tourist* is a temporarily leisured person away from home in order to experience a change.[2]

Employment Opportunities

Those employed in the travel and tourism domain are involved in assisting people with arrangements such as travel tickets, transportation to sites of interest, actual operation of transportation systems, operation of tourist attractions, and other activities associated with travel. Persons working in the travel and tourism domain may serve as guides, travel agents, social directors, or hostesses and hosts. The travel and tourism industry overlaps with the hospitality industry (to be discussed later in this chapter) in that both involve the operation and management of hotels, motels, food services, and other activities that serve "tourists." Table 2-2 presents some of the organizations and job opportunities that might be found in the travel and tourism domain.

Historical Perspective

The early settlers in America were motivated to travel for a number of reasons: the prospect of new land, religious freedom, gold, and, occasionally, wanderlust. Only the hearty and highly motivated traveled, however. Hazards such as robbers, bad roads, and bad weather conditions were commonplace. The accommodations that did exist were often primitive and

* For a in depth treatment of commercial leisure services refer to John R. Kelly, *Recreation Business*, New York: John Wiley & Sons, 1985.

TABLE 2-2. A Sampling of Job Opportunities in Travel and Tourism

Type of Business	Sample Jobs
Airline	Group Sales Manager Chief Flight Attendant Reservation Agent Flight Attendant
Tour Bus Line	Manager Tour Bus Driver Bus Host or Hostess
Tour Boat Line	Owner Manager Captain Sightseeing Guide Steward
Steamship Company	Cabin Superintendent Social Director
Travel Agency	Owner Sales Manager Group Sales Manager Sales Representative Travel Counselor Reservation Agent Travel Clerk
Tour Promoter/Operator	Manager Sales Manager Promotion Manager Sales Representative Travel Counselor Reservation Agent Tour Guide Travel Clerk

costly. The common carriers of the day, stage coaches and sailing ships, were uncomfortable. Until the development of the railroads in the middle 1800s, few people traveled for leisure.

Around 1860, the race to link the east and west coasts together by steam had begun, the Union Pacific Railroad building west across the plains, the Central Pacific Railroad building east from California. They met at Promontory Point, Utah, in 1869. The railroads provided relatively safe transportation.[3]

Between 1860 and 1920, steamship companies such as the Hart Line, through its branch, the Okeehumkee Line, ran passengers up the St. Johns, Oklawaha, and Silver rivers in Florida. These paddle wheelers were a great tourist attraction.

By 1905 the automobile had made its appearance in American towns. It was first considered a novelty, not worthy of serious consideration. But the appearance of the automobile and the 57-second flight of the Wright Brothers at Kitty Hawk, North Carolina, on October 10, 1902 marked the unofficial beginning of modern-day travel and tourism in America.

Travel to foreign countries is affected by both domestic and world economic conditions. A strong dollar usually encourages Americans to travel abroad, because the travel dollar buys more goods and services. (John Bullaro)

Leisure activities during the nineteenth and early twentieth century were class related. This was especially true of travel. The urban poor visited parks on Sunday and went to circuses, parades, and sporting events. With the development of movie theaters, the poor found additional escape from the drudgery of their lives. It was only the well-to-do who "cruised, travelled, and created, by their patronage, the resort business."[4]

Around the turn of the century people "just wanted to go somewhere."[5] In the east, the Cottage City of America and Gay Head on Martha's Vineyard were popular places. Hostelries at that time charged $2.50 to $3.50 a day—modest by today's prices but more than a day's wages for an industrial laborer.

The affluent frequently traveled to such places as the William Henry Hotel at Lake George, New York. Rates in 1900 were $17.50 to $28.00 a week. The hotel featured a fast-running elevator and hourly stock market reports. The prohibitive costs barred the less wealthy from visiting such resorts; it was an artificial yet effective barrier by which the wealthy isolated themselves from the poor. (These weekly room rates were approximately equal to the average weekly wage for a factory or office worker.)

By 1935, America was deeply mired in the Great Depression. With 25 percent unemployment, travel and tourism remained a prerogative of the wealthy. It was not until the end of World War II that tourism and travel as we have come to understand them emerged.

The Impact of Disposable Income on Tourism and Travel

There are two widely held definitions of disposable income. In the literature about recreation and leisure, disposable or discretionary income refers to personal funds available for leisure goods and services after the necessities of life are paid for. The necessities of life include rent or mortgage payments, food and clothing costs, medical care, and, often, some form of savings. Economists on the other hand refer to disposable income as personal income less personal taxes; that is, disposable income is the amount of income

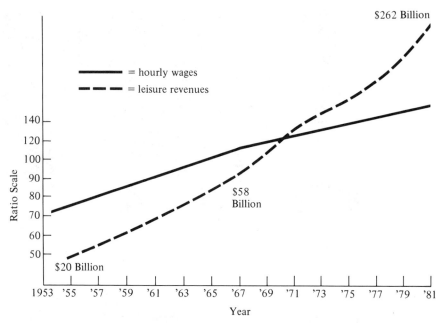

FIGURE 2–1. Comparison of hourly wages and expenditures on leisure (tourism included).

households have to dispose of as they see fit. Researchers of the leisure industry have simply narrowed and refined the economists' definition to gain a clearer picture of leisure expenditures. We are referring to the former definition when discussing disposable income.

Figure 2-1 illustrates a contradiction to an assumption widely held by those who study leisure, namely, that there is a positive correlation between growth in personal income and growth in personal expenditures for leisure. In fact, such an assumption is incorrect. Wages have not kept pace with the basic cost of living expenses (food, shelter, utilities), but consumers have used creative strategies to generate increases in disposable income. Travel and tourism thus grew from a $4 billion market in 1953 (20 percent of $20 billion) to a $52 billion market in less than thirty years (a 350-percent increase) while hourly wages only increased about 150 percent.[6] During this same period, personal consumption of all goods and services grew from $235 billion to $1,600 billion, or an increase of 300 percent. What is the source of the difference between wage income and personal expenditures? Part of the answer is that in 1950 consumer debt was $15.5 billion and by 1980 this figure had increased to over $303.8 billion. Personal debt has contributed significantly to personal consumption of all goods and services, including leisure activities.

People generate dollars for leisure pursuits in ways other than by earning surplus income and borrowing. They buy smaller cars, cheaper homes, and less expensive food. Individuals will rearrange their budgets before dropping their leisure interests. Mobley has stated "Economic conditions will have to get a lot worse before people cut back substantially on leisure."[7]

But travel industry analysts note that there are changes shaping up in this field. The new "have nots" tend to travel closer to home, eat at fast food restaurants, and take shorter vacations. By contrast, there is a growth in the number of "haves," who continue to spend freely with few worries about debt. For example, when the American Express travel division initiated a deluxe nine-day "Sentimental Journey" featuring a private railroad car from New York to Los Angeles, the trip sold out weeks in advance of departure—at a cost of $2,229 per person. Or consider a Royal Viking cruise; an eighty-eight-day, nineteen-port voyage including stops at Penang in Malaysia, Colombo in Sri Lanka, Majuro Atoll in the Marshall Islands and Mahé in the Seychelles. Suites, which cost $52,000 for the trip, are always the first to be booked. The ultimate vacation experience for the "haves," however, is probably an around-the-world tour in a penthouse suite aboard the Cunard Line's *Queen Elizabeth II* at a cost of $235,000.

Current Status

People travel to satisfy a variety of needs: to fulfill a promise to themselves, to visit relatives, for the purpose of education, to conduct business, for military service, or perhaps to search for the elusive self. Regardless of why people travel, millions of them do every year, making travel and tourism one of the largest industries in the United States. For example, the Under Secretary for Travel and Tourism of the United States Department of Commerce noted the following facts about tourism and travel in the United States for 1982 and 1983.[8]

Travel in the United States in 1982:
- was the second largest retail industry in the U.S., following only food stores.
- was the second largest private employer in the Nation, accounting for 8 percent of the total U.S. labor force.
- was one of the top three employers in 39 states.
- accounted for $194 billion in domestic and foreign visitor spending, 6.3 percent of the gross national product.
- directly employed 4.5 million Americans at every skill level and another 2.2 million workers indirectly.
- generated over $41 billion in wages and salaries and more than $20 billion in federal, state, and local tax income.
- was a highly diversified industry with more than one million component companies ranging from small travel agencies to large airlines and hotel chains, with 99 percent of these companies classified as small businesses.

International Travel to the United States in 1983:
- accounted for 21.6 million total foreign arrivals and receipts of $13.8 billion (including international transportation payments to U.S. carriers).
- netted this nation 7.5 percent of total world international arrivals (286.5 million) and 11.6 percent of global foreign tourism expenditures ($96.2 billion).
- resulted in federal, state, and local tax revenues of more than $1.1 billion.*
- directly and indirectly generated approximately 600,000 U.S. jobs.
- accounted for one third of the business services exports.

* $640 million of the $1.1 billion was federal tax revenues.

Changes in Travel and Tourism for the 1980s

The travel imperative is strong and will continue to be a major factor in the gigantic leisure market. There will be adjustments stimulated by the changing economic fortunes of Americans. For example, the American Automobile Association reported that requests for trip information were up 15 percent in 1981, although most trips were less than 300 miles from home.

Travel has an impact on the other domains of leisure service. Theme parks are prospering, as are other attractions close to population centers. Resorts such as Sherburne Corporation's giant Killington Ski Area in Vermont are also prospering. This particular resort has plans to operate on a year-round basis. National parks are jammed, but federal budget reductions will curtail expansion. Van Doren noted that travel in Texas was up 13 percent for 1981. Van Doren went on to state that he believes people are becoming more hedonistic about travel, i.e., do it now, tomorrow is uncertain, and that modern stresses necessitate a let's-get-away attitude.[9]

Low cost travel programs will become increasingly popular. River rafting, backcountry pack trips, train rides, bus trips, bargain cruise-ship junkets, all will enjoy continued growth in the years ahead.

Travel Agencies

Travel agencies represent a major marketing channel for the travel and tourism industry. By definition, a travel agency is a local retail outlet that plans travel itineraries and secures tickets on common carriers for its clients. Travel agents also book reservations at various hospitality establishments around the world. Travel agents earn their fees from commissions paid by the common carriers and other businesses that provide travel and tourism services. Travel agents book about 10 percent of the nation's travel business and 40 percent of the domestic air traffic.

The small, independently owned travel agency is giving way to the large chain operation, which, through operating efficiency and aggressive marketing programs, is making it difficult for the independents to successfully compete. An example of a large travel agency chain is the American Express Company.

Hospitality and Food Services

The hospitality and food services industry is devoted to the lodging and feeding of travelers and tourists. Hotels, motels, inns, and resorts are examples of organizations providing hospitality and food services. Historically, the hospitality and food service industry has focused upon the care of travelers and tourists; however, there has been tremendous growth in the food service industry, extending its scope beyond the care of travelers and tourists. This is especially the case in the areas of fast food restaurants and theme restaurants.

Size and Scope of the Industry

Hotels are to be found in every country of the world, from large cities to places with fewer than 500 inhabitants. It is no wonder that the hospitality industry ranks high among the largest worldwide industries.

46

In America, hotel-keeping is the seventh ranked service industry. There are approximately 22,000 hotels in the United States, with a total of 1 million rooms. These hotels can accommodate over 2 million guests each night of the year and can offer dining facilities for over 1 million people. Total hotel receipts are presently about $5 billion a year, and hotels have an annual payroll expense of approximately $1.5 billion.

Traditionally, the hospitality industry has been one of individual ownership. In recent years, however, skyrocketing costs have resulted in a trend toward corporate ownership and professionally trained managers.

The Beginning of the Industry

The growth of hospitality services was inextricably tied to increases in trade opportunities. A major impetus to trade and travel was the Industrial Revolution, which began in England between the years 1750 and 1790. This revolution caused the changeover from an agrarian, home-based economy, in which farmers grew their own food and made their own clothing and tools, to an industrial economy, in which products for which there was a need and for which needs were created were manufactured by others and sold or traded to others. The increased trade created the need for roads, which linked villages, and a corresponding increase in the movement of people. As people traveled away from home, the need for food and lodging facilities grew.

The English inn had its origin in London and quickly spread throughout Europe. Although English innkeepers succeeded in making their facilities available to the ordinary traveler, they were content to maintain their businesses without any thought of innovation or change. It was not until inns opened in American seaports that the industry started to undergo dramatic changes. The first inn in America was built in Virginia in the year 1607. Thereafter inns were opened in various locations.

There are several important reasons for the rapid ascendancy of the hospitality industry in America. The first and perhaps most important reason is that inns were open to all, not only to the rich as were the European inns. The second is that early American hotelkeepers were innovative and constantly searched for better ways to serve their guests.

In 1794 the City Hotel was built in New York; it contained 73 rooms. In 1829, only 35 years later, the Tremont House was built in Boston, marking the beginning of the industry as we know it today.

At the turn of the century some dramatic changes took place in America's economy. As the country expanded there were more and more commercial travelers; transporation became easier and cheaper. Many people had an urge to travel. All these factors combined to create the need for more and larger hotels that would truly meet the needs of the average traveler in service, quality of food, cleanliness, and price of accommodations.

In 1908, the entrepreneur Ellsworth M. Statler made a study of the hotel industry. He opened his first hotel in Buffalo, New York in the same year. The Buffalo Statler boasted many new features such as fire doors, door locks with the keyholes above the knobs for easy access, light switches just inside the door, private baths, full-length mirrors, circulating ice water for every room, and a free morning newspaper for every guest. The combination of the room rates, which were within reach of the average traveler, and the innovations assured the success of the venture and led to the establishment of the Statler Hotel chain. Statler is to the hotel industry what Henry Ford is to the automotive industry. Statler's Buffalo hotel became the model for hotel construction for the next forty years.

Hospitality Industry Today

During the period between 1900 and 1960 the hotel industry developed four different kinds of hotels:

1. The commercial or transient hotel, created by Ellsworth Statler, which served the needs of traveling salespeople and middle-class tourists
2. The residential hotel, which developed to serve the needs of long-term residents
3. The luxury hotel, such as the Plaza in New York and the Marriott in Los Angeles, which catered to the rich and offered the ultimate in service, cuisine, and comfort at a price most people could not afford
4. The resort hotel, such as the Sands or Caesar's Palace in Las Vegas, which was developed to provide the maximum in comfort, food, and entertainment at a price that the middle class could afford.

Between the end of World War II and 1960 a new dimension to the hospitality industry came of age—the motel. Motels emerged from the tourist court concept; a tourist court is a cluster of tiny cabins that offers little convenience to the traveler except a place to sleep.

Motels are a major supplier of sleeping accommodations in America today. They primarily meet the family's need for low cost accommodations that are accessible to adults traveling with children. (John Bullaro)

Commercial Leisure Services

The first motels were built horizontally, usually with twelve to twenty-four rooms in a row. They offered guests a comfortable room with a private bath. The guests could park their cars in front of their rooms, thus providing quick check-in and check-out procedures and eliminating the expense of tipping. Most of these early motels were "perimeter facilities," that is, they were located away from the center of town, usually along main highways. The perimeter motel became a transient facility catering primarily to tourists.

The next development in the growth of the motel was the in-city motel, which has many of the characteristics of a hotel such as restaurants and swimming pools. In-city motels are known as motor inns and cater to commercial travelers as well as tourists. Their rates are generally higher than those of a perimeter facility, but they offer more conveniences as well as access to central city attractions and commerce centers.

Perhaps the most innovative concept to emerge in the hospitality industry was the budget motel. William Becker, a retired contractor, originated the budget motel with the basic Motel 6 in 1963. The real growth of the budget motel occurred during 1970 as a response to double-digit inflation and corresponding high hotel room rates. By 1975 there were approximately 125,000 budget motel rooms in the United States. *Venture* magazine reported that the budget segment of the hospitality industry has captured about 8 percent of the total lodging dollar by offering rooms 20 percent to 50 percent below average rates.[10] This has been accomplished by foregoing food services and other public-space amenities in favor of fairly plush, standard-size rooms. *Venture* also reported that the budget motel segment of the hotel industry is "booming and will grow much faster than the lodging industry as a whole."[11] Examples of companies offering franchise opportunities are Econo Lodges of America Inc., Super 8 Motels, Inc., and Quality Inns International Inc.

Criteria for Success

When Ellsworth Statler was asked to list the three most important things to consider when buying or building a motel or hotel, he said location, location, and location. The message here is obvious; location is the primary consideration. Other factors, all really involved with location are:

1. The volume of traffic passing the site.
2. The proximity of a major highway or interchange.
3. The closeness of an airport, industrial park, college, or city.
4. The location of the nearest competition.
5. The rates of the competition.
6. Planned food services.
7. The inclusion of retail shops.
8. The necessity and size of meeting rooms.
9. The number of rooms required.
10. New highways being planned that might bypass the facility.

These ten considerations are guidelines for those who are contemplating building or buying any kind of facility that caters to the tourism trade. Anyone interested in starting a business in this field would be well-advised to seek professional assistance from a consultant specializing in the hospitality field.

Employment Opportunities

Because this is a very diverse field, job opportunities range from managing a hotel or resort to serving as a housekeeper, sales representative, convention manager, camp director, cook, or purchasing manager. Table 2-3 presents some of the job opportunities in the hospitality field. A discussion of other factors pertinent to the field, such as chain operations, franchising, and the personal and educational requirements, follow.

Franchising. One route to hotel ownership is franchising. Franchising is selling or leasing to an individual or organization the right or privilege to use, rent, or buy the franchiser's name, product, and services. The independently owned business operating as a franchise appears to be part of a large chain, thus giving the establishment instant recognition and credibility. Franchising is not unique to the hospitality industry. Campgrounds, restaurants, bowling centers, day-care centers, bus lines, and recreational vehicle (RV) dealerships are just a few examples of franchises.

In the hospitality industry, brand name recognition often determines success or failure for an enterprise. Being a part of a national organization thus can be an important consideration in buying a franchise. Franchises, it should be noted, are different from company-owned (chain) operations.

Chain Operations. For the customer, chain operations in the hospitality industry serve the same function as a franchise operation; they provide a familiar environment with a predictable level of service within a known price structure. In a chain, each unit or establishment is owned by the parent company. Company managers operate the facility. Career development often takes an individual to a variety of locations as one "moves up the ladder." A chain establishment is, as we mentioned, different from a franchise, which is independently owned. The consumer often overlooks this difference, however.

One of the largest hotel chain operations in the hospitality industry is Holiday Inns. It has many facilities spread from coast to coast, often several within one city.

Outlook for Employment. The tremendous growth that is taking place in the hospitality industry has had an impact on all types of hotels and motels. Many of the hotels and motels now under construction will provide increased services and activities. As a result, existing hotels and motels may have to modernize and expand in order to remain competitive. The result will be increased employment opportunities in the hospitality services domain.

Most colleges have a student placement service. Often they include job listings for hotel trainees. If your college placement service does not list positions in hotels, apply to the personnel department of a particular hotel or hotels. Also, there are hotel associations in every state that act as clearing houses for all members of the association. They send out regular lists of available positions. Contact any hotel for the address.

TABLE 2-3. A Sampling of Jobs in the Hospitality Industry

Type of Business	Sample Jobs
Resort	Manager
	Resident Manager
	Convention Manager
	Front Office Manager
	Service Superintendent
	Executive Housekeeper
	Reservations Clerk
	Front Desk Clerk
Convention Center	Convention Manager
	Sales Manager
	Front Office Manager
	Service Superintendent
	Executive Housekeeper
	Reservations Clerk
	Front Desk Clerk
Hotel	Manager
	Resident Manager
	Sales Manager
	Convention Manager
	Front Office Manager
	Salesman
	Service Superintendent
	Executive Housekeeper
	Reservations Clerk
	Front Desk Clerk
Motel	Manager
	Front Office Manager
	Reservations Clerk
	Desk Clerk
Guest House	Manager
	Lodging Facilities Attendant
Catering Service	Owner
	Manager
	Cook
	Kitchen Supervisor
Restaurant	Owner
	Manager
	Executive Chef
	Chef
	Baker
	Cook
	Kitchen Supervisor
	Food Controller
	Maitre d'
Fast Food or Concession Stand	Director of Food and Beverages
	Purchasing Manager
	District Manager
	Chef/Cook
	Kitchen Supervisor
	Food Controller

When making out a list of hotels to contact, you could refer to the *Hotel Red Book*.* The *Hotel Red Book* is the "bible" of all hotels in this hemisphere. Use it as an address book of job leads.

Positions in hotel management that are particularly suited to students studying leisure services and would offer them an opportunity to use their skills are convention manager, sales representative, or events manager. These positions involve working with consumers and assisting them in conducting conferences, conventions, seminars, workshops, or clinics. Students with backgrounds in leisure studies are very adept at understanding the steps in planning, organizing, and implementing such programs. It should be noted that it is often necessary to hold a degree in hotel management in order to obtain work as an upper level manager in larger hotel and motel chains.[12]

Remuneration.　There is a tremendous cross section of trades and occupations in the hospitality industry (see Figure 2-2), and pay scales are commensurate with the specific job. Many jobs depend on outside income (tips and service charges), therefore salary scales do not always truly reflect real earnings. In addition, some hotels provide meals and services for employees. In general, salaries range from a few dollars a week (augmented by tips, meals, lodging, and services, depending on the hotel) to thousands of dollars annually for top-level executives. Persons can carve their own niche in the hotel industry according to their ability and performance.

Personal Requirements.　Probably the most important factor for success in the hospitality industry is the ability to get along with all kinds of people in all situations. In this regard self appraisal is essential: "Do I like all people well enough to overlook their personal idiosyncrasies?" If so, then the hospitality industry may be for you. A person should be socially aware, tolerant, understanding, intelligent, industrious, humane, have a flair for detail, and have initiative. As Kalt paraphrased Kipling, "if you can mingle with cabbages and walk with kings, then you're not only a man, but more important, a genuine hotel man."[13]

Educational Requirements.　Of the top executives in the hospitality industry today, 80 percent started at the bottom and worked their way up to top management jobs. Some began as buspersons, bellhops, and room clerks. When many of these individuals started out, few schools gave courses in hotel management and operations. Because hotels have became a major industry, a large number of schools have created special classes or complete courses in hotel management. However, you should acquire a general education first; a general education background will shape you into a well-rounded person. It is difficult to set up a rigid schedule for the educational preparation necessary for entrance into the hotel industry because of the many job specialities.

Some hotels offer on-the-job training. Since most hotels operate on a three-shift system, it is easy for students to work and go to school.

* Published each June by the American Hotel Association Directory Corporation, 888 Seventh Avenue, New York, NY 10019. The Hotel Red Book is available in most libraries.

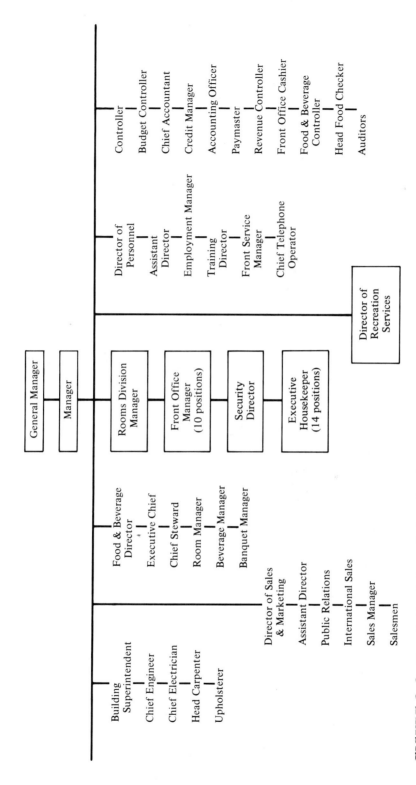

FIGURE 2–2. Organizational chart of a large hotel.

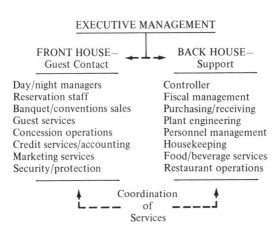

FIGURE 2-3. Overview of hotel functions.

Components of a Hotel

Each hotel is divided into two parts, the front house and the back house. The front house includes those operations that deal directly with and are seen by the public. Front house departments include service, front office, accounting, credit, office management, protection, banquet, advertising, public relations, sales, resident management, executive management, and all subdivisions of these departments. Back house departments include food and liquor, chief steward, room service, wine steward, kitchen, restaurant, and housekeeping (see Figure 2-3).

Sources of Customers

Anyone contemplating a career in the hospitality industry must have an understanding of the market. Hospitality customers essentially come from two primary sources: the community and travelers.[14]

The community can be the immediate area surrounding a hotel or it can be a geographical area of many miles. The community must have sufficient resources (disposable income) to motivate a resident population to visit the business for food, beverages, and entertainment. Affluent communities, such as Beverly Hills, California, have many fine restaurants and hotels. The residents of this community make up a significant part of the users of these facilities.

If the community in which a hotel is located is perceived as an attractive place to spend vacation time, that is, it has attractions of historical significance, geographical beauty, or cultural resources, then a sufficient number of travelers will be attracted to support the hotel. Often the presence of other successful hotels is an indication that the demand is present.

Hospitality Services and Natural Resources

There is a direct relationship between the economic benefit to a community of its natural resources and the presence of hospitality services. Visitors to a community with natural resources, such as a lake or hiking trails, may generate little revenue unless there are rooms, meals, and related hospitality and leisure services to buy. This has created much controversy between

Small concessions such as private beaches and camp grounds generate revenues for a community with natural resources. Development of natural resources is not without its controversy, however. (John Bullaro)

developers and environmentalists. Environmentalists, politicians, and entrepreneurs must continually weigh the economic benefits of resource exploitation with the need for resource banking (protecting a resource from development).

Bed and Breakfast Inns (Country Inns)

There is a rapidly growing segment of the hospitality industry called the country inn. A smaller unit is the bed and breakfast inn. These hospitality facilities are usually renovated lodges, hotels, farmhouses, or Victorian homes. The bed and breakfast inn is showing the most remarkable growth in North America today.

A bed and breakfast inn provides tourists with sleeping accommodations and a light breakfast. However, this definition fails to grasp the charm and uniqueness of these inns. Usually a renovated Victorian home or an old farmhouse, the facility is often furnished with antiques and historic items of the period in which it was built. Some rooms have private baths, but more likely guests share toilet facilities. Depending on the area of the country and the season, room rates vary from $50.00 to $150.00 per night.

Historically, bed and breakfast inns trace their beginnings to England. During the latter part of the eighteenth century, industrialization created a middle class that demanded reasonable accommodations. While most English inns catered to the nobility, these were small, private homes opened to accommodate the middle class traveler. The guest often shared meals and accommodations with the host family. This family style arrangement is carried on by the bed and breakfast inns of today.

Employment opportunities in bed and breakfast inns are rather limited given the fact that most inns are owned and operated by people who feel that their personal involvement with the guests is essential for success. However, the larger, more elaborate country inn frequently employs managers and other assistants. These country inns sometimes have full kitchen

The warmth and charm of bed and breakfast inns make them a growing favorite with tourists who are not on a limited budget. These inns are frequently located near natural resources such as lakes or rivers. Inns are often rich in historic significance and produce a feeling of living in a bygone era. (Ridenhour Ranch House Inn)

facilities and have three meal seatings a day. Often such restaurant operations are open to the public. Persons seeking employment in a country inn or a bed and breakfast inn should visit their local library and secure a copy of *Country Inns of America.** Select the area and the type of establishment in which you want to work and send a resume and a cover letter (see Chapter 3).

The bed and breakfast inn provides an excellent opportunity for an entrepreneur who wants to enter the hospitality field and offer a unique service. These quaint hospitality facilities offer a pleasant working environment and the potential for profit for the right individual. Anyone contemplating ownership of a bed and breakfast inn should possess a high degree of personal warmth and charm, and the ability to put guests at ease.

The amount of capital required to start a bed and breakfast inn depends upon the cost of the original structure and the extent to which the structure needs renovation. These costs can range from $250,000 to well over $1 million. A country inn requires a higher initial investment because it offers more services, such as a restaurant. Chapter 5, Starting a Commercial Leisure Service Business, will provide you with a track to follow to arrive at a total cost.

The future outlook for country inns, including bed and breakfast inns, is tied directly to the nation's economy. Since these types of accommo-

* Or write to The Complete Traveler, 235 East 44th Street, New York, NY 10017.

dations represent the extras of tourism, any economic downturn would most likely have an immediate effect on revenues. Yet the outlook for future growth and profits is excellent. With the rapid growth of entrepreneurism in America today, the rate of new entrants into the bed and breakfast business should be brisk.

Prospects for Profit for the Hospitality Domain

With its history of boom and bust, the stability and financial solvency of the hotel industry are viewed somewhat apprehensively by investors. In reality there have been only two great boom periods in the hospitality industry, the 1920s and the mid-1950s to mid-1960s. The constantly nagging question is, has the industry over-built?

The hotel industry today is on a much firmer financial base than in 1929. This is partly due to the greater affluence of the middle class, which has an increased amount of dollars available for travel. It is also partly due to improvement in other economies of the free world, which means that more foreign travelers are coming to America. There are, however, many clouds on the economic horizon that could spell problems for the hospitality industry—none is more ominous than inflation.

Beggs and Lewis stated:

> One of the most pervasive influences on the hotel industry during the past decade, as on everything else, has been inflation. On the demand side, the industry is generally considered to be greatly affected by the level of disposable income and consumers' increasing resistance to higher prices. Yet, until 1980 the overall industry response has been to raise room rates even faster than the steep increases in the Consumer Price Index. Average room rates at the end of 1980 were 58.3 percent higher than they were in 1975. During the same period the CPI increased by 47 percent and disposable income increased about 50 percent.[15]

Yet the business recovery of the 1980s should spawn new growth in the hospitality industry, albeit a different type of growth than in the past. This growth will be in the chains, franchises, specialty organizations such as bed and breakfast inns, and the budget motels.

Increases in labor costs, food and beverage costs, energy costs, and other variable expenses as well as in fixed costs of insurance, taxes, rent and interest provide a constant upward pressure on food and beverage prices and room rates. Increases in costs that push room rates and food prices higher might be expected to dampen demand. However, one industry consultant, C. DeWitt Coffman, has stated that "never in industry has the public been so acclimated to rate increases as they are today. Unless you realize this and raise your prices, you can't be a winner in the hotel industry."[16]

Travel figures suggest that the hospitality industry is a growth industry. Eighty million Americans traveled in 1979. They took 120 million pleasure trips, an estimated 145 million business trips, and 14 million traveled abroad. In the same year, there were 21.6 million foreign arrivals. The 1981 *Travel Market Yearbook*[17] projected that there are another 20 to 30 million Americans who have not traveled; these people represent the potential for growth.

However, the number of persons who resist travel because of the "hassle of traveling" has grown from 13 percent to 24 percent according to the *Travel Market Yearbook*.[18]

Travelers (customers) are looking for specific conditions before they will spend their dollars.

1. More than ever before, people are looking for *value*—not just price, but value. This suggests that customers are more enlightened consumers. They are evaluating the leisure experience in terms of what it has done to please them; they do not just want to fill time.
2. People want *information*. They want to know what to expect and they do not want surprises. They want honesty in communications between the organization delivering the service and themselves.
3. People want *excitement, adventure, the new, and the different*. Most people do not want peace and quiet when they travel.[19]

In order to succeed in the hospitality industry, persons must become strategic planners. They must anticipate consumer demands for a significant experience. The organizations serving this market must hire good people, have rigorous and thorough training programs, and high standards of service. As in all industries, it is vital to have managers and an organization that cannot only predict and prepare for change, but creatively manage change as well. In addition, they must be able to control costs, yet not be miserly in their administrative philosophy.

Entertainment Services

Entertainment services are involved with entertaining or amusing people during their leisure. Such interesting, diverting, or amusing events as shows or performances fall within the category of entertainment services. Entertainment is some action external to the participant that produces a diversionary effect on the attention of the participant. Entertainment can be an experience that is shared by two or more people, yet the experience has a unique impact on each participant. Thus, a movie or stage play affects each viewer differently although each viewer is experiencing the same external event. The common motivating force that moves people to seek an entertainment experience is anticipating the suspension of reality. Joseph Levy, in his book *Play Behavior*, defines the suspension of reality as

> the loss of the 'real self' or 'imaginary self.' Through this form of make-believe, individuals achieve freedom from the real world (e.g., rules, roles, expectations, etc.) to experience their inner egoless personality.[20]

If the business of children is to play, the business of adults is to work, raise a family, get along with peers, and try to succeed. As tensions and stresses build, a child can escape into play, but adults must seek entertainment, which like play can help them transcend the world of reality. The entertainment opportunities available to the consumer are many. They may vary from spectator sports, theme parks, movie theaters, live theater, television, and music or dance performances to video game centers. Some of these activities overlap with the category of travel and tourism services because they are destination points for travelers; for example, many people travel to the Superbowl. Movies are usually catagorized as entertainment services; however, an international movie festival might also fall within the travel and tourism domain.

Employment Opportunities

Job opportunities in the entertainment industry are varied. They range from work in theme parks to work in professional sports, bowling alleys, movie theaters, video arcades, and ski resorts. Table 2-4 presents some of the types of organizations and job opportunities available in the entertainment industry.

TABLE 2-4. A Sampling of Job Opportunities in the Entertainment Industry

Type of Business	Sample Jobs
Racetrack/Raceway	Owner Manager Publicity Director Patrol Judge Course Clerk Paddock Judge Jockey/Driver Animal Attendant
Professional Athletics	Owner Publicity Director General Manager Athlete Manager Coach Athlete Umpire/Referee
Night Club	Owner Manager Booking Agent Maitre d'Hotel Host/Hostess
Ticket Agency	Ticket Broker Counter Clerk
Rodeo	Rodeo Manager Performer Animal Keeper
Movie Theater	Manager Booking Agent Sales Manager Projectionist
Circus	Superintendent Trainmaster Foreman Master of Ceremonies Performer

TABLE 2-4. (Continued)

Type of Business	Sample Jobs
Entertainment Bureau	Promoter Booking Agent Artist Manager Road Manager
Zoo or Aquarium	Director Publicity Director Head Animal Person Animal Helper Tour Guide Attendant
Bowling Alley	Owner Manager Desk Attendant
Carnival	Manager Supervisor of Rides Supervisor of Games Ride Operator Game Operator
Amusement Park	Manager Supervisor of Rides Supervisor of Games Ride Operator Game Operator

The Theme Park Industry

The genesis of the modern theme park can be traced back to 1955 when Disneyland opened its gates on a 65-acre tract of land in Anaheim, California, and introduced the world to a new era in family entertainment. The phenomenal success of Disneyland spawned a host of imitators, albeit smaller ones, usually based on regional rather than national or international tourist markets. Today there are twenty-eight regional theme parks in the United States. Table 2-5 illustrates major theme park corporations, their park names, and locations.

The Disney model can be summarized as follows:

1. Atmosphere: an infinite number of harmonious details are blended together to create a sense of well-being and safety.
2. The park provides sophisticated entertainment for the entire family.
3. The park is clean.
4. Employees are selected for charm, manners, and good humor.
5. Employees undergo intensive training courses stressing the philosophy of cleanliness, safety, courtesy.
6. Employees are considered performers, on stage at all times.
7. Employees must conform to a rigid dress and behavior code—the Disney look: A well-scrubbed, kid-next-door wholesomeness that rules out such sophisticated "corruptions as eye shadow, teased hair and colored nail polish."[21]

TABLE 2-5. Leading Theme Park Vendors and Their Locations

Corporation	Theme Park Name	Location
Walt Disney Production	Disneyland	Anaheim, California
	Walt Disney World	Lake Buena Vista, Florida
Six Flags	Six Flags over Texas	Arlington, Texas
	Six Flags over Georgia	Atlanta, Georgia
	Six Flags over Mid-America	Eureka, Missouri
	Astroworld	Houston, Texas
	Great Aventure	Jackson, New Jersey
	Magic Mountain	Valencia, California
Taft Broadcasting	Kings Island	Kings Mills, Ohio
	Kings Dominion	Doswell, Virginia
	Carowinds	Charlotte, North Carolina
	Canada's Wonderland	Maple, Ontario
Marriott	Great America	Gurnee, Illinois
Anheuser-Busch	The Dark Continent	Tampa, Florida
	The Old Country	Williamsburg, Virginia
Independents	Knott's Berry Farm	Buena Park, California
	Cedar Point	Sandusky, Ohio
	Opryland	Nashville, Tennessee

The Disney formula produced swift results. Disneyland attracted 3.8 million customers in its first year of operation. By 1977 it had attracted over 110 million visitors. In 1965, Walt Disney Productions acquired 27,400 acres of land twenty miles west of Orlando, Florida for construction of a second park, Walt Disney World's Magic Kingdom. By 1977, total investment for this project reached $750 million. The park attracted 58 million customers during its first five years, with over 13 million customers in fiscal year 1976. This one-year attendance generated gross revenues of nearly $257 million. On this same Orlando, Florida site is the Disney World showcase EPCOT Center, where pavilions from the world's nations create a permanent world's fair.

A 1977 study of the amusement park industry claimed gross revenues in the United States to be $1.3 billion, with Walt Disney World and Disney World Showcase attracting a third of all American theme park attendance and 40 percent of the gross revenue.[22]

Professionals working in the theme park industry draw a distinction between today's theme park and yesterday's amusement park. The latter featured thrill rides, side shows, games of chance, and fast food concessions. The primary market was the single young adult and teenager. Marriott Corporation offers a definition for a theme park that the industry generally accepts.

> A family entertainment complex oriented to a particular subject or historical area, combining the continuity of costuming and architecture with entertainment and merchandise to create a fantasy-provoking atmosphere.[23]

Large theme parks evolved over the years to become a major provider of entertainment services in the United States. Today's theme park is a safe and clean establishment catering to the family. Walt Disney is credited with establishing the high standards of operation that characterize the industry today. Six Flags Magic Mountain, Valencia, California, is a leader in providing thrilling and safe rides. (Six Flags Corporation)

Evolution and Historical Perspective

Theme parks are thought to have evolved from such attractions as amusement parks and circuses. Amusement parks, popular in America during the 1920s and 1930s, fell from customer favor because of the disreputable aspects of many of them. Amusement parks were an idea transplanted from Europe in the late nineteenth and early twentieth centuries. Movie houses and television also helped to bring their era to an end. But it was the "atmosphere" of these early amusement parks that ultimately closed down most of them.

The circus, more than the amusement park, provided the philosophical focus for the modern theme park. It caters to the family market and provides the customer with a wide variety of entertaining acts. While the format of the circus is always familiar, the acts were usually different when the circus reappeared in town each year. The evolution of the modern circus is very interesting.

During the nineteenth century three types of traveling enterprises emerged: the menagerie, the circus, and the combined circus and menagerie.[24] A menagerie is a collection of animals that customers can view for a fee. A circus is a troupe of performers.

A menagerie consisting of birds, reptiles, snakes, and quadrupeds toured the eastern part of the United States in 1781. About this same time, European circus troupes began coming to America. Some early troupes were Lailson and Jaymond (1797), Pepin, Breschard, and Giutano (1806), Don Felipe Lailson's Royal Circus (1809), and Cayetano and Company (1810). Circuses and menageries were essentially separate entities until the 1800s, when an innkeeper in Somers, New York, Hachaliah Bailey, bought and exhibited an elephant by the name of "Old Bet."[25]

His son, James Anthony Bailey, launched a show knows as "The Crusades" in 1856, which featured elephants and a hippopotamus. The show was both a circus and a menagerie and is thought to be one of the earliest shows to combine the specialized acts of circus performers with a collection of animals.

Phineas Taylor Barnum was eighteen years old when he visited with Hachaliah Bailey in 1828. The elder Bailey's account of his experience as a showman may have influenced the young Barnum. In 1835, Barnum entered show business by purchasing an aged Negro slave named Joice Heth and exhibiting her for several months as George Washington's nurse.[26] Barnum then formed a show consisting of a juggler, a black singer and dancer, and some musicians. The project failed, and Barnum abandoned it in the summer of 1838. For the next fifty years Barnum operated a small circus. In 1887 P. T. Barnum and J. A. Bailey joined forces and created Barnum & Bailey's Greatest Show on Earth. They became the giants of this entertainment format.

P. T. Barnum died on April 7, 1891, at the age of eighty, but Bailey had complete charge of operations long before Barnum's death. James A. Bailey died in New York on April 11, 1906 at the age of fifty-eight. Bailey's career started at the age of twelve and earned him a reputation for uprightness, fair dealing with employees, and generosity toward associates in responsible positions.[27] These qualities are also a part of the Disney success formula.

The passing of the two great showmen, Barnum and Bailey, created changes in the direction of the company. In the spring of 1919 Ringling Brothers' World's Greatest Show and Barnum and Bailey's Greatest Show on Earth were merged. Like its successor, the theme park, the circus survived by following a formula of success laid down by early pioneers in entertainment.[28] The formula stressed entertainment, variety of shows, a fantasy–provoking atmosphere, family attractions, educational value, and a perception of value received by the customer. These qualities are also characteristic of today's modern theme park.

Current Scene. Florida epitomizes the theme park industry's battleground for the consumer's dollar. Of Florida's top ten tourist attractions, five are owned by California companies, with a total capital investment of more than $2 billion. Table 2-6 depicts this scenerio.

Disney's Experimental Prototype City of Tomorrow (EPCOT) was drawing nearly 1 million admissions each month in 1983, driving down attendance at neighboring parks. Many theme park corporations are concerned they will not be able to compete with EPCOT. MCA, Inc. is delaying plans to construct a Florida version of its successful Universal Studio Tour in California. Mattel, Inc. reported that attendance was off at Circus World, which is located eight miles west of Disney World. Six Flags Corporation, the Los Angeles-based theme park operator acquired in 1981 by Bally Manufacturing Corporation of Chicago, cites EPCOT as the reason for declining attendance at the Stars' Hall of Fame near Orlando.

Disney management concedes that EPCOT has put neighboring parks in a difficult competitive position but that the market requires a constant infusion of capital into the parks in order to attract tourists.[29] For example, Walt Disney World opened in 1971 with a capital investment of $282 million; since then its total capital investment has been increased to $700 million. It is the success of Walt Disney World that generates the capital necessary to keep the park attractive, thus making it increasingly difficult for other parks to compete in the same market.

Marketing. The marketing challenge of the theme park industry is to keep the park vital and interesting enough to make tourists want to return and to urge friends to make the trip. The theme park industry is faced with the challenge of producing enough revenues to allow for constant rebuilding and upgrading of attractions while at the same time ensuring profitability.[30]

This requirement of reinvestment of capital is forcing some theme park corporations to re-evaluate their plans to stay in Florida. Mattel, Inc. (Circus World) feels that they would be better served in terms of overall profitability

TABLE 2-6. California Companies' Investment in Central Florida Theme Parks

Walt Disney World	
Magic Kingdom	$700 million
EPCOT Center	1.2 billion
Universal Studios-Florida	203 million
Circus World	35 million
Stars Hall of Fame	10 million
Sea World	50 million
Wet'n Wild	8 million

by investing large amounts of capital in other segments of their business rather than in their Florida-based theme park.

Other theme parks continue to upgrade their attractions. For example, construction is underway at Sea World of Florida on a new $15 million "Shamu Stadium." Wet'n Wild is spending $2 million to expand its capacity and is contemplating other additions that may cost $5 million to $6 million in the next couple of years. The point is that the theme park industry is fiercely competitive and requires strong financial support to maintain its market share. This industry would be difficult at best and most likely impossible to enter without an enormous financial investment. On the other hand, hospitality services and certain other small businesses (i.e., transportation companies, travel agencies) and recreation facilities, such as tennis courts, ice and roller skating rinks, movie theaters, bowling centers, swimming pools, and gymnasiums, have a great potential for feeding off of the attendance flow of the large theme parks.

At present, the number of new theme parks that can be launched in the United States is limited for several reasons other than capital requirements. These reasons include accessibility to large population areas, the existence of tourist traffic, site availability, the presence of competitive parks and other competing recreational activities, and the length of time required to obtain necessary governmental approvals.

Foreign Markets.   Impending market saturation and increasing competition among existing theme park operations in the United States has led the major operators to consider possible expansion into foreign markets. Walt Disney Productions moved into Tokyo, Japan in 1976 with their Oriental Disneyland. The total investment in this foreign operation exceeded $300 million. Economics Research Associates and R. Duell and Associates, two of the major consultants in the field, have identified other foreign markets: Saudi Arabia, Kuwait, Australia, and Great Britain.

Employment opportunities in the theme park industry can be classified into one of the following general areas:

1. Ride Operators. These are usually part-time entry level positions.
2. Food Services. These are usually part-time or full-time entry level positions, except for management or supervisory personnel.
3. Entertainment. Entertainment positions usually require a background in set design, wardrobe, or drama.
4. Personnel. Positions in personnel usually require graduation from college with a background in human resource management. Training level positions are often available to four-year college graduates lacking the requisite experience.
5. Marketing. Positions in this area require formal training in marketing and experience in entry level areas such as ride operations, entertainment, or food services.
6. Park Maintenance. Maintenance positions generally require a strong technical background for full-time managerial positions. Besides the general maintenance of the park, this department is responsible for the safe operation of all attractions.

7. Engineering and Design. Positions in this area usually require a technical degree in a related field with experience in maintenance. Experience can often be substituted for a degree; however, this is becoming increasingly more difficult.

8. Finance. Along with marketing, this job classification is usually associated with a park's top management. Students aspiring to top-level management in this and other large leisure service corporations are well advised to have a background in marketing and finance. It should be understood that a four-year degree (often an M.B.A.) is "highly desirable" or "required," as is amusement park experience.

Prospects for Growth

After two disappointing years (1981–1982), the nation's theme parks are experiencing a rebound as vacation-minded travelers are once again swelling attendance figures. Walt Disney Productions increased its projection for the 1983–1984 year from 20 million to 23 million visitors. Still, that is below the 1980 attendance level of 25.3 million. This resurgence of attendance parallels the economic growth in the general economy. As people gain confidence in a sustained economic recovery, they feel comfortable about releasing discretionary funds for the travel and theme park experience.

The Disney philosophy, that none of its parks is ever completed, is shared by the industry generally. Thus, future theme parks will be different from today's parks in attractions, pricing, and marketing. Specifically what they will resemble is only conjecture, but it seems safe to speculate that much of the electronic technology of today will become part of the milieu of future theme parks. The success of such motion pictures as *Star Wars* and *ET* suggest that ride designers will be constructing attractions where the participant will take a more active role in the outcome of the experience. A flight simulator would be an example of such an experience, where the participant gains "control" of the "craft" and competes with a robot in war games or tries to successfully land, all without leaving an enclosure.

If new entrepreneurs are to gain entrance to the theme park business, they will probably have to do so on a smaller scale than present parks. Perhaps electronic attractions such as flight simulators can be adapted to regional shopping centers where "ride" formats could be changed regularly without the enormous cash outlays usually required for traditional attractions. Of course, these shopping center parks would require a new market analysis, pricing strategies, and advertising objectives. One would not seek tourist dollars here but would attempt to capture the same leisure dollars being spent in video arcades.

Other Entertainment Services

Commercial entertainment organizations catering to the public also include bars, nightclubs, dance halls, pool and billiard halls, and video arcades. Entertainment in the form of dining out (as distinguished from food services for tourists) is rapidly becoming a popular family entertainment activity close to home.

Commercial Leisure Services in the Natural Environment

Within the commercial leisure services field is a group of leisure service organizations that use the natural environment as a "resource." Leisure services in the natural environment encompass voluntary leisure activities that involve the use, understanding, or appreciation of natural resources or a combination of these. Organizations that provide commercial leisure services in the natural environment will be referred to as the *commercial outdoor recreation system*. Those who purchase these products or services will be referred to as *outdoor recreation consumers*.

Historical Perspective

Americans have exercised the spirit of enterprise in the out-of-doors. As individuals moved west in pursuit of economic and religious freedom, they often paid guides to help them reach their destinations. In the early history of the United States, people who ventured into the wilderness areas did so primarily for purely practical purposes, rather than recreational ones. They were involved in the search for land, shelter, food, and so on.

Historically, interest in pursuing entrepreneurial activities in the natural environment provided the basis for the beginning of our outdoor recreation system as we know it today. In 1870, a group of individuals were meeting around a campfire in Wyoming Territory in an area today known as Yellowstone. These individuals had been sent by the federal government to determine the accuracy of reports concerning the beauty of the scenery and natural wonders of the area. As they sat around the fire, they discussed the possibility of establishing a private corporation to purchase the land so that tourists would come and pay to see it. These individuals felt that there would be great profit in such a venture. However, Cornelius Hedges, a judge from Helena, Montana, took the position that such land should be held in public trust for the enjoyment of all people and that it should be set apart as a great national park. In 1872, President Ulysses S. Grant signed a bill that set aside 3,000 square miles for "pleasuring ground" for the people. Thus, Yellowstone became America's and the world's first national park.

From the onset, Yellowstone park was managed as a tourist attraction. Concession operations were arranged between the government and private entrepreneurs. There were luxurious lodges and convenient transportation. In these early days camping activities were not encouraged. Most management activities were directed toward drawing people to the national park and serving the visitors once they had arrived. At times, park managers and concessionaires were carried away in their efforts to attract tourists. They engaged in such activities as attracting bears to the hotels by feeding them garbage, focusing colored spotlights on Old Faithful, and putting soap in it so that it would erupt at "times convenient to visiting park patrons." This was done with the blessing of the Director of the National Park Service, Stephen T. Mather.

As a result of such unbridled commercialism, there has been conflict between entrepreneurs and environmentalists. Often environmentalists have felt that entrepreneurs were exploiting the environment purely for the sake of profit. Ironically, much of our contemporary concern for the environment is a result of such early exploitation.

As the demand for outdoor recreation services has grown during the last century, commercial opportunities have also increased. We have seen the development of numerous and diverse facilities and services. Often private facilities have been built on leased public lands, like camps, ski resorts, and marinas. The organized camping movement can be traced to the early 1800s where Joseph Cogswell developed a camp for boys of the Roundhill School in 1823. The resort movement in America flourished with the onset of automobile transportation in the 1920s. Ski resorts are among the most popular commercial leisure services facilities in the out-of-doors, although the first mechanical rope tow in the United States was built just over a half a century ago. Private campgrounds such as Kampground of America (KOA) exemplify the commercial leisure service company operating in the natural environment in recent decades.

Many individuals who make their living operating commercial leisure services in the out-of-doors today are active environmentalists. They know that the environment must be protected in order for their businesses to flourish. Also, many of these entrepreneurs have entered their businesses because of their appreciation and love for the out-of-doors.

Employment Opportunities

Job opportunities in this area range from fishing guide to zoo director, river raft guide, counselor, marina operator, ski resort operator or instructor, outdoor instructor, and trail guide. Table 2-7 gives a sampling of the job opportunities available in the commercial outdoor recreation system.

The Commercial Outdoor Recreation System

The commercial outdoor recreation system can be described in terms of its basic elements and their interrelationships. These elements and their economic correlates are as follows:[31]

System Elements	Economic Correlate
• Users ⟶	• Demand
• Outdoor leisure services (and products) ⟶	• Supply
• Delivery of services ⟶	• Profitability
• Marketing strategies ⟶	• Distribution

Users and their Characteristics (Demand). Exact figures on expenditures in the area of outdoor recreation in terms of the total spent annually on all leisure services are difficult if not impossible to determine, but it is estimated that outdoor recreation consumers spend billions of dollars on products and services annually. Several factors contribute to the problem of determining income generated by the outdoor recreation system. Carlson, MacLean, Deppe, and Peterson, addressing the issue of why estimates of income generated by the outdoor recreation system vary, state:

> There is . . . considerable duplication in the figures for total national expenditures. For example, estimates of vacation costs might include costs for fishing,

TABLE 2-7. Sampling of Environment-Based Service Jobs

Type of Business	Sample Jobs
Resident Camp	Owner Camp Director Program Director Activities Director Head Counselor Head of Waterfront Counselor
Pool, Beach, Lake, Waterfront, River	Director of Aquatic Facilities and Programs Swimming Pool Manager Senior Lifeguard Swimming and Life Saving Instructor Lifeguard River Raft Guide Sailing Instructor
Ski Resort	Manager Publicity Director Head of Ski School Ski Instructor Head of Ski Patrol Ski Patrolman Ticket Seller Lift Attendant
Campground	Director Office Clerk Site Attendant

boating, or other activities for which separate estimates are made, so that when total costs are added, the same item might be included twice.[32]

U.S. News and World Report reported that recreation has grown into a $244 billion market[33] and projects that the market will climb to $300 billion by the end of 1985.[34] If we accept as realistic this projected total revenue of $300 billion for leisure for 1985, we can work backwards from that figure to arrive at a less-than-ideal estimate of the monetary dimension (revenue only) of the outdoor recreation system for 1985.

In Table 2-8 we estimate the total expenditure for outdoor recreation (products and services) to be $85 billion. If we are to further grasp the economic significance of outdoor recreation service income, we must deduct $50 billion in sales for hot tubs, recreational vehicles (including motorcycles and snowmobiles), pleasure aircraft, and vacation homes. After making this adjustment, the $35 billion remaining represents an estimate of the amount of money spent by outdoor recreation consumers for services. This figure ($35 billion) represents the third largest income category in the entire commercial leisure market in the United States.

Outdoor Leisure Services (Supply). The supply component of the commercial outdoor recreation system, as we have just determined, generates approximately $35 billion in annual revenues. Table 2–9 depicts the broad spectrum of business interests serving this market.

TABLE 2-8. Estimating Outdoor Recreation Expenditures

Items to Be Deducted	Annual Expenditures (Billions)
Gambling (1980 estimate)	$75
Hospitality and tourism	65
Recreation-related personal items	45
Books, magazines, other leisure literature	12
Motion pictures, performing arts	2
Spectator sports	2
Theme parks	2
Government expenditures (grants, subsidies)	2
Miscellaneous (including fitness center revenues)	10
Total of non-outdoor leisure revenues	$215
Projected total expenditures for leisure by 1985 (billions)	$300
Less items to be deducted	−215
Estimate of annual expenditures for outdoor recreation system in 1985 (billions)	$ 85

Data adapted from R. E. Carlson, J. R. MacLean, T. R. Deppe, J. A. Peterson, *Recreation and Leisure: The Changing Scene*, 3rd Ed. Wadsworth Publishing, 1983, pp. 60–67; and "Disney's Lure is Hurting Other Florida Parks," *Los Angeles Times*, September 18, 1983, pp. 4–6.

Some outdoor recreation services share the same consumers. For example, consumers can select a vacation experience from among competing leisure businesses (i.e., rafting trips, deep sea fishing trips, or pack trips to the mountains). On the other hand, some businesses support each other, as in the case of a tour bus operator who brings guests to a resort or who

Wilderness lodges often depend upon a variety of other vendors to market their services: pack station operators, wilderness guides, and travel agents. Most wilderness operators operate under a permit issued by the U. S. Forest Service and frequently use land leased from a governmental agency. (John Bullaro)

Commercial Leisure Services

incorporates a raft trip into their travel itinerary. Thus, various elements of the commercial outdoor recreation system compete and cooperate.

Table 2-9 presents a list of suppliers of outdoor recreation services. It is not exhaustive by any means. For example, some other suppliers include hang gliding and sky diving sales outlets and schools. Hang gliding has attracted an estimated 45,000 enthusiasts since 1970. Piloting ultralight aircraft, which are hanggliders with motors, is a relatively new sport that is attracting hundreds of new participants each year. Equestrian activities, in many ways a very specialized activity and requiring large capital outlay for equipment and participation costs, boasts 8 million participants. Other suppliers provide organized bicycle tours, which may include luxury accommodations for the evening stops, wilderness living experiences for business executives, and still others provide opportunities for sailing, big-game hunting, desert motorcycle racing, SCUBA diving, soaring (in sailplanes), surfing, shark fishing, ballooning, ice boating, canoeing, and kayaking.

While we have separated product sales from service sales, there is a service to be performed in the sale of a product. In the case of a backpacking speciality shop, for instance, the customer generally pays a higher price for a given piece of equipment than if he or she shopped at a discount

TABLE 2-9. Suppliers of Outdoor Leisure Services (Ranked by Number of Annual Participants)

Supplier	Activity	Annual Participation by Consumers (Millions)
Swimming schools, pool construction	Swimming	105
Bicycle shops, tour guides, classes	Bicycling	70
Sporting goods shops: baseball, football, archery, handball	Outdoor sports	61
Campgrounds, private reserves, private youth camps	Camping	60
Fishing excursions, retail shops	Fishing	55
Tour bus and guide services	Touring	50
Boat sales, storage, instruction, maintenance	Boating	38
Triathalon shops, clubs, training centers	Jogging	36
Backpacking shops, classes, excursions	Backpacking	30
Hunting trips, guides, lodges, instruction	Hunting	22
Water skiing instruction, product sales	Water skiing	15
Snow ski shops, rentals, instruction	Skiing	11
Retail outlets: crafts, photography including oil painting	Nature study	10
Motorcycle shops, retail, repair	Motorcycling	9
River rafting companies	Rafting	6
Mountaineering instruction and guide service	Mountain climbing	5
Skin and scuba diving shops, classes, excursions	Diving	5
Wilderness outfitters	Wilderness packing	5

Data adapted from Arlin Epperson, *Private and Commercial Recreation*, 1977, N.Y.: Wiley, p. 61. *U.S. News & World Report*, August 10, 1981, p. 63. Standard and Poor's Industry Survey, August 31, 1980, L8–L38. Douglas M. Knudson, *Outdoor Recreation*, New York: Macmillan, p. 125, 1980.

store. Because of the complexity associated with selecting good equipment, the consumer must depend upon knowledgeable sales personnel. The customer goes to the speciality shop expecting the higher price but also expecting expert guidance in selecting the appropriate item. Normally, this expertise is not available at a discount store. The difference in price for these identical items represents the value the customer puts on the service provided by the knowledgeable speciality shop personnel.

Delivery of Services. Profitability is the third economic correlate of the commercial outdoor system. Two factors that determine profitability in delivering a leisure service are pricing strategies and resource utilization.

Pricing strategies for commercial leisure services are dealt with in detail in Chapter 6. Suffice it to say here that if market factors such as competition, demand, and economics are working properly, the price of any service must be in line with those of competitors and will be at sufficient level to allow the owner/manager to earn a profit.

Resource utilization, on the other hand, refers not only to fiscal responsibility in the use of resources but also to employing sound strategies in the utilization of employees and establishing functional operational policies. Operational policies include such decisions as hours of operation, employee training programs, relationships with consumers, image building with consumers and the community, and establishing positive working relationships with the governmental agencies that manage the natural environment. Recognizing the organization's responsibility to the entire outdoor recreation system is sound management and will help ensure the long-range profitability of the entire commercial outdoor recreation system in this country.

Leisure service organizations in the commercial outdoor recreation system should be aware of such governmental documents as the Nationwide Outdoor Recreation Plan of 1973 produced by the Bureau of Outdoor Recreation. This plan reviewed policies and programs and compared existing resources with current and projected participation rates. A new plan was published in 1979. Subsequent plans were to be prepared every five years by the Department of the interior. Budget cutbacks have suspended these publications however.

The Wilderness Acts of 1964 and 1965 have had considerable impact on the federal land management agencies. These agencies, the National Park Service, the U.S. Forest Service, and the Bureau of Land Management (BLM), regulate the resources many commercial outdoor recreation service providers use in their business. Operations policy must be sensitive to the ever-changing resource policies of the federal government, and there must be participation by these commercial outdoor recreation owner/managers in the establishment of land use policies.[35]

Marketing Strategies. The fourth element in the commercial outdoor recreation system is marketing. This subject is covered in detail in Chapter 6. All who provide services in the commercial outdoor recreation system must be cognizant of the factors that make up the recreation experience: anticipation, participation, and reflection.

In marketing an outdoor recreation experience, the organization providing the experience should understand that the consumer comes away with only an experience. In buying the experience, the customer expects to feel better for having made the purchase than before. By contrast, tangible products speak for themselves. They have status, utility, and can be viewed periodically as the need arises. On the other hand, the value of a leisure service experience depends to a large extent on a pleasant recollection of the experience.

Geographic Distribution of Commercial Outdoor Recreation Suppliers

A survey by the Bureau of Outdoor Recreation pointed out that most of the 130,000 private enterprises in outdoor recreation are remote from large concentrations of people, indicating that most of these enterprises, like those of government, are resource oriented. The figures in Table 2-10 demonstrate that areas with low population density have the most private outdoor recreation enterprises.

A private sector study of outdoor recreation enterprises by Chilton Research Services for the Bureau of Outdoor Recreation indicated that most private outdoor recreation facilities are relatively small, averaging about 230 acres each, yet they serve about seven times as many people per acre per year as federal and state areas. This is not accomplished, says the report, through "a lessening of environmental quality. In many cases, commercial facilities and resources are superb."[36] The private sector, including both commercial and nonprofit interests, is the country's largest supplier of outdoor recreation resources and facilities.

Camping Resorts

Club Med is perhaps the best known of the camping resorts. As a camping resort, Club Med offers a planned program, meals, sleeping accommodations, and trained staff to guide activities. Originally begun as an international vacation network of exotic facilities for single persons, the new target of Club Med is young families, particularly those of middle to upper middle income professionals. Some of the locations are exclusively for single travellers, however. Club Med's marketing strategy is based on providing a package tour with a minimum of extras for a reasonable price.

The Midwest Adventurers' Club, another travel club, was started in Chicago by Ron Phillips. Phillips loved to travel but found it difficult to do

TABLE 2-10. Private Outdoor Recreation Enterprise Distribution

	Total Enterprises	%	Cities and Towns	%	Rural Settings	%
United States	131,849	100	43,315	33	88,534	67
Northeast	23,703	100	9,377	40	14,326	60
North Central	40,170	100	16,066	40	24,104	60
South	43,936	100	7,491	17	36,445	83
West	24,040	100	10,381	43	13,659	57

Source: Bureau of Outdoor Recreation, *The Recreation Imperative.* United States Department of Interior, Superintendent of Documents, Washington, D.C., 1974, p. 197.

so on his income, so he "indulged his own interests," and involved others with similar interests and founded what might be termed a "travel camp resort."[37] Joining the club costs $20 a year and entitles the member to be placed on a computerized mailing list. Once on the list, the member will receive regular announcements of upcoming trips, excursions, and socials organized by Phillips. Club members have available one-day canoe trips, four-day rafting trips in Canada, ski trips in Michigan, or hiking and bicycling trips around the Midwest. The marketing theory behind the Midwest Adventurers' Club is to provide a variety of activities within a short, easy drive of the members' homes. There are monthly meetings in the Chicago area.

A most unusual resort is tucked away in Maho Bay on St. John in the Virgin Islands. This resort attracts tourists with a series of arts and nature festivals.[38] The owner, Stanley Selengut, organizes the festivals by offering musicians, dancers, and lecturers a free, two-week vacation on St. John in exchange for four performances. In 1982 the resort earned a profit of $200,000 on revenues of $1.5 million. Selengut's future plans include a second resort at Nanny Point on the other side of the island. The 58-acre resort will derive electricity from windmills and solar cells, and water will be distilled from sea water using solar stills.

Retail Outlets

Retailing is a means whereby services and products are delivered to consumers in a manner that is convenient to them. Most commonly, a retailer acts as a middleman between a producer or wholesaler and the consumer. For example, in the area of sportswear sales, a retailer might purchase sportswear from a wholesaler and, in turn, sell it to consumers at a profit. Retailing is a facet of the distribution process (discussed in Chapter 1).

Historical Perspective

At the conclusion of the Civil War, most individuals still bought their goods at the community general store. Purchases were made by working with a sales clerk or owner who assisted consumers in their choice of products and physically procured their merchandise for them. In the general store the use of credit was commonplace. The owner often had to wait for customers to sell their crops before receiving full payment for goods.

The modern retailing system was started sometime after the Civil War, at the same time the Industrial Revolution came to the United States. Many of the different types of retail outlets that exist today were started during this same period. In 1872 Montgomery Ward launched a mail-order business. This was a new approach to servicing consumers in rural environments. It was very successful because it provided individuals with a greater selection of merchandise, which was often sold at a lower price than the local stores could manage.

As the nation became more industrialized in the late nineteenth and early twentieth centuries, people began moving into urban areas. During this period of time, the department store emerged. The department stores offered one-stop shopping to consumers with lower priced goods. Department stores flourished because they appealed to all types of consumers.

Retail outlets will continue to be a promising source of profits for the entrepreneur who enjoys working in a specialized leisure product/service center. Retail outlets also provide an excellent laboratory for persons wishing to gain experience working in a business environment and dealing with the public. (John Bullaro)

For example, the bargain basement was for consumers who could afford only less expensive products. Department stores also established a single price policy (eliminating price haggling) and established the money-back guarantee that is standard in the industry today. Department stores aggressively promoted their merchandise, making extensive use of window displays and newspaper advertising.

After World War II, retailing changed very dramatically in the United States and Canada. The decentralization of our urban areas gave rise to the modern suburb. This change was a boon to the small independent retail establishment as well as franchise operations. Another development that occurred after World War II was the emergence of shopping centers and malls. These types of complexes included both department stores and small independent retail stores in one area for one-stop shopping.

Today, there are numerous specialty stores that focus exclusively on leisure products and services, including sporting goods stores, outdoor outfitters, toy stores, video and audio stores, hobby shops, fitness centers, music centers, bookstores, and so on.

There are a variety of factors that have historically influenced the development of retailing of leisure services and products, including the following.

1. The emergence of the automobile. The automobile has enabled consumers to have greater access to a variety of places where leisure products and services can be purchased. For example, the automobile has allowed people to travel to distant places where exclusive leisure services are provided, and they can do it more frequently.
2. Informed consumers. A major factor influencing the retailing industry has been the fact that consumers are more informed and knowledgeable

in this area than most others. There seems to be a greater desire for more information about products and services on the part of these consumers.

3. Discretionary income. The increase in the discretionary income of consumers has led to greater purchase of leisure products and services. The growth of the leisure market has been tremendously affected by this factor.

4. Discretionary time. Increased leisure time has resulted in greater opportunities for individuals to participate in leisure pursuits that require the purchasing of leisure products and services.

5. Pluralism. Diversity of choice in leisure activities has led to the creation of many different kinds of retail outlets providing specialty items for consumers.

6. Mass transportation. The development of mass transportation has enabled consumers to have greater access to retail outlets and retail services.

Types of Retail Outlets

The types of retail businesses are almost limitless. Not only are there many, many types of retail leisure businesses already in operation, but more new leisure businesses come into being every year. Retail sales outlets are distribution centers that offer specialized products and services directly to the consumer. These outlets for leisure services (or products or both) may be classified as store or nonstore outlets.

Store Outlets.   Retail outlets in the leisure industry include such establishments as restaurants, music stores, sporting goods stores, backpacking shops, bicycle shops, and toy stores. In addition, there are personal service stores, such as motion picture theaters, bowling centers, and fitness centers.

Although there are a variety of types of retail stores that sell leisure products and services, in general, there are only two basic types. The first is known as the food-based store and includes the convenience store, supermarket, box store, warehouse store, superstore, and combination store. The second type of retail store is involved with the retailing of general merchandise. The focus of our discussion will be on the latter category. Some of the general merchandise stores selling leisure products and services include the following.

1. *Specialty Store.* This type of store usually provides a very narrow selection of merchandise either competitively priced or priced to cater to specific income niches in the market place. Athletic footwear stores are an example of this type of store.

2. *Variety Store.* This type of store usually provides a large assortment of merchandise competitively priced. National chains such as Woolworth fall into this category.

3. *Department Store.* The department store also provides a wide assortment of merchandise. Service provided in these types of stores is excellent and often they are associated with prestigious merchandise. Macy's and the Neiman Marcus store are examples of these types of stores.

4. *Full Line Discount Store.* The full line discount store provides merchandise of average to good quality. Key features of this type of store is that it is price-oriented. This type of store often resembles a department store, but the merchandise is priced much lower. K-Mart is an example of this type of store.

5. *Retail Catalog Showroom.* This type of store promotes self service and use of catalogs. Merchandise is selected in a showroom, but retrieved from an adjacent warehouse. Jafco and Consumer Distributing are examples of this type of store.

6. *Off Price Chain.* This type of store provides minimal service to the consumer. Typically the merchandise is overruns or cancelled orders. Off priced stores are often run as a spin off to major department stores. The Macy's Discount Warehouse is an example of this type of store.

7. *Factory Outlet.* Factory outlets are stores operated by businesses that manufacture goods. They sell goods directly to the public including items that have been closed out, irregulars, cancelled orders, or merchandise that has been discontinued. One of the most popular leisure clothing outlets on the west coast is the Esprit Factory, located in San Francisco, California.

8. *Flea Market.* It is estimated that there are over 200 major flea markets in the United States. Flea markets sell a variety of types of goods, both new and used. The flea market in San Jose, California is one of the largest in operation.

Nonstore Outlets. In the nonstore outlet mode the owner/manager (retailer) takes his or her service to the prospect's home or business. In other words, the sale is usually made on a client's "turf." An example of this type of retail operation is the growing area of industrial recreation consulting. In this case the leisure business owner is likely to set up a sales interview with a corporate officer and make a sales presentation in the executive's office. In all likelihood the industrial recreation service will be performed on the premises of the business or at some facility close by that the industrial recreation consultant has leased.

Another type of nonstore retail outlet that has generated millions of dollars in annual revenues from the leisure market is mailorder sales. REI of Seattle, Washington and L.L. Bean of Freeport, Maine have become two of the most famous nonstore (mail-order) businesses in the United States. Each of these outdoor leisure product retailers have retail stores in addition to their nonstore business; however, it was their nonstore operations that gave them national visibility.

Video Ordering Systems. It is projected that one of the more significant retailing innovations in the years to come will be that of video ordering systems. It is predicted that up to 50 percent of households in the United States by 1990 will have cable television. In addition, the same percentage of households will own videocassette players by 1990. These two types of media will provide tremendous opportunities for the direct retailing of products and services to individuals in their homes.

People will be able to turn to a television channel and to view products for sale. By using the telephone, the mail, or perhaps their home computer terminal they will be able to buy and pay for the product. The implications of this for leisure are enormous. For example, a person interested in golf equipment could view the actual use of a piece of equipment and judge its desirability. Further, individuals interested in purchasing a service, such as tickets to the theater, a nightclub act or a movie, could sample the performance prior to making reservations. People desiring to take a vacation could play videocassettes advertising the vacation site prior to making the purchase. The possibilities are exciting and virtually unlimited.

The Fitness Industry: A Case Study

One of the growth industries in the commercial leisure field is the fitness industry. It provides a good example of the development and opportunities of a retail service oriented outlet.

Millions of Americans today are engaged in some kind of regular fitness program. It is estimated by a variety of sources that over 50 million adults exercise regularly. In the last two decades, the number of commercial leisure service organizations providing fitness programs has grown dramatically. This retail leisure service has grown in annual revenues to over $5 billion (including the purchase of specialized publications and equipment). Some historians credit our national passion for fitness to President Kennedy's administration. In addition, the commercial success in the 1960s of television's Jack LaLanne's early morning exercise show further spurred the fitness craze. Much of this exercise is performed in fitness centers. Fitness centers offer a wide variety of exercise formats, personal amenities, and cost to the participant.

Current Status.   Fitness centers are often referred to by names such as aerobic studios, health clubs, sports and fitness centers, athletic clubs, fitness clubs, health spas, wellness centers, racquetball/sports centers, or figure salons. The cost of participating in fitness center programs can range from $99 to $1,500 per year. Besides basic fitness programs, fitness centers offer a variety of other programs such as diet consultation, massage, pro shops, child care services, and instruction for handball, racquetball, tennis, martial arts.

To make memberships easier to sell, many fitness centers have arranged reciprocity agreements with other fitness centers around the country. Thus, a business person who anticipates travelling a great deal can have facilities available in a variety of locations to encourage maintenance of the fitness program.

The fitness industry offers a variety of employment opportunities for properly trained people. Persons with a physiology background should find instructor positions readily available because the industry is rapidly expanding and the turnover of employees in this classification is frequent. This turnover has many causes, not the least of which is the relatively low salaries paid to fitness instructors.

Many of the "good" instructors leave to start their own centers or private consulting firms. One such case is Jake Steinfeld.[39] Steinfeld grew up in Brooklyn, New York. After high school, Jake moved to Santa Monica, California to train for body building competition. He found employment in a local health club, where he helped some of the movie studio managers and actors improve their level of fitness. He then began helping a few actors improve their fitness by going to their residence and supervising personalized fitness programs. The idea caught on, and "Body By Jake" was born. Steinfeld added a 17-foot trailer with special equipment to his housecall business. Business has now grown to the point where "Body By Jake" programs are being franchised nationally.

The more lucrative positions in the fitness center industry are in management and sales. It is essential that the aspiring manager have some fitness background. Persons seeking employment as a manager or sales agent must look physically fit and follow good personal health habits.

Future Outlook. The fitness market seems to be in a state of steady growth. The future is bright and potentially very profitable. New growth areas include fitness camps for adults, videocassettes aimed at the home instruction market, and the manufacture and sale of specialized clothing and equipment.

Employee fitness programs are becoming easier to sell on a consulting basis to small- and medium-sized companies. Corporate Aerobics, a Los Angeles-based fitness and wellness company, was founded in 1982 to provide on-site fitness and wellness programs to businesses concerned with the health and well-being of their employees. Corporate Aerobics, Inc. sells nonstore franchise opportunities nationwide. The company has clients such as Bonnie Bell of Lakewood, Ohio, Sentry Insurance Company of Stevens Point, Wisconsin, and Xerox Corporation of El Segundo, California.

Individual fitness consultants can earn between $3,000 and $4,000 a week in large metropolitan areas.[40]

Because of the rapid growth of the fitness market and the concomitant opportunity for profit, many inexperienced practitioners are flooding the field. This will probably give rise to legislation regulating the minimum amount of formal training necessary to enter the field.

Employment Opportunities

There are numerous job opportunities available in the retail area. Most of these center on sales jobs, for example a salesperson or sales representative. There are, however, other opportunities in the retail area in such diverse areas as accounting, merchandising, sales promotion, advertising, and management. In smaller retail outlets all of these functions may be undertaken by the owner or manager and a few employees. In larger organizations, the staffing scheme may be more complex, requiring an extensive recruitment, selection, and training program for employees. Table 2-11 is a sampling of job opportunities in retail outlets.

Contracting and Retail Outlets

A most exciting and new business opportunity in the leisure field has been the growth of consulting and contracting services. This service area offers many opportunities because of growth in the demand for specific services and the relatively small capital investment required to launch an enterprise.

Providing public services as a business was discussed in a recent article in *Venture.*[41] Entrepreneurs are beginning to make money by selling services once provided by the various levels of government. This "privatization" of services includes providing fire department services, mail delivery serv-

TABLE 2-11. A Sampling of Job Opportunities in Retail Outlets

Type of Business	Sample Jobs
Recreational Vehicle (automobile, boat, motorcycle)	Owner Manager Sales Person
Outdoor Sports Products	Owner Manager Sales Person
Souvenirs/Antiques	Owner Manager Auctioneer Collector Sales Person
Toys, Games, Home Entertainment	Owner Manager Sales Person
Leisure Consultation Planning and Investments	Owner Manager Consultant Investment Analyst Researcher Planner Technical Information Specialist Data Collection/Analyst
Music Center	Owner Manager Demonstrator Sales Person
Dance Studio	Manager Sales Person Dance Instructor
Ice Rink	Manager Supervisor, Hockey Leagues Instructor Referee/Umpire Clerk
Hobby Shop	Owner Manager Model Builder Sales Person Clerk
Golf Club	Manager Golf Pro Caddie Master Golf Course Manager Caddie Golf Range Attendant
Health Spa or Club	Owner Manager Fitness Instructor Trainer Equipment Handler Masseuse

TABLE 2-11. (Continued)

Type of Business	Sample Jobs
Tennis or Racquet Club	Owner
	Manager
	Tennis Pro
	Equipment Manager
	Maintenance Person
	Schedule Clerk
Aquatic Complex	Director
	Swimming Pool Manager
	Senior Life Guard
	Swimming Instructor
	Lifeguard

ice, air traffic control, emergency medical services, prison services, schools, mass transit, and park maintenance and recreation program services.

Aside from providing excellent entrepreneurial opportunities, privatization has saved taxpayers money. By operating with less expensive labor, achieving economies of scale, choosing dynamic markets, and applying business principles, entrepreneurs are succeeding where the government has often failed. The President's Private Sector Survey on Cost Control determined that privatization saved the government a total of $37 billion over a three-year period.[42]

Contracting and consulting services have, for some time, been an important service arrangement in the public sector. Public recreation agencies historically have hired specialists such as construction crews, lawyers, doctors, and other professionals to perform critical services the agencies, for a variety of reasons, could not provide for themselves. The economic problems recently facing public agencies has prompted an expansion of the contract service arrangement. In these relationships, public agencies and commercial leisure specialists form a cooperative relationship to ensure delivery of a service or services at reasonable costs.

The contractor provides a variety of services: program maintenance, fund raising, marketing, or whatever special services the community deems essential. This cooperative effort can take several forms such as corporate gifts to the public agency, a manager's working with nonprofit fund raising agencies and other sharing programs (Adopt-a-Park, Executive Loan, etc.), joint capital development (such as lease-back programs where a public facility is leased for a private business), and private contracting (for facility maintenance, facility management, or major program services).

But there can be problems for both the public agency and the commercial business engaged in private contracting arrangements. They must solve the problem of establishing a legal relationship that ensures that an independent contractor is in fact independent and not an employee. For example, Jane Wagner-Tyack, Director of Public Affairs for California Parks and Recreation reported the case of two former contractors who filed with the California Unemployment Insurance Appeals Board for unemployment insurance benefits after their contract was terminated by the cities of Long Beach and Redondo Beach. The cities interpreted the contract arrangement to exempt them from unemployment insurance tax liability. The California Employment Development Department (EDD) granted them employee status. It was determined that both cities were in violation of the Revenue Taxation Code for failing to pay unemployment insurance premiums and not withholding income tax for certain program personnel. The cities had treated these people as independent contractors, but the EDD ruled they were, in fact, city employees, and demanded payment of unpaid state income taxes, penalties, and interest.[43]

Independent Contractor Guidelines. Whether you are addressing the issue of employee contractor status as outlined above or are establishing an independent consulting relationship with a corporate client to deliver employee recreation programs on contract, it is essential for federal and state income tax purposes to be certain the relationship is indeed one of an independent contractor. Otherwise certain business expenses are not deductible and both parties face sanctions by taxing authorities.

The characteristics of an independent contractor are:

1. He or she has a place of business (space, phone, utilities, equipment) in his or her name.
2. He or she advertises to the general public (business cards, stationery, classified advertising in the telephone book).
3. He or she has employees.
4. He or she has an account number for tax purposes.
5. He or she performs work under contract, written or oral, usually for more than one party.
6. He or she has a significant amount of capital invested in facilities and equipment.
7. He or she has, or should have, a business license.
8. He or she holds a franchise (the expressed written authority to act on behalf of the principal).
9. He or she, having the expertise in a specialized field of endeavor, determines how the task is to be performed and what hours are to be worked, and proceeds to accomplish the end product or service (within a specified time span) as set forth by the principal.

Not all these elements above must be met, however, because any challenge by taxing authorities to a claim by an individual that he or she is an independent contractor will be made from the integrated picture of the entire working relationship drawn from a significant grouping of the above factors. Of course, all contracts of this sort should be reviewed by legal counsel.

In the future there will be increased opportunities for individuals to deliver commercial leisure services as independent contractors and consultants. Neil C. Smart, former Parks and Recreation Service Manager for the City of Santa Cruz, California noted, "I see a future for contractors and the private sector to provide eliminated and/or diminished recreational and park services, especially as economic crises are faced in the public sector."[44]

Undoubtedly, as the future unfolds, entrepreneurs will seize new opportunities in the leisure market to build new programs, new leisure service organizations, and take the field in new directions.

Summary

An overview of five categories of commercial leisure services has been presented in this chapter. These five areas are: (1) travel and tourism; (2) hospitality services; (3) entertainment services; (4) leisure services in the natural environment; and (5) retail outlets.

Travel and tourism is a major revenue producer ($60 billion annually). It is not an isolated service entity, but is inextricably linked to the hospitality industry and, less directly, to the entertainment industry. Tourism is one of the top three revenue producers in thirty-nine of the fifty states; 8 percent of the total U.S. civilian labor force is employed in a tourism-related enterprise.

Tourism in America became a significant industry after the invention of the automobile. World War II marked the beginning of rapid growth in the travel and tourism domain because of easy credit and economic prosperity.

There are new trends in tourism on the horizon. The recent economic downturn has created a realignment of the "haves" and "have nots." The latter group tends to travel closer to home, eat at fast food restaurants, and take shorter vacations. The "haves," on the other hand, represent a growing segment of the market who spend money freely with few worries about debt. They are consuming expensive travel programs.

The history of the hospitality and food service industry parallels that of the travel and tourism industry. Accommodation services grew in response to increases in travel. Between 1900 and 1960 the hotel industry developed four different kinds of hotels: (1) the commercial or transient hotel; (2) the residential hotel; (3) the luxury hotel; and (4) the resort hotel. After World War II a new dimension was added to the hospitality industry—the motel.

Because rooms at an average hotel for one night can exceed $100, today's consumers are looking for value in their lodging needs. This need for value has seen the rapid growth of bargain accommodations such as the Motel 6 chain.

Bed and breakfast inns are also experiencing rapid growth. While a poor employment source, these inns are excellent vehicles by which an entrepreneur can enter the hospitality field.

Theme parks in America were launched in 1955 by Walt Disney Productions with the opening of Disneyland in Anaheim, California. The theme park was vastly different from its predecessor, the amusement park. The latter was not always a well-maintained facility and was frequently the site of antisocial behavior. Disneyland, on the other hand, established a theme park formula that corrected these conditions. Today the Disney formula is copied by almost every major theme park in the country.

The circus, more than the amusement park, was the progenitor of the theme park. The circus features acts that change yearly, a variety of adult-oriented as well as child-oriented performances, and attractiveness to families. In this respect, it is similar to the Disney formula for theme parks.

The circus is a combination of two early performance formats; human performers and the menagerie or animal acts.

The theme park industry is, at best, difficult to enter as an owner. The capital investment in a new theme park could easily reach $300 million. However, theme parks support many other leisure service businesses such as motels, novelty shops, campgrounds, tour bus operations, and theaters.

Variety is the prime characteristic of leisure service organizations in the natural environment. Yet despite this variability of services, there is evidence of cooperative relationships between services in this category. This category therefore is referred to as the outdoor recreation system. Characteristics of organizations in the system are that they use the natural environment as a stage, they have a symbiotic relationship with other system members, they frequently deal with governmental agencies, and they often serve the same customers as other system members. The commercial outdoor recreation system has been described in terms of four elements and their economic correlates:

1. Users and their characteristics (demand)
2. Outdoor leisure services and product sales at the retail level (supply)
3. Delivery strategies of services (profitability)
4. Marketing strategies (distribution)

Retail outlets are businesses that offer products or services directly to consumers in convenient quantities and at convenient locations. Retail outlets may be classified as store or nonstore (e.g., mail order).

Retail contract services permit organizations (e.g., public recreation departments) to enter into an agreement with a recreation service provider (an independent business) to operate the community's recreation program. The community is contracting for services, in this case recreation programming, that it is not equipped to provide itself by reason of economics or expertise.

Contract services and consulting practices dealing with leisure organizations is a growing area. Many of the nation's medium and large companies, for example, are turning to leisure consultants to organize, plan, and direct industrial recreation and leisure services for their employees.

Study Questions

1. List and describe the five areas of service that constitute commercial leisure services.
2. What were the factors that contributed to the growth of the travel and tourism industry?
3. What factors prompted the growth of the hospitality industry?
4. List and define the various categories of lodging.
5. What are the advantages to opening up a hotel as a franchise?
6. How could leisure services increase revenues to a community that is situated near a lake?
7. Explain the difference(s) between a theme park and an amusement park.
8. Describe the Disney formula for success for a theme park.

9. List and describe the elements and their economic correlates of the commercial outdoor recreation system.
10. What are the guidelines that determine that an individual operating under a contract service arrangement is self-employed (an independent contractor) and not an employee?

Experiential Exercise

I. In order to gain a better grasp of the magnitude and variability of the commercial leisure service field, you should begin a "literature search." Find at least five advertisements or articles from each of the commercial leisure services domains discussed in the text. These advertisements or articles should be bound into a portfolio under the appropriate headings and shared with other members of the class or study group. In this way, each participant's understanding will be broadened by sharing the examples uncovered by colleagues. The categories are:

1. Travel and tourism
2. Hospitality and food services
3. Entertainment services (theme parks)
4. Leisure services in the natural environment
5. Retail outlets: store and nonstore

II. Refer to Table 2-1. Categorize each of these services into one of the five domains. How many new services can you come up with? Place them in appropriate domains. Can you identify an additional domain?

Notes

1. Valene L. Smith, *Hosts and Guests: The Anthropology of Tourism*, Philadelphia: University of Pennsylvania Press, 1977, p. 2.
2. Ibid.
3. Oliver Jensen, Joan P. Kerr, Murray Belsky, *American Album*. New York: American Heritage Publishing Co., 1968, p. 321.
4. Ibid.
5. Ibid., p. 322.
6. Campbell McConnell, *Economics*, 7th ed. New York: McGraw Hill, 1978.
7. Tony Mobley, quoted in "Goodbye to the Good Life?" *U.S. News & World Report*, Aug. 4, 1980, p. 48.
8. Undersecretary for Travel and Tourism, U.S. Department of Commerce, Unpublished Monograph, April 25, 1984, Washington, D.C.
9. "Quest for Fun on a Shoestring," *U.S. News & World Report*, Aug. 10, 1981, pp. 60–64.
10. Larry Reibstein, "Franchise Facts—Action in Budget Motels," *Venture*, Dec. 1983, p. 130.
11. Ibid.
12. Nathan Kalt, *Introduction to the Hospitality Industry*. New York: I.T.T. Educational Services, 1971, p. 24. Kalt paraphrases Kipling.
13. Ibid., p. 9.

14. A. Pizam, R. C. Lewis, P. Manning, "Introduction," in A. Pizam, R. C. Lewis, P. Manning (eds.), *The Practice of Hospitality Management.* Westport, CT: AVI Publishing, 1982, p. 12.
15. T.S. Beggs, R.C. Lewis, "The Future Impact of Inflation on the Hotel Industry," in A. Pizam, R.C. Lewis, P. Manning (eds.), The Practice of Hospitality Management. Westport, CT: AVI Publishing, 1982, pp. 499–510.
16. Pizam et al., p. 13.
17. The Consumer Travel and Tourism Consultants International, *Travel Market Yearbook, 1981.* Cherry Hill, NJ: The Consumer Travel and Tourism Consultants International, 1981, pp. 45–66.
18. Richard P. Friese, "Travel Industry Overview," in *Travel Market Yearbook, 1981.* Cherry Hill, NJ: The Consumer Travel and Tourism Consultants International, 1981.
19. James M. Cameron, Ronald Bordessa, *Wonderland Through the Looking Glass.* Maple, Ontario: Belsten Publishing, 1981, p. 16.
20. Joseph L. Levy, *Play Behavior*, New York: John Wiley & Sons, 1978, pp. 12–14.
21. Cameron and Bordessa, p. 493.
22. Patricia McKay, "Theme Parks: USA," *Theater Crafts,* September, 1977, p. 56.
23. Ibid.
24. George L. Chindahl, *The History of the Circus in America.* Caldwell, IA: The Caxton Printers, 1959, p. 1.
25. Ibid., p. 2.
26. Ibid., p. 67.
27. Ibid., p. 137.
28. Ibid., p. 145.
29. Kathryn Harris, "Disney's Lure is Hurting Other Florida Parks," *Los Angeles Times,* Sept. 18, 1983, p. 6.
30. Cameron and Bordessa, p. 16.
31. Douglas M. Knudson, *Outdoor Recreation,* New York: Macmillan, 1980, p. 11.
32. R. E. Carlson, J.R. MacClean, T.R. Deppe, J.A. Peterson, *Recreation and Leisure: The Changing Scene,* 3rd ed., Belmont, CA: Wadsworth Publishing, 1979, p. 60.
33. "The Boom in Leisure," *U.S. News & World Report,* May 23, 1977, p. 62.
34. "Our Endless Pursuit of Happiness," *U.S. News & World Report,* Aug. 10, 1981, pp. 58–60.
35. Carlson et al., p. 66.
36. Bureau of Outdoor Recreation, *The Recreation Imperative,* Washington, D.C.: U.S. Department of the Interior, 1974, p. 196.
37. Sharon Balderson, *Weekend World Press,* July 15, 1983, p. 1.
38. July Greenwald, "Arts and Profits in the Virgin Islands," *Venture,* October, 1982, pp. 78–79.
39. Mary A. Fischer, "When Jake Steinfeld Barks, Spielberg, Presley, and Garr Jump (and Stretch and Bend)," *People,* May 9, 1983, pp. 56–59.
40. "Lifting Physical Fitness to New, Lucrative Heights," *San Diego Union,* March 25, 1984, pp. C1–C4 (Business/Sports Section).
41. Kevin Farrell, "Going Private—Public Service in Private Hands," *Venture,* July, 1984, p. 34.
42. Ibid., p. 36.
43. Jane Wagner-Tyack, "The Contractor/Employee Controversy," *California Parks and Recreation Society,* February/March, Vol. 37, No. 2, p. 29.
44. Personal communication: Neil C. Smart, Parks and Recreation Services Manager, City of Santa Cruz, California, November 16, 1982.

Close-up: Lazy "J" Ranch Camp

Jerry and Arnold Johnson moved to California from Chicago in 1949. Jerry is a graduate of Northwestern University with a degree in Art. In California she began teaching art at the exclusive Marlbourogh Girls' School in Los Angeles. Arnold was employed as a civil engineer for the Edison Company of Los Angeles. At that time Jerry and Arnold lived on a small farm in the San Fernando Valley.

During her tenure as an art teacher, Jerry would arrange for her talented art students to make weekend trips to the farm to provide them with an opportunity to see first hand a variety of farm animals. Within a year of the first weekend excursion, Jerry was receiving calls from parents asking her to take their children on a regular basis. They praised the Johnsons for the stimulating and entertaining environment the farm provided.

Jerry soon found her farm-art program expanding. Holidays and summers had become periods of high demand. The Johnsons discovered there was a need for a specialized camp program geared to youngsters who had interest in art and horsemanship. They sold their small five-acre farm and bought a forty-acre ranch not far away. Word-of-mouth advertising soon established the Lazy "J" Ranch Camp as one of the quality programs of its type in California.

Arnold left his job with the Edison Company to take over the equestrian program while Jerry assumed the duties of camp director in addition to her involvement with the arts and crafts program.

By the middle of the 1950s, the Lazy "J" Ranch was entertaining over 150 campers and had a staff of twenty. Summers were usually booked up a year in advance. Many of Hollywood's stars enrolled their children in the Lazy "J" program. Counselors often stayed on the staff for five or more years.

Jerry Johnson stressed professionalism at all levels of her operation. Counselors were expected to be mature, energetic, skilled in one or more activities, and above all else, to like children. The close family feeling engineered by Jerry and Arnold required the counselors to exhibit a high degree of loyalty. Counselors who did not live up to the high standards set by the Johnsons were quietly yet decisively asked to leave. There is always a waiting list of counselor replacements through the Lazy "J" Camp counselor-in-training program.

Eventually the camp also became well known for its equestrian teams. Campers could bring their own horses and board them on the property or train on one of the many horses owned by the Lazy "J" Ranch. The program expanded to include an inclusive animal husbandry program for campers between the ages of seven and ten. Campers in this age group were assigned to care for specific animals and could earn an award at a camp fair held during the latter part of each two-week period.

In the 1960s the camp moved to Malibu. The new Lazy "J" Ranch Camp is a 180-acre ranch built in the 1930s located on a mountain top overlooking the Pacific Ocean. The original owner was actor William Boyd, who played Hopalong Cassidy in the movies. Facilities include a large recreation hall, a fifty-foot swimming pool, equestrian facilities, an archery range, an athletic field, and many historic buildings. The main house is a 6,000-square-foot replica of a Spanish hacienda.

The Lazy "J" Ranch has served over 5,000 children in its forty years of service. Many of the campers today are the children and grandchildren of some of the early campers. The Johnsons have employed over 600 professionals and are credited with launching the careers of over two dozen professional recreation specialists.

When asked the secret of her success, Jerry Johnson answered unhesitantly, "the staff is the single most important ingredient for success. Second, children must have fun—they come to camp to have fun." Regarding the facility design, Jerry stated most emphatically, "the approach is that the camp must have charm and make you feel happy to have arrived."

Thirty-five years after the founding of the Lazy "J" Ranch Camp, it is still the most popular and successful commercial children's camp in the western United States.

3

Career Development

There are a number of steps that should be considered in planning for a career in the commercial leisure services area. To assist individuals in understanding them, we will present a four-step career development model. Components of this model include: self assessment of personal interests and skills; career exploration; academic preparation and reality testing; and job search strategy. All of these components are interrelated in that the information gained in one helps in understanding others. *You* are at the center of the career development model; you must analyze, evaluate, and integrate information in order to determine a successful course of action for yourself. This chapter will prepare you to begin your personal career quest.

In addition to presenting a career model, this chapter will compare self-employment (entrepreneurship) with salaried employment as two major and distinct career tracks. A curriculum is presented that should assist you in preparing for professional employment as either an owner/manager or an employee of a commercial leisure service organization.

The remainder of the chapter will focus on strategies for securing employment as a corporate employee. These strategies include resume building, letter writing, and preparing for employment interviews.

The Career Development Model

Career planning consists of a series of actions that will teach persons how to plan and achieve their career goals. This process can best be explained through the use of a career development model. The four major components of this model and the person's role as an agent of change are illustrated in Figure 3-1.

This model stresses the need for persons to know themselves, to know the world of work, and to combine this knowledge when making a career decision. It is not necessary to move sequentially through the process; you may need to reconsider or reevaluate an issue confronted in an earlier step. It is recommended, however, that self-assessment be the first step undertaken in the career development process.

Self Assessment

Shakespeare said, "go to your bosom; knock there, and ask your heart what it doth know." Within each person lies the source of success. Professional success is realized by choosing the right career path, which should be more than a job that yields a paycheck. Your work should be an expression of your self.

It is essential to identify your interests. Interests are those things in life that hold your attention. Interests should not be confused with curiosity. Curiosity may be a passing desire to learn or know about something. An interest, by contrast, is a sustained focus. The things that interest us do

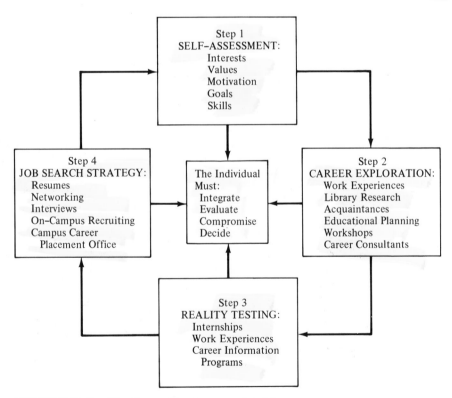

FIGURE 3–1. The Career Development Model.

change, of course, but not readily. Our interests often guide our decisions. Of course, as our interests change or mature so do our personal objectives, such as career goals. Counseling centers at universities and colleges usually have tools for measuring personal interests.

The study of interests has probably received its strongest support from vocational and educational counseling. In terms of vocational success, achievement is a result of aptitude and interest. Although these two variables are positively correlated, a high level in one does not necessarily imply a high level in the other. A measure of both permits a more effective prediction of performance than would be possible from the measurement of either alone.

Perhaps the most reliable and popular interest inventory is the *Strong Vocational Interest Blank.* The inventory consists of 325 items grouped into seven parts. For the first five parts, occupations, school subjects, activities (e.g., making a speech, repairing a clock, raising money for charity), amusements, and day-to-day contacts with various types of people (e.g., very old people, military officers, people who live dangerously), the respondent records a preference by marking whether they like, dislike or are indifferent to the choices. The remaining two parts require the respondent to express a preference between paired items (e.g., dealing with things versus dealing with people) and marking a set of self-descriptive statements "yes," "no," or "?."

Another widely used instrument in the area of self-assessment is the *Study of Values,* which was prepared by Allport, Vernon, and Lindzey. This inventory was designed to measure the relative strength of six basic values in the respondent: theoretical (discovers truth by empirical, rational, or intellectual approach), economic (emphasizes useful and practical values conforming closely to the prevailing stereotype of the average businessman), esthetic (places highest value on form and harmony), social (is altruistic and philanthropic), political (interest in personal power, influence, and renown), and religious (concerned with the unity of all experience).

A third instrument is the *Work Value Inventory,* which was designed for use in academic settings. This self-report inventory explores the sources of satisfaction a person seeks in his or her work. The Work Value Inventory measures creativity, intellectual stimulation, associates, economic return, security, prestige, and altruism.

Career Exploration

Once a person has a suitable idea of his or her personal strengths and limitations, it is time to actively explore career options.

Those who have opted for a career in the leisure field should further narrow the career selection process. This involves limiting the career field to a choice between working in the public sector or within the commercial-private sector. Often this choice is predicated on the availability of current employment opportunities. We will explore this idea of job availability.

Not a few scholars in the leisure field have chided university departments of recreation and leisure across the country for producing more graduates than the field can absorb. Viewed from an historical perspective this criticism may be deserved. But the leisure field has changed. No longer is the public sector the primary provider of leisure services. The private sector has emerged as the largest provider of leisure services in the United States. The unparallelled growth in private leisure businesses, particularly small commercial leisure businesses, is producing numerous opportunities for employment in the leisure field. Of course, the job descriptions and job titles may be unfamiliar, and one may have to look outside of the "Help Wanted—Recreation Leader" listings to locate these opportunities. What is needed is an overhaul of college and university leisure studies curricula to reflect the changes in the employment market in leisure services.

Staying current on employment trends in the leisure industry is crucial for those wishing to enter the commercial leisure services field. Many of the future jobs in leisure services will be created by technology and the explosive growth in entrepreneurial endeavors. Naisbitt noted, as mentioned in Chapter 1, ". . . in 1950 we were creating new businesses at the rate of 93,000 per year. Today, we are creating new companies in this country at the rate of about 600,000 a year."[1] Six million new jobs have been created in small business since 1976—a significant contribution to the job market by small business in the past six years. While the figures for leisure enterprises started each year are not separately identifiable, we can assume that many of these 600,000 new starts annually are commercial leisure service organizations.

What, generally, will the employment market look like in the coming decades? In a special edition of *U.S. News & World Report,* May 9, 1983, dealing with "The Next Fifty Years," the editors made the following points regarding the future employment market:

1. American industry will be rebuilt.
2. Only one out of ten workers will work in industries that symbolize the industrial revolution: auto, steel, textile.
3. Most workers will be earning their living providing information, advice, and services to society.
4. Entrepreneurs will find big companies wanting their services, especially in services and high technology fields.
5. During the next fifty years, scores of new occupations will crop up, reflecting advances in computers and health care and a growing demand for services and leisure activities.
6. We will be a society less dependent upon manufacturing and more devoted to providing services.
7. By the year 2000, more than a million geriatric workers will be employed.
8. Because of the complexity and constant changes in technology, few workers will hold one job for life.
9. Retraining programs will become commonplace in most large private firms.
10. There is a coming revolution in culture. For example, one forecaster sees "communities of consciousness" where computers will link networks of people sharing common ideologies and interests.[2]

We might conclude from this and from personal observation and evaluation of daily events that professional preparation must accommodate variable goals. Furthermore, leisure itself is undergoing a major transfor-

Commercial Leisure Services

mation, viz., a shift from public to private services, home entertainment centers, leisure programs embracing the consciousness growth phenomena, and the move into the retraining field. Perhaps we are beneficiaries of the old Chinese curse, "may you live in interesting times."

There seems to be great pressure on students today to select a career goal early in their college education. This is difficult. It is difficult because of the personal changes that take place in the learning process (at any age) and the changeability of the job market. Yet the idea behind a college "major" suggests that students need to reach some decision about a career at least by their third year of college. As suggested in Figure 3-1 (steps 2 and 3), work experiences, campus career days, personal acquaintances and their friends, and the appraisal of personal interest and values should suggest a course of study or career track.

Academic Preparation and Reality Testing

Chapter 2 makes it clear that the choice of a career in a commercial leisure service business has opportunities and obstacles. The opportunities are born out of the rich diversity of services that constitute the field of commercial leisure services.

This diversity also poses problems for educators and students in identifying specific competencies that will facilitate success in a specific leisure service business. For example, how does one prepare academically to own, operate, or work for a company specializing in river raft excursions? Or consider a person interested in owning and operating a private children's camp. What experiences, educationally and job related, would assist this person in gaining entrance to and succeeding in this specific area? It is suggested, then, that one's career goals and plans be directed more toward one of the five major service domains identified in Chapter 1 and discussed

High adventure recreation requires extensive training in leadership and outdoor skills. (John Bullaro)

more fully in Chapter 2 than toward a specific commercial leisure service organization.

When we consider each of the five types of commercial leisure service organizations, (see Figure 1-1, Chapter 1), and use the variables of function and focus of service, identifiable skills and competencies emerge that are common to all the businesses in that particular service domain. Taking the river raft excursion enterprise and private camp examples, we can identify some broad competencies common to both employment environments.

1. Leadership
2. Orienteering (map and compass skills)
3. Emergency procedures
4. Ecological insights and resource management
5. Public speaking
6. Written communication
7. Budgeting and finance
8. Marketing of leisure services

Thus, a person who prepares for a career in the domain of leisure services in the natural environment, for example, will be preparing for a variety of career opportunities, gaining, perhaps, specific career-related skills through a well-chosen internship program or part-time employment. Later in this chapter you will find a section entitled "Planning an Educational Package" that details general skills and competencies identified by a select jury of experts to be common to all commercial leisure services.

Tour leaders require extensive training in foreign languages and international law and economics and should possess a great deal of patience and understanding. (John Bullaro)

Reality testing is nothing more than taking a plan (in this case a tentative career choice or major course of study) and determining if it feels right for you and if career opportunities exist that will meet your needs. This "testing" is accomplished through part-time employment and internships. Not a few individuals opt to become recreation majors on the notion that this field is fun and an easy way to earn a degree. Taking courses in recreation programming, leisure research, public administration, and the history and philosophy of leisure (among others) might quickly bring them back to reality and demonstrate that the leisure studies curriculum is indeed a demanding one. An internship at a private resort, for example, could quickly open the door for meaningful and profitable professional employment and subsequent career contacts. In any case, reality brings before us the information we need to make sound decisions.

Job Search Strategy

The search for the right job frequently requires "pick and shovel" work. Preparing a resume is time consuming and needs to reflect the area under consideration. For example, if a person has skills in leading leisure programs and in product or service sales, one of these areas of expertise should be highlighted over the other, depending on the nature of the position for which he or she is applying. Thus, it is difficult to have one resume that will be effective for all positions in the commercial leisure services field. We will discuss this process thoroughly later in the chapter.

Selecting a Career Path

For the person who choses to work in the leisure field, the next question to answer is "Do I want to work for myself or someone else?" To determine if business ownership is appropriate or not is usually not an easy matter. Research over the years has suggested that having an entrepreneurial parent is frequently a contributing factor to a person's disposition towards this employment mode. Shapero suggests that the prime factor motivating people to become entrepreneurs is their having been "dislodged from some nice, familiar niche."[3] This dislocation can result from several types of situations:

1. Being an emigrant
2. Being fired or passed over for promotion
3. Having an opportunity arise (such as an inheritance or meeting a particular person) that jars original career goals
4. Being transferred by an employer

Thus, personal history, stage in life, and personal philosophy can combine in some unique way to move a person towards entrepreneurship. Deciding which career path to follow, whether to engage in business ownership or work as an employee, can be an adventure in self discovery.

Step one of the career development model should help a person decide which of these two options, self employment or employee status, is right for them. In addition to the self-assessment process outlined in Figure 3–1, completion of the following exercise on the traits of enterpeneurs will provide further insight into selecting between self employment or working for someone else. The review of the biographies of successful entrepreneurs featured in *Venture* between January, 1981 and July, 1983 suggests a list of "psycho-philosophical traits of successful entrepreneurs." This list of traits is reported here. The answers to the questions can prove insightful.

(Answer each of the following questions and place a check mark under the appropriate column.)

Psycho-philosophical Traits of Successful Entrepreneurs

Issue	Yes	No
1. I prefer to be a care giver rather than care taker.	____	____
2. An important person's opinion easily directs my behavior.	____	____
3. I want to make an impact on society.	____	____
4. I prefer to do all phases of a particular task as opposed to just one or two.	____	____
5. I understand and support with enthusiasm the free enterprise system.	____	____
6. I work best with no supervision.	____	____
7. I hold people in authority in high regard.	____	____
8. I enjoy teaching others.	____	____
9. I see myself as a parent figure.	____	____
10. I am not afraid to make unpopular decisions.	____	____

No single test or other measuring device exists that can predict success in business to any acceptable level of reliability. However, assembling a mosaic of test scores, attitudinal surveys, and personal history assessments coupled with a specific opportunity appraisal can yield a success potential profile.

In the case of the issues in the above list, the statements were the most mentioned "yes" traits in biographies of successful entrepreneurs. Still, if you marked all yeses or mostly yeses, it only suggests a propensity for self employment. However, being psychologically or philosophically oriented to entrepreneurship is a good starting point for further investigation.

On the other hand, recognizing that you are not of an entrepreneurial bent is an equally important discovery, one that can save thousands of dollars and hundreds of unpleasant if not futile hours. Both self employment and salaried employment are discussed further in the following sections of the book.

Self Employment

The successful entrepreneur is often pictured sitting behind an elegant desk, surrounded by mementos of material success, and looking confident. Here is a person, we say to ourselves, who has grabbed control of his or her life, who is no longer a "wage slave," and who makes events happen instead of waiting for luck to make a visit.

In fact, once the commitment is made to "go it alone," one's world takes a radical change—sometimes for the better, too frequently for the worse. Many small businesses fail in their infancy. In fact, of the 600,000 new businesses born each year in the United States, only half live as long as eighteen months and only one in five lives as long as ten years.[4] Our archetypical hero who emerges among the survivors is indeed self reliant, strong, and not infrequently affluent.

If you have completed the exercise on the psycho-philosophical traits of entrepreneurs above, you should have, a sense of your personal orientation to the two career paths (self- or salaried employment) under consideration here. Additional considerations will be presented that will aid you, we hope, in deciding which path to choose.

Frequently one of the first questions a career researcher asks is, "am I the type of person who can handle the special demands of small business ownership," in other words, "can I take the heat in the kitchen?" To develop insight into this fundamental question, you need to first answer some secondary questions. Would you hire yourself and do you have the qualities necessary to succeed? Would you hire someone with your strengths and weaknesses? This is the time for frankness about your personal "balance sheet." Perhaps a friend or acquaintance (preferably an entrepreneur) would help you with this personal appraisal (see Table 3-1).

A U.S. Small Business Administration study showed that successful managers possessed superior amounts of certain personality characteristics.[5] "Success" in this study was measured by the satisfaction of the owners and others who dealt with the owner including the community at large. Five characteristics showed a significant correlation to success. They were drive, thinking ability, human relations ability, communications ability, and technical knowledge (see Figure 3-2).

1. *Drive* is defined as a blending of responsibility, vigor, initiative, persistence, and health.
2. *Thinking ability* consists of original, creative, critical, and analytical thinking.
3. *Human relations ability* is composed of ascendency (one has control or power in his or her life), emotional stability, sociability, cautiousness, personal relations, consideration, cheerfulness, cooperation, and tactfulness.
4. *Communications ability* is composed of verbal comprehension, oral communication, and written expression.
5. *Technical knowledge* is the information an entrepreneur had regarding the physical process of producing the product or carrying out the service and the ability to use this information purposefully.

At the end of this chapter is an experiential exercise that requires the use of Table 3-1. You are urged to complete this exercise and rate your score. This exercise will not only assist you in self assessment but will give you an idea of how much your perception of your personality conforms with that of others. It is not essential to be a paragon of strength in every area, but it would be foolish to risk personal and borrowed resources unless a weak profile can be strengthened.

Causes of Failure

According to Walker, "most entrepreneurs are miserably prepared to enter business."[6] Some people have considerable business experience in a par-

TABLE 3-1. Rating Scale For Personal Traits Important to a Small-Business Owner

Instructions: After each question place a check mark on the line at the point closest to your answer. The check mark need not be placed directly over one of the suggested answers because your rating may lie somewhere between two answers. Be honest with yourself.

Are you a self-starter?	I do things my own way. Nobody needs to tell me to get going.	If someone gets me started, I keep going all right.	Easy does it. I don't put myself out until I have to.
How do you feel about other people?	I like people. I can get along with just about anybody.	I have plenty of friends. I don't need anyone else.	Most people bug me.
Can you lead others?	I can get most people to go along without much difficulty.	I can get people to do things if I drive them.	I let someone else get things moving.
Can you take responsibility?	I like to take charge of and see things through.	I'll take over if I have to, but I'd rather let someone else be responsible.	There's always some eager beaver around wanting to show off. I say let him.
How good an organizer are you?	I like to have a plan before I start. I'm usually the one to get things lined up.	I do all right unless things get too goofed up. Then I cop out.	I just take things as they come.
How good a worker are you?	I can keep going as long as necessary. I don't mind working hard.	I'll work hard for a while, but when I've had enough, that's it!	I can't see that hard work gets you anywhere.
Can you make decisions?	I can make up my mind in a hurry if necessary, and my decision is usually o.k.	I can if I have plenty of time. If I have to make up my mind fast, I usually regret it.	I don't like to be the one who decides things. I'd probably blow it.
Can people trust what you say?	They sure can. I don't say things I don't mean.	I try to be on the level, but sometimes I just say what's easiest.	What's the sweat if the other fellow doesn't know the difference?
Can you stick with it?	If I make up my mind to do something, I don't let anything stop me.	I usually finish what I start.	If a job doesn't go right, I turn off. Why beat your brains out?
How good is your health?	I never run down.	I have enough energy for most things I want to do.	I run out of juice sooner than most of my friends seem to.

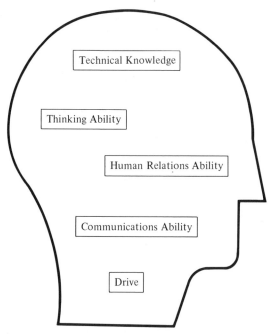

FIGURE 3–2. Characteristics correlated with successful management.

ticular field but find themselves technically or emotionally unprepared to be "the creator of ideas, the boss and the person who has to meet the Friday-night payroll."[7] Walker goes on to say that only about 40 percent of the firms started this year will be operating five years from now. Supporting this view, Broom and Longenecker cite a 1977 report by Dun & Bradstreet that states that management seems to be the number one problem of the enterprise. These management failures, report Broom and Longenecker, are in the areas of competition, capital, location, and premature expansion.[8] A closer look at the causes of business failure reveals:

1. Owners do not know or understand their market.
2. Owners mismanage money. Having access to large sums of money frequently calls out the demon of misappropriation, i.e., buying things that do not produce profit.
3. No attention is paid to costs or cash flow requirements. A business must generate more cash than it spends to conduct its business.
4. Owners have accumulated too much inventory and follow a pricing strategy that is too low. When this is the case, Walker suggests improving the service or doing something unique and charging more.[9]

If we were to compile the chief causes of business failures into one category, it would be poor management. Most failures are attributable to management error. Competent management requires the entrepreneur to exercise a high level of stewardship over the funds of the business. The overriding requirement for successful business ownership is financial competence. This means initially planning for and getting the requisite amount of money needed to start and keep the business running without getting into cash flow troubles. An entrepreneur who excels in this area will have a wider margin for error in other management areas. This axiom does not work in reverse, however.

There are factors that adversely affect individual firms over which the owners have little control. As was noted above, however, even in such cases the astute manager can often soften the blow or sometimes change adversity into an asset. These uncontrollable factors are

1. Overall poor business conditions
2. Relocations of highways
3. Sudden changes in consumer interests
4. The replacement of existing services (and products) by new services (or products)
5. Local politics

The leisure service organization, while affected by these exigencies of the marketplace, often has the flexibility to respond quickly because little cash is tied up in "fragile" inventory.

Salaried Employment

While dreams continue to motivate prospective entrepreneurs to launch their own enterprise, it behooves the entrepreneurial aspirant to weigh the two career paths carefully. As mentioned, each path has advantages and disadvantages that need to be seriously evaluated in light of personality strengths and weaknesses and current market conditions. The list below indicates the advantages and disadvantages of working for someone else. This comparison is not an exhaustive analysis because each work setting may differ, but it is a strategy you should follow in selecting and evaluating your personal career choice.

Advantages of Salaried Employment	Disadvantages of Salaried Employment
• No risk to personal savings	• Rigid salary prospect
• Security and fringe benefits	• Measure of worth by others
• Fixed working conditions	• Residence mobility limited
• Sense of security	• "Deadly" politics
• Career growth delineated	• Extrinsic controls

Risk. In considering the advantages of salaried employment, you might start with the assumption that it is preferable to earn a yearly salary of $15,000 to a profit of $15,000. Remember, to earn the profit you must invest considerable money—some personal, some borrowed. Setting aside any tax advantages or personal pride that often accompany business ownership, the fact remains that risking money is something some people cannot tolerate.

Small Business Reporter, which is published by the Bank of America, illustrated that a bicycle shop must have annual sales of $100,000 to generate a net income, before taxes, of $21,000. To launch this enterprise, the investor/owner will need a minimum investment of $36,000. Let's assume the entrepreneur invested $20,000 of personal funds and borrowed the balance from a bank or friends. If this same individual had salaried employment paying $15,000 a year and kept his or her $20,000 invested in a certificate of deposit at the bank, which might pay 10 percent interest without risk of capital, the total income realized before taxes would be $17,000. If one gives up a salary greater than our example, then the argument for salaried employment becomes stronger.[10]

Security/Fringe Benefits. Most employers provide paid group medical insurance, retirement plans, paid holidays, and frequently pay for trips to professional conferences. The business owner must provide these benefits for himself or herself (not to mention for his or her employees) at a cost that could exceed 10 percent of monthly payroll, or in our illustration of a $15,000 net profit before taxes, an additional $125 per month ($15,000 ÷ 12 × .10 = $125.00).

Fixed Working Conditions. When an employee is hired, he or she is usually expected to perform the duties described in a specific job description. In most instances the employee knows what performance is expected from the onset and may soon find these expectations rather confining intellectually. However, at the end of the work day the employee returns home and is free to do other things with his or her leisure time. In time, and as the employee ascends the corporate ladder, this rather benign scenario changes radically. By some estimates, middle and upper executives work more than 60 hours a week. Usually this schedule is self-imposed, yet to stay in the "race" and succeed as an employee, it is often required.

In contrast to the employee with long weekends, paid vacations, and multiple fringe benefits, we often find the new business owner working twelve hour days, six and not infrequently seven days a week, dealing with payroll, accounts receivable, and numerous governmental regulations: rarely having any time off. Unless a partnership exists, our entrepreneur also may have a sense of loneliness and isolation when it comes to sharing the burdens of management.

Sense of Security. Being a member of a corporate team often engenders a sense of family in the employee, although it can be a short-lived experience. Rewards for playing on the team take many forms: expense accounts, a company automobile, a private office, cash bonuses and profit sharing, access to company secrets, and paid membership in a country club. Less obtrusive rewards are a warm salutory greeting in the hall, invitations to the "in" social events, secret tips on money-making opportunities, and other fraternal gestures. Lest this picture appear padded, keep in mind that most large organizations must offer an ever-expanding array of "perks" (benefits) to keep highly talented personnel.

Career Growth. Career goals should be selected early. Choosing one area over another in the leisure market usually means learning a particular set of skills that may not be applicable in another area. For example, an entry level position in the travel industry may require you to learn federal regulations and industry procedures for ticketing passengers on various common carriers. The time spent learning these skills may not be of value in the amusement park business or in the resort management field. As our society becomes more technical, skills frequently become so specialized that transferring to other areas becomes difficult.

Whichever path you choose, you will rarely spend your entire career with one organization. The career path frequently involves three to five moves before retirement. In the initial stages of career development, it is essential to select a company or employer who will teach basic skills rather than one who offers attractive "perks." These will come later. "Pay your dues" is a cliche but one worth following.

The disadvantages to salaried employment are implied in the above discussion. Fixed salary schedules and clearly delineated job descriptions frequently frustrate the ambitious and creative employee. These rigid limits of employment are, in a sense, the way the organization defines the worth of an employee at a given time. Frequently this perception is not shared by the employee and not infrequently creates what Albert Shapero calls the displaced, uncomfortable entrepreneur. Shapero sums up other displacement factors:

> In one set of studies we interviewed 109 people who had formed companies in Austin, Texas. They were founders of technical, accounting, advertising and publishing firms, and boat and hi-fi stores. In 65 percent of the cases, the sole or primary influence (for striking out on ones own [sic]) was negative. We heard the same comments over and over again: "I was fired," "I was told I was going to be transferred to Hoboken by my company and I just didn't want to go," "I worked for the company for 10 years, day and night, and then they brought in their idiot son as my boss," "my boss sold the company."[11]

It is interesting to note that the Shapero study reported that entrepreneurs, when asked "what they would do if they lost their companies," replied "that they would promptly start a new one."[12] Clearly, business owners seem to believe in personal ownership of their means of income and seem to be committed to this option. This willingness to begin again suggests that entrepreneurs find a unique kind of personal satisfaction in owning their own business. Gail Sheehy, author of the bestseller *Pathfinders* (a book devoted to determining how people create lives characterized by a high level of well being), states: "the most satisfied people are the most highly educated . . . are likely to be running their own smaller businesses or to be self-employed." "A disproportionate percentage," writes Sheehy, "of younger men who scored high in life satisfaction are self employed."[13] Sheehy discovered that persons in white collar jobs or who were "stuck in middle management" were least likely to feel satisfied with their lives.

Careers get derailed for many reasons. These are identifiable "fatal flaws" that keep corporate executives from reaching the upper levels of management. This list of flaws might help you in planning your educational and employment strategies to include a run for the coveted prize of chief executive officer of a major leisure service corporation.

In an article in *Psychology Today*, McCall and Lombardo presented a study of corporate leadership characteristics. They compared "twenty-one derailed executives—successful people who were expected to go even higher in the organization but who were fired or were forced to retire early—with twenty 'arrivers'—those who made it all the way to the top . . ." Members of both groups possessed remarkable strengths and significant weaknesses.[14]

The following ten "fatal flaws" were given as the reasons for failure by those "derailed." No one person had all the flaws cited, in fact an average of only two were found in each of the derailed executives.

1. Insensitive to others.
2. Cold, aloof, arrogant.
3. Betrayal of trust (rarely related to honesty but more "a one-upping of others, or failure to follow through on promises that wreaked havoc in terms of organizational efficiency.").
4. Overly ambitious: thinking of next job, playing politics.
5. Specific performance problems with the business (job performance: inability to change; failure to admit problems; covering up; blaming others).
6. Overmanaging: unable to delegate or build a team.
7. Unable to staff effectively.
8. Unable to think strategically (take a broad, long-term view).
9. Unable to adapt to boss with different style.
10. Overdependent on advocate or mentor.

McCall and Lombardo concluded "that executives were derailed for four basic reasons, all connected to the fact that situations change as one ascends the organizational hierarchy."[15]

1. Strengths become weaknesses (i.e., loyalty becomes overdependence or cronyism; ambition eventually viewed as politicking).
2. Deficiencies eventually matter (i.e., an insensitive person at lower levels becomes highly visable at upper levels; useful interpersonal skills at lower level not effective at a higher level).
3. Success goes to their heads.
4. Events conspire ("done in politically, or by economic upheavals—were not lucky.").

Comparing the two groups:

1. Under pressure arrivers were calm, confident, and predictable while the derailed were moody or volatile.
2. Although neither group made many mistakes, arrivers handled their mistakes with poise and grace while the derailed tended to react to failure by going on the defensive.

Marketing Yourself

So far we have defined the small business environment and some of the entrepreneurial characteristics needed to succeed. By contrasting the entrepreneurial mission with a career track as a salaried employee we hoped to give you insight into making a tentative commitment to one track. Either track, however, requires strong leadership qualities, albeit the different career environments call for somewhat different leadership "expressions."

The owner or manager must be comfortable in a jack-of-all-trades role (at least early on in the life of the business) while the salaried employee must be capable of working toward group value and organizational goals in meeting his or her own needs.

Moving around the career development model (Figure 3-1) it becomes crucial to plan with vision your educational program (step 2), to locate work experiences, to reality test your career decision (step 3) and to begin thinking about your "personal advertising literature," the resume (step 4). At each of these steps keep in mind that ultimately this "package" of accomplishments will be viewed by a prospective employer as a "product to purchase (to hire) or not to purchase."

Planning an Educational Package

The following discussion will focus on an educational package that will prepare a student for a career in commercial leisure services. No attempt will be made to differentiate between the owner or manager and salaried employment tracks. It is our contention that the undergraduate curriculum should not be so specialized as to diminish employment opportunities for the graduate. Furthermore, there is a consensus among educators, practitioners, and salaried counselors that there are useful skills common to both tracks.

One pioneering study was completed by Robert Langman in 1974.[16] This study concluded that most recreation graduates already possess many of the competencies required for success in commercial recreation, namely:

1. General study and research skills attributable to all college and university graduates.
2. Strong people orientation—works well with groups and is cognizant of the role of public relations for the leisure delivery systems generally.
3. Sensitive to unethical practices, thus are moved to act in an ethical way.

In addition to the above "human relations skills," Langman's study judged the following personality and technical skills as necessary.

1. Be an effective communicator—written and oral expression.
2. Be competitive.
3. Possess a positive attitude.
4. Be self-disciplined.
5. Have clearly defined goals and demonstrate persistence in their attainment.
6. Be empathetic.
7. Be willing to communicate to the proper authority one's ability to do the job.
8. Reason well.
9. Use time wisely.

One conclusion of the Langman study points up the suitability of recreation graduates for a career in commercial recreation "because the competencies they do possess (human relations skills, for one) [sic] are not skills that can be easily taught."[17]

The education of a commercial leisure services professional should begin with basic leisure studies core classes. This leisure studies education should be mixed with a rich selection of classes from management, marketing, economics, law, finance, computer science, and accounting.

The following is a composite "commercial recreation" course of study gleaned from programs of six western universities and a western two-year college and two eastern schools offering baccalaureate degree programs in commercial recreation.*

Leisure Studies (specific unit credit varies)
1. Basic Programming
2. History and Philosophy of Leisure
3. Commercial Recreation
4. Industrial Recreation
5. Resource Management
6. Community Relations
7. Leadership
8. Research Methods
9. Principles of Administration and Supervision
10. Introduction to Tourism
11. Field Experiences
(Approximate unit value—30 to 36 semester hours.)

Business Related Courses
1. Marketing of Leisure Services
2. Micro-Macro Economics
3. Personal Finance
4. Organizational Behavioral Science
5. Business Law I–II
6. Introduction to Computer Applications for Business Use
7. Accounting I–II
(Approximate unit value—18 to 20 semester hours.)

Related Courses—(electives)
1. Public Speaking
2. Physiology of Exercise
3. Social Anthropology
4. Statistics
5. Non Profit Leisure Service Organizational Management
6. Recreation for Special Populations
7. Leisure Counseling
8. Outdoor Recreation
9. Fundamentals of Retailing
(Approximate unit value—10 to 12 semester hours.)

* Brigham Young University, University of Utah, Michigan State University, University of Oregon, California State University, Northridge, Texas A & M University, De Anza Community College (a two-year school included in study), Fresno State University, and the George Washington University.

Individual educational objectives can be met by selecting courses from the list of related courses. There is a rather uniform opinion among the institutions surveyed about the core requirements and specific business-related courses. The course content will undoubtedly vary between schools, yet the nature of the program is rather uniform. Contracting for leisure services, for example, can be found in such courses as Marketing of Leisure Services, Commercial Recreation, or Principles of Administration and Supervision. Each region of the country has its special requirements, and they too will be reflected in the various course outlines.

Graduate education in commercial recreation has not gotten the attention it deserves. Perhaps a marriage between leisure studies departments and schools of business could produce the courses for a Master of Business Administration degree with a specialty in Commercial Recreation. The George Washington University and Cornell University (for example) have designed exceptional programs in Travel and Tourism and Hotel Management (respectively) at both the undergraduate and graduate levels. This specific graduate training is possible, in part, because tourism and hotel management are recognized as separate employment markets capable of absorbing most of the graduates in these specializations. This is not the case with most other specializations within commercial recreation.

Work Study Experiences

Because of the diverse and multidimensional aspects of commercial recreation, the sincere student should supplement the above course of study with supervised off-campus work experiences. Curriculum planners have long recognized the value of supervised work experience. Without these experiences as part of the formal curriculum package, any professional preparation program would be lacking.

Many educators are recommending work experience at the lower division and upper division levels. The relevant work experience at lower-division levels places students in the leisure work environment so that they can, among other things, test their resolve to follow this profession when it is still early enough in their academic lives to change directions should that be necessary. The upper division field work should be in the students' main area of interest. Hopefully they will continue involvement in this area after completing the program. It should be noted that employers weigh these work experiences heavily in the selection process for full-time entry level positions. Likewise, loan officers in financial institutions look more kindly on an application for a business loan where the applicant has experience in the particular business.

It is worth noting that while the above educational package is aimed at producing future employees and entrepreneurs for the commercial leisure services field, the student is not limited to this choice. In fact, the strength of a commercial recreation education lies in the breadth of employment choices available to successful graduates. In a study completed by Carol Bobys, a master's student at California State University, Northridge, in 1979, it was concluded that employers in business generally are not as concerned that applicants have a strong business background as they are that they demonstrate strong human relations skills and have completed college.[18] When shown resumes of business school graduates and general recreation graduates, "employee selectors" said they would look to extracurricular activities in selecting candidates to be interviewed. However, given candidates of equal strength in this area, the students with business backgrounds would prevail in the final selection process. Thus, we might conclude that recreation graduates, with their propensity for working with people and their usual gregarious nature, with a strong general business foundation would be successful in gaining employment in other fields requiring these skills.

Applying and Interviewing for a Job

The information in this chapter thus far has been generally applicable to both the owner/manager and salaried employee career tracks. The remainder of this chapter will focus on topics more germane to persons desiring salaried positions.

Preparing a Resume

Undoubtedly the resume is the first step in the active search for professional employment. The resume is crucial for several reasons. First, it presents the prospective employer with an historical sketch of the applicant. Second, because the personality of the applicant cannot impress the reader, everyone is screened objectively. Finally, a resume can be focused toward a particular career by having relevant facts embellished while others are played down. Following are suggestions for the type of information that should be included in a resume.

The Personal Inventory

Identification of the Applicant. Your name, address, and telephone number (including your area code), heads the resume. An alternate phone number is strongly recommended. This information is centered at the top of the page or placed to one side. Do not use headings such as "Name," "Address," "Telephone," or "Resume." This information is self-evident and the headings are unnecessary. Additional information that might also be included at the top is whether you are willing to relocate or travel for a specific position, any special skills you might have, such as being bilingual, and so forth.

Personal Data. Personal data includes such information as your date of birth, marital status, health, height, weight, and so forth. This is generally extraneous information and often is best left out. You may, however, want to include some of this information, especially if it is beneficial for you to do so.

Career/Occupational Objectives. Career objectives are optional on the resume. They are most often placed in the cover letter. In either case, they should be clearly defined, concise, and address the position for which you are applying. This statement tells the reader that you are not looking for just anything that might come along. It is the *key* to an effective resume. Three, four, or even more different resumes may be necessary, depending upon the variety of positions being sought.

Education History.   Start with the most recent and work backwards. Limit the number of schools attended. Whatever you put on your resume, let there be a purpose, a reason for doing so. Ask yourself this question, "Does it strengthen my resume?" Your most advanced degree should come first, followed by the month and year of graduation; then, the institution attended; the major and option, if appropriate. You may wish to list major subjects, internships, or practicums, that contributed to your job aims. Omit course information if you have been out of school for several years or if you have had extensive work experience directly related to the position you wish to obtain.

Credentials (for persons seeking teaching or other school-related positions).   Persons with credentials should list those credentials along with the information concerning degrees. List the credentials accurately, when completed, whether clear or partial, and where completed.

Honors and Extracurricular Activities.   The honors and extracurricular activities category can include data such as club and professional memberships, awards, honors, high grade point averages (3.0 or better), and so forth. Mention only those activities that called for significant leadership on your part or those in which you were an active contributing member. Explain your activities or clubs (abbreviations and Greek letters connote nothing to an employer). This category can be omitted if your work experience has been significant.

Work Experience/Accomplishments/Skills.   The heading for this category will depend on the format you choose: chronological, functional, skills related, or a combination of these. If you choose a chronological format, list your most current job first and work backwards. List employment dates (in most cases, month and year is sufficient), names of the employers, cities and states (eliminate street addresses), and your job titles. Write in *action* verbs as much information as possible about your job. List not only your job duties, but what you created and accomplished. An example of this type of statement might be: "Successful in raising the volume of sales in the department 25 percent within the first six months of employment." Be sure to include summer, part-time, and volunteer work. If your professional experience warrants the use of a functional or skills resume, use various job functions or major skills headings with appropriate achievements noted under each heading. (Salary information is usually left off the resume unless requested by the employer.)

Special Skills, Hobbies, Travel, Interests.   If you have special skills or hobbies, have traveled extensively, or have interests that relate directly to the job for which you are applying, include these under an appropriate heading; if you have no such skills or interests, omit this category. This category usually appears near the end of the resume. As mentioned before, if you are bilingual or have a skill that is highly important to the job for which you are applying, you may want to place it in the Personal Data category or under a separate heading near the beginning of the resume.

References.   Current feeling is that it is not necessary to list references. You can omit them or you can simply indicate that they are available. Credentialed applicants seeking teaching or other school-related positions should establish a professional file and list it as being available.

Final Note.   The resume is a very individualized document. What you decide to include, to leave off, or the format you use will depend on the job you are seeking and your personal background and experience. Your resume must say clearly and unmistakably to the employer: "Call me. Let me appear for a personal interview."

Types of Resumes

The information in resumes can be arranged chronologically, functionally, in a skills-related manner, or in a combination of these.

Chronological.   The basic feature of the chronological resume is that employment experience is listed according to the order in which you held the jobs, starting with the most recent and ending with the earliest.

Functional Resume.   Those who have acquired a variety of skills and achievements through a number of experiences may want to consider a functional format. This style allows the applicant to highlight select areas that relate strongly to the job being sought. The information is also ranked from the most important to least important down the page. This ranking is not arbitrary, but is based on a knowledge of the skills the potential employer may be seeking.

Skills-Achievement Resume.   Applicants with little or no work experience often have difficulty composing an effective resume. This may also be true for the more mature applicant who has not worked for a number of years. The salient feature of a skills-achievement resume is that it is not limited to education and work experience but encompasses all aspects of a person's life—school work, community involvement, family duties and activities, church and volunteer work, and so forth.

A skills-achievement resume is shown in Figure 3-3. The resume shown here is that of an applicant with a strong academic and scholastic record who has had little if any paid work experience but who has had extensive involvement in department/campus activities. The skills developed by this applicant through study in the major field along with other course work related to the business world have been enumerated, followed by a systematized listing of individual skills and achievements under appropriate headings. Marital status and birth date were included because the applicant felt this information would be beneficial for the type of employment being sought. Advantages of the skills-achievement resume are that it can spotlight all of life's experiences, it is highly individualized, and it can eliminate the need for dates and employment record. Disadvantages of the skills-achievement resume are that it is difficult to write, assistance in identifying

18013 Lindley Ave., #221   Marital Status: Single
Northridge, CA 91330   Birth Date: April 12, 1953
(213) 363-4853 or   Willing to Relocate
John Roberts (213) 358-1122   or Travel

EDUCATION

> Bachelor of Science degree in Recreation and Leisure
> Studies, California State University, Northridge,
> California. Graduated with Distinction. Awarded
> the President's Scholarship 1980-81. Grade Point
> Average 3.6.

Skills developed through the study of recreation

- Evaluated and analyzed programs critically
- Conducted independent research
- Synthesized data, weighed conflicting evidence,
  and arrived at a conclusion or recommendation
- Understood cause-and-effect relationship among
  events
- Wrote narrative and analytical reports

Special business-related courses:

Business Management	Accounting	History of Tourism
Economic History	Economics I	Industrial Psychology
Statistics	Economics II	
Marketing	Bus. Law I	
	Bus. Law II	

SKILLS AND ACHIEVEMENTS
ORGANIZATIONAL/LEADERSHIP

- Coordinated informal seminars, conferences, and
  cultural and social activities for several volunteer
  organizations
- Organized, publicized, and promoted the Valley
  Recreation Society
- Initiated, developed, and coordinated the Special
  Olympics
- Reorganized the Recreation Majors Club into a viable
  and integral part of the Recreation Department
- Researched and organized land use maps that became
  the basis for a professor's dissertation

COMMUNICATIVE

- Wrote, produced, and distributed newsletters for
  several volunteer organizations
- Wrote articles on California leisure that are
  presently being considered for publication
- Spoke before several high school groups on the
  "Relevance of Recreation"
- Lectured and debated in undergraduate classes while
  a graduate student
- Conducted an informal seminar on the career
  opportunities in commercial recreation

HUMAN RELATIONS

- Resold merchandize to displeased customers and
  mediated their complaints
- Counseled students on all types of grants, loans,
  and other financial assistance available toward
  educational support
- Counseled and advised students about the opportunities
  and requirements of a career in leisure services
- Worked as a teaching assistant for professor in
  outdoor recreation class

FIGURE 3–3. Sample of a skills/achievement resume.

skills and achievements is often needed, it has no standard format, and employers often are not familiar with the format.

It is important to use *work words* or what are called *action verbs* in describing your experience on your resume or in an interview. Words such as administered, coordinated, developed, supervised, consulted, managed, or prepared are keys in telling employers (verbally or in writing) what you have accomplished. Listed below are a few of these *Action Verbs:*

Achieved	Effected	Motivated
Administered	Established	Negotiated
Analyzed	Evaluated	Operated
Arranged	Executed	Originated
Attended	Expedited	Organized
Built	Expanded	Performed
Clarified	Experienced	Pioneered
Conceived	Formed	Planned
Constructed	Formulated	Prepared
Consulted	Founded	Promoted
Controlled	Generated	Provided
Converted	Handled	Purchased
Coordinated	Improved	Researched
Correlated	Implemented	Reduced
Created	Increased	Reorganized
Conducted	Innovated	Supervised
Delegated	Initiated	Simplified
Demonstrated	Inspired	Solved
Designed	Installed	Succeeded
Detailed	Integrated	Sold
Developed	Interviewed	Tailored
Devised	Invented	Transformed
Directed	Justified	Trained
Discovered	Keynoted	United
Doubled	Managed	Verified
Earned	Maintained	Wrote

Letter of Application

Every resume should be accompanied by a letter of application. This letter will personalize the resume even more and will demonstrate your writing skill. Figures 3-4a and b are a general outline for a letter of application and interview postcard and Figure 3-5 shows a sample of an actual letter.

Opening Paragraph
1. The opening paragraph on the letter of application states the position for which the applicant is applying.
2. It specifically states the name of the company in the body of the letter.
3. It quickly capsulizes the applicant's academic preparation for the position.

Middle Paragraph(s)
1. It points out assets as they relate to the requirements of the jobs, i.e., previous knowledge of public relations, community organizations, and so forth.
2. The tone of the letter indicates self-confidence.

```
┌─────────────────────────────────────────────────────────────────┐
│                          Applicant's Address                       │
│                          Applicant's Phone Number                  │
│                          Date of Letter                            │
│                                                                    │
│      Use complete        Employer's Name and Title                 │
│      title and           and Address                               │
│      address                                                       │
│                                                                    │
│      If you know the                                               │
│      name, use it        Salutation:                               │
│      rather than                                                   │
│      "Dear Sir"          Opening Paragraph:  State why you are     │
│                          writing, name the position or type of     │
│                          work for which you are applying, and      │
│                          mention how you heard of the              │
│                          opening or organization.  If appropriate, │
│                          state your academic preparation and how   │
│                          it relates to the job.                    │
│      Make the                                                      │
│      addressee want      Middle paragraph (s):  Explain why you    │
│      to read your        are interested in working for this        │
│      resume              employer and specify your reasons for     │
│                          desiring this type of work.  If you have  │
│      Be brief but        had relevant work experience, be sure     │
│      specific; your      to point it out along with any other      │
│      resume contains     skills or abilities you have as they also │
│      details             relate to the job for which you are       │
│                          applying.  Be sure to do this in a        │
│                          confident manner, and remember that the   │
│                          reader will view your letter of           │
│                          application as an example of your         │
│                          writing skills.                           │
│                                                                    │
│                          You may refer the reader to your enclosed │
│                          resume (which gives a summary of your     │
│                          qualifications) or whatever medium you    │
│                          are using to illustrate your training,    │
│                          interests, and experience.  Do not        │
│      Top and bottom      reiterate your entire resume.             │
│      margins should                                                │
│      be equal            Closing paragraph:  Have an appropriate   │
│                          closing to pave the way for the interview │
│                          by indicating the action or steps you     │
│                          will take to initiate an interview date.  │
│                          Enclosing a self-addressed post card,     │
│                          similar to the one below, is an excellent │
│                          way to facilitate this process.           │
│                                                                    │
│                          Sincerely,                                │
│      Always sign                                                   │
│      letters             Your signature                            │
│                                                                    │
│                          Your name typed                           │
│      If a resume or                                                │
│      other enclosure     Enclosure                                 │
│      is used, note                                                 │
│      in letter                                                     │
└─────────────────────────────────────────────────────────────────┘
```

FIGURE 3–4a. General outline for a letter of application.

Ending Paragraph

1. Applicant takes the initiative by enclosing a self-addressed and stamped interview date postcard or by indicating what action they will take regarding setting up an interview date.

The Employment Interview

Why do employers make a hiring decision on the basis of an interview rather than only an application or resume? The fact is that some important

```
┌─────────────────────────────────────────────────────────────────┐
│                    INTERVIEW INFORMATION CARD                      │
│                                                                    │
│       Company Name _____         │
│                                                                    │
│       Address _____         │
│                                                                    │
│       Date _____         │
│                                                                    │
│       Time _____         │
│                                                                    │
│                Interviewer _____         │
│                                                                    │
│                Title _____         │
│                                                                    │
│                Signature _____         │
│                                                                    │
└─────────────────────────────────────────────────────────────────┘
```

FIGURE 3–4b. Sample format for an interview date postcard that may be included with letter of application.

factors about you could never be discovered by merely reading your resume or application.

Employers want to learn about your personality, attitudes and motivations, communication skills, and appearance, as well as to assess your strengths and abilities in relation to the position. You, in turn, have the opportunity to find out important information about the organization and details about the position as well as about the people for whom and with whom you will work. The interview, therefore, is a way for you and a prospective employer to exchange information about each other that can only be done by meeting in person.

At the heart of a successful interview will be your own belief in yourself and a determination to approach the process with a positive attitude. Convince yourself that there will be a good outcome, then you can convince the employer. This attitude will generate enthusiasm and help to create a favorable impression on the interviewer. It is also important to remember that the interviewer wants and needs to hire and is responsible for finding and offering employment to qualified applicants. Remember, you must present yourself and your qualifications to the employer more effectively than anyone else.

Employers report that there are several critical areas in which a job seeker should be well-prepared in order to encourage an offer of employment.

1. Know what position you want. Do your research before the interview and be prepared to explain why you are seeking the position and why you would be successful in the job.
2. Research the company or agency and its products or services, so that you can converse intelligently about the organization.
3. Remember that you have a basic responsibility during the interview to give the employer substantial reasons why you should be hired. This means what you can do for the employer, not what the employer can do for you. An inability to provide this information is a major cause of failing to get job offers.

```
Date


Mr. Harvey J. Brown
Executive Director
African Wildlife Safari
1717 Overland Way
Roseburg, Oregon 97408

Dear Mr. Brown:

I am interested in the position of Public Relations
Coordinator with African Wildlife Safari.  I feel that
my education, skills, and desire to work in this area make
me a strong candidate for this position.

My education has helped me develop sound analytical
abilities and has exposed me to the public relations
field.  My involvement with public relations and community
organizations has provided me with a working knowledge of
the profession.  These experiences have also reinforced
my desire and interest to pursue work in this field.

Please review the enclosed resume.  If I have not heard
from you regarding an interview date within the next ten
days, I will phone your office to arrange a mutual time
and date.

Sincerely,


Denise M. Johnson
18411 Antioch Drive
Northridge, California 91330
(213) 886-1234

Enclosure
```

FIGURE 3–5. A sample application letter.

4. First impressions are lasting. Grooming and selection of clothes should reflect the professional look for the position you are seeking. *Dress for Success* is more than just the title of a well-known book.
5. Most employers recommend attending a basic interview workshop and doing some practice with other students in a group setting. This tends to alleviate preinterview jitters and prepares you to express your qualifications more effectively.

Remember, you can learn the techniques that will greatly increase your odds of getting the position you want. Your willingness to practice what you learn is the key to your success.

Assertive Interview Technique. *Assertiveness* in the context of the interview is a form of behavior that demonstrates to the interviewer your self-confidence, your interest and enthusiasm for the work you are seeking, and your optimistic outlook toward the outcome of the interview.

It is demonstrated by the applicant in two ways.

1. Verbally—Information-giving.
2. Nonverbally—Body language.

Information giving refers to the quality of the information you provide verbally. Use the following assertive techniques.

1. General to the specific
2. Positive self-reference
3. Volunteer relevant information
4. Use of transitional statements
5. Use of action verbs

Body language refers to behavior the employer sees or hears and includes the following:

1. Alert posture
2. Good eye contact
3. Good handshake
4. Smile
5. Voice modulation

General characteristics employers tend to assess during the interview are:

1. Qualifications
2. Leadership/initiative
3. Motivation/goals
4. Communication skills

Your best preparation is to:

1. Know your own abilities, strengths, and skills and be able to draw logical connections between them and what you know the employer is seeking.
2. Know what you want and why you are seeking it.
3. Know what characteristics the employer seeks for the position.

Some questions which may be asked during the employment interview are:

1. What are your future career plans?
2. In what school activities have you participated? Which did you enjoy the most?
3. In what type of position are you most interested?
4. Why do you think you might like to work for our company?
5. What jobs have you held? How were they obtained and why did you leave?
6. What courses did you like best? Least? Why?
7. Why did you choose this particular field of work?
8. What percentage of your college expenses did you earn? How?
9. What do you know about our company?
10. What qualifications do you have that make you feel that you will be successful in your field?
11. Why do you think you would like this particular type of job?
12. What do you think determines a person's progress in a good company?
13. Tell me about yourself.
14. When did you choose your college major?
15. Do you feel you have done the best scholastic work of which you are capable?
16. What is your major weakness?
17. Would you describe for me your greatest strengths?
18. What have you done that shows initiative and willingness to work?
19. How do you feel about working overtime?

We do not recommend you memorize answers to these questions. It is important to be aware of the scope of questions that could be asked. Your best approach is to know yourself well and know what you want the employer to know about you.

Here are fifteen "knockout" reasons why candidates receive rejection replies:

1. Lack of proper career planning—purposes and goals ill defined—needs direction.
2. Lack of knowledge of field of specialization—not well qualified—lacks depth.
3. Inability to express thoughts clearly and concisely—rambles.
4. Insufficient evidence of achievement or capacity to excite action in others.
5. Not prepared for the interview—no research on company—poor presentation.
6. No real interest in the organization or the industry—merely shopping around.
7. Narrow location interest—unwilling to relocate later—inflexible.
8. Little interest and enthusiasm—indifferent—bland personality.
9. Overbearing—overaggressive—conceited—cocky—aloof—assuming.
10. Interested only in the best dollar offer—too money conscious.
11. Asks no or poor questions about the job—little depth and meaning to questions.
12. Unwilling to start at the bottom—expects too much too soon—unrealistic.

13. Makes excuses—evasiveness—hedges on unfavorable factors in record.
14. No confidence and lack of poise—fails to look interviewer in the eye—immature.
15. Poor personal appearance—sloppy dress—inappropriate choice of clothes.[18]

The Follow-up Letter

The follow-up letter can be used for two different purposes.

1. It can be used as an opportunity to thank the employer for the interview, to reinforce your interest in the position you are seeking and the organization with which you have interviewed. This type of follow-up letter is usually sent within ten days after the initial interview.
2. In the event that you have not heard from the employer regarding the outcome of your initial interview (generally, applicants are told by the employer by what date they will be notified of the results of the interview), the follow-up letter can serve to re-establish contact with the employer. (This can also be done by phone if desired.)

Applicant's Address
Applicant's Phone Number
Date of Letter

Employer's Name and Title
and Address

Salutation:

Opening paragraph: Thank the employer for the interview and express appreciation for the courtesy or consideration extended to you. Be sure to remind the reader of the position for which you were interviewed and the date of the interview.

Middle paragraph (s): Reaffirm your interest in the position and the organization. Mention anything you have done since the interview that demonstrates your interest in the opening (i.e., additional research on the employer, conversations with local representatives, etc.). You may also add information that you failed to give in the interview at this point.

If the employer does not already have a copy of your resume, it can be sent with this letter. Express willingness to provide additional data if requested.

Closing paragraph: Close with a suggestion for further action, such as your availability for additional interviews at the employer's convenience.

Sincerely,

(Your signature)

Type your name

FIGURE 3–6. General outline of a follow-up letter.

```
18111 Nordhoff Street
Northridge, CA 91330
(213) 885-2381
June 10, 19xx


Mr. John Johnson
College Relations Officer
Hunt Corporation
345 North East Street
Los Angeles, CA 90011

Dear Mr. Johnson:

I want to thank you for giving me the opportunity to
discuss my interest in and qualifications for the position
of Sales Representative with you on Monday, June 2.

After my interview with you, I sought out a Sales
Representative with Hunt and was able to spend some time
with her discussing the rewards as well as the challenges
of the work.  This has reaffirmed my interest in the
position and my confidence that I could do well in this
field.

In the event you would like additional information
regarding my background, please feel free to contact me.
I will be looking forward to hearing from you soon.

Sincerely,


Richard Long
```

FIGURE 3–7. A sample follow-up letter.

A general outline and a sample follow-up letter are shown in Figures 3-6 and 3-7. It is important, however, that you write a letter to fit the situation using your own words.

Summary

This chapter has focused on four main issues: assessing your interests and talents relative to a career in commercial leisure services; selecting either an entrepreneurial or an employee career track; developing an academic program to prepare for a career in either track, and steps for "selling" your credentials to prospective employers.

As we have seen, career planning and assessment is a continual process. It starts while you are pursuing your education, and because of rapid market changes, it must continue throughout your professional life. The leisure market will continue its historical pattern of fluctuation and change.

Because of these changes, today's satisfied employee can become tomorrow's new entrepreneur.

Entrepreneurs have readily identifiable traits: drive, enthusiasm, thinking ability, human relations skills, communications skills, and knowledge of the field. On the other hand, working for someone else also requires special skills such as an understanding of group operations and corporate politics. While the entrepreneur builds businesses, it is the employee that keeps these businesses successful.

Career development, in effect, is building a personal background that is marketable. This background should show academic preparation, interest in people, and work experience. Relevant work experience during academic training is essential for securing professional level jobs.

In preparing a resume, it is important to understand the variations in style that can be used. It is also important to determine which style would best serve a particular purpose. When writing letters of application, it is desirable to use action verbs whenever possible. All letters should be typed and contain a statement about current career objectives and where you can be reached.

In preparing for an employment interview, be aware of your strengths and weaknesses, the job requirements, and the background of the potential employer. You can also prepare for an interview by quizzing yourself on questions commonly asked in interviews.

Study Questions

1. Describe the components of the career development model.
2. Identify and discuss competencies that are necessary for individuals entering the commercial leisure service profession.
3. Describe the advantages and disadvantages of self-employment and salaried employment.
4. What are some of the "fatal flaws" that derail individuals as they move up the executive ladder?
5. Identify three different types of resumes. Develop one of each type.
6. Why do employers make hiring decisions based on an interview rather than on an application or resume? How might you prepare yourself for a job interview?
7. What type of academic program might you develop to prepare for work in the commercial leisure services field?
8. Discuss the steps in selling your credentials to prospective employers.
9. Why must a resume be a highly individualized document?
10. How can you explore different career opportunities? What are some of the sources? How might you go about locating job opportunities?

Experiential Exercise

Review the rating scale for personal traits of small business owners (Table 3-1, p. 98). Complete this scale. Make a copy of this scale and ask a friend to locate someone else who knows you well (but whose identity is unknown to you) and have that second person complete this form for you. Review the degree of agreement between your assessment of yourself and that of the unknown rater. (It would be helpful if the unknown rater was a business owner.)

Write a summary of your findings and make a conclusion about which career track seems appropriate for you.

Notes

1. John Naisbitt, *Megatrends*, New York: Warner Books, 1982, p. 16.
2. "The Next Fifty Years" *U.S. News & World Report*, May 9, 1983, pp. A25–A26.
3. Albert Shapero, "The Displaced Uncomfortable Entrepreneur," *Psychology Today*, November, 1975, p. 24.
4. Nicholas C. Siropolis, *A Guide to Entrepreneurship*, 2nd ed., Boston: Houghton Mifflin, 1982, p. 12.
5. U.S. Small Business Administration, *Small Business Management Aid No. 1*, Washington, D.C.: U.S. Government Printing Office, 1973, pp. 1–4.
6. Gene C. Walker, "Starting a New Business—Pitfalls to Avoid," *U.S. News & World Report*, July 13, 1981, pp. 75–76.
7. Ibid., p. 75.
8. H.N. Broom and Justine Longenecker, *Small Business Management*, 5th ed., Cincinnati: Southwestern Publishing, 1979, p. 47.
9. Glen C. Walker, "Starting a New Business—Pitfalls to Avoid," *U.S. News & World Report*, July 13, 1981, pp. 75–76.
10. "Bicycle Shop," *Small Business Reporter*, Vol. 14, No. 8, 1976, p. 9, San Francisco: Bank of America.
11. Shapero, p. 25.
12. Ibid., p. 26.
13. Gail Sheehy, *Pathfinders*, New York: Bantam Books, 1981, pp. 23–24.
14. Moran McCall and Michael Lombardo, "What Makes a Top Executive," *Psychology Today*, February, 1983, pp. 26–32.
15. Ibid., pp. 26–31.
16. Robert R. Langman, "Development of a Commercial Recreation Curriculum," Unpublished doctoral dissertation, University of Utah, June, 1974.
17. Ibid.
18. Carol Bobys, "The Effectiveness of a Commercial Recreation Degree in Securing Employment Interviews in Private Leisure Companies," Unpublished Master's thesis, California State University, Northridge, June, 1981.
19. Frank P. Endicott, Director of Placement, Northwestern University, Evanston, IL: Northwestern University Placement Center, n.d.

Close-up: Fitness Designs

Fitness in America is big business. According to the *U.S. News & World Report*,* home exercise equipment sales stand at $1 billion. The National Sporting Goods Association reports that sales in 1984 were $15 billion.

The position paper that follows came to the attention of the editor of the *San Diego Union*, the city's major daily newspaper. The paper then ran an article on Judy Myers in its business section.** Judy Myers's position paper signaled a major change in her career. Within a short period of time, Myers became a major fitness consultant in California. She is currently developing an instructor training program for substance abuse programs in the state. Myers is also planning a national campaign to sell her program of "How to Start and Operate a Fitness Consulting Business." What makes this story unique is that it demonstrates the power of an idea whose time has come.

We wish to thank Judy Myers of Fitness Designs for permission to reprint her original position paper.

As a professional in the field of physical education, I'm sick and tired of seeing women *waste* their time on fitness programs that don't give the kind of results they promise. All women want to look like Victoria Principal, Linda Evans, and Joan Collins (no matter what they say)! These actresses have written best-selling health and diet books and signed lucrative commercial contracts, all under the guise of being *the* "gurus" of fitness. They may be aware, but they lack the knowledge and formal education to become authorities on fitness.

The program I have designed will enable women who are serious about getting in shape to obtain dramatic results and save years of wasted effort. If I were able to "bottle and sell" my program, every women in the country would beat a path to my door.

In the last year, personal trainers have been getting a great deal of attention from the media (re: John Travolta's training for "Staying Alive" and Sylvester Stallone's training for "Rocky III"), primarily in Los Angeles and New York. It is going to be the trend of the future. . . . The fitness movement has developed in various stages. First there were the Y's and people like Jack LaLanne, then the health clubs. As people's interest grew, magazines, workshops, and other sources became available for the consumer. Eventually the consumer became very sophisticated and is now creating a demand for individual attention that health clubs, aerobics, jazzercise, and so forth, cannot meet.

The people in this country want to get in shape and stay that way. The people in health clubs thought they were meeting the demand by providing people with facilities stocked with equipment, machines, large rooms for

* "Fitness in America," Special Report, *U.S. News & World Report*, Aug. 13, 1984, pp. 23–28.
** Donald C. Bauder, "Sculptress Carves Out Career in One-on-One Fitness Counseling," *San Diego Union*, March 25, 1984, p. 1 (Section I, The Economy Page).

aerobics, and so forth. Since most of the employees in these facilities (dance teachers, exercise instructors, etc.) have had no formal or relevant education to speak of, I have actually witnessed minimal instruction on the machines and have seen people exhibit poor form on these and in exercise classes. Not surprisingly, their workouts are having either little, no, or a detrimental effect. It upsets me to see this.

The public has become frustrated by their inability to improve, but they are determined to become fit. Some of the more committed are now seeking "trainers" to work with them on a one-to-one basis. In my travels and research in cities such as Los Angeles, San Francisco, and New York, I have recognized the trend gaining momentum, particularly in Los Angeles where it has become a very big business—so big that health clubs are starting to offer trainers an opportunity to freelance in hopes of selling memberships and getting a piece of the action. Fees range from $30 to $100 per hour.

The trainers who are "cashing in" on this trend are "nouveau" trainers who generally lack a formal education. There is a bandwagon effect going on right now, and some people are becoming trainers who shouldn't. They make promises, and the workouts I have seen actually do more harm than good.

The timing couldn't be better for me. I have been catapulted by the very nature of my education, experience and interest into the forefront of an important national trend, a trend that is of the highest interest and importance to many people. I have decided not only to go into business for myself as a personal trainer, but have just completed an "Instructor's Manual for Personal Trainers" (I intend to publish this myself but I am not opposed to an interested publisher). This gives the aspiring fitness entrepreneurs a good introductory understanding of what they must know to succeed and offers in the process a step-by-step guide and sample of my twelve-week course complete with the client's workbook and diary. Each step is personalized and based on actual experiences.

4

Starting a Leisure Service Business

There are numerous decisions that must be made and plans that must be formulated before engaging in a commercial leisure service business. The entrepreneur who does not engage in proper planning and who does not investigate market conditions and the other factors that influence a business venture increases the risks associated with operating a commercial leisure service business. It is surprising how many businesses start without proper planning, their owners instead using a "seat of the pants" approach. It therefore is not so surprising that a large number of small businesses fail.

In this chapter, we will discuss the various steps that are involved in establishing a commercial leisure service business. For example, a prospective business owner desiring to launch an entirely new venture must first have an idea around which to build the business. A prospective owner must also decide whether to start a new business or purchase an existing one and what form of legal operation the business will take. Decisions must be made regarding the type of business (retail, wholesale), the location, the capital requirements, and sources of capital. Finally, there are miscellaneous details related to the laws governing business operations that must be attended to. In order to address these and other business-related topics in a systematic manner, the potential owner should develop a formal business plan. A format for a formal business plan preceded by a preplanning exercise is also presented in this chapter.

Ideas That Sell

The creation and refinement of an idea that will sell is one of several informal but nonetheless crucial preplanning steps. A person who desires to launch a new business must have an idea upon which the venture will be based. There is nothing mysterious about an idea. Powerful and profitable ideas can and do occur to everyone at one time or another. A sound idea for a leisure business may come while you are walking along the beach, browsing in a store, reading a book, or looking at the travel section of the Sunday newspaper.

There are three important factors involved in the creation of any idea.

1. The person and his or her experiences.
2. The environment and the stimuli it provides.
3. The transactions and interactions between the person and the stimuli.

These three steps are frequently causative, i.e., the idea originates in step 1 and matures through steps 2 and 3, although each step can be a source of individual ideas.

The best idea in the world is worth nothing until it is made tangible and communicated to others. An idea, then, to have commercial value, must have three parts:

1. The concept itself.
2. A plan or purpose of action.
3. The execution of that plan.

Ideas happen in three distinct and definable ways: consciously, subconsciously, and by accident (see Figure 4-1).

The Conscious Effort. The conscious desire to produce an idea often results from a need to solve a problem. In order to attempt to produce an idea that will solve a problem, one must first formulate a problem statement. For example, what if the problem is to identify a leisure service that can be sold at a profit, has a potential market, is one that you are qualified to

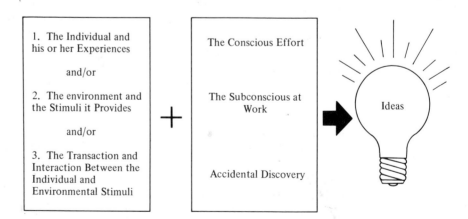

FIGURE 4–1. Factors involved in the creation of ideas.

perform, and one that you would enjoy? By stating your problem or objective in this way, your conscious search would already have several definable guidelines. Your search might be quite different if, for example, your problem statement was to identify a leisure service that would simply make money. In the first instance you would be guided by your personal criteria: profit, marketability, personal qualifications, and personal satisfaction. In the second instance, any profitable business would fulfill your needs. The act of formulating your problem often leads to creative solutions or ideas. This process can also help a person to use the process of elimination to refine ideas. In the example given, many types of leisure services would be eliminated from consideration based upon their failure to meet the criteria involved. The conscious effort, then, is based upon the use of "scientific" reasoning—in this case deductive—to achieve a new perspective or "idea."

The Subconscious at Work. The subconscious works in ways that are often puzzling. In the conscious act of creating ideas, the subconscious plays a supportive role. According to Arthur Koestler, the subconscious can be invoked by shifting our attention to a seemingly irrelevant aspect of a phenomenon.[1] This side-stepping, "shift of emphasis" produces a changeover from one frame of reference to another.

For those who doubt the existence of a subconscious mind, recall the last time you got in your car and found that you had driven yourself to a wrong location "automatically." This type of occurrence is a result of your subconscious mind, not your conscious mind. There are those who say that the subconscious mind is more active when people are in a semi-awake state, as when you are going to sleep or just waking up. Solutions to problems or ideas often will occur at this time or while relaxing and daydeaming. This, then, is the subconscious at work. It can be tapped by attending to such ideas and solutions to problems as they come to you.

Accidental Discovery

Accidental discovery occurs not only when something new is observed, but also when new relevance is attached to an observation, whether the observation is new or old. In order to be prepared for a new discovery, two conditions are necessary: a knowledge of the subject area, and an open mind. Accidental discovery is most likely to occur when a mind is active. In addition, accidental discovery is often related to prior work experience, since a knowledge of the subject area is prerequisite. In fact, according to Broom, "Work experience may well be the most productive of all venture-idea sources."[2]

Other sources of ideas that might serve as a basis for the creation of a commercial leisure service are:

1. Hobbies or personal interests.
2. The answer to the question, "Why isn't there a . . . ?"
3. Shortcomings in the services of others.
4. Extraordinary uses for ordinary things. (Advertisements in magazines and newspapers are a good source of "ordinary things.")
5. Opportunities for social change.

Create a New Business or Purchase
an Existing Business?

One of the major decisions that a prospective business owner must make is whether to create and develop a new business or purchase a business that is already in operation. There are advantages and disadvantages to each course of action, although purchasing an existing business is the most common avenue of business ownership.

Creating a New Business

Never before in the history of North America have there been so many small businesses created each year than at the present. Many of these businesses are created and developed in order to introduce new products or services that cannot be accommodated by existing businesses. Other small businesses are created by owners who wish to have the creative control that a new business offers over such factors as location, personnel, policies, design, and organization.

As just discussed, a person creating a new business must first have an idea that will sell. Once an idea has been developed around which a business can be formed, a prospective business owner should first engage in preplanning and should then develop a comprehensive formal business plan. Development of a formal business plan is crucial to the successful organization of a new business venture. Such a plan includes information about the type of business and the business's history, market, capital requirements, plan of operation, marketing strategy, sales tactics, sales projections, and long- and short-range objectives. Formats for a preplanning exercise and a formal business plan are offered in the latter half of this chapter.

Some of the specific advantages and disadvantages of creating a new business firm have been outlined by Van Voorhis.[3]

Possible Advantages of Starting a New Firm
1. Great opportunity to orient firm toward personal goals.
2. Flexibility in selecting products, services, location, facilities, and customers.
3. Policies and procedures established as desired.
4. Work force trained your way.
5. Possibility of unknown lawsuits and contingent liabilities minimized.
6. Smaller capital investment because the owner does not have to pay for "goodwill" or reputation.
7. Potential for great profit because the product or service may not have been available to consumers previously.

Possible Disadvantages of Starting a New Firm
1. Uncertainty about market demand for products and services.
2. Hidden costs of getting started and building business.
3. Extensive time and personal energy required.
4. Time lag between investment, cash flow, and profitability.
5. Potential customers difficult to attract to new firm.

6. Competitors able to undercut and prevent successful establishment of firm.
7. Investment capital difficult to obtain at attractive interest rates and repayment terms.

Purchasing an Existing Business

If a person is considering the purchase of an existing business, it is important that an attempt be made to evaluate and analyze the business as comprehensively as possible. Such an evaluation will help the prospective buyer determine the advantages and disadvantages of ownership of the business. It is important to note that any business will have some drawbacks. However, an assessment must be made about the seriousness of any problems within the business and the degree to which they would be correctable with proper management. What are some of the specific things that should be considered when examining a business to be purchased? A business can be evaluated in terms of its tangible and intangible assets, personnel, legal commitments (contracts, lawsuits if any, zoning), competition, predicted area developments, financial records, and the owner's reason for selling (see Figure 4–2).

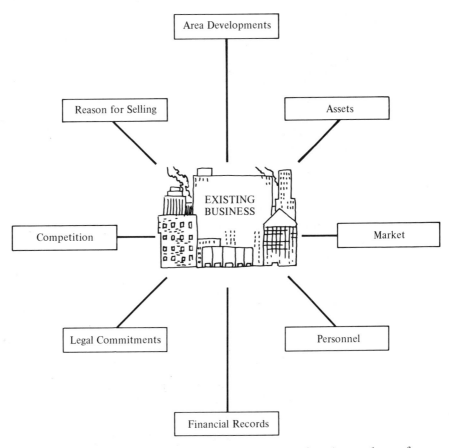

FIGURE 4–2. Factors that should be considered before the purchase of an existing business.

Assets.   A business will have both tangible and intangible assets. Tangible assets, such as physical facilities, inventory, equipment, and so on, should be examined and checked against the owner's claims regarding the condition of the business and the amount of inventory present. The intangible assets of a business can also be checked. Intangible assets include the business's reputation among clients, creditors, investors, and within the community at large.

Financial Records.   The financial records of the business should be examined, in particular the income statement, balance sheet, and cash flow statements. Various types of financial statements and their purposes are detailed in Chapter 7. It is often recommended that the prospective buyer hire an accountant to conduct an independent audit to confirm the accuracy of the financial statements.

Using the balance sheet, the net worth of a business can be estimated by determining the difference between total assets and total liabilities. However, it should be kept in mind that the assets listed on a balance sheet may differ somewhat from their real value. The net worth of a business can also be estimated by using a business's income statement. The prospective buyer can use an income statement to determine the net income or profit expected from the business and then compare this with the dollar amount of investment that would be required to earn the estimated profit. This dollar amount of investment can be said to be the value of the business.

In addition to examining the financial statements of a business, a prospective buyer should attempt to gain an overall picture of the sales of the business over a period of years. Is the business in a strong growth period? Is it a mature business? Is the business just beginning a decline? A graph of sales over a period of time should yield a curve that is indicative of the future prospects for the business. If the business is just beginning to decline, the prospective buyer should determine whether or not the decline can be turned around with proper management or by infusing new ideas into the business.

Personnel.   Before purchasing a business, a prospective owner should attempt to determine whether key employees intend to stay with the company if it changes ownership. The future prosperity of a business may depend upon the continuity of such key employees. In addition, the prospective owner should attempt to interact with key employees to ascertain whether they appear to be effective, productive, and happy. If unqualified to assess whether or not employees are doing their jobs in a productive manner, the prospective business owner should engage the services of a consultant who is familiar with the type of business being investigated.

Market.   The prospective owner should personally investigate the market for which the products or services of a business are intended. This topic is discussed in this chapter and in greater detail in Chapter 6.

The prospective business owner should consider the availability and cost of supplies for a business, the demand for its products or services, and the possibilities for expanding its market. Societal factors that might affect the future growth of the business's market should be considered as well.

Reason for Selling. When a person sells a business, he or she has a reason for doing so. The reason is most likely self serving and is not intended to offer a golden opportunity to someone else. The prospective business owner should determine the real reason for the sale of the business being considered. If there are problems within the business, they should be identified and evaluated in terms of their possible consequences. It is important that the prospective business owner be able to make an *informed* decision regarding the purchase of a business. Information that can be used in assessing an owner's reason for selling a business can be gained from its financial statements, conversations with employees, and investigation of the business's reputation with customers, creditors, and investors. Determining the owner's reason for selling may help the prospective buyer in negotiating a fair price for the business.

Legal Commitments. The prospective business owner should identify and evaluate the legal commitments that have been made by a business. Although a business might appear to be in good financial health, legal commitments regarding zoning; long-term contracts with customers, suppliers or others; property use restrictions; law suits; and delinquent taxes or union contracts might affect the future prosperity of the business. Therefore, it is important that such legal commitments be examined in light of their possible future consequences to the business.

Competition. The prospective owner should identify and assess the competition of a business. The competition should be evaluated in terms of the number of competing businesses in the market area, their proximity, and their size and effectiveness. By simply viewing first-hand a business for sale and its competitors over a short period of time, a prospective owner can usually determine how the business compares with its competition.

Area Developments. Planned developments within the area in which a business is located can have a great influence upon its future prosperity. Such factors as changes in zoning ordinances, changes in street traffic, and lack of or addition of bus routes, can affect a business either positively or negatively. It is probably safe to assume that a seller will inform a prospective buyer of any developments that will increase future business; however, the prospective owner should make sure that there are no planned future community developments that will adversely affect the business.

Once a prospective business owner has considered the above mentioned factors, he or she should be able to determine the advisability of purchasing the business and negotiate an acceptable price for it. Van Voorhis has outlined some of the specific advantages and disadvantages of purchasing an existing business.[4]

Possible Advantages of Buying a Going Concern
1. Less uncertainty about market demand for products or services.
2. No lag time in receiving initial returns on investment.
3. Known capabilities of facilities, equipment, and personnel.
4. Established sources of supply for materials.
5. Easier financing if track record of firm is good.
6. Less time, effort, and personal pressure for new owner in takeover and start-up.
7. Opportunity to purchase exceptionally low-priced firm (be especially careful here!).
8. Proven record of earnings.

Possible Disadvantages of Buying a Going Concern
1. Compromising of purchaser's goals to match firm's.
2. Existing customers leaving business along with previous owner.
3. Poor selection or condition of goods or both.
4. Inefficient physical layout and deteriorated equipment.
5. Ill-will from previous dealings accepted along with goodwill.
6. Questionable policies and practices difficult to change.
7. Apparent bargain found to be high-priced purchase.
8. Larger investment as a result of purchase of "goodwill" and reputation.

Determining Your Type of Business

Joseph Vosmik started a business selling and renting boats. He considered himself in the marina business. When he needed cash for expansion, Vosmik discovered he was in several businesses; he was in a dockside cafe business, serving meals to boating parties; he was in the real estate business, buying and selling local lots; and he was in the boat-repair business.

Vosmik was trying to meet a vast array of customer needs and in the process discovered he was not doing *one* thing well. Before he could make a profit, Vosmik had to decide what business he wanted to be in and concentrate on it. Reviewing his markets and personal strengths, he saw that his business was really that of a recreation shopping center. After defining his business and its goals, his profits grew.[5]

By determining or pinpointing his or her type of business, an owner or manager can set the focus of the service to correspond with the organization's mandate. It also encourages the entrepreneur to direct his or her energy toward those areas that will move the business, as defined, forward productively.

Determining Your Market

Knowing the type of business to be operated helps an owner or manager determine the market to be served. Unless a market exists for the product or service produced by a commercial leisure service business, it will be unsuccessful. Therefore, it is critical that market analysis be conducted before engaging in a business.

It is because of the diverse and multidimensional interests within the leisure market that the aspiring entrepreneur must invest time, effort, and money into identifying potential customers for the service. Table 4-1 illustrates the multidimensional aspects of the leisure market. It is essential for the entrepreneur to research to what extent segmentation variables affect his or her target market. This information is invaluable in reaching potential users by guiding the advertising message and media selection. For example, it would be useful for a sporting goods store owner to know that persons attending throughbred racing are likely to bowl and fish. A unique advertisement in a racing guide sold at a near-by race track could produce positive results. In the same vein, Louie's U-Bake Pizza parlours centered in Oregon have a mutual agreement with American Video stores that they will advertise one another's products in their establishments. The premise is that pizzas and rentals of video recorders and movies go hand-in hand. It is important to understand that services such as these and the others listed in Table 4-1 frequently share the same customer. Chapter 6 discusses the marketing of leisure services comprehensively and offers suggestions for determining a business's target market or population.

Realistic marketing research is the cornerstone of sound business planning. It results in the sales forecast, which is one of the most important documents in the business plan. It is also the basis for all financial projections. Dible says of market research and the subsequent sales forecast:

> In its preparation, the founders must compromise between the optimism necessary to ensure an agressive assault on the marketplace and the sensible projection that will interest the investor.[6]

Market preparation is essential if a new leisure service organization is to be successful. The leisure market can be characterized as growing, diverse, changing and faddish, financially robust, difficult to define, fickle, and alluring for the profit-motivated person. To enter this market without in-depth research and a thorough understanding of the service area is foolhardy.

TABLE 4-1. Marketing Survey of the Spectators and Participants in the Leisure Industry

Spectators	Attendance (millions)	Participants	(millions)
Automobile racing	51.0	Swimming	105.4
Thoroughbred racing	50.1	Bicycling	69.8
Major-league baseball	43.7	Camping	60.3
College football	35.5	Fishing	59.3
College basketball	30.7	Bowling	43.3
Harness racing	27.4	Boating	37.9
Greyhound racing	20.8	Jogging/running	35.7
NFL football	13.4	Tennis	32.3
Minor-league baseball	12.6	Pool/billiards	31.9
NHL hockey	11.5	Softball	28.5
Soccer	11.4	Table tennis	26.9
NBA basketball	10.7	Roller-skating	25.4

Reprinted from "The Quest for Fun on a Shoestring," *U.S. News & World Report*, August 10, 1981, pp. 62–63.

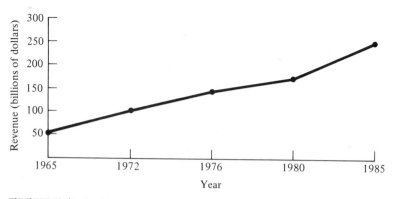

FIGURE 4–3. The growth of revenues for total leisure expenditures, 1965–1985.

Figure 4-3 charts the growth of dollar revenues for total leisure expenditures over the past twenty years. It dramatically illustrates the growth in revenues from leisure expenditures. What makes these figures especially alluring is that they show growth through the years of energy shortages and recession, which supports the notion that the leisure market as a whole has great vitality. While cursory examination of the data is encouraging, it must be tempered with caution, because these figures are confounded by unobtrusive product fad fluctuations and the inclusion of revenue from socially controversial leisure activities, such as liquor consumption and gambling. Yet the data show that the leisure consumer is seeking personal fulfillment through leisure activities, and there is cause for optimism that growth and opportunity in the leisure field will continue.

Obtaining Initial Capital and Credit

Initial capital consists of owner capital and creditor capital. Conservative guidelines set forth by Broom and Longenecker suggest that "owner capital in a new firm should be at least two thirds of the total initial capital."[7] This conservative "two thirds" dictum is recommended because a large percentage of small business failures each year are attributable to inadequate ownership equity.

The Business Failure Record of Dun and Bradstreet, Inc. for the year 1976 illustrates that 54.8 percent of the businesses that failed were less than five years old.[8] This same report states that monetary weakness was a root cause of 75.3 percent of all business failures in 1976.

Another cause of potential monetary weakness is sales volume. While new (as well as seasoned) entrepreneurs should maintain optimism regarding market acceptance of their product or service, a touch of pessimism is not out of line. There is a group of factors that have been identified by Broom and Longenecker that negatively effect sales:[9]

1. Inadequate market research to measure sales potential.
2. Poorly planned advertising and promotional activities.
3. Obsolete products (or service offering without market appeal or incorrectly priced) and product packaging. For our discussion, service pack-

Wilderness schools are growing in popularity. They are relatively easy to start because they do not require large amounts of venture capital. (John Bullaro)

aging includes facility design, professionalism of personnel, and location.

The person planning financial estimates for a new business must act as a critic. He or she must play the devil's advocate to ensure realistic appraisals of potential expenses and revenues. In this way, the potential for business success is greatly enhanced. Regardless of the extent of market research and the caliber of one's advisors, there are, as we have seen, uncontrollable events that can and will arise to threaten the fledgling enterprise. But that's where the excitement is—meeting the unknown and winning.

Sources of Capital

Estimating capital requirements will be discussed later in this section. What are some of the sources of funds for a new leisure service organization? According to the Internal Revenue Service,[10] 40.3 percent of the capital of small corporations and other business firms is supplied by the owner or owners. But where, specifically, does capital for new ventures originate? Most new businesses get their economic lift from personal savings of the owners, commercial bank loans, trade credit, equipment loans and leases, and from friends, relatives, and local investors. (See Figure 4-4.)

Personal Savings.   It has already been stressed that the two-thirds dictum, which states that two thirds of start-up capital should come from personal savings, is the safest and soundest approach for a new entrepreneur. This dictum applies only to new organizations; expanding or modernizing an existing business requires other considerations.

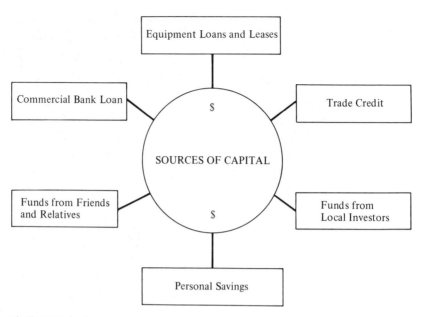

FIGURE 4—4. Sources of capital for starting a new business.

Commercial Bank Loans. Banks do not normally finance start-up costs of new ventures. However, if equity capital (the two-thirds dictum) is adequate and the entrepreneur is of good character, a commercial bank may loan on the basis of signature only. More often, collateral or personal guarantees are required.

Collateral arrangements can be made whereby such assets as life insurance policies, real estate, personal investments, and selected personal property (e.g., an automobile) may be pledged to secure a loan. A line of credit should be arranged in advance of actual need, and the potential business owner should apply for the maximum amount of projected need. "Last ditch" financing (going back for more) is next to impossible to arrange. The actual dollar amount of future credit needs should evolve from the formal business plan.

Long-term borrowing is usually for a period in excess of ten years, and the money is generally used for working capital and fixed assets. Lending policies of banks are not uniform. However, most banks consider a person in terms of personal reputation, prior credit history, purpose of the loan, changes and the plan for debt repayment, and collateral. Frequently, a co-signer is required.

The borrower should remember that banks are in the business of lending money. As such, it is to their advantage to do business with reputable persons and firms. Before developing a relationship with a bank, check out the bank's reputation as a friend to the borrower. In times of economic stress, the entrepreneur usually turns to his or her banker for support and flexibility. This information can be obtained from other businesses in the area. Real estate brokers, insurance agents, and accountants are additional sources of reliable information on a particular financial institution's banking practices.

Trade Credit. Trade credit is where a supplier (seller) sends merchandise to a business firm (buyer) and bills it at a later date. Trade credit is of short duration, usually thirty days. Most leisure service organizations will not have trade credit available. Yet some commercial leisure businesses, such as bicycle shops, backpacking stores, and tennis shops, while having service as a major component of their product offering, do have trade credit available.

Suppliers set the upper limit of trade credit they are willing to extend to the buyer. This limit is set by the supplier's confidence in the buyer and the nature of the business. Suppliers are inclined to extend trade credit to a new firm because of their interest in developing new customers.

Equipment Loans and Leases. Small businesses such as restaurants, ski resorts, marinas, and private camps often utilize equipment that may be purchased on an installment basis. A down payment of 25 to 35 percent is ordinarily required, and the contract period normally runs from three to five years.

Equipment leasing is an arrangement whereby the equipment supplier retains title to the asset, and the user makes a modest deposit and monthly payments as in a purchase agreement. At some time in the future, generally three to five years depending on the item being leased, the equipment is returned. Often new equipment is substituted. Cars, trucks, and business equipment are examples of assets that may be obtained by leasing. The two major advantages to leasing are that it enables a business to keep a large capital deposit available for other uses, and a business is less likely to be stuck with obsolete equipment.

Funds from Friends, Relatives, and Local Investors. Friends and relatives frequently share the new entrepreneur's excitement and are willing to support the venture. If it is necessary to tap this source of funds, it is desirable that the money be repaid within the first six months of operation.

Local investors, often referred to as venture capitalists, are a good source of funding but they usually require an equity position in the new organization. Where an equity position is not requested, a venture capitalist will be looking for a much larger rate of return on his or her money than is available elsewhere. Furthermore, the entrepreneur must also surrender some degree of control in this type of financing. The use of venture capitalists should be given careful consideration. Venture capitalists can be located in the advertising section of business and financial publications such as the *Wall Street Journal* and *Venture* Magazine.

Estimating Capital Requirements

In estimating capital requirements, it should be noted that the amount of initial capital required will vary from business to business. The size of the commercial leisure service business, the type of service provided, selling and buying terms, as well as variations in economic conditions and seasonal variables all can influence the amount of working capital that a business will need.

There are several approaches that an owner or manager may use in estimating capital requirements. One relatively simple approach is the use of worksheets that estimate the start-up costs of a business and estimate its monthly expenses. For your convenience, these are identified as Worksheet 1 (Estimating Starting Costs) and Worksheet 2 (Estimating Monthly Expenses). In Worksheet 1 (Estimating Starting Costs), the form is set up in three columns: the item, estimated monthly cost, and an explanation for the expenditures. In this case the first item, fixtures and equipment, might have a cost estimate of $2,000. This expenditure might be used to purchase or rent desks, computers, typewriters, and other fixtures and equipment necessary to operate the business. Estimated starting costs are only paid once. The second worksheet (Estimated Monthly Expenses), can help the owner or manager develop a detailed projection of the cost to run the business on a monthly basis. The form has categories similar to Worksheet 1.

The goal of an owner or manager in determining starting costs and monthly expenses using these worksheets is to calculate as accurately as possible an estimate of these costs. In order to increase the accuracy of these estimates, the owner or manager·can obtain industry-wide average operating ratios for the type of business under consideration and then multiply the projected sales volume times these ratios. The estimate of sales volume is, of course, also a key factor in the accuracy of the estimation of capital requirements. The owner should consider the size of business, its location, its market, and other similar variables when estimating sales volume. It is not recommended that a business rely solely on this method for estimating capital requirements.

A second approach that can be used to estimate capital requirements is the development of a projected or estimated income statement, a projected cash flow statement, and a break even analysis. To illustrate these tools we will look at a hypothetical leisure service business—The Happy Hills Day Camp.

The camp begins on January 1 with $7,500 in expenses for bus rental, advertising, program supplies, and salary for a counselor, and $12,000 in

Worksheet 1: Estimating Starting Costs

Item		Cost Estimate Explanation
Fixtures and equipment	_____	Desks, Computers, Chairs, etc.
Decorating and Remodeling labor	_____	Designing appropriate ambience for installation of equipment
Promotional flyers/event	_____	Grand Opening Celebration
Initial advertising	_____	Special Media Announcement
Program equipment	_____	Camping gear, canoes, pool tables, etc.
Deposits with public utilities	_____	Refundable
Legal and professional fees	_____	Incorporation Costs/Accounting
Licenses and permits	_____	Statutory Requirements
Beginning inventory	_____	Initial stock for sale
Two months' living expenses	_____	Owners' living expenses should be secure during initial start up
Total Start-up Costs: Transfer to Item 7A (2) of Outline for Business Plan (page __)	_____	

Worksheet 2: Estimating Monthly Expenses

Item	Your Monthly Cost Estimate	Explanation
Salary: Owner or Manager	_____	Based on living expenses
All other salaries or wages	_____	Employees/contractors
Rent or mortgage payment	_____	
Advertising	_____	On-going program
Transportation expenses	_____	Pick-up and delivery service for clients. Auto expenses for self and employees
Office supplies	_____	
Program supplies	_____	Any consumable items used in camps, resorts, health clubs, etc.
Communication expenses	_____	Telephone, telegraph, computer services
Other utilities	_____	Including trash pick-up
Insurance	_____	Health, auto, fire, casualty
Payroll expense, including social security	_____	See page ___this chapter
Loan payments	_____	Business loans, repayment to investors, Visa/Mastercard
Maintenance	_____	
Legal and other professional fees	_____	Accounting services, lawyers or retainer
Entertainment/travel	_____	Expenses incurred in acquiring new business
Miscellaneous	_____	Other costs that will be on-going monthly items
Total Monthly Expenses: (Refer to 7. (7) (c) of Formal Business Plan, page ___this chapter.)	_____	

cash. The director pays his bills promptly and bills the parents of the campers with a 30-day-due requirement. The director keeps supplies and other expenses equal to sales expected during the next 30 days.

One month later, the camp director looks at his first income statement proudly and reflects on the $2,500 profit (see profit for January in Table 4-2). The next day the director's banker calls to say the business is out of cash. Shocked, the director laments, "I made a profit of $2,500 in January. How can I be out of cash?"

Table 4-3 tells the story. The missing cash is tied up in program supplies and in bills owed by customers. The director had plowed his profits of

TABLE 4-2. Income Statement

Actual	January	February
Sales Revenues	$10,000	$16,000
Expenses	7,500	12,000
Profits	$ 2,500	$ 4,000

TABLE 4-3. Cash Flow Statement

	January	February	March
Sales Revenue	$10,000	$16,000	$20,000
Cash received from sales	0	10,000	16,000
Cash expenditures (monthly)	12,000	15,000	15,000
Cash gain or loss	$12,000	$ 5,000	$ 1,000
Beginning cash	12,000	0	5,000
Ending cash	0	$ 5,000	$ 4,000

$2,500 back into supplies and equipment in anticipation of February sales of $16,000. He had used the $12,000 cash on hand (beginning cash as of January 1) for the same reason.

The director learned that dollars do not necessarily return when they are most needed. This revenue lag, in our example, could be partially offset by requiring fees to be paid in advance and borrowing from a prearranged line of credit to carry the business forward until the camp begins to pay its own way. When will this glorious day occur? A simple break-even formula can answer this question (see Chapter 7).

The break-even formula shows how sales volume, selling price, and operating expenses affect profits. A break-even calculation tells an entrepreneur of a service business how many service units (clients, rented spaces at a campground, campers at camps, etc.) must be generated before the business is profitable. Preparation of the complete version of this and the other financial statements can be frustrating to the new entrepreneur who lacks financial knowledge. For help, the new entrepreneur should seek professional assistance. However, these preliminary strategies will be sufficient to provide realistic goals and guidelines.

To continue on with our Happy Hills Day Camp saga, let us assume the director now decides he wants to know how many campers each month he must have to make a profit (to reach the magic break-even point—the BEP).

To answer that question, the camp director (with a little help from his accountant) has made the following estimates:

1. Variable costs (program supplies) will be $.20 on each dollar of sales (fees paid by campers).
2. Fixed costs (bus rental, salaries, telephone, facility rental) will be $3,000 a month.
3. The average camper will spend $100 a month.

First he would estimate the contribution to fixed costs made by each camper ($100 monthly fee − $20 variable cost = $80). This means that $80 out of each $100 monthly fee is left over to cover fixed costs (fixed costs usually do not vary with the sales column). He would then divide this unit contribution into monthly fixed costs:

$3,000 per month/$80 per camper = 38 campers a month needed to cover fixed costs and begin to make a profit

While a BEP of 38 campers gives the director a sales target for profitability, it lacks the versatility of the completely illustrated break-even chart, which can answer questions about expansion timing, the hiring of additional personnel, and safety margins for sales.

In estimating capital requirements, a final word of warning is in order. It is prudent for the beginning business to borrow more than projections indicate will be needed. A business can be in a cash bind if it overestimates its sales or even if it *underestimates* them. A cash buffer in excess of projected financial needs can be used to offset unexpected problems that arise. A new business as a general rule of thumb should have sufficient funds to operate for its first month without inflow of additional cash.

Selecting a Location

Location variables differ among types of businesses. However, for the majority of commercial leisure service organizations selecting the proper location can be vital for success. Certain characteristics of businesses will determine the importance of location: Do customers travel to the business (day-care centers, backpacking shops, bowling centers) or does the entrepreneur travel to the customer (home swimming lessons, leisure counseling, contracting services)? Does a business offer a special product or service with little local competition? Is convenience a key selling point in what the business offers a customer?[11] There are a few basic guidelines that should be considered by owners of commercial leisure service organizations:

1. Select a community, town, or city that is appealing for personal reasons.
2. Select an area within the city or town that complements the business.
3. Select a specific site that will encourage business.

Selecting the City or Town. It is important that individuals like where they live. Do not disregard personal preference when deciding on a specific city or town. Often persons raised in large cities prefer the fast pace and cultural diversity of that type of environment to the quiet and somewhat limited cultural and social opportunities of a small town. Yet keep in mind that personal contacts are important to the new entrepreneur and to move to a new area miles from these contacts could be shortsighted.

Demographic Considerations. There is also the question of customer demographics that will have an impact on the selection of a business location. For example, certain types of businesses require a minimum population base (see Table 4-4). The number of inhabitants per store indicates the population necessary to support one enterprise of the kind listed. For example, it is recommended that an area (a particular geographic boundary) have a minimum of 27,000 inhabitants to support one sporting goods store. If an area of this size already has a sporting goods store, it would be wise to consider locating in another area. Of course, other market variables must be considered such as psychographic factors (see Figure 6-5, Chapter 6).

Then again, the nature of a leisure business may dictate whether it should be located in an urban or rural area. Campgrounds, resident camps, resorts, marinas, and high-country packing and raft excursion companies

TABLE 4-4. Inhabitants per Store for Selected Service Businesses

Kind of Business	Number of Inhabitants per Store
Candy, nuts, and confectionary store	31,400
Restaurants, lunchrooms, caterers	1,580
Drinking places (alcoholic beverages)	2,414
Record Shops	112,144
Musical instrument stores	46,332
Boat dealers	61,526
R.V. dealers (trailers)	44,746
Book stores	28,584
Hobby, toy and game shops	61,430
Sporting goods	27,063

Source: Census of Retail Trade, Number of inhabitants residing in the United States (excluding Armed Forces). Washington, D.C.: Bureau of the Census, U.S. Department of Commerce, 1979.

usually are located in remote areas with contact centers in or near large urban populations. Some private campgrounds are located in population centers, but keep in mind that land costs are usually prohibitive today in these areas; charging the fees necessary to cover land acquisition costs would price a new urban campground out of the market.

If an organizaton's business comes primarily from local inhabitants, certain questions must be answered: Is the population increasing, stationary, or declining? Are the people native-born, mixed, or chiefly foreign? What do they do for a living? Are they predominantly laborers, clerks, executives, or retired persons? What age group is dominant? To help you gauge buying power, find out the average rental fees for housing in the area, the average real estate taxes for homes, and the per capita income.

The zoning ordinances, parking availability, transportation facilities, and physical barriers such as hills, bridges, and freeways are also important in considering the location of any kind of business.

Selecting a Site. In site selection for a retail store or service business, check on such factors as:

1. Nearest competition.
2. Traffic flow.
3. Parking facilities.
4. Street location.
5. Physical aspects of the building.
6. Type of lease.
7. Cost per square foot of space.
8. Elevator service for handicapped persons.
9. The quality of transportation.

If the service is located in a large urban area, it is important to determine the incidence of crime in the area. This factor alone can have a chilling effect on any business[12] (see Table 4-5).

TABLE 4-5. Score Sheets on Sites

(Grade each factor: "A" for excellent, "B" for good, "C" for fair, "D" for poor.)

Factor	Grade
1. Centrally located to reach my market	_____
2. Merchandise or raw materials available readily	_____
3. Nearby competition situation	_____
4. Transportation availability and rates	_____
5. Quantity of available employees	_____
6. Prevailing rates of employee pay	_____
7. Parking facilities	_____
8. Adequacy of utilities (sewer, water, power, gas)	_____
9. Traffic flow	_____
10. Taxation burden	_____
11. Quality of police and fire protection	_____
12. Housing availability for employees	_____
13. Environmental factors (schools, cultural, community activities, enterprise of businessmen)	_____
14. Physical suitability of building	_____
15. Type and cost of lease	_____
16. Provision for future expansion	_____
17. Overall estimate of quality of site in ten years	_____
18. Crime rate	_____

Other Considerations

There are several other crucial considerations in starting a commercial leisure service business. A form of business ownership must be chosen, and a lawyer, accountant, banker, and insurance agent must be selected. In addition, requirements for licenses and permits, sales taxes, self employment tax, employer taxes and worker's compensation insurance must be met.

Form of Legal Organization. One of the things that the potential business owner must decide is the way in which a business will be organized. Basically, there are three types of business ownership: sole proprietorship, partnership, and corporation. A good deal of thought should be given to the advantages and disadvantages of each of these approaches in terms of the needs of the business. Some of the specific advantages and disadvantages associated with each form of ownership can be found in Chapter 5.

Licenses and Permits. No textbook discussion can cover specific details on licenses and permits because regulations vary among states, counties, and cities. In some regulatory jurisdictions, an occupational license is required of any business activity or profession. Costs vary but are usually nominal. The exception is liquor. If liquor is being sold and a new license is required, it can be costly. Some areas have limits on the number of liquor licenses, and the cost of this license is a significant factor in the sale of an existing business that has a liquor license.

Before launching any new enterprise, check with the local chamber of commerce and local offices of the Small Business Administration for information on licenses and permits.

Sales Taxes. Most states levy a sales tax on all items sold. Check with the state department of revenue in order to comply with the law in terms of amounts to be collected and all reporting procedures.

Self Employment Tax. If an owner or manager earns at least $400 per year, he or she must pay a self-employment tax. Check with the local Internal Revenue Service office.

Employer Tax. If a business hires employees, it must withhold federal (and perhaps state and city) income taxes as well as social security taxes from employees' wages. The business must also pay its own share of the social security tax and taxes (or premiums) for unemployment insurance. It is recommended that prospective business owners or managers obtain two useful publications from the IRS: *Mr. Businessman's Kit*, which contains tax forms, and *Guide for Small Business*, which explains how to fill out the necessary tax forms.

Workers' Compensation. Those businesses that hire employees must carry workers' compensation insurance. This protects workers from loss of income because of injury on the job.

Preparing a Business Plan

Once a prospective business owner has an idea around which to build a business, preplanning should be done, followed by the development of a formal business plan. At just what point in the process of launching an enterprise the formal business plan should be developed is a matter of judgment. It is recommended that this project be undertaken when the prospective entrepreneur determines that his or her resources, interest, and desire to proceed are sufficiently strong to warrant the time and energy necessary to develop this document.

Preplanning

Preplanning activities such as pinpointing and defining the business to be engaged in, defining the business's intended market, and research of competitors, should be completed before commitment of time and resources to a formal business plan. Figure 4-5 outlines a three-week preproposal planning exercise. If, at the end of this exercise, you, the aspiring entrepreneur, are still committed to the project, then it is time to prepare a formal business plan. The preplanning exercise allows you time to gather information needed for the formal plan, provides an exit point if interest wanes, and provides a departure point from which to continue to develop the business. Although relatively little time and effort are involved in preproposal planning, it requires a serious appraisal of the enterprise and should settle some of the doubts that the prospective business owner may have.

The Formal Business Plan

Starting a commercial leisure service business requires a well-thought-out plan. A formal business plan is the most important document in the life

Task

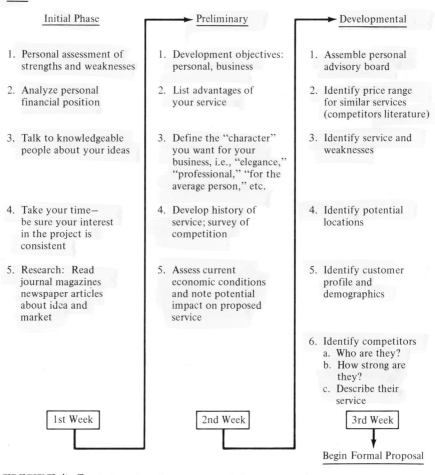

FIGURE 4–5. A three-week preproposal planning guide.

of a business. It is the midwife for its birth. As depicted in the outline below, every key aspect of the business should be discussed in detail. The preparation of such a plan is advantageous in that it requires the prospective business owner to be disciplined and organized in his or her planning efforts, it provides a guide for the operation of the business, and it can be used as a tool in attempts to obtain financing from outside parties, e.g., bankers or investors. The prospective business owner should endeavor to communicate a sense of thoroughness in the business plan and a feeling that all contingencies have been explored.

A business plan should answer such questions as:

• What business will I be in?
• What do I want? What am I capable of doing?
• Do I really want to do this? Why would someone want to loan me the money?
• Why would a potential customer want to do business with me?
• What are the most workable ways to achieve my goals?

Outline for Developing a Commercial Leisure Service Business Plan

1. Introduction
   A. Description of your proposed business.
      1. Describe your product or service.
      2. Support with diagrams, illustrations, or pictures (if available).
   B. Summary of proposed marketing method (see Chapter 5 for detailed plan).
      1. Describe the market segment you are aiming to reach.
      2. Describe in detail the service(s), character of the organization, and proposed location.
   C. Summary of your financial estimates.
      1. State a sales projection total for each of the next three years.
      2. State the estimated profit for each of the first three years.
      3. State the estimated starting capital you will need.
2. Statement of objectives.
   A. Statement of the desirability of your product or service.
      1. Describe the advantages of your product or service, its improvements over existing products or services.
      2. State the long-range objectives and the short-range subobjectives of your proposed business.
      3. Describe your qualifications to run the business; include a personal resumé.
      4. State why you feel you will be successful.
   B. List metaobjectives you may feel are pertinent.
3. Background of proposed business.
   A. Brief summary of existing conditions in the business you are intending to enter (the "state of the art" as it is now).
      1. Where the product or service is now being used.
      2. How the product or service is now being used.
   B. Detailed explanation of your place in the state of the art.
      1. Describe the projections and trends for the leisure industry for the next five years.
      2. Describe competition you face (place competitors' advertisements and brochures in the appendix at the end of your prospectus).
      3. State your intended strategy for meeting competition.
      4. Describe the special qualities of your product or service that make it unique.
4. Marketing strategy (market plan in Chapter 5 should be completed).
   A. A comprehensive description of marketing strategy.
      1. Describe the segment of the market you plan to reach.
      2. Describe in full detail the distribution channel you plan to use to reach your market segment: retail, mail order, direct sales.
5. Selling tactics.
   A. An outline of the activities to be used in selling the product or service.
      1. State the methods you expect to use to promote your product or service: direct calling, telephone, advertising, mail, radio, television, or other.
      2. Include a sample brochure or dummy, advertisements, announcements, or other promotional literature.
      3. Present data supporting your ability to meet your sales goals: actual orders, personally known prospective key accounts, and potential customers.

4. Explain the margins of safety you have allowed in your sales forecasts (underprojecting figures obtained in market research—overprojecting cost to acquire business).
6. Plan of operation.
    A. Description of the proposed organization.
        1. Show an organization chart describing the needed business functions and relationships.
        2. Describe the key positions and identify the persons to fill them.
        3. Give resumes of the key persons.
        4. List equipment or facilities and the space and location required.
7. Supporting data.
    A. Information required to support the major points in the business plan.
        1. Include a detailed description of the service to be offered.
        2. Show a list of material(s) needed to renovate facility or work required to ready facility.
        3. List the capital equipment you will need and its estimated cost.
        4. Provide a layout of your proposed business site.
        5. List a price schedule for your service.
        6. Include your detailed market survey data.
        7. Supply the following financial data:
            a. Projected balance sheet for the end of each of the first two years.
            b. Income statement for each of two years (balance sheet).
            c. Cash flow projection for two years by the month.
            d. Break-even chart for two years, by the year.
8. Conclusions and summary.
    A. A statement of proposed approach in starting the new organization.
        1. State the total capital you will need and the safety factor you have used.
        2. State how much profit you expect and when you expect to show it.
        3. Tell what percentage of ownership you want for yourself and your partners.
        4. Indicate the total amount of capital you need and how it is to be made up.
            a. Your share of the starting investment.
            b. How much more you will need from others and when you will need the money.
            c. State what share of the business you will give to the investors or lenders for this additional capital.
        5. State your planned schedule for starting your business.

Preparation of a formal business plan requires commitment on the part of a prospective business owner. Distractions, such as indecision about the project, family problems, educational pursuits, or vacations may affect the quality of the business plan. Such distractions should not be present if the formal business plan is to come together into a well-organized, comprehensive, and useful document. In other words, this project should be the prospective business owner's primary focus for the immediate future once the commitment has been made to prepare it (see the "Outline for Developing a Commercial Leisure Service Business Plan").

The business plan is a highly confidential document. If it were to get into the wrong hands, it could jeopardize the success of a business project.

The document should be treated with respect and should be bound and appear professional. The prospective business owner should not hesitate to include pictures of the location, product, or facilities. In addition, the document should honor the reader: important charts should be easy to locate, it should be double spaced, and it should be free of typing and spelling errors.

Caveats

There are no universally set rules regarding business plans, but some common sense rules may improve the chances of getting the plan read and getting the plan funded. According to *Venture,* "large venture capital firms (organizations whose business it is to finance new enterprises) typically receive 500 to 1,500 business plans in the mail."[13] Most of these plans do get one reading. Only 10 percent of the business plans go beyond the first reading, however. Ninety-nine out of 100 business plans that are received by venture capitalists are never funded.

To improve the odds of receiving funding, the prospective entrepreneur should observe the following caveats:

1. A report should be as brief as possible while still giving the impression of completeness. *Venture* Magazine states that reports are measured in terms of inches—no more than ¼ to ½ inch thick.[14]
2. Venture capitalists are not impressed with computer-generated business plans. The people funding business plans want to know if somebody really sat down and thought about the numbers. A professionally prepared business plan should be avoided.
3. A business plan must show clearly the idea (focus) of the service, who will buy the service and why, the amount of money needed, and the data to support this figure including sales and earnings forecasts, and the profile of the business owners/managers.
4. Be certain that the individual or firm reviewing your proposal is interested in your type of enterprise.
5. A business plan is like a job seeker's resume; its purpose is to secure an interview for its writer.
6. Make a phone call or send a letter to introduce the business plan to the reviewer before it is delivered. An introductory call from an accountant or attorney who knows the firm will be most helpful. Without this tactic the chances of getting the plan reviewed are greatly reduced.
7. A business plan must be neatly typed and free of poor grammar and spelling errors. However, it should not read like a sales brochure.
8. Long, detailed, down-to-the-last-nickel financial forecasts are not necessary. Sales projections, earnings, and cash flow on a monthly basis for the first or second year are usually adequate.
9. Be careful about unrealistic assumptions, e.g., receivables of thirty days, high attendance figures, low operating costs, underpricing the competition.
10. Business plans that budget the new owners with high salaries, large expense accounts, and large monthly lease payments for cars are "turn-offs" to potential investors. An executive of Ventana Growth Fund, San Diego, stated in *Venture:* "In an entrepreneurial environment you don't get high salaries, you get stock."[15]

Buying a Franchise

An alternative form of business ownership is franchising. A franchise is an agreement that permits the buyer (franchisee) to sell a product or a service of the seller (franchisor). The International Franchise Association defines a franchise as a continuing relationship between the franchisor and the franchisee in which the sum total of the franchisor's knowledge, image, success, manufacturing, and marketing techniques is supplied to the franchisee for a consideration (usually money).

By purchasing a franchise, the franchisee gets a ready-made business. The franchisee can forego the effort required to build a business step-by-step as outlined in the preceding section. In most cases, the franchisor will provide the franchisee with everything necessary to open his or her door for customers, including a key to the door.

Total sales by business franchises topped $80 billion in 1981, up from $79 billion in 1980.[16] According to the Bank of America, the number of businesses doing business under franchise arrangements increased from 253,000 in 1979 to 291,000 in 1981.[17] Among the newer and growing types of franchises are ethnic food restaurants, home computer stores, business aids and services, car repair centers, employment agencies, and equipment rental stores. In the leisure service field, two franchise opportunities stand out: KOA (Kampgrounds of America, Inc.) and Krazy Horse Campground, Inc. Other opportunities include bookstores, motels, restaurants, and preschools.

At its best, business franchising combines the expertise and marketing sophistication of big business from the home company (franchisor) with the entrepreneurial motivation and investment capital from the buyer (franchisee). The franchisor can expand his or her business by using the capital of the franchisee and by penetrating more markets with franchise units. In return, the franchisee obtains a business that might take years to develop alone.

Owning a franchise is not for everyone, however. The would-be entrepreneur must be willing to give up some personal authority and be subjected to outside control on various operating matters. There often are restrictions on selling the business that could effect the franchisee's long-term personal financial objectives.

There are, unfortunately, some unsavory franchisors. Many of these companies have names of movie stars and sports heroes as their only big selling point. If the franchise plan is not based on solid business principles and it fails, it also wipes out the individual franchisee.

Each year, about 2,000 companies sell franchises in the United States. To select the best investment from the many options available, prospective franchises may begin their search by consulting several sources that list franchise opportunities.

- Franchise directories. These list the names of franchisors and their franchise opportunities, including assistance available to the prospective buyer. The U.S. Department of Commerce can provide information on franchising opportunities.[18]

- Newspaper and business magazines. The classified sections of these generally carry advertisements of current franchise offers.
- Trade shows. Trade shows featuring franchisor exhibits are held in major cities around the country. Trade associations and local chambers of commerce can provide show schedules.
- Professionals. Professionals such as accountants and management consultants who specialize in franchising often know of franchises for sale.
- Franchise brokers. These are agents who may represent several franchisors and can provide listings of franchise offers.

Evaluating the Franchise

Keep in mind that buying a franchise is buying a service. The franchisor is being paid to deliver a set of services that are crucial to the success of the enterprise. The franchisor is trying to make a profit and is often tempted to cut some of these services to increase profits. Before buying any franchise, the prospective franchisee should investigate the opportunity in detail. One of the best sources of information about a company is the disclosure document provided by the franchisor to interested buyers.

Generally, franchisors are required by federal law to provide interested buyers with detailed information on company operations before they agree to invest in a franchise. Under the 1979 Federal Trade Commission rule, "Disclosure Requirements and Prohibitions Concerning Franchising and Business Opportunity Ventures," franchisors must give prospective franchisees a disclosure statement. This statement must be provided at least ten days before the buyer signs a contract or makes a payment, whichever comes first. This federal trade rule and other pertinent information are available from the International Franchise Association.* The disclosure statement must include the following information.

1. Identifying information about the franchisor.
2. Business experience of the franchisor's directors and key executives.
3. The franchisor's business experience.
4. Litigation history of the franchisor and its directors and key executives.
5. Bankruptcy history of the franchisor and its directors and key executives.
6. Description of the franchise.
7. A statement of the total funds that must be paid by the franchisee to obtain or start the franchise operation.
8. A statement of continuing payments that the franchisee is required to make to carry on the franchise business.
9. A list of persons, either the franchisor or any of its affiliates, with whom the franchisee is required or advised to do business.
10. Realty, personal property, and other property or services that the franchisee is required to purchase, lease, or rent and a list of any persons with whom these transactions must be made.
11. Consideration, such as royalties and commissions, paid by suppliers to the franchisor or any of its affiliates as a result of a franchisee's purchase from the suppliers.

* International Franchise Association, 7315 Wisconsin Ave., Suite 600W, Washington, D.C. 20014.

12. Any franchisor assistance in financing the purchase of a franchise.
13. Restrictions placed on a franchisee's conduct of his or her business.
14. Required personal participation by the franchisee.
15. Termination, cancellation, and renewal of the franchise.
16. Statistical information about the number of franchises and their rate of termination.
17. Franchisor's right to select or approve a site for the franchise.
18. Training programs for the franchisee.
19. Celebrity involvement with the franchise.
20. The franchisor's financial information, which generally includes audited financial statements for each of the last three fiscal years.

If the prospective buyer is still interested in the franchise after a review of the disclosure document, further review of the arrangement with the following list in mind is the next step in deciding whether to pursue a particular franchising opportunity[19] (see Figure 4-6).

1. *Company.* Does the company have a solid reputation in its field, a good credit rating, an image of honesty and fair dealing with franchisees, a

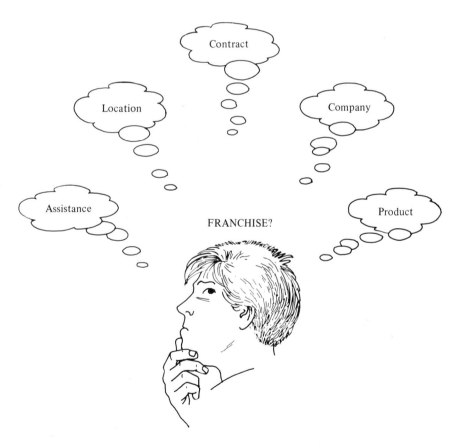

FIGURE 4–6. Factors to evaluate when considering the purchase of a franchise. (Adapted from Peter Van Voorhis, *Entrepreneurship and Small Business Management*, Boston, Allyn & Bacon, 1980, p. 122.)

good training program and merchandising, experienced management, and adequate resources?

2. *Product.* What is the current availability of the product, its market penetration, pricing and packaging, durability and ease of use, manufacturing source and standards, purchasing and distribution requirements, comparison with competing products?

3. *Location.* What are the quantity and quality of areas available? Is there protection of exclusive rights to the franchisee, franchisor assistance in selecting a desirable site, lease or purchase arrangements.?

4. *Assistance.* Does the franchisor offer a promise of help both initially and on a continuing basis in such decisions as store layout and display, inventory selection and control, market research, financial analysis, promotion, and advertising?

5. *Contract.* Is the contract complete in all terms, such as what each party must do, payments to be made, inventory purchase and sales quotas, limitations on franchisee's other activities, provisions for sale of business and termination of the contract?

If after obtaining answers to the foregoing questions, interest is strong, Voorhis suggests the next step.

> If you do feel that the opportunity looks good based on the answers to these preliminary questions, have your lawyer study the proposed contract paragraph by paragraph and clause by clause. Although many of the well-known national franchisors are extremely rigid in the wording of their contracts (and have waiting lists of potential franchisees willing to accept all terms as offered), you'll want to consider carefully whether the overall impact of the agreement is in the best interests of achieving your personal and business goals. If it isn't, then tell the franchisor what parts are objectionable and make a counterproposal about their wording.[20]

It is important that the prospective buyer to satisfy himself or herself that all the issues presented above are understood. Like any business venture, franchising has its risks; however, good franchises have an overwhelming record of success. Perhaps the best known franchisor, McDonald's hamburger system, is worthy of note in this regard. The franchisor claims that not a single outlet has ever lost money. It is the success of McDonald's and other well-known franchisors that has lured many prospective entrepreneurs to this business format. Yet caution should be the motto of anyone considering the purchase of any franchise.

Summary

This chapter has presented a series of steps necessary to start a commercial leisure service business.

Starting a commercial leisure service business requires an idea that will sell. Ideas come from observing a phenomena such as a gap in the market, a conscious desire to produce an idea, letting the subconscious work, accidental discovery, personal hobbies or interests, answering the question, "Why isn't there a . . .?", or opportunities flowing from the technological changes taking place today.

We discussed three ways of getting into a commercial leisure service business: buying an existing business, starting a new business, or purchasing a franchise. Creating a new business requires a sound idea, extensive market research, and the preparation of a formal business plan. It is important to determine the type of business one is in. This step sets the stage for determining the market to be served because the leisure market is diverse and multidimensional. The aspiring entrepreneur must invest time, effort, and money into identifying potential customers.

Some of the disadvantages of buying an existing business are that the entrepreneur must purchase "goodwill" and reputation and customers may leave with the previous owner. It is often difficult to attract new customers, particularly if the previous owners have damaged the organization's image. It must be remembered that when an individual sells a business, he or she is not doing so to offer a golden opportunity to someone else.

A third alternative in business ownership is franchising. A franchise is an agreement that permits the buyer (franchisee) to sell a product or a service of the seller (franchisor). There is a continuing relationship between franchisee and franchisor in which the latter, for a fee, provides knowledge, image, marketing techniques, and management assistance.

The aspiring entrepreneur must determine where he or she will go to obtain the initial capital and credit to launch the enterprise. Capital may come from commercial banks; trade credit; equipment loans and leases, or funds from friends, relatives and venture capitalists. Determining capital requirements necessitates the preparation of a cash flow chart, a starting costs worksheet, and a list of estimated monthly expenses.

Selecting a location for a commercial leisure service involves the review and assessment of many variables. These variables include personal preference for one area or city over another, the demographics of the intended target market, zoning ordinances, transportation facilities, physical barriers, and the nature of the enterprise itself.

Once the foregoing information has been assembled, a formal business plan should be drawn up. The formal business plan should not only answer key questions about the service, competitors, markets, and capital requirements, but it should also be an operational blue print for the next few years.

Study Questions

1. What are the primary decisions that an aspiring entrepreneur must make before launching a commercial leisure service business?
2. Where do ideas come from? What is your most recent idea about a product or service that you feel would be successful?
3. List and describe three ways of obtaining a business of your own.
4. Why is it important to define the business you are in?
5. List and discuss the various ways of obtaining initial capital and credit to start a commercial leisure service business.
6. List and discuss the various financial statements necessary to launch a new enterprise.
7. Which financial statement do you feel would be of greatest interest to a prospective investor (lending institution)?
8. What are the key variables in selecting a location for a commercial leisure service organization such as a private youth camp?

9. In selecting a site for a retail store, what factors should be considered?
10. What value is there in engaging in preplanning activities before writing a formal business plan?
11. What questions should a formal business plan answer?
12. What is a franchise? What are some of the advantages and disadvantages of buying a franchise?

Experiential Exercise

On page 143 of this chapter is a preproposal planning guide. Select a personal hobby or other leisure interest and "walk" the idea through the various steps of the guide. This should not be an elaborate exercise, such as one likely to be executed before the preparation of a formal business plan, but a short excursion into the preplanning process using the knowledge you already possess about your hobby or leisure interest or knowledge you might easily obtain from a visit with a friend or to the library. Write out this exercise and share it with colleagues or friends for their input and evaluation.

Notes

1. Arthur Koestler, *The Art of Creation*, New York: Dell, 1964, p. 189.
2. H.N. Broom, Justine Longenecker, *Small Business Management*, 5th ed., Cincinnati: Southwestern Publishing, 1979, p. 21.
3. Peter Van Voorhis, *Entrepreneurship and Small Business Management*, Boston: Allyn & Bacon, 1980, p. 122.
4. Ibid., p. 115.
5. U.S. Small Business Administration, *Business Plan for Retailers*. Small Marketers Aid No. 150, Washington, D.C.: U.S. Government Printing Office, 1973, p. 3.
6. Donald M. Dibble, *Up Your Own Organization*, Santa Clara, CA: The Entrepreneur Press, 1974, p. 176.
7. Broom and Longenecker, p. 103.
8. Dun & Bradstreet, Inc., *The Business Failure Record: 1976*. New York: Dun & Bradstreet, Inc., 1977, pp. 12–13.
9. Broom and Longenecker, p. 49.
10. Internal Revenue Service, *Statistics of Income for 1972*. Richmond, VA: Internal Revenue Service, 1972, p. 11.
11. N.C. Siropolis, *A Guide to Entrepreneurship*, 2nd ed., Boston: Houghton Mifflin, 1982, p. 198.
12. Wendell O. Metcalf, *The Starting and Managing Series*, Vol. 1, 3rd ed., Washington, D.C.: U.S. Small Business Administration, 1973, p. 15.
13. Sabin Russell, "What Investors Hate Most About Business Plans," *Venture*, June, 1984, p. 52–53.
14. Ibid., p. 52.
15. Ibid., p. 53.
16. "Buying a Franchise," *Small Business Reporter*, Vol. 15, No. 8, San Francisco: Bank of America, 1979, p. 1.
17. Ibid., p. 2.
18. U.S. Department of Commerce, *Franchise Opportunities Handbook*, Washington, D.C.: U.S. Government Printing Office, 1980.
19. Van Voorhis, p. 125.
20. Ibid.

Close-up: Hydrotube

Brent Marshall is the manager of an indoor water slide. This business, known as Hydrotube, caters to individuals of all ages, but focuses primarily upon youth. The facility itself consists of two fiberglass tubes that have a 60-foot vertical drop and a 17,000-gallon splash pool. It takes approximately 20 to 30 seconds to traverse the water slide. According to Marshall, this leisure experience "must be exciting since people come back—we try to make it an exciting and safe experience."

As the manager of this facility, Marshall supervises (during the peak season) eighteen part-time and full-time employees. All employees are certified lifeguards. These employees are responsible for carrying out the various functions necessary for the operation of the Hydrotube facility. This includes lifeguarding responsibilities, cashiering, maintenance, and regulation of persons riding the Hydrotube. According to Marshall, his greatest challenge as a manager is to maintain a positive work environment. He does this by "giving the employees a certain amount of autonomy, responsibility, and independence." In order to allow his employees this type of independence, he hires people with outstanding qualifications and professional skills. He feels that people respond negatively to an overbearing supervisory stance. He notes that his staff "is very capable of operating in a professional manner with minimal supervision."

Because a large percentage of the Hydrotube customers are young children, Marshall notes that it is "important to convey an image to parents of absolute safety. Many parents drop their children off at the Hydrotube while they shop or run errands, and it is important that they feel comfortable doing so." The Hydrotube experience involves a certain minimal amount of risk. However, controlling this risk is very important. Marshall notes that with sales of over 70,000 individual rides, there have been fewer than 70 minor accidents, such as cuts or bruises (less than 1 percent).

The construction costs associated with the development of indoor water slides, according to Marshall, are great. A water slide can cost between $500,000 and $1 million depending upon its size, complexity, and the amenities offered in conjunction with it. The expectation of the investors in this Hydrotube operation is that they will recoup their investment in three to five years. Marshall notes that "as is the case with many leisure activities and programs, the risk to the investor is high (since this may be a fad), therefore the investors have targeted an early date for the return on their investment." Although the risk is high in this type of venture, the potential for profit is also high. The product life cycle of the Hydrotube is not one that will follow a normal distribution; that is, with a gradual build-up of business, a peak, and a gradual decline. They expect immediate high interest and peak consumer participation, at which point they will realize their greatest profits, followed by a gradual decline over a number of years. Marshall notes that the water slide market may have already passed the saturation point in terms of new facilities.

Brent Marshall sees his involvement at Hydrotube as a good investment in the future. He feels that he has been able to learn how to deal with people effectively as well as learn some of the important realities of business (such as trying to keep overhead low). In addition, he has learned how to deal with the media in promoting his product and how to effectively manage employees. He feels that his experience working in a leisure-oriented business has enabled him to develop skills that can be used in other business settings. For the future, he sees himself working as a district manager and is pleased that many of his management and program ideas have been used in other Hydrotube operations.

5

Organizing and Managing Commercial Leisure Service Businesses

The organization and management of commercial leisure service organizations is the topic of this chapter. Initially, three types of business ownership—sole proprietorship, partnership, and corporation—will be presented. Also discussed will be the development of an approach for managing a commercial leisure service venture. In this discussion we stress the importance of the development of an organizational philosophy. We also focus attention on the importance of select management skills, the manager's style, management systems, the organizational structure, and methods that can be used in working with staff. All of these are variables that the owner or manager of a commercial leisure service venture must address in order to operate it successfully.

Types of Business Ownership

In the United States and Canada there are three basic types of business ownership: sole proprietorship, partnership, and corporation (see Figure 5-1). Sole proprietorships occur when a single person owns a business. When two or more persons own a commercial leisure service venture it is known as a partnership. A corporation is not owned by one person or a few people, but rather has a legal existence of its own, as if it were "a person." These types of business ownership, all of which can be applied in the management of commercial leisure service organizations, will be dis-

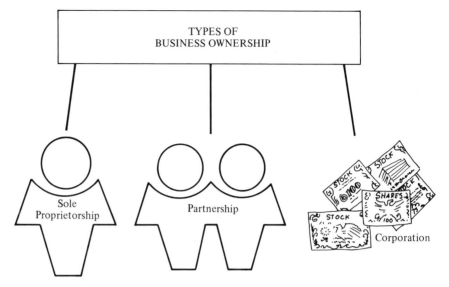

FIGURE 5–1. Types of business ownership.

cussed in detail. However, first we will present some statistics regarding these types of business ownership.

An analysis of businesses in the United States and Canada reveals a number of interesting patterns. By and large, the majority of businesses in North America are sole proprietorships or what could be termed small business ventures. The U.S. Small Business Administration has established guidelines for various types of businesses delineating what constitutes a large versus a small business operation. Since our focus is primarily on organizations providing commercial leisure services and retail outlets selling leisure goods and products, our comments will be confined to these two types of businesses. A small commercial leisure organization is one that has annual sales receipts under $2 million.[1]

When viewing all businesses, it is interesting to note that the Internal Revenue Service suggests that over 95 percent of the businesses in the United States can be described as small businesses.[2] In terms of total employment, small businesses employ nearly 60 percent of the entire labor force, whereas large businesses employ the remaining 40 percent. In terms of total sales, however, larger organizations account for approximately 60 percent of our gross national product. If one takes into consideration the emphasis placed on decentralization, economies of scale, and the ability to respond rapidly to changes in the leisure market, it would appear quite evident that smaller commercial leisure service organizations have an exceedingly important role to play in providing leisure services both now and in the future.

Sole Proprietorship

A sole proprietorship is the most common form of business ownership. Basically, a sole proprietorship exists when a commercial leisure service business is owned by one person. This person is financially responsible for the business, and if the business succeeds and makes a profit, he or she reaps the benefits. If the business is not successful and experiences a loss, a sole proprietor is liable for the expense of the loss. Most small commercial leisure service businesses are sole proprietorships.

The sole proprietor is responsible for managing the business or hiring someone to act in the role of manager within the business. However, the authority and responsibility for decision making, acquisition of resources, financial remuneration, and other business decisions clearly are the responsibility of the person who owns the business.

Advantages

Archer has written that the principle advantages of the sole proprietorship are that it provides a high personal incentive for the owner, it provides freedom to act, it is less expensive to establish, its financial statements are private, it offers an opportunity for tax savings, and it can be dissolved simply[3] (see Figure 5-2).

High Personal Incentives. Sole proprietors of commercial leisure service organizations know that any profits resulting from their investment in the business in terms of time, energy, and money will return to them. As a result, their motivation to invest time, effort, and money is great. Such persons may be motivated to work overtime and to reinvest part or all of their personal resources or salaries back into their business. Persons who do not own the businesses for which they work may not be so motivated because, being salaried, their realization of profit will not likely rise dramatically or proportionately with the amount of profit realized by the organization.

Sole proprietors may also have a creative interest in the businesses in which they are involved. They may feel that they are expressing themselves and their personal interests through their work. This can also result in a high degree of personal incentive.

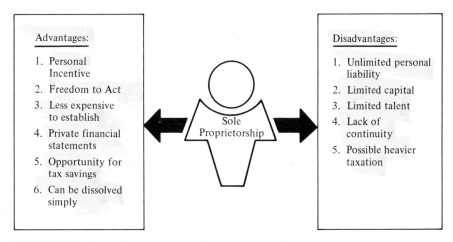

FIGURE 5–2. Advantages and disadvantages of a sole proprietorship.

Freedom to Act.   The sole proprietor has the ability to act in an independent fashion and to make decisions without consulting others. All decisions regarding the leisure services to be provided, costs, staffing, facilities, equipment, supplies, and organizational policies are made by the sole proprietor independently. This freedom to act in many situations provides an opportunity to respond rapidly to changes in the market. In the leisure market, the ability to respond quickly to changing fads and styles often may make the difference between success or failure. This is especially important among distributors of goods and services. Small commercial leisure service organizations acting independently can choose freely from among various product lines, selecting those that are currently in demand in their target markets.

Sole proprietors' freedom to act is also reflected in their ability to structure their job situations as they choose. For example, sole proprietors can choose the hours that they want to work, the days of the week that they want to work, their own salary, their own benefits, their own subordinates, and the location at which they want to be although they may have to work within certain financial or practical business limits.

Less Expensive to Establish.   A sole proprietorship can be less expensive to establish than a partnership or a corporation. The establishment of a sole proprietorship does not require legal agreements that entail legal fees nor does it require the fees associated with incorporation. Furthermore, when a sole proprietorship is dissolved, it is a simple and inexpensive process as contrasted with the dissolution of a partnership or corporation.

Privacy in Financial Statements.   Basically, a commercial leisure service business organized as a sole proprietorship does not have to publish its financial statements. Only the owner, the Internal Revenue Service, and those persons with whom the owner wishes to share his or her statements can have access to financial information regarding the business. This type of privacy also applies to other contractual arrangements made by the sole proprietor. This can be an advantage when business operations require confidentiality. In fact, the sole proprietorship is the form of business ownership that best ensures privacy and secrecy of operations.

Tax Savings.   For income tax purposes, the sole proprietor can include profits or wages earned from the business plus personal income on income tax returns. Unlike a corporation, a sole proprietorship is not subject to special taxes. Thus, the commercial leisure service business organized as a sole proprietorship offers an opportunity for tax savings.

Ease of Dissolution.   The sole proprietorship can be dissolved simply by the owner deciding that he or she no longer wishes to conduct business. The sole proprietor does not have to involve others in the decision to dissolve.

Disadvantages

There are also a number of disadvantages of operating a business as a sole proprietorship. Some of the disadvantages include unlimited personal liability, limited capital, limited talent, lack of continuity, and possible heavier taxation.[4]

Unlimited Personal Liability. A sole proprietorship carries with it an opportunity for great personal gains. It also carries the risk of personal loss. The sole proprietor is responsible for the debts of the organization. He or she may have personal property and belongings attached in order to pay for debts incurred by the business. Because of the high risk of failure of small commercial leisure businesses, those interested in sole proprietorships certainly will want to be aware of the extent to whch they are exposing themselves to personal loss. This is often a crucial decision, and it must be made in an intelligent and sound financial manner.

Limited Capital. It is not unusual for a person to have sound ideas and a good managerial background yet lack the capital needed to develop a concept. Sole proprietorship places a restriction on the nature and extent of the amount of money that a person can use to develop an idea. Because the sole proprietor is liable for all debts incurred by the business, his or her ability to borrow funds is proportional to personal assets. Again, many good ideas have remained undeveloped as a result of a lack of capital.

Limited Talent. One of the serious disadvantages of a sole proprietorship is limited talent. It is rare when one person has all of the necessary technical, managerial, and financial skills to move a business forward effectively. This lack may be especially felt at the initial development stage of a commercial leisure service venture. Many ideas go undeveloped because a person lacks the talent to carry them out. Although appropriate human resources can be purchased by the sole proprietor, such people will not have a vested interest in the business and may not be as motivated as an owner.

Lack of Continuity. A serious disadvantage of a sole proprietorship is the possibility that the continuity of the business could be interrupted. A commercial leisure service organization may be established as a sole proprietorship and operate successfully for a number of years. However, if the proprietor dies, decides to give up the business, or becomes unable to continue business operations, the continuity of the business venture may cease. Obviously, a person can sell a business to another person, but this does not ensure that the business will operate in a manner consistent with the philosophy of its predecessor.

Possible Heavier Taxation. As indicated, in a sole proprietorship the owner is taxed on earnings and profit. As a business progresses financially and as the individual owner makes a decision to pay himself or herself more or to retain more of the profit, his or her individual taxes increase. At a point in the tax structure it becomes more advantageous for the sole proprietor to consider the possibility of incorporation to offset tax burdens. This will be a decision each owner must make, based on personal factors, as well as the financial status of the commercial leisure service venture.

Partnership

As indicated, a partnership exists when two or more persons combine their talents, energies, capital, and interests to engage in business. In addition, a partnership implies that co-owners agree to share in the risks and the profits inherent in their common business. Partnerships are common in service industries. Why do individuals join forces to engage in a business venture? The reasons for partnerships are numerous. Partnerships often help to offset the disadvantages of the sole proprietorship. A partner may provide capital, technical competence, or managerial skill that complements the work of another person. For example, a partner may be a person who provides capital to help develop a business, or a partner may be a person who has a great deal of technical competence in a particular leisure area (i.e., outdoor recreation, aquatics, childrens' play, or dance); however, this person may not possess the managerial skills necessary to form and profitably operate a business venture. Furthermore, neither of these two individuals may have the necessary capital to purchase the appropriate equipment, supplies, or other facilities necessary to move the venture ahead. It may very well be that a combination of three persons, all with different types of "assets," would be needed in order to pursue a business venture.

Forming a partnership can be done by verbal or written agreement. In addition, a partnership may be formed by implication. When two or more people agree verbally or in writing to establish a partnership, it is known as an expressed agreement. A partnership by implication occurs when it is determined legally that the two parties intend to act together. Generally speaking, unless otherwise agreed to ". . . partners share equally in their initial investments, in their decision-making authority, in their respective shares of risk and profit, and in other important business considerations."[5]

There are two basic patterns that emerge when persons form partnerships. The first is known as a *general partnership.* General partners share equally in the profits of the business and also share, from a legal standpoint, unlimited liability for the debts of a business. A written document known as *Articles of Partnership* is drawn up between two individuals. This document serves as the legal tool to bind each of the individuals in the partnership. Persons can participate in a general partnership in a number of different ways. For example an *active partner* within a general partnership is a person who is actively involved in the business and is identified as a part of the organization. A *silent partner* within a general partnership is a person who is involved in the business venture but whose name is not public and whose involvement is "behind the scenes." Another type of general partner is an *ostensible partner.* An ostensible partner may lend his or her name to the venture, usually in exchange for a fee, but does not have an investment in the organization and is not involved in organizational decision making.

The second type of partnership is known as a *limited partnership*. The limited partnership is a way of legally specifying the extent and amount of responsibilities that each individual assumes in the business venture. For example, an individual might want to limit his or her liability to a specific dollar figure. When establishing a limited partnership individuals usually draw up a formal written agreement. This written agreement will specify the name of the business venture, the names of the partners, and the terms to which the partners have agreed. This written agreement is usually recorded publicly. A limited partnership is usually established when outside investors contribute funds to assist in the establishment or expansion of a business. In this way, outside investors may be drawn to a business for specific terms. The information that should be included in the articles of partnership is presented below.

Taxation for a partnership is similar to that for the sole proprietorship; that is, each partner in the business venture is taxed on his or her earnings. The organization is not taxed, as is the case of the corporation. This may be advantageous in certain business ventures, whereas it may be disadvantageous in others. It is an important factor to keep in mind in the selection of a type of business ownership (see Figure 5-3).

Advantages

There are a number of advantages to operating a business as a partnership. Some of the more obvious are "more capital, better credit standing, more

Information That Should be Included _____
in the Articles of Partnership*

- Date of the formation of the partnership.
- Name and address of all partners.
- Statement of fact of partnership.
- Statement of business purposes.
- Duration of the business.
- Name and location of the business.
- Amount invested by each partner.
- Sharing ratio for profits and losses.
- Partners rights, if any, for withdrawal of funds for personal use.
- Provision of accounting records and their accessibility to partners.
- Specific duties of each partner.
- Provision of dissolution and for sharing the net assets.
- Restraint on partner's assumption of special obligations, such as endorsing the note of another.
- Provision for protecting a surviving partner's descendents, estate, etc.

* From: H. N. Broom, Justin G. Longenecker, and Carlos W. Moore, *Small-Business Management*, 6th ed. Cincinnati: South-Western Publishing Company, 1982, p. 171.

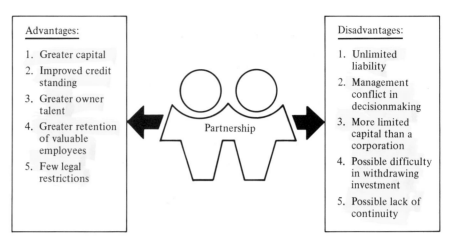

Advantages:		Disadvantages:
1. Greater capital		1. Unlimited liability
2. Improved credit standing		2. Management conflict in decisionmaking
3. Greater owner talent	Partnership	3. More limited capital than a corporation
4. Greater retention of valuable employees		4. Possible difficulty in withdrawing investment
5. Few legal restrictions		5. Possible lack of continuity

FIGURE 5–3. Advantages and disadvantages of a partnership.

owner talent, retaining valuable employees by personal incentive, and few legal restrictions."[6]

More Capital.   Combining the financial resources of partners in a business means greater financial resources. It is not unusual for a person to have an idea but lack the funds to develop the concept. By working with one or more other people, it is possible to increase the amount of capital available and thus the scope of the commercial leisure service business venture. Simply put, the collective personal wealth of two or more people will be greater than that of one person.

Better Credit Standing.   According to Archer, two or more people may obtain credit more easily than a single person. He suggests that banks and other lending institutions will look favorably on lending money to several people because they will be able to look to several persons for repayment rather than just one. In the event that one person experiences financial reversals, the others may be able to pick up the slack.

More Talent.   An obvious advantage to a partnership is the increase in talent. Different people bring different skills and abilities to a business. One person in a partnership may have the necessary technical skills, whereas another may have important organizational skills. For example, persons engaging in ownership of a camp for children might find it advantageous if one partner were skilled in management, if another possessed outdoor skills, and if still another partner were skilled in the area of games and activities. As an organization grows, the need for people with a variety of skills often increases. In addition, the more involved these people are in decision making processes, the greater the stake they will have in the business venture.

Increasing Personal Incentive of Valued Employees.   When an employee is particularly valuable to a business, it may want to increase the personal incentive of such a valued employee by making him or her a partner. For the organization, the ability to offer a partnership allows it to retain the services of people whose talents are valuable and who contribute greatly to its effective operation. For the employee, the possibility of a partnership may offer an incentive to strive for peak individual performance. A partnership offers the employee the ability to have greater influence within the organization, greater personal satisfaction, and greater financial gain.

Few Legal Restrictions.   A partnership, like a sole proprietorship, is relatively easy to establish, although it does often involve the development of an agreement between the parties and the filing of that agreement with a legal authority. For example, in Oregon, Articles of Partnership are filed with the Oregon Corporation Commission. In addition, most states require a small fee to accompany the processing and recording of the agreement. In Oregon, the fee for such transactions is $25.

Disadvantages

As is the case with the sole proprietorship, there are also disadvantages to a partnership. Some of the disadvantages of a partnership include unlimited liability and management conflict. Although a partnership usually has access to more capital than a sole proprietorship, the amount of capital for partnership business ventures is limited when compared with corporations.[7] Also, partners cannot easily withdraw their investment or their profits from a business venture, as can sole proprietors or shareholders in corporations.[8] In addition, the continuity of a business based on a partnership may be in jeopardy if one of the partners dies or becomes incapacitated in some way.

Management Conflict.   When two or more individuals are partners in a business, disagreements may occur regarding major and minor issues related to the business. Whereas in a sole proprietorship one person makes all decisions regarding the direction of the business, in a partnership it is often necessary to reach a consensus among partners in order for the business to move forward. This can be a stumbling block to efficiency, effectiveness, and the ability of the business to react quickly to changes in the business climate. Later in this chapter we will discuss the importance of resolving conflicts as a managerial skill.

Unlimited Liability.   Like the sole proprietorship, a partnership carries with it the opportunity for great risk. Each partner can be held responsible for the debts incurred by the business in which he or she is involved. This responsibility for payment of debts can extend to the partners' personal property and wealth. In other words, the personal property of partners can be claimed by those to whom the business owes debts. The fact that each partner has unlimited financial liability is complicated by the fact that any one of the partners can enter into contracts or agreements on behalf of the business that then hold the other partners accountable as well. One partner, for example, can purchase supplies without the consent of the others, yet the others are financially responsible for payment for the supplies.

Constraints on Capital.   A partnership is usually able to generate more capital than a sole proprietorship; however, in comparison with a corporation a partnership is more limited in terms of the numbers of individual investors. In other words, a partnership is not public and the business partnership cannot sell shares of stock to generate additional revenue.

Difficulty in Liquidating Investments.   Both sole proprietors and shareholders within a corporation can easily withdraw their financial investment in their respective business ventures. A sole proprietor can simply decide that he or she wishes to cease business operations and withdraw any capital investment or profits from the business. Shareholders in a corporation can simply sell their stock and thereby withdraw their financial investment from the corporation. Individuals engaged in a business partnership do not have this type of mobility regarding their financial investment. If a partner chooses to withdraw from a partnership, considerable time may elapse before he or she can regain his or her financial investment. The other partners typically must either buy out the departing partner or approve a new partner who is to buy into the business.

Continuity of Business.   When a partner decides to leave a partnership, the other partner or partners must approve a new partner or purchase the share of the departing partner. If neither of these options is feasible, the partnership will dissolve, threatening the well being and stability of the business. Death of a partner can also affect the stability and continuity of the business. When a partner dies the partnership is dissolved unless prior legal provisions have been made by the partners collectively. It is not uncommon for partners to agree to purchase the business from one another in the case of death or disability of one of the partners. This option can be covered through purchase of appropriate insurance.

Corporation

A corporation is a separate legal entity that has specific rights and privileges. Although it may be composed of many people, it can act as if it were a single person. It is empowered to buy and sell, own property and equipment, create and distribute services, and bring lawsuits. A corporation has its own life; it is not dependent upon a single person or group of people for its continuity.

One of the chief factors distinguishing a corporation from a sole proprietorship or partnership is the ease with which ownership rights are transferred. A corporation obtains its funds through the creation of shares of stock. These shares of stock can be bought and sold and are especially useful in raising capital when additional investors are desired. There are two types of shares that can be distributed by a corporation: common and preferred. *Common shares* of stock are those that entitle the shareholder to certain benefits, such as voting at shareholders' meetings, sharing in organizational profits and sharing in assets of the organization if it is liquidated. *Preferred shares* of stock are those that entitle the shareholder to a "preferred" position in terms of assets and profits. In particular, preferred shareholders are entitled to a dividend on their shares before any dividends are distributed to the common shareholders. If the corporation is liquidated, preferred shareholders are also entitled to receive a share of the remaining assets before they are further divided among the common shareholders.

In order to set up a corporation, several conditions must be met. According to Van Voorhis, most states require the following:[9]

1. Registration of the name of the corporation and operating game plan (generally called *Articles of Incorporation*).
2. Payment of filing fees and an organizational tax in the state where it is formed.
3. Payment of similar fees in other states where it wants to do business and is viewed in legal terms as a "foreign corporation."
4. Compliance with various other statutory procedures that may be specified.

Because the procedures for incorporation as well as the fees may vary from state to state, it is important to be aware of the specific requirements in the area within which the corporation is being established.

As indicated, a corporation is owned by its shareholders. The shareholders of a corporation elect directors who are responsible for the success or failure of the business venture. Often a board of directors will hire a manager to oversee the operation of the business. The board of directors is also responsible for the allotment of shares, the distribution of dividends, the appointment of officers, and other affairs necessary to move the corporation forward in a productive, effective, and profitable manner.

Advantages

There are numerous advantages to establishing a business as a corporation. Among the most important are increased ease in raising capital, ease in transferring ownership, continuity of operations, and limited liability of owners. (See Figure 5-4.)

Limited Liability of Owners. A major advantage of a corporation is the limiting of the legal liability of the owners to the amount that they have invested in the business venture. In other words, persons purchasing shares in a corporation are legally responsible only for the amount that they have

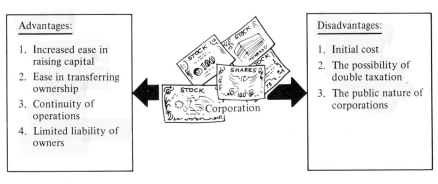

Advantages:

1. Increased ease in raising capital
2. Ease in transferring ownership
3. Continuity of operations
4. Limited liability of owners

Disadvantages:

1. Initial cost
2. The possibility of double taxation
3. The public nature of corporations

FIGURE 5–4. Advantages and disadvantages of a corporation.

risked or invested in the corporation. Unlike the sole proprietorship or partnership, if a commercial leisure service venture organized as a corporation is unsuccessful, the personal assets of the investor cannot be attached or confiscated to pay the outstanding debts of the organization. The implication of this limited liability is that investors are attracted to this type of investment. This, in turn, means that it is easier to raise capital.

Ease in Raising Capital. When a corporation offers shares of stock publicly, it creates a larger pool of investors. This, in turn, produces more capital. With more capital an organization is able to grow and develop new services, facilities, and other programs. Thus, the potential for growth is great in a corporation.

Ease in Transferring Ownership. In a corporation, transfer of ownership is done by selling shares. This can be done simply and quickly; it does not require the permission of a partner. In addition, transfer of ownership allows investment opportunities to take place relatively easily. A person can make the decision to invest in the corporation and if that investment is profitable and the value of the shares increases, he or she may sell these shares and earn a profit. In addition, ease in transferring ownership allows corporations to enhance the personal incentive of virtually all employees by establishing plans whereby employees can buy shares in the corporation. Many large corporations have established programs where they match the contribution that the employee makes toward buying shares. This benefit provides an incentive for each employee to become personally involved in the ownership of the corporation. This can be an important factor in the retention of valued employees.

Continuity of Operation. The last major advantage of a corporation is that it ensures continuity of operations. Within the bylaws of a corporation there are procedures and mechanisms to replace members of the board as well as to replace people in management positions. As people retire or otherwise vacate their positions, the corporation, as a separate legal entity continues by replacing these key persons with others.

Disadvantages

There are three major disadvantages of establishing a business as a corporation: the initial cost involved, the possibility of double taxation, and the public nature of corporations.

Cost Involved in Establishing a Corporation. Because it is a separate legal entity and operates as if it were a person, the cost of establishing a corporation is more expensive than the other two forms. Not only are the fees charged by state regulation agencies higher in many cases, but legal counsel often must be sought in the preparation of formal documentation. Although legal counsel may be necessary to establish a sole proprietorship or a partnership, it is not usually as extensive.

Double Taxation. A corporation is taxed just like a person. Furthermore, shareholders who receive dividends from a corporation must pay taxes on them. Therefore, shareholders pay double taxes. In the United States, double taxation can be avoided in some cases if the Subchapter S provisions of the Internal Revenue Service are followed. In this case, corporate income is treated as personal income if certain conditions can be met.

Public Nature of Corporations.   Corporations, unlike sole proprietorships or partnerships, must disclose information regarding their assets, liabilities, and so forth to their shareholders. Because of this broad distribution of information, competitors can gain information fairly easily regarding the organization's financial status. Sole proprietorships and the partnerships both offer more privacy if such information is sensitive.

Developing an Approach for Managing Your Business

Managing a commercial leisure service business is not unlike any other facet of your life. If you manage your personal affairs, your finances, and your relationships with others well, if you plan for the future, if you learn from your mistakes, if you continue to grow in a positive way, you will probably prosper in your personal life. The same rule of thumb can be applied to a commercial leisure service business. If you are prudent in financial matters, plan ahead, maintain positive harmonious relationships with employees and consumers, and grow and learn, your business will probably prosper.

Well-designed and managed resorts are a response to the competition that characterizes leisure services in the natural environment. Time-share vacation homes are gaining in popularity throughout America. Time-share involves the purchase of a resort accommodation for a specified period each year. Purchasers often have the option of trading locations with time-share purchasers from other parts of the country. (John Bullaro)

One of the important factors influencing the success of an organization is the extent to which the values of the owner are communicated to employees at the operational level. The way in which an owner or manager interprets his or her values to employees will have a direct bearing on the quality of services, the relationship that is established between the organization and its consumers, whether or not the organization is able to live within economic reality and become profitable, and the way in which it meets its ethical responsibilities. Patterns of behavior can be taught to employees. People see the behavior of others and model their behavior accordingly. This behavior can become a part of the value structure of the organization. Thus, it seems appropriate that the first concern that an owner or a manager would have in developing an approach to management of a commercial leisure service organization would be to identify the philosophy, values, and attitudes that he or she wishes to communicate to his or her employees and consumers.

The philosophy, values, and attitudes of a commercial leisure business are often held only in the mind of the owner or owners. Because the communication of this information, both to employees and consumers, is so important to the well being and success of a commercial leisure service venture, we feel very strongly that an organization should first attempt to formally identify and set down in writing its goals and its reason for existence. The identification of written goals is important because it provides a tangible form of communication that can be taught, discussed, and referred to as a benchmark. A philosophy or the goals of an organization should be stated in simple terms that are "significant, durable and achievable."[10] In discussing organizational goals, Pascale and Athos have suggested that effective goals tend to fall into one or more of the following categories (see Figure 5-5)[11]:

1. *The company as an entity.* The entire organization is reinforced as an entity one lives within, identifies with and belongs to and which is deserving of admiration and approval from employees and society (e.g., Delta's belief in the "family feeling").
2. *The company's external markets.* The emphasis is on the value of the company's products or services to humanity and on those factors important in maintaining this value, that is, quality, delivery, service, and consumer needs (e.g., Matsushita's belief in advancing the standard of living in Japan by distributing reliable and affordable electric products).
3. *The company's internal operations.* Attention is focused on such things as efficiency, cost, productivity, inventiveness, problem solving, and customer attention (e.g., Delta's emphasis on "service" and Matsushita's dedication to class production engineering).
4. *The company's employees.* Attention is paid to the needs of groups of people in reference to their productive function and to individual employees as valued human beings in a larger context; that is, human resource systems, growth and development, opportunity and rewards, individual attention and expectations (e.g., Matsushita's commitment to developing employees not only for the firm's benefit but to contribute to each employee's growth over a lifetime).

FIGURE 5–5. Factors that influence the structuring of the philosophy and goals of a business.

5. *The company's relation to society and the state.* The values, expectations, and legal requirements of the surrounding larger community are explicitly honored, such as beliefs in competition, meritocracy, the necessity of obeying the law, or being sensitive to the customs of other nations (e.g., Matsushita sees itself as a major contributor in restoring Japanese status and prestige).

6. *The company's relation to culture (including religion).* The underlying beliefs about "the good" in culture are honored (in the West beliefs largely derived from Judeo-Christian tradition including honesty and fairness; in the case of Matsushita, the strong influence of religion in shaping its philosophy, which reinforces many Confucian and Buddhist values including harmony, solidarity, discipline, and dedication).

Is it realistic to assume that, especially for a small commercial leisure service business, a philosophical statement can be written that reflects accurately the intentions and values of the owner in relation to these six categories? Consider the philosophical statement found in the box entitled "A Company Philosophy." This philosophical statement for a small business presents information that employees can easily understand, learn from, and to which they can refer. It sets forth in straightforward terms the goal of the business; that is, *excellence.* It sets forth a definition to help each employee understand that excellence is the pursuit of the possible. The statement also clearly identifies what constitutes "success" within the or-

A Company Philosophy

If there is a single word that describes the philosophy we are dedicated to, it is excellence. Excellence in the products and service we supply. Excellence in attitude. Excellence in our interactions with each other and our customers.

To understand our dedication, our definition of excellence must first be understood. To us, *excellence is the pursuit of the possible.* Not what is possible given all the limits we believe must exist, but what is possible given the human ability for innovation, insight, desire to achieve, and dedication to results.

Dedication to excellence is not always easy. In fact it carries with it many risks, not the least of which is the potential for failure. There is no assurance of success. The path is not always apparent and many times must be looked at closely and with discipline. It many times appears to be the most difficult way to go. However, we feel the rewards are worth the risks and go forward.

Given this philosophical definition, let's look at how it applies in our everyday business enterprise, since that is the arena in which we have chosen to excel. We must never forget that we ARE in business, and that is our only reason for coming together. All additional benefits that come about as a result of this relationship are extremely welcome, but not at the expense of business success. This success can be clearly defined: *A profitable, well-organized, highly innovative business that does all that it does in the best possible way in which it can be done.*

This approach could be called *pragmatic idealism,* or more simply, an approach that recognizes the real-world needs while striving for the excellence that few ever achieve given their desire for immediate comfort.

The desire for immediate comfort frustrates all but those who have a clear goal in sight, the proverbial light at the end of the tunnel. Most of us are not willing to "pay our dues" to get lasting value and results. Instead we turn back at the slightest hint of tough going. Running away from the goal is suddenly more comfortable than slowly crawling forward. It is only by staying focused on the goal and inching forward that we make any true progress.

All of us have turned and run without even realizing it. Usually not until we have run far from our original objective do we realize the truth of the situation. We have all been guilty of it; we've all been known to fail the test. That doesn't mean we have to make it a habit. We must consciously focus on the objective and block out the easy exits. Otherwise failure becomes a way of life. Cynicism sets in. Personal disbelief crops up. Self-indulgence and childishness become the norm. We've all seen it around us daily. It's not a particularly enjoyable sight.

Given this option, let's get down to the business at hand.

We consider ourselves to be specialists in our field. We take our work seriously and work hard to reach the objectives we have established for ourselves. It is therefore important that you understand our dedication to excellence, desire to share in it, and use your own personal objectives and your Position Contract with this firm as tools to reach your goals. If you are willing, we commit ourselves both as individuals and as a firm to assist you in reaching your objectives, on the way to reaching ours.

* Adapted by Larry's Autoworks, Mountain View, California, and Michael Thomas Company, San Mateo, California. Used by permission.

ganization: *"a profitable, well organized, highly innovative business that does all that it does in the best possible way that it can be done."* Furthermore, the statement sets forth the limits or "real world" conditions in which the organization must operate. The statement also speaks to the character and nature of the human spirit. Thus, when discussing the need to become disciplined "to get lasting value and results" the statement provides very practical guidelines for personal conduct within the business.

A philosophy statement should be written in a simple and straightforward manner. It should also be written in a way that elicits an emotional commitment from the employees of the organization. It should provide a clear vision for people within the organization and bring together people with diverse interests to work toward common organizational goals. It should promote a sense of pride in the organization and dedication to its values and ideals.

The statement on page 175 entitled "The Disneyland Story" describes the philosophical underpinnings of Disneyland. It is written in a direct manner and is easily understandable. According to this statement, Disneyland is "a place for people to find happiness and knowledge. . . . a place for parents and children . . . for teacher and pupils . . . the older generation, . . . and the younger generation. . . . [A place] dedicated to the ideals, dreams and hard facts that have created America." It is a statement that can evoke an emotional commitment from people and is a philosophy that is durable and has been achieved.

The McKinsey Company has developed a conceptual model that presents the variables that affect an organization's operations. As one can see from Figure 5-6, the conceptual model places seven variables into an integrated framework. This is known as the 7-S system of management. At the core of an organization are its "superordinate goals." In other words, its philosophy, values, attitudes, or shared cultural beliefs. The other six variables are influenced by and have an influence upon the superordinate goals. These six factors include structure, systems, style, staff, skills, and strategy. Since we have already discussed the superordinate goals referred to in this figure—philosophy, values, attitudes, and shared cultural beliefs of an organization—we will focus our attention on the other variables in the model, what we interpret as management skills, managerial style, management systems, staff, and organizational structures. These are areas that the owner or manager of a commercial leisure service business can act upon to achieve defined organizational goals.

Skills of the Manager

Those persons working to own, operate, or manage commercial leisure service organizations must possess or develop both technical and managerial skills. Technical skills are important because they give the person unique knowledge or technical information related to the product or service line produced. For example, if an individual wanted to establish a river raft excursion company, technical knowledge about guiding and outfitting as well as knowledge of specialized equipment and supplies would be essential. Without this technical knowledge, an individual would be at a severe disadvantage when attempting to organize a competitive small commercial

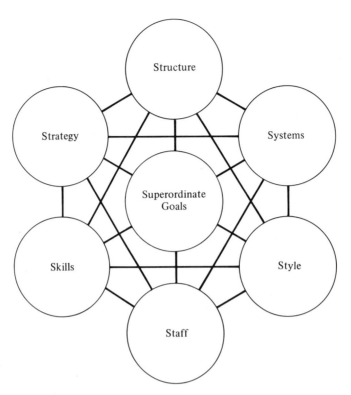

FIGURE 5–6. "Mc-Kinsey 7-S Framework." (From *In Pursuit of Excellence: America's Best-Run Companies* by Thomas J. Peters and Robert H. Waterman. Copyright © by Thomas J. Peters and Robert H. Waterman. Reprinted by permission of Harper and Row, Publishers, Inc.)

leisure service organization. As an organization grows in size, it can hire people with expertise to assist it. For example, an organization might want to hire someone to assist in the maintenance of financial records, data processing, advertising, market research, and so on. It is interesting to note that many larger successful companies require that their managers "work their way through the system" to acquire appropriate technical knowledge before assuming a management position.

When we speak of managerial knowledge, we mean the knowledge necessary to acquire and transform resources to produce leisure experiences. A manager works with fiscal resources, physical resources, technological resources, and most importantly, human resources to produce leisure experiences. Because we have focused upon fiscal resource management, product development, and the use of technological resources in other chapters, our discussion of managerial skills here will not address these topics again but will focus on the management of human resources.

Most managers work in environments that involve a few people at a time. Therefore, the manager should focus attention on the development of managerial skills that are conducive to working with people in small groups. From our perspective, some of the skills that the manager should possess or develop in the area of small group management include the ability to organize, the ability to make decisions, the ability to create and

Commercial Leisure Services

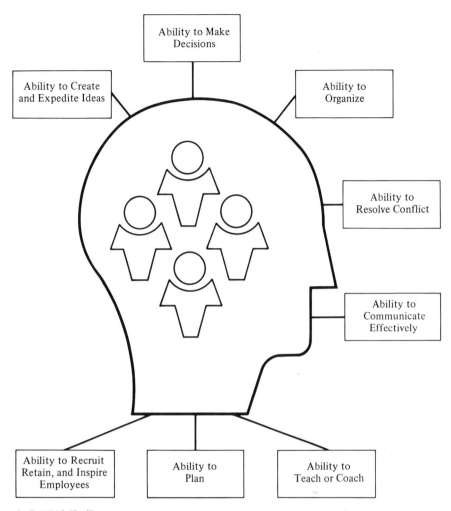

FIGURE 5–7. Skills that a manager should possess or develop.

expedite ideas, the ability to teach or coach, the ability to resolve conflict, the ability to facilitate communication, the ability to plan, and the ability to recruit, retain and inspire employees. (See Figure 5-7).

Ability to Organize. This is the ability to arrange various organizational components and resources in order to attain the goals and objectives of the leisure service organization. When we speak of the manager's ability to organize, we are referring to a person's ability to put the organization into "working order." Organizing involves understanding the broader goals of the organization (these can be stated in terms of desired profitability, service, growth, customer satisfaction, employee morale, and so on). It also involves the ability to analyze these goals in terms of the tasks needed to accomplish them and then assigning the human, fiscal, physical, and technological resources needed to accomplish the goals.

Ability to Make Decisions. Within a commercial leisure service organization, managerial decision-making deals exclusively with judgment regarding the allocation of organizational resources. The ability to commit organizational resources decisively may mean the difference between a successful and an unsuccessful organization. Knowing what amount of resources to commit and when are strategic organizational questions to be considered in the management of a commercial leisure service organization.

Decisions that occur within organizations often involve weighing the alternative strategies and methods that can be used in achieving the goals and objectives of the organization. Reviewing and assessing the respective values assigned to a given course of action can help the manager in making a decision. Decisions based on short-term profitability alone when compared with long-term consumer satisfaction and retention are often unwise. Managerial decisions should be firmly grounded in the principles outlined in Chapter 1 relating to quality, value, reliability, consistency, consumer relations, and so on.

The Ability to Create and Expedite Ideas. The generation of new and innovative ideas is an important dimension in the long-term success and well being of a commercial leisure service organization. A person should not expect to possess all of the ideas that are necessary to move a business forward; however, the manager should have the ability to use good ideas that are offered by employees and consumers. A good manager will work to assist persons in the development of their ideas by bringing to bear the resources necessary to encourage such creativity.

Successful organizations pay close attention to the generation of new ideas. Organizations often will formally create mechanisms whereby employees can contribute their ideas. Simple mechanisms such as suggestion boxes and evaluation forms are common practices in many organizations. Recently, the idea of *quality circles* has been adopted by many American corporations after its successful use by the Japanese. The quality circle concept is one of the generation of ideas aimed at increasing productivity, quality, employee satisfaction, consumer satisfaction, and organizational profit.

The Ability to Teach or Coach. Although many persons in managerial roles perceive their job as one of directing people, we feel that it is essential that the manager view himself or herself as a teacher or coach in order to be successful. Teaching involves the transmittal of the technical knowledge and values necessary to run an organization. Technical knowledge is often easy to acquire or to teach; however, it is much more difficult to teach the values that are essential for organizational success.

The Ability to Resolve Conflict. The most difficult type of conflict to be resolved by the manager is that involving interactive patterns between and among employees rather than one involving issues. In other words, the more personal a conflict is, the more difficult it is to resolve in a positive fashion. For example, one person may have a great aversion to the personal "style" of another. He or she may perceive the other person to be too wishy-washy, too passive, too indecisive, or too slow in action. The manager must be able to discriminate between issues involved in conflict and such differences in personal interaction to determine the "real" issues involved.

The Disneyland Story

The idea of Disneyland is a simple one. It will be a place for people to find happiness and knowledge.

It will be a place for parents and children to share pleasant times in one another's company; a place for teacher and pupils to discover greater ways of understanding and education. Here the older generation can recapture the nostalgia of days gone by, and the younger generation can savor the challenge of the future. Here will be the wonders of Nature and Man for all to see and understand.

Disneyland will be based upon and dedicated to the ideals, the dreams, and hard facts that have created America. And it will be uniquely equipped to dramatize these dreams and facts and send them forth as a source of courage and inspiration to all the world.

Disneyland will be something of a fair, an exhibition, a playground, a community center, a museum of living facts, and a showplace of beauty and magic.

It will be filled with the accomplishments, the joys, and the hopes of the world we live in. And it will remind us and show us how to make these wonders part of our own lives.

This is the major task of the manager in conflict resolution. The manager should drive for a win–win situation for all persons involved in a given conflict. The manager involved in conflict resolutions should also ensure that he or she is in possession of all relevant facts from dependable sources. Finally, the manager should develop an awareness of when intervention is appropriate and when it is not. A manager should not waste time intervening in petty issues and squabbles but should reserve his or her expertise for issues and situations that have implications for the organization as a whole.

The Ability to Communicate Effectively. The ability to communicate effectively is an essential skill of the manager. Communication involves both transmitting and receiving information. The purpose of communications is to influence the behavior of individuals. Within commercial leisure service organizations, there are two types of communication: interpersonal and organizational. Interpersonal communication is communication that takes place between the manager and his or her subordinates. This can be done one-to-one or it can occur in small groups. Interpersonal communications can obviously directly influence employees' development of values and acquisition of knowledge. It is through interpersonal communication that the manager creates a sense of order, harmony, builds rapport, fosters and promotes enthusiasm, and motivates his or her employees.

The second type of communication—organizational communication—is also very important. Organizational communication is the official communication that takes place between the commercial leisure service organization and its target or market group. It is through organizational communication that the commercial leisure service business conveys to its consumers its goals, information about its services, and its reputation. Organizational communications are often systematized in order to ensure consistency in dealing with consumers. For example, a commercial leisure service organization may standardize the way in which sales staff greet and interact with consumers. Attention to detail in organizational communications is very important. The way in which a receptionist answers the phone to how an organization's logo is used and presented to its public, all must be evaluated by the manager and systematic plans developed to facilitate effective communication.

There are many forms of communication. The most common form is that of the spoken word. Other forms include written, graphic or visual, and technological communication. In the coming decades, use of technological innovations such as the personal computer will greatly increase access to information. This will assist managers in making more precise and accurate decisions, as well as increase the volume of information that can be processed and assimilated.

The Ability to Plan.   Planning is the process of developing objectives and the methods for achieving them. The role of short-term and long-term planning in commercial leisure service organizations is critical. Leisure products and services tend to have extremely short life cycles. As a result, thorough and proper planning to ensure long-term profitability is an important skill for the manager to possess.

Setting forth objectives and the process necessary to achieve them is useful in helping the commercial leisure service manager identify the types of consumers the organization is targeting, the types of services or products that will meet the needs of these consumers, and the types of resources necessary to produce the services required by the target group. Furthermore, plans encourage the manager to determine the type of organizational structure that should be used to transform resources into services.

The establishment of organizational objectives provides benchmarks by which the organization can measure its success and growth. Objectives can be stated in terms of profitability, consumer retention and satisfaction, employee retention and job satisfaction, community visibility, and so on. They enable the commercial leisure service manager to establish standards of performance and control. In this way, objectives serve to tell the manager when the organization is veering off course. Many organizations are built around the theme or goal of the pursuit of excellence. As you will recall from the philosophy statement in Chapter 1, excellence is the pursuit of the possible with the highest standards of quality, value, and service to the consumer.

The Ability to Recruit, Retain, and Inspire Employees.   The human resources within an organization are its most important asset. The ability of the manager to attract and retain good employees and to inspire their best efforts is directly related to organizational success. The manager who takes time to carefully invest in people will, by and large, be more successful than one who overlooks this critical element. To attract excellent people, a commercial leisure service organization must be willing to make an investment. This investment should not only be reflected in the financial remuneration of individuals but also in the growth and development of employees. When employees within an organization are growing and developing, the organization itself will also grow and develop.

Inspiring the best efforts of others is also in important skill for a manager. We refer to this as motivation. Although this will be discussed later in the chapter, it may be important for you to think at this point about the ways in which you have been inspired by others to excel. Did you strive for excellence because you were well paid? Because you were appreciated? Because you felt that you were a part of a quality organization? Because you were treated with respect? Because you had an opportunity to share your ideas and see them grow? Because you had the opportunity to fail and learn from your failure? Because you were recognized and rewarded for your individual contributions? Because you had an opportunity to experience growth and learning? Because you had input into the design and development of your job? All of these factors can serve to inspire or motivate people to achieve excellence within an organization.

A manager should not only have the ability to inspire employees to accomplish their best in terms of their performance, but must also inspire them to do this within the economic boundaries of the organization. Within existing limits of financial resources, the manager should be able to inspire employees to operate effectively, creatively, and profitably. This is one of the greatest challenges to the commercial leisure service manager, to motivate employees to operate within "reality" in a way that moves the organization forward.

The Manager's Style

The manager's style is the way in which he or she interacts with others; it is the individual's mode of behavior. It is the individual's management method, manner, or way. An individual's managerial style is best observed and understood by reviewing his or her actual behavior. In other words, managerial style is reflected in how a person interacts with others, controls and manages finances, plans, deals with consumers, involves subordinates in managerial decision making, follows the chain of command, is a problem solver, welcomes new ideas, is willing to take risks, and is willing to help the business grow. As one can see, it is the actual behavior of people in management positions rather than what they say, write, or otherwise communicate that determines their management style.

Different situations require different managerial styles. The management literature today suggests that a contingency approach to one's managerial style is essential. Fiedler,[12] Reddin,[13] and Hersey and Blanchard[14] have suggested that the manager must have the ability to flex his or her style to meet the needs of a given situation. For example, consider the product life cycle. As a product moves through various stages of the cycle, different managerial leadership styles may be necessary in order for the manager to be successful and effective. Kroeger[15] has suggested, for example, that in the initiation stage of the product life cycle, the best managerial qualities might include innovation, independence, self confidence, risk taking, and vision (see Table 5-1). The basic skills in the first stage of the life cycle are perceptual and conceptual. In the developmental stage of the product life cycle such managerial qualities as planning, evaluation, judging, organizing, negotiating and decision making are needed. In this stage, the basic skills are analytical, focusing on interpersonal relations.

TABLE 5-1. Relationship of Basic Managerial Skill and Capability to the Stages of the Life Cycle

Life Cycle Stage	Managerial Role	Managerial Qualities	Basic Skill Requirement	Primary Functional Emphasis
1. Initiation	Originator-Inventor	Innovation Independence Self-confidence Risk-taking Vision	Perceptual and Conceptual	Technology
2. Development	Planner-Organizer	Investigation Planning Evaluation Judging Organizing Negotiation Decision making	Analytical, External-Behavioral Interpersonal Relations	Finance
3. Growth	Developer-Implementer	Leadership Delegation Motivation Supervision Achievement Decision making	Budgeting, Scheduling, Controlling, Intergroup Relations	Production Marketing
4. Maturity	Administrator-Operator	Maintenance Coordinating Efficiency Seeker	Internal Intergroup Relations	Marketing
5. Decline	Successor-Reorganizer	Type A— Innovative Change Agent Risk-taking Vision Strategic Planner	Perceptual and Conceptual, External Interpersonal Relations	Technology
		Type B— Efficiency Seeking Change Agent	Budgeting Controlling Internal Intergroup Relations	Finance

Source: Carroll V. Kroeger, "Managerial Development in the Small Firm." © 1974 by the Regents of the University of California. Reprinted from *California Management Review*, volume XVII, number 1, pg. 43, by permission of the Regents.

The third stage of product life cycle, the growth stage, finds the qualities of delegation, motivation, and supervision being important. The basic skills necessary are those of budgeting, scheduling, controlling, and intergroup relationships. When one is attempting to manage during the maturity stage of the product life cycle, the qualities that are needed are those of maintenance, coordination, and efficiency. In the last stage of the product life cycle, decline, a manager must be innovative, able to act as a change agent, visionary, and able to seek out efficiency in operations. The basic skills in this stage are similar to those found in the initiation stage and the growth stage.

Although there are number of conceptual models of management styles, we feel that there are three that have particular significance for the management of commercial leisure service organizations: Blake and Mouton's Management Grid, the Tannenbaum and Schmidt Leadership Continuum, and Hersey and Blanchard's Tri-Dimensional Leader Effectiveness Model.

The Tannenbaum and Schmit Leadership Continuum

The Tannenbaum and Schmidt Leadership Continuum supports the idea that specific organizational situations in which a manager finds himself or herself will affect the type of managerial style adopted. They suggest that a variety of variables can influence the type of style. For example, they note that the climate of the organization, its goals, and its structure are variables that can influence the type of management style selected. They note that the type of work in which people are engaged, the type of technology employed, and the type of employee to be managed can also influence the managerial leadership style adopted. In addition, the individual manager's experience, background, and goals will affect his or her selection of management style.

Figure 5-8 presents a continuum of management behavior. At one end of the continuum is the manager who is "boss centered," and at the other end of the continuum is the manager who is "subordinate centered." As one can see, the boss-centered managerial leadership style involves more use of authority by the manager. On the other hand, the subordinate-centered style gives the individual employees more freedom within limits defined by the superior. Tannenbaum and Schmidt suggest that a subordinate-

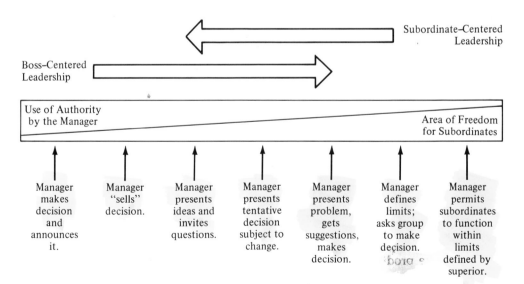

FIGURE 5–8. A continuum of management behavior. (Robert Tannenbaum and Warren H. Schmidt. "How to Choose a Leadership Pattern." *Harvard Business Review*, May–June 1973, p. 166. Copyright © 1973 by the President and Fellows of Harvard College, all rights reserved.)

centered managerial style is appropriate when people are committed to the goals of an organization, desire freedom and responsibility, and seek authority for making decisions. It assumes that employees are performing their jobs in an exemplary manner and can and will control their own behavior. It is important to note that people can operate independently if taught the values of the organization.

The Blake and Mouton Managerial Grid

The Blake and Mouton Managerial Grid was developed to help people understand what type of leadership behavior produces organizational excellence. They developed a system that expands upon the authoritarian employee-centered continuum of Tannenbaum and Schmidt. They felt that it was difficult to categorize persons as having either an autocratic or democratic style or a production-oriented versus a people-oriented style. As they note in the preface of their original book, "These labels have been admittedly inadequate and confusing. The stress on terms which represent extremes has placed many managers in a position where they felt that they could not accept either alternative."[16]

Figure 5-9 represents the Blake and Mouton Managerial Grid. On the

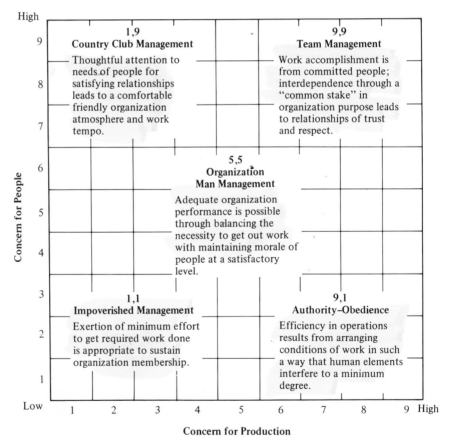

FIGURE 5–9. The Blake and Mouton Managerial Grid. (*The New Managerial Grid*, Robert R. Blake and Jany Srygley Mouton, Houston: Gulf Publishing Company, Copyright © 1978, page 11. Reproduced by permission.)

vertical axis they have placed the variable "concern for people" and on the horizontal axis they have placed "concern for production." Using a nine-point scale on both variables, they have identified five basic management styles:

1.1 *Impoverished Manager.* This management style reflects no concern for either people or production.

9.1 *Authority-Obedience.* This management style represents high concern for controlling variables in the work environment and a low concern for people.

1.9 *Country Club Management.* The manager using this style is concerned primarily with the well being of employees in the organization and has little concern for production or output goals.

5.5 *Organizational Management.* The manager using this style attempts to balance relationships between people and production requirements in order to strike a balance or compromise within the work environment.

9.9 *Team Management.* The 9.9 management style is one in which the manager has a high concern for people, open communication, trust, and commitment to both the goals of the organization and the goals of the individual employee.

Blake and Mouton suggest that the most appropriate management style is the 9.9 Team Management. They suggest that this approach will result in high productivity and greater employee satisfaction.

The Hersey and Blanchard Tri-Dimensional Leadership Model

Hersey and Blanchard have developed a management style or leadership model that adds an interesting dimension to the Blake and Mouton Management Grid. Basically, Hersey and Blanchard suggest that a person's style is an interplay of three variables: task behavior, relationship behavior, and task-relevant maturity. Task behavior refers to the ability of the manager to direct the work of the organization. In other words, the ability of the manager to "get things done." Relationship behavior is the level of social-emotional support given to employees. This is the concern that the manager would show for the welfare of his or her employees. Last, task-relevant maturity refers to the "maturity" of followers. This is an important dimension of the Hersey and Blanchard model. Maturity of followers is defined by Hersey and Blanchard as the followers' desire for achievement, their ability and willingness to accept responsibility and the knowledge they have that is relevant to successfully undertaking a particular task.

As illustrated in Figure 5-10, the Hersey and Blanchard model suggests that the style of the manager or owner should depend upon the level of maturity of the individual employee. As one can see, they have identified four basic management styles. The first, S1 (Telling) is a high task/low relatonship management style. Managers would use this style in situations in which they perceive that employees need to be told what to do and how to do it. The next management style, S2 (Selling), suggests that there is a need to continue to direct people but with a higher degree of social-emotional support. The third management style, S3 (Participating), finds the

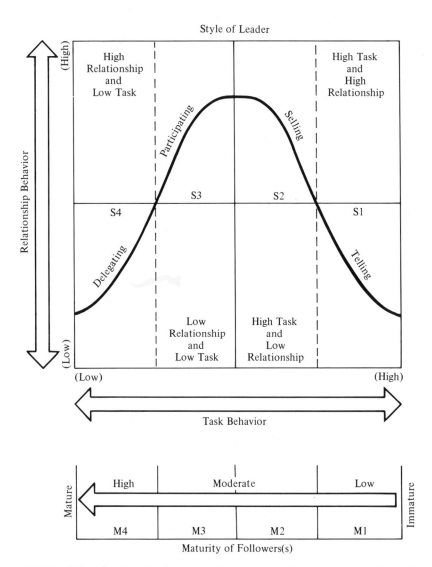

Style of Leader

High
Relationship
and
Low Task

High Task
and
High
Relationship

Participating

Selling

S3

S2

S4

S1

Delegating

Telling

Low
Relationship
and
Low Task

High Task
and
Low
Relationship

(Low)

(High)

Relationship Behavior

(High)

(Low)

Task Behavior

		Mature	Moderate	Low	Immature

High · Moderate · Low

M4 · M3 · M2 · M1

Maturity of Followers(s)

FIGURE 5–10. The Hershey and Blanchard leadership model. (Paul Hersey and Kenneth Blanchard, Center for Leadership Studies, California American University, 1977.)

manager using a high relationship/low task orientation. In a sense, the manager here is reinforcing and encouraging people who possess the necessary skills to do their jobs. Last, the S4 (Delegating) management style finds the manager using a low relationship/low task orientation. Here the assumption is that the individual employee has the necessary skills, attitudes, and desire to achieve a work situation. Basically, the manager in this situation would want to allow the individual employee to operate independently, exercising self control.

Organizational Structure

The placement of human resources within a business is usually done in a formal way. This process often results in the creation of an organizational structure. The creation of an organizational structure allows an organization to coordinate various components within the organization. Furthermore, it allows the owner or manager of a commercial leisure service venture to determine who is accountable for various activities. Thus, the creation of an organizational structure is very important within a commercial leisure service venture.

In most business ventures, there is an attempt to create a structure that recognizes the need for the accomplishment of three primary functions. The first of these is the production or creation of services. The second is the marketing of services. Last is the control of financial resources. These are known as *line functions* within an organization. Other roles, such as personnel, inventory supply and control, research and development are referred to as *staff functions*. There is no one best way to structure an organization. Consideration must be given to the character and nature of the services, the size and complexity of the organization, and the abilities of the people within the organization.

There are a number of different types of organizational structures that can be employed by commercial leisure service organizations. Two factors seem to be prevalent in terms of the adoption or selection of a given organizational design. The first is the type of environment in which the organization operates; the second is the type of technology employed. An organization's type of environment refers to the conditions within which the business operates. For example, in some businesses, environmental conditions are extremely stable; in others they tend to be more fluid and subject to change. Interestingly, certain types of organizational structures seem to be best fitted to stable environments, where the market conditions are highly predictable. Whereas other organizational structures work effectively in unstable environments, where there is a need for the rapid movement of organizational resources. The type of technology employed by an organization refers to the processes used to create and distribute services. Certain processes require more freedom and independence of action on the part of the person providing the leisure services, whereas others require a great deal of control.

Organizational structures can be viewed as a continuum. At one end of the continuum are what are known as *organic structures*. At the other end of the continuum are what are known as *mechanistic structures*. Organic structures are more flexible, whereas mechanistic structures are more rigid. Mechanistic structures have very well-defined rules of order and specific roles; organic structures tend to be more open, with emphasis on the knowledge or expertise of the person. There are a number of different types of organizational designs. We will describe some of the more prevalent ones starting with those that are mechanistic in nature and moving to ones that are more organic in nature.

- *Autocracy.* An autocracy exists when one person has absolute authority, power, or influence within a group. One could argue that a sole proprietorship is an autocracy. However, seldom does an individual owner dictate to consumers; rather he or she responds to their needs.
- *Bureaucracy.* A bureaucracy is the most common form of organizational structure. It is based on the idea that there is a rational model of organ-

ization that can be put in place and applied to all organizations. It is built on the assumption that authority flows from the top down and that there is a division of labor within an organization.

- *Project or Modular Organization.* The project or modular organizational design is one in which specific units are created to perform desired functions. In other words, rather than separating production, sales, and finance for a specific product line, they may be combined to form a project unit to carry out a specific task. Many large conglomerates use this method to encourage competition within their corporations.

- *Matrix.* The matrix organizational design gained popularity during the 1960s and 1970s in corporations. It is a way of reorganizing the work of an organization into special projects while leaving the traditional organizational structure intact. For example, most commercial recreation and leisure service organizations would be lumped into three functional areas: sales, finance, and service component. Often there is a need to bring together people from various parts of an organization to use their talents for a specific project. Usually, a project director oversees the operation and completion of such special projects. As long as the normal functions of the "project team" members are carried out, their added contribution of working on a special project may serve an organization well.

- *Systems.* The manager implements a systems organizational design by looking at the relationships that exist between various components within the organization and integrating hem into an orderly, logical and sequential system in order to create and distribute services. To organize a systems design, it is necessary to identify the task involved, the materials and equipment needed, and the processes that can be used to integrate the tasks with one another. Furthermore, it is necessary to identify the standards that are to be met by the integrated organizational system.

- *Decentralization.* Decentralization is an organizational structure that attempts to disperse decision making at lower levels within a business. Decentralized organizations are ones that place decision-making authority as close as possible to those who are expending organizational resources rather than with persons at the top of the organizational hierarchy. In other words, the organization attempts to give decision-making authority to those with the best perspective on what resources are needed to meet both organizational and consumer needs.

- *Collegialism.* The collegial model of organization is especially prevalent in knowledge-based or information-based organizations. The traditional superior/subordinate relationship, as a way of coordinating and controlling the activities of people is not used in this approach. This model allows for a great deal of innovation, while at the same time providing opportunities for people to specialize. Basically, professionals in the organization operate within their areas of specialization as equals and are assisted by support staff.

In discussing organizational structures, Bannon has argued that managers should be aware of the games that executives can play in changing or rearranging organizational charts.[17] He suggests that an organizational structure should be used as a point of reference and that the manager should quickly understand how the informal organizational structure works to move a business ahead productively. We agree with Bannon's analysis and feel that very careful consideration should be given to the type and form of structure used in a commercial leisure service venture. The selection of an appropriate organizational structure may very well provide the margin of profit that is necessary to successfully operate a commercial leisure service venture.

Working with Staff

The human resources of an organization, especially a service-oriented one, are its most precious asset. They are also its most costly and unpredictable asset. The successful management of human resources within an organization will have a direct effect on the ability of a business to achieve its goals. Working with people can be fun, exciting, and stimulating if there are relationships of trust, confidence, and mutual respect within the organization. In situations where people feel abused, exploited, or misused there can be severe problems. Thus, when working with the staff within an organization, great care and energy should be used to ensure that the staff members have confidence and trust in one another.

How does one create an atmosphere of confidence and trust? Basically, this results from an open environment in which people communicate freely, understand and are committed to the goals of the organization, and understand and respect the limits within which they must operate. One of the most difficult limits for employees to deal with is the economic "reality" of the organization. Staff members should also be carefully taught in a positive way the values of the organization. These values must be reinforced; this is not something that can be left to chance or circumstance. The values of the organization must be carefully analyzed, identified, and taught systematically to staff members. The values of an organization are *not* simply the rules by which the organization operates; rather, they are the attitudes, ethics, and principles that underlie the organization.

In order to work with staff members in a manner that is productive to the organization, an owner or manager must recognize the need to create a motivating environment. A motivating environment is one in which individual needs are addressed while at the same time organizational goals are met. Although in an ideal sense we would like to assume that people are selfless, reality tells us differently. People are self centered; they are occupied with their own needs, wants, and interests. The role of the manager is to determine what needs, wants, and interests a person has and to meet these as far as possible in a way that also assists the organization.

There have been numerous theories regarding employee motivation. One of the more interesting of these theories is that proposed by McClelland.[18] McClelland notes that people have three basic motives: the need for achievement, the need for power, and the need for affiliation. The need for achievement refers to an individual's desire to achieve a goal or to take some personal responsibility for solving a problem. The need for power refers to a person's desire to influence and control others. This need for affiliation refers to an individual's desire to establish and maintain positive, friendly relationships with others. People want to be liked by others. It is interesting to note that entrepreneurs are often people who are highly motivated by the desire for achievement. On the other hand, managers of large corporations tend to be persons who are highly motivated by a desire for power.

We believe in motivating employees through the use of positive reinforcement. One can create positive reinforcement by arranging the work environment in such a way that employees are allowed to meet their needs in a constructive and positive way. For example, the need for affiliation can be met through company social activities. The need for achievement can be met by offering employees tangible or intangible rewards. Tangible rewards include monetary awards, certificates, plaques, and so on; intangible rewards include extra privileges, promotion, and verbal praise. The need for power can be met by allowing persons to have authority over others, to operate independently when possible, and to participate in decision making.

There is of course a negative side to the topic of employee needs. When employees' desires for meeting their own needs becomes so strong that it robs them or others of dignity, self worth, or self esteem, the pursuit of the need is detrimental. It is detrimental to the person, to fellow employees, to the organization, and to society as a whole. For example, one must be careful in exercising power to ensure that others are not abused. One must be careful in seeking affiliation that some individuals are not excluded. In seeking individual achievement, one must be careful to retain a perspective of the organization as a "team." There is often a very delicate balance between meeting one's needs and the needs of others in a positive way and meeting one's needs at the cost of others or the organization. The dividing line between right and wrong can be very thin.

The key to whether an owner, manager or employee is operating "honorably" rests with each person and his or her intentions. Either people intend to operate ethically or they do not; often they are the only ones that know for sure. The task of the manager is to find a way to help people within the business to develop an "organizational conscience" that enables them to view themselves as part of a harmonious, ethical, cooperative, diligent, and productive work force within the organization.

Management System

A management system is the operating procedure employed within a commercial leisure service organization to move the business to action. A management system should be viewed as a vehicle to achieve the goals of the organization; a management system should never be viewed as an end in itself. This is often the case, and one must guard against it. An analogy illustrating this point might be the selection of a car to drive from point A to point B. A Cadillac, or Porsche, or a Toyota could be used to travel the distance, depending upon the situation and the needs of the driver. One is formal, one is fast, and the other is efficient. Similarly, some management systems are formal, some expedite communications and decision making, and others are more cost effective.

When selecting a management system, the owner or manager of a commercial leisure service business should take into consideration the benefits of the system as they relate to the goals of the organization. If the benefits are complementary to the goals of the organization, then it is possible to consider the use of that particular system. Careful consideration should be given to the advantages and disadvantages of a given management system. There is a tendency within organizations to adopt popular management systems without considering their implications for the organization as a whole.

With the above information about the adoption of a management system in mind, we offer three examples of management systems that can be employed by commercial leisure service organizations: management by objectives, zero-based budgeting, and quality circles.

- *Management by Objectives (MBO).* Management by objectives was introduced by Peter Drucker in 1954 in his book, *The Practice of Management.*[19] Management by objective, or MBO, is a results-oriented program. Success using an MBO plan is measured in terms of the achievement of selected performance objectives by employees. A good MBO program enables an owner or manager to establish realistic, attainable goals for members within the organization as well as delineate a course of action to achieve these goals. A format for an MBO system is depicted in the box entitled "Action Plan Format." The major attraction of management by objectives is that it enables a manager and his or her subordinates to sit down and discuss the goals and objectives that the organization *and* the employee would like to see achieved. Following this discussion, a plan is written out specifying the employee's objectives and steps for achieving them. This plan is reviewed and re-evaluated periodically. In this way, teaching, coaching, and directing can take place formally.
- *Zero-Based Budgeting.* Initially established at Texas Instruments Corporation in the 1970s, zero-based budgeting is a widely adopted budgetary/management system. Like Program Planning Budgeting System (PBBS), zero-based budgeting involves the establishment of decision-making packages. The major difference is that managers are required to rejustify or go back to zero every year in calculating their budgeting needs for the coming year.
- *Quality Circles.* Quality circles offer a method for improving employee involvement, self regulation, and productivity. They generally consist of two to ten employees per quality circle group; an organization may have many such groups. Basically, quality circles provide an opportunity for employees to contribute directly to the decision-making process in terms of product innovation, product standards, and working conditions. Such groups of employees meet together and determine where problems exist within their areas of responsibility in the organization and what could be done to improve these problems. They report their findings and suggestions to management. Quality circles have recently gained widespread attention because of their successful use in Japanese companies. The box entitled "Quality Circles" presents additional information regarding them.

Again, careful consideration should be given to the adoption of a management system. The benefits of each should be carefully weighed and

Action Plan Format ———————————————————

What is your objective? To (action or accomplishment verb) (single key result) by (target date) at (cost).

Action Steps	By When	Costs $	Hours	By Whom Us	Them

Action Plan Format. (Copyright 1973 by George L. Morrisey, MOR Associates, Buena Park, CA 90622. Reprinted with permission of Addison-Wesley Publishing Company).

planning should occur in order to ensure that employees understand and acknowledge the benefits of the system as it relates to the entire organization.

It may not be unusual for several management systems to be used in conjunction with one another. For example, organizations will set goals and objectives using an MBO process. This may be related to a budgeting process, or tied to other management systems affecting the operation of the organization.

Quality Circles

What Is a Quality Circle?

A quality circle is a group of people who voluntarily meet together on a regular basis to identify, analyze, and solve quality problems and other problems in their area.

Who Makes Up a Quality Circle?

Members of a quality circle come from your organization. Ideally, members of a particular circle should be from the same work area, or should do similar work, so that the problems they select will be familiar to all of them.

How is the Quality Circles Program Different from Other Programs?

Quality circles as a program is different in a number of ways from other programs that have been tried. Consider these characteristics: members select the project or problem they want to study; members analyze the problem; members use management presentations for communications and recognition; leaders and members receive formal training; participation is voluntary; the agency pays for the meetings.

What Are the Objectives of Quality Circles?

In a parks and recreation setting, quality circles have two areas of impact. A more traditional role of quality circles can be found in maintenance and park operations. An emerging role of quality circles in the human services field finds great potential among recreation programming staffs. There are three broad goals that serve the human services phase of quality circles. These are:

- Improvement of quality of work and life
- Improvement of program operations
- Improvement of staff office operations

More specific objectives of quality circles are to:

- Inspire more effective teamwork
- Promote job involvement
- Increase employee motivation
- Create a problem-solving capacity
- Build an attitude of "problem prevention"
- Improve agency communications

What Are the Outcomes of Quality Circles?

A number of outcomes have accrued as the result of involvement in quality circles. Some of the benefits strengthen program services in a recreation department. Among others, these include:

- Team building
- Improved internal communications
- Improved attitudes both at home and work

The *most important outcome* of quality circles is their effect on people's attitudes and behaviors.

How Does the Process Work?

Discovery Stage	▸	Development of Plan	▸	Pre-imple-mentation Stage	▸	Initi-ation	▸	Review and Evaluation

Problem identification comes from the circle members, management, and staff. Typically, several problems are identified.
Problem selection is a prerogative of the circle.
Problem analysis is performed by the circle, with assistance, if needed, by the appropriate experts.
The circle makes its recommendation directly to its manager using a powerful communication technique described as "The Management Presentation."
There are three vital factors to the success of any quality circles program.

- Selecting the right problem
- Work of the leader
- Participation of the group

* Used with the permission of Daniel D. McLean, Ph.D., Recreation Commission, Cedar Rapids, Iowa and Carlton F. Yoshioka, Ph.D., Assistant Professor, Leisure Studies Curriculum, Iowa State University.

Hiring, Compensating, and Training Staff

Almost all commercial leisure service organizations require the hiring, compensation, and training of staff members in order to ensure that products and services are delivered efficiently and effectively to consumers. We usually refer to these functions within an organization as personnel management. Hiring and placing qualified staff members is a management activity that requires thoroughness to ensure that the most competent and qualified people that can be found are recruited into the system and placed in appropriate roles. Compensating a person refers to the creation of a wage or salary structure that is fair and *competitive* in terms of the market as well as the individual needs of the organization. Training personnel ensures that the job is done correctly and existing skills are reinforced and new knowledge is introduced into the work environment as required.

In large organizations, a personnel manager will be hired to oversee these diverse functions. This person will, in turn, hire other people in support of their work, such as a benefits administrator. On the other hand, in many small commercial leisure service organizations, the leisure service manager will be personally responsible for each of these tasks. In this latter case, the owner or manager will be challenged to be familiar with a variety of factors related to personnel management. For example, this person might be challenged to know the law as it relates to hiring as well as the most up-to-date procedures that can be employed in training individuals.

Hiring Staff

It is no secret that the quality of the organization is directly related to the excellence of its human resources. Therefore, an organization that pays particular attention to the recruitment and hiring of employees will be more effective than one that that neglects this area. How does one go about establishing an effective recruiting process? First, the recruitment and hiring of a person does not occur by happenstance. It occurs because the commercial leisure service organization has developed a systematic plan or procedure for recruiting and selecting personnel.

Initially, the recruitment process requires a complete understanding of the role that is to be filled by a person. This is usually embodied in a job description. A job description details the responsibilities and functions that a person is to perform in an organization. A job description will also present the qualifications required for the position in terms of experience and education. A well-written job description can be used as a major evaluative criterion for the selection of an employee. If the competencies required to perform a particular job are spelled out clearly in the job description, it may very well serve as the most effective screening mechanism that can be employed. An illustration of a job description for a position in a commercial leisure service organization is given in the section "American Fitness Complex" on the next page.

Once the job description has been developed, the next step in the process of recruitment is to let qualified people know that the position is available. This can be done in a variety of ways, such as working with educational institutions, professional organizations, state employment agencies, commercial employment agencies, executive search firms, newspapers and other advertising media, labor unions, and unsolicited applications.

1. *Educational Institutions.* Educational institutions are excellent resources for recruiting part-time, seasonal, and full-time employees. Colleges, universities, technical insitutions, and high schools often operate placement services. Services range from listing positions to holding job fairs where organizations come to the campus to interview potential employees.

2. *Professional Organizations.* Professional societies and associations often have job placement services. These usually consist of job listings, job bulletins, newsletters, or professional magazines. Usually, the types of jobs listed through professional associations are managerial or those that require highly specialized skills.

3. *State Employment Agencies.* Listing positions with state employment agencies is a common way to advertise. This can be especially useful in securing individuals for part-time or seasonal positions or positions that fall into categories that are nonprofessional or nonmanagerial. State employment services can assist an organization in their screening process by matching a person's work experience and education with the requirements of a particular job. State employment offices also provide

American Fitness Complex
Job Description for Pool Manager

General Description

The Pool Manager employed with the American Fitness Complex is responsible for managing, programming, and maintaining the Complex's swimming pool. The Pool Manager's major responsibility is to ensure the establishment of an aquatics program that meets the needs and interests of the Complex's participants and also results in the efficient financial operation of the aquatics facility.

Supervision Received

This position comes under the direct supervision of the General Manager of the American Fitness Complex. The Pool Manager is responsible for following and carrying out all of the policies of the Complex's Board of Directors.

Supervision Exercised

The Pool Manager is responsible for the direct supervision of both full-time and part-time employees. Specifically, he or she is responsible for the supervision of the Pool Operator, Lifeguards, Instructors, and Cashiers.

Duties

1. To plan, organize, and implement a year-round comprehensive aquatics program that meets the needs and interests of the Complex's members.
2. To hire and supervise staff members relative to performance of duties connected with each position. Submit periodic evaluations, as required, to the General Manager of the Complex.
3. To schedule the work of the entire staff on a weekly basis and present such a schedule to the General Manager of the Complex for approval.
4. To requisition and maintain all equipment and supplies necessary to carry out of the safe and successful operation of the pool during the times that it is open.
5. To provide periodic in-service training to staff members.
6. To supervise maintenance of the aquatic facility and assign duties among staff members.
7. To act in the capacity of lifeguard or instructor when the pool load requires additional staffing.
8. To ensure the safety of all swimmers by continuous reinforcement of rules and regulations.
9. To administer first aid in the event of injury.
10. To maintain all records and forms as required, including having daily receipts deposited.
11. To make sure the pool is open and closed on time and that the facility is clean and orderly and in good operating condition.
12. To perform other duties as may be assigned by the General Manager of the American Fitness Complex.

Qualifications

A Baccalaureate degree in Park and Recreation Management or Physical Education from an accredited university. A minimum of three (3) years of progressively responsible part-time experience in the aquatics area is also required, or six (6) years of full-time professional experience in the park and recreation field with an emphasis in aquatics and academic training in aquatic management. In addition, the Pool Manager must be certified as a Water Safety Instructor and in Red Cross Advanced Life Saving or YMCA Senior Life Saving, CPR, and first aid or equivalent.

Skills

The Pool Manager must have the ability to organize and supervise the operation of an aquatics facility. This involves knowledge of efficient and safe pool operation, knowledge of water hazards, life saving techniques, and first aid methods, knowledge of pool maintenance, the ability to get along well with the public, to communicate effectively, and the ability to hire, supervise, schedule, and evaluate staff members.

---

psychological testing services. In the United States, there are over 2,400 employment offices.

4. *Commercial Employment Agencies.* Commercial employment agencies are those that assist businesses in finding qualified employees for a fee. The fee may be paid by the business hiring the person or by the person seeking employment. Fees are commensurate with the level of importance of the position. Such agencies have the know how and means to recruit highly qualified people. The fee paid to such an agency may actually represent a savings to a business seeking an employee when compared with the time and effort it might have to expend to perform the task itself.

5. *Executive Search Firms.* Executive search firms specialize in recruiting top level management personnel. This can often be a difficult and demanding task because it involves having a thorough knowledge of the needs of the business as well as first-hand knowledge of highly competent persons who can fill management roles. Executive searches must often be carried out with a great deal of discretion and confidence. The fees for this type of search can be very high and depend upon the level of pay of the position.

6. *Newspapers and Other Advertising.* Newspapers are also a good way of attracting people to positions within a commercial leisure service organization. They are often helpful in informing people who might not otherwise be aware of the position opening through connections with professional organizations. The cost of newspaper advertisements depends upon the circulation of the paper and the amount of advertising copy requested. Newspaper advertisements can be useful in attracting prospective employees for both full- and part-time positions.

7. *Labor Unions.* From a historical standpoint, labor unions have been an excellent source of employees, especially in the trade areas. Today there are numerous occupations that are represented by labor unions. In fact, many occupations that claim professional status are unionized.

8. *Unsolicited Applications.* It is not unusual for people to approach an organization with unsolicited applications in the event of a job opening. Commercial leisure service organizations, like other businesses, should have a systematic way of handling such applications. Even if there are

no jobs currently available, applications should be filed away to form a readily accessible pool of persons for various positions. In addition, the organization should send an acknowledgment of applicaions received and comment on the status of jobs within the organization.

Screening.   Once applications have been obtained by the organization for a position, the work of the leisure service manager or owner focuses on screening. Screening is a process of narrowing down the field of applicants to the most qualified people. It usually involves a review of the applicants' educational qualifications, work experience, and other special qualifications. The screening process should be done as objectively and rationally as possible. The overall goal is to get the most qualified person for the position. This usually involves establishing some systematic method for ranking the credentials of the applicants. One such method that can be employed and that is especially useful when hiring full-time employees is the matrix system.

The matrix system is an objective and rational method for assessing the qualifications of potential candidates. It involves identifying general areas of competence and then specific evaluative criteria to measure each person's credentials in each area. Evaluative criteria are weighted numerically so that an overall score can be obtained and compared with other scores. The next page presents a matrix system for fitness center manager. There are five areas of competence by which applicants can be judged. These include their administrative skills, knowledge of financial management, planning and research skills, public relations skills, and personnel management skills. Using this system, the organization evaluates applicants in terms of each of these areas of expertise and the evaluative criteria listed. By assigning a numerical value to each of the evaluative criteria, an applicant's "score" for all of the criteria can be added and used for comparative purposes.

Interviewing.   The interview process is the most important factor in the selection of an employee. It provides a method for a business to assess the capabilities of the final candidates for a position. Depending upon the level of responsibility of the job to be filled, the interview will be more or less complex. For example, it is not unusual to require psychological testing and present opportunities for role playing and other simulated activities for top management positions within an organization. Regardless of the level of the position within the organization, the interview should be structured so that it provides information that is useful in selecting a qualified candidate.

The interview should be viewed as a two-way process; that is, it should provide an opportunity for each individual applying for the job to explore the nature of the job itself as well as the goals, priorities, and problems of the organization. On the other hand, it provides the commercial leisure service business with an opportunity to determine the job skills, knowledge, and potential of the individual as they relate to the needs of the business. Creating a two-way process of communication can be an essential step in building positive and harmonious relationships between the individual and the organization. Even if a person is not offered a job, the organization

194

American Fitness Complex
Matrix for a General Manager

Name _____

	Possible Points	Candidate's Points

1. *Administration and Programming*

   a. Experience working with a corporate Board of Directors.

(4)	(0)	(4)	_____
(yes)	(no)		

   b. Evidence of managerial leadership.

     1) Number of FTE supervised

(1)	(2)	(3)	(6)	_____
1-5 FTE	5-10 FTE	11 + FTE		

     2) Level of responsibility

(2)	(4)	(6)	_____
supervisory	managerial		

     3) Length of time

(1)	(2)	(3)	(6)	_____
0–3 yrs.	3–6 yrs.	over 6		

   c. Experience in fitness and wellness

(2)	(2)	(2)	
Fitness	Nutrition	Weight Loss	
(2)	(2)	(2)	(12) _____
Recreation & Leisure	Smoking Clinics	Aquatic Services	

   d. Property management

     1) Areas (grounds, athletic fields, etc.)

(2)	(0)	(2)	_____
yes	no		

     2) Facilities (recreation buildings, shelters, etc.)

(1)	(0)	(1)	_____
yes	no		

     3) Equipment (mowers, vehicles, Recreation, etc.)

(1)	(0)	(1)	_____
yes	no		

   e. Aquatic facility management

(3)	(3)	(3)	(3)	(12) _____
Program organization & development	Instructional skills	certification	mechanical operations	

Total Administration and Programming   (50)   _____

2. *Financial Management*

   a. Size of budget administered

(2)	(4)	(6)	(6)	_____
0–$150,000	$150,000–250,000	$250,000 +		

   b. Fiscal control procedures

(2)	(2)	(2)	(6)	_____
Purchasing	Auditing	Contract Law		

   c. Fee and revenue management

(3)	(3)	(6)	_____
Administering	Received		

   d. Budget Process

(4)	(3)	(7)	_____
Budget preparation	Level of responsibility		

Total Financial Management   (25)   _____

3. *Planning and Research*

   a. Have you been involved in policy development?

(10)	(0)	(10)	_____
yes	no		

   b. Have you been involved in facility development?

(2.5)	(2.5)	(5)	_____
Maintenance	Improvements		

   c. Have you been involved in planning?

(5)	(0)	(5)	_____
yes	no		

   d. Have you been involved in market research?

(5)	(0)	(5)	_____
yes	no		

Total Planning and Research   (25)   _____

4. *Public Relations*

   a. Marketing plan experience (brochures, flyers, reports, etc.)

(10)	(0)	(10)	_____
yes	no		

   b. Professional relations experience (state, regional, national)

(5)	(0)	(5)	_____
yes	no		

			Possible Points	Candidate's Points

c. Written communications

(0)	(0)	(2)		
Poor	Below Average	Satisfactory		

(3)	(5)		(10)	_____
Above Average	Outstanding			

d. Presentational/public speaking experience   (10)   _____

(2)	(2)	(2)	(2)	(2)
Business Groups	Service Clubs	Park & Recrea-tional Organiza-tions	Govern-ment	Self Improve-ment

e. Community relations

(3)	(3)	(3)	(1)	(10)
Membership & Participation	Public Service	Professional	Government	

Total Public Relations   (45)   _____

5. *Personnel*

a. Experience in *hiring* and *termination* of employees   (13)   _____

(13)	(0)
yes	no

b. Personnel Administration

(5)	(5)	(5)
Systems Evaluation	Performance Appraisal	Job Descriptions

(5)	(5)	(5)	(32)
Wage & Salary Administration	Grievance	Affirmative Action	

c. Training and Development

(5)	(5)	(10)
Orientation	In-Service	

Total Personnel   (55)   _____

Total Administration & Programming   (50)   _____

Total Financial Management   (25)   _____

Total Planning & Research   (25)   _____

Total Public Relations   (45)   _____

Total Personnel   (55)   _____

Grant Total   (200)   _____ should strive to make that person feel good about the interview experience and the organization.

Some of the specific guidelines for interviewing applicants follow.

1. Determine the skills, knowledge, and abilities of the individual.
2. Assess the applicant's personality characteristics in relation to the needs of the organization and the position.
3. Determine if the person will "fit" into the organization and relate well to other staff members.
4. Determine how this person might react to pressure situations or problems that the business may be facing.
5. Determine whether the person has a working knowledge of the information portrayed on his or her resume and application.
6. Determine the ability of the individual to "think" on his or her feet, responding in a thorough and positive manner.

Creating the Interview Climate. In order to ensure a successful interview procedure, a positive climate should be established between the interviewer and the interviewee. This is usually done by attempting to create a friendly and open rapport.

There are a number of ways of structuring an interview. An organization can establish a number of predetermined questions, or it can be more "freewheeling" without a predetermined "script." An organization might want to conduct an interview that requires actual demonstration of knowledge and skills in real-life or simulated situations. We feel that a modified pattern, wherein a set of questions are formulated in advance, is the best interview approach. By "modified," we mean that the interviewer should have the flexibility to probe in depth in areas that are of special interest. This approach usually provides more complete and consistent information from candidate to candidate and therefore is more reliable in comparing candidates' interview responses.

When conducting interviews, there are several guidelines that can be followed. First, it is important that the interviewer(s) review the job description for the position and also the credentials of the candidates that will be interviewed. A very poor and all-too-common practice is where the interviewer reviews the resume and application of the interviewee for the first time at the onset of the interview while the interviewee waits uncomfortably. Second, interview questions should be goal-oriented; that is, the interview process should provide information that helps in the employment decision. It is important to focus on the task at hand and not to go off on irrelevant tangents. Third, interviewees should be given an opportunity to respond fully to questions. The interviewer should also attempt to clarify the response of candidates. Last, the interviewer(s) should look for inconsistencies in responses to questions by the interviewee.

After the interview process has been conducted, an important step in the process of hiring a person is checking references. References are usually provided upon request by the applicant to the business reviewing their credentials. Reference checks can be conducted by telephone or by written request. At the very least a commercial leisure business should require that a person submit letters of reference from previous employers, educators, and other persons who can provide an objective appraisal of the candidate.

Caution should be taken in contacting present employers of individual applicants. One should check with the applicant that they have informed their current employer about their decision to seek out and investigate other employment opportunities.

Compensation

When we think of compensation, we usually think of financial incentives. However, there are a variety of ways to compensate employees within a commercial leisure service business. Because the greatest cost is personnel in service-oriented industries, careful consideration should be given to the development of a compensation program. Such a compensation program must satisfy the needs and desires of employees, while at the same time remaining within the financial limits of the organization. Remember, businesses are established to earn a profit. A compensation plan must reinforce this basic principle.

Financial Incentives. Financial incentives are usually thought of as wages, salaries or commissions paid to an employee. Wages are hourly; that is, the employee is paid by the hour for services performed. A salary is a fixed amount of money that is paid to an individual usually on a monthly or yearly basis. In other words, rather than being paid for each hour of work, the employee is paid for services rendered over a broader time frame. Salaries are usually paid to permanent full-time employees in contrast to wages, which are often associated with part-time, seasonal, or semi-skilled work. Still another method of financial compensation is that of commissions. When we think of commissions we usually think of sales commissions. A sales commission is an amount or percentage that a person receives for selling a product or service based upon the price. This financial incentive creates a direct relationship between the work of the employee and the amount that he or she earns.

Another form of financial incentive is that of the employee benefit. Different types of benefits are provided to employees, often in the areas of life, health, and dental insurance. Other forms of benefits include bonuses and the opportunity to purchase company stock at a discount rate. Because many of these benefits are taken for granted within large corporations, employees often forget the cost of these to the business itself and do not view it as a financial reward. Benefits can add an additional 30 to 40 percent to an employee's paycheck. A business owner may want to periodically inform employees of the amount that the business contributes for these benefits for each individual employee. This information can be added to employees' paychecks, for example.

Nonfinancial Incentives. By nonfinancial incentives, we mean those "perks" or benefits that affect the quality of employment but are not directly tied to the "pay" that an employee receives. This does not mean that such "perks" do not cost the business money. In fact, they can be costly. These benefits range from child care, company cars, employee fitness centers, and fitness programs to employee recreation associations and coffee and donuts during office breaks.

Nonfinancial incentives are often termed "psychic income." The power of such incentives to hold employees in a work environment is very strong.

Other nonfinancial incentives that may attract people are such things as the organization's image within the community and its physical and psychological work environment (people like to work in places that are clean and harmonious). Today, many electronics corporations attempt to attract and retain employees by building facilities that are park-like and meet the other criteria mentioned.

Laws Affecting Wages.   Consideration must be given to federal statutes when establishing a compensation system. There are two laws that have a great impact upon the establishment of compensation systems: the Fair Labor Standards Act and the Equal Pay Act of 1963. The Fair Labor Standards Act is the federal statute that provides for minimum wage rates and overtime rates for work performed over 40 hours per week. The Equal Pay Act of 1963 provides for equal pay for jobs that require the same work, effort, skill, or responsibility. This is intended to prevent discrimination between men and women performing equal work under similar work conditions in the same establishment.

Training

Commercial leisure service organizations, like other businesses, require competent, appropriately trained staff if they are to succeed. No organization should risk approaching the orientation and training functions in a haphazard way. The need to think through the tasks that need to be completed, the policies that need to be reinforced and maintained, and other essential components of the organization's operations would seem to be self evident. However, it is surprising how often organizations approach this management function with little planning and delegate it to individuals ill-prepared to orient and train new staff.

One of the most interesting areas of staff training that can help us understand the importance of its value to an organization is that of consumer–staff relationships. In the leisure service area, the relationship that is developed between the leader and the consumer may be a significant factor in the success of a leisure experience. Persons within businesses can be effectively trained to understand the importance of their role in this concept. For example, at Great America in Santa Clara, California, hosts and hostesses are encouraged in their training to adopt ". . . a genuine attitude of graciousness, friendliness, courtesy, and service toward each guest."[20] The point is that training creates an opportunity to shape the thinking, attitudes, and behavior of employees so that they are consistent with the goals of the organization.

What is training? Training is a process of educating persons within an organization to do required tasks, form attitudes and values, and otherwise assimilate information that might not be known. Training exists to provide information to new employees as well as to reinforce the values and beliefs of persons who are already within the organization. In addition, training can be used to introduce new knowledge, skills, and technology to existing employees. For example, the half-life of management knowledge is said to be seven years. This means that in seven years one-half of one's management knowledge will be obsolete. This suggests that managers will need access to new management theories and concepts in a relatively short period of time in order to remain current in their management knowledge.

Another dimension of training is that of preparing employees to advance within an organization. To ensure that an organization has employees who are capable of assuming managerial roles, it is necessary to create a training program for this purpose. Although we more frequently see this type of training program in larger organizations, it might also be useful in smaller organizations to ensure successful continuity as a business expands or as staff changes occur. Supervisory or managerial training programs often focus on equipping employees with the skills that provide them with a broader orientation to the organization and its activities. In other words, the focus of the training program might be on developing effective human relations skills, understanding financial goals, and training persons in ways that will help them in the long-range planning for the organization. This is contrasted with training that tends to be more task-specific and focused on particular job skills.

Training has a tremendous impact upon employees, both initially and after a person has been employed by an organization for a period of time. The initial training an employee receives has the potential to make a lasting impression. This is the time when the basic values of the organization are transmitted. It is the time when new employees get a sense of the dynamism, commitment to excellence and service, and commitment to employees' welfare of an organization. This training offers an opportunity to influence the whole tone of the organization.

Training that occurs after a person has been with an organization for a period of time is termed in-service or on-the-job training. Participation in this type of training often is received by employees as a sign of the organization's commitment and willingness to invest in their continued development. It offers a way to indicate to employees that an organization cares about their future and wants to make them a part of the business's growth and development. Dynamic organizations are constantly looking for new products, services, and ways to improve the delivery of these services to consumers. This type of training affords an opportunity for employees to be a part of that creative process.

Summary

In this chapter we have discussed the organization and management of commercial leisure service organizations. We have reviewed different types of business ownership and have discussed a variety of different factors that influence the management of an organization, including the establishment of superordinate goals, management skills, managerial style, working with staff, organizational structures, and management systems.

There are three types of business ownership: sole proprietorship, partnership, and corporation. A sole proprietorship occurs when a business is owned by one person. The advantages of this type of business ownership are that it provides high personal incentive, freedom to act, privacy in financial statements, tax savings, and ease of dissolution. The disadvantages of this type of business ownership are that it creates unlimited personal liability, limited capital, possible lack of talent, possible lack of continuity, and potential heavy taxation. A partnership occurs when two or more people engage in a business activity. The advantages of a partnership include more capital, better credit standing, more talent, increased personal incentive of valued employees, and few legal restrictions. The disadvantages of this type of business ownership include management conflict, unlimited liability, constraints on capital, difficulty in liquidating investments, and possible lack of continuity of the business. Last, a corporation is a separate legal entity. Its chief advantages are the limited liability of owners, ease in raising capital, ease in transferring ownership, and continuity of operations. The disadvantages of this type of business ownership include the cost involved in establishment, the potential for double taxation, and the public nature of corporations.

We have suggested that managing a business is like managing your personal life. If you are successful in your personal, financial, and other affairs and are achievement oriented, you will probably succeed as an entrepreneur. Perhaps the most overriding factor in the success of an organization is the philosophy that is established and communicated to employees at the operational level. We feel that it is essential for a manager to have a number of skills. These include the ability to organize, to make decisions, to create and carry out ideas, to teach or coach, to resolve conflict, to communicate, to plan, and to inspire employees.

Management style refers to the way in which a manager interacts with others within the organization. There is no one best management style. We suggest that a manager use a management style that meets the needs of the situation within which he or she is operating. A key factor in determining which management style should be employed is evaluation of the task-relevant maturity of employees.

Organizational structure can be thought of as the establishment of organizational roles. Like the manager's style, the type of organizational structure employed should also be selected depending upon the situation. Some of the structures that can be employed are autocracy, bureaucracy, project or modular organization, matrix systems, decentralization, or collegial organization.

Managing the human resources of an organization is especially important. This is particularly true in service-oriented organizations. We believe that the manager should provide positive reinforcement to employees by arranging the work environment in such a way that the needs of the individual employee and the needs of the organization are simultaneously met. In this chapter we have also discussed the adoption of management systems. The manager should be careful to weigh the advantages and disadvantages to the organization as a whole of various management systems when selecting one. A management system should be viewed as a vehicle that helps the organization achieve its primary mission.

Study Questions

1. Define a sole proprietorship. What are the advantages and disadvantages?
2. Define a partnership. What are the advantages and disadvantages?

3. Define a corporation. What are the advantages and disadvantages?
4. Discuss the importance of establishing an organizational philosophy.
5. What skills does the commercial leisure service manager need to have to operate a commercial leisure service venture successfully?
6. How would you appraise your own management skills? What technical skills do you have?
7. Define the term "management style." What type of management style do you feel you have?
8. Identify and define seven different types of organizational structures.
9. How do you build relationships of trust, confidence, and mutual respect within commercial leisure service organizations?
10. What is a management system? What factors must you guard against when adopting and using a management system?

Experiental Exercise

In Chapter 2, we identified five different types of commercial organizations. These included travel and tourism, entertainment, hospitality and food service, leisure services in the natural environment, and retail outlets. In this exercise, we would like you to develop two specific statements. First, we would like you to develop a statement of philosophy for your business. This statement should be approximately two pages long, typewritten. Keep in mind that you want to communicate not only the purpose and objectives of your business, but also the values that must be shared by all members of the organization in order to ensure its success. This will not be an easy task, because you will need to communicate many "intangible" ideas in a way that is easily understandable. Second, we would like you to use the outline on page 161 for the development of articles of partnership to draw up your own articles of partnership for a leisure service business of your choice. Do this with another person who will be your "partner." Remember, there are items that you will want to negotiate in the area of finance as well as in the management of the business.

Notes

1. U.S. General Services Administration, *Code of Federal Regulations*, Section 121.3-10, Washington, D.C.: Office of the Federal Register, 1977.
2. U.S. Internal Revenue Service, *Statistics of Income—Business and Corporation Income Tax Returns*, Washington, D.C.: Internal Revenue Service, 1975.
3. Maurice Archer, *An Introduction to Canadian Business*, 2nd ed., Toronto: McGraw-Hill Ryerson Ltd., 1974, p. 29.
4. Ibid., p. 30.
5. Kenneth R. Van Voorhis, *Entrepreneurship and Small Business Management*, Boston: Allyn & Bacon, 1980, p. 86.
6. Archer, p. 41.
7. Ibid., p. 43.
8. Ibid.
9. Van Voorhis, p. 43
10. Richard Tanner Pascale, Anthony G. Athos, *The Art of Japanese Management*, New York: Warner Books, 1981, p. 289.
11. Ibid., p. 289–290.

12. Fred Fiedler, *A Theory of Leadership Effectiveness*, New York: McGraw-Hill, 1967.
13. William J. Reddin, *Managerial Effectiveness*, New York: McGraw-Hill, 1970, pp. 41–43.
14. Paul Hersey, Kenneth M. Blanchard, *Management of Organization Behavior: Utilizing Human Resources*, Englewood Cliffs, NJ: Prentice-Hall, 1977.
15. Carroll V. Kroeger, "Managerial Development in the Small Firm," *California Management Review*, Vol. 17, No. 1, 1974, p. 43.
16. Robert R. Blake, Jane S. Mouton, *The Managerial Grid*, Houston, TX: Gulf Publishing, 1964, p. vi.
17. Joseph J. Bannon, "The Organizational Chart: The Manager's Toy," *Leisure Today*, April, 1982, p. 47.
18. David C. McClelland, *The Achieving Society*, Princeton, NJ: D. Van Nostrand Co., 1961.
19. Peter F. Drucker, *The Practice of Management*, New York: Harper & Row, 1954.
20. Marriott Corporation's Great America, "Supervisory Training," p. 4.

Close-up: Early Winters

About ten years ago, Bill Nicolai had a dream. As a self-described "mountain bum," Nicolai left a well paying job as a computer programmer to climb mountains. While on one of his trips, Nicolai's tent blew apart in high winds. Returning home, he set out to design and build his own tent. Impressed with his creation, Nicolai began to think of supporting himself and his lifestyle manufacturing and selling his tent. Nicolai marketed his tents at Seattle street fairs and West Coast sporting goods stores. While mild success resulted from this effort, it was not until 1976 that the level of success Nicolai hoped to achieve would become a reality.

It was at this time that a salesman called on Nicolai to demonstrate a new fabric that was supposedly waterproof and breathable. Although skeptical, Nicolai and his new partners made a tent from this new material (called Gore-Tex). To test the material's usefulness Nicolai and his partners went into the field. It lived up to its promise.

Nicolai and his partners renamed the company Early Winters after a group of peaks in the Cascade Mountains of Washington. They decided to manufacture a line of Gore-Tex equipment. The distribution strategy was changed from personal sales effort and trade show promotion to mail order.

The year was 1977 and people were becoming energy conservation minded, so the convenience of catalog shopping made sense. Also, 76 million Americans born between 1946 and 1964 were in their late teens and early twenties, which is the entry stage for backpacking. The Early Winters management identified their market by using their own list of campers who had expressed interest in their new tent design. The company's initial mailing was 7,000 flyers promoting its new 3½-pound Gore-Tex tent. The mailings doubled every year. With this new marketing focus, sales shot from $6,000 to $35,000 per month.

The company now has 300 employees and distributed six million catalogs in 1983.

Early Winters still makes various products, including about 450 Gore-Tex tents a year. But 80 percent of its 500 items come from other manufacturers. The company prides itself on unique products such as the Danish Fisherman's Cap, Thousand Mile Socks, Japanese Picnic boxes and insoles made in Germany from sphagnum moss. Items range in price from a $2.50 thermometer that attaches to a zipper (87,000 sold) to $4,995 for a hot air balloon (no orders received).

Sales for Early Winters in fiscal 1984 were $17 million and earnings after taxes were $600,000. Since 1982, Early Winters has opened two retail outlets, but mail order continues to account for 85 percent of sales.

If there is a secret to Early Winters' success, it lies in their unique catalog items and their policy of placing customer service as a high priority. To this end, Early Winters runs classes for its employees covering what each product does, how it does it, and who it's for, so they can give better customer service. Nicolai stated in an interview that "customers can use our products for thirty days and if they don't like them they get their money back. We also repair equipment no matter how long a person has had it or what's wrong with it."* Nicolai feels that this type of policy will, in the long run, "win the hearts" of their customers and build a company everyone can be proud of.

* Elizabeth McGown, "Behind the Label—Early Winters," *Backpacker*, November, 1983, p. 8.

6

Marketing for a Commercial Leisure Service Organization

This chapter will present the steps involved in developing a marketing plan for a commercial leisure service organization. It also will present basic marketing theory and define the terms necessary for understanding the theory and practice of marketing. Steps involved in conducting preliminary market research will be discussed as well. This discussion of marketing research will focus on procedures for identifying and measuring the breadth (boundaries) of a specific user group (target market) and for measuring the market's potential for profit. Following the measurement of the market, we will present a format for developing a plan to penetrate the market. The marketing plan will review several promotional strategies with emphasis on conceptualizing, developing, implementing, and evaluating an advertising program. Special attention will be focused on the use of creative selling to help the organization achieve profitability.

What Is Marketing?

Edginton and Williams have stated that marketing is a systematic process that controls an organization's activities in such a way that the consumer's needs are efficiently identified and fulfilled.[1] To be more specific, marketing is a course of action that facilitates an exchange of something of value between two parties, i.e., money, goods, or services (see Figure 6-1). The

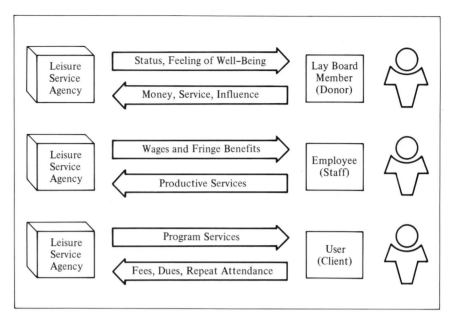

FIGURE 6–1. Examples of exchange transactions. (Adapted from Philip Kotler, *Marketing for Non-Profit Organizations*. Englewood Cliffs, NJ: Prentice-Hall, Inc. 1975, p. 24.)

marketing process includes the activities of analysis, planning, implementation, and control.

The primary objective of marketing is to ensure that a commercial leisure service organization becomes and remains a profitable and dynamic organization. To accomplish this objective, the organization must attract sufficient resources (money, facilities, personnel), convert these resources into leisure services and programs, and ensure that these services and programs are delivered to the public desiring them. For a commercial leisure service organization, these activities must translate into profit.

The foundation of marketing is *exchange*.[2] Exchange is the offering of something of value in return for something of value. As depicted in Figure 6-1, the exchange process is crucial to nearly all interactions between persons, agencies, and institutions in social settings. The concept of exchange clarifies and simplifies the "why" and "how" in motivating potential customers, creditors, and employees to act in a manner consistent with the goals of the organization.

Why Consumers Buy a Leisure Service

Why *do* consumers buy a leisure service? Why do consumers buy a service or product of any type? Whether a consumer purchases a river raft excursion or a Frisbee, he or she anticipates that some benefit will be derived from the purchase. For example, some leisure services offer an opportunity to learn a skill, gain prestige, or feel a sense of achievement. Others provide an opportunity for escape, fantasy, or risk. Still others provide an opportunity for social contact or opportunities for viewing the beauty and majesty of our environment.

| Anticipation | → | Participation | → | Reflection |

FIGURE 6–2. Three phases of a leisure activity that have an impact upon the consumer's desire to purchase or repurchase a service or product.

A consumer's desire to benefit from participation in leisure activities is a function of his or her basic needs. This is an important concept in the marketing of leisure services. The thrust of marketing efforts is to help consumers meet their perceived needs by purchasing from a business the products or services that they feel will benefit them. Consumers are not only influenced to purchase services and products by emotional motives related to needs, but are influenced by economic motives as well. In appealing to consumers, consideration should be given to both of these factors.

Regardless of the type of leisure service or product, there are three phases of the leisure experience that have an impact on the consumer and that influence his or her decision to purchase or repurchase a service or product: anticipation, participation, and reflection (evaluation) (see Figure 6-2).

Anticipation is the stage at which advertising is directed. In the *anticipation* stage, consumers either recognize a need for something of value (money, goods, or services), or they are committed to participate in a service to be performed sometime in the future.

Participation is the stage during which the user is involved with the service. It is at this time that a lasting impression of the service, the individual practitioner, and his or her organization is being formed. Since the only thing the user will take away with him or her is an impression, it is important for the owner or manager of a service organization to be sensitive to the impression the user takes away. It is the client's evaluation of the service that will determine whether the client will become a repeat customer or recommend the service to a friend.

Reflection is the impression the user is left with once the service has been performed. If the impression is positive, the likelihood of repeat business or referral business is great.

What Is a Market?

A market is a potential arena for the trading of resources of value. Runyon expands this definition to say that "a market is a group of people with purchasing power who are willing to spend money to satisfy their needs."[3] In a narrower sense, then, a *leisure market* is composed of people willing to exchange something of value (i.e., money) to satisfy their leisure needs.

Markets may be evaluated and segmented in order to help a business define and pinpoint its *target market*. A target market is a homogeneous group of consumers to whom a business intends to try to sell its products and services.

Runyon stresses that people, purchasing power, and willingness to spend are essential criteria in determining whether a market exists (see Figure 6-3).[4] Leisure expenditures have historically come from discretionary or surplus income. It is felt by many that the growth in the market for

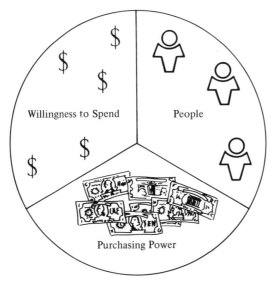

FIGURE 6–3. Prerequisites of a market.

leisure products and services is a direct result of the growing affluence of North American workers and the reduced work hours required to produce a higher standard of living. This confluence of factors produces discretionary funds.

Discretionary income is that portion of income that is not required for maintenance or debt reduction. It was this discretionary income margin that some economists used to support the explanation that the growth of leisure expenditures in this country was a valid measure of the good life. In Chapter 2 we saw that between 1953 and 1981 expenditures for leisure grew from $20 billion to $262 billion, an increase of 763 percent. During this same period, however, salaries and wages grew by only 150 percent. Some of this increase in leisure spending was the result of increased consumption of products and services, but much of this increase was caused by inflation (reduction of purchasing power of the dollar). The point is that expenditures for leisure grew at a faster rate during the past thirty years than disposable income (the source of leisure dollars), which means that individual and family budget allocations for leisure must be accounted for in some other way. This increased availability of leisure dollars in the budget could reflect a *leisure imperative*, that is, a force or tendency that moves people to no longer consider leisure a luxury. Discretionary income may be only one measure of market strength for leisure, while people's perception of leisure as a necessity (leisure imperative) may be an equally valid measure of market strength, albeit a less quantifiable and identifiable one.

Leisure dollars come from several sources: couples have fewer children, both husbands and wives work, consumers purchase small, inexpensive, and energy-efficient cars, families buy cheaper and smaller homes, and people borrow more money. In regard to this last factor, there has been a dramatic increase in consumer debt; it is now approaching the $1 trillion mark.

Figure 6-4 illustrates that spending by individuals, businesses, and the government between 1971 and 1990 is projected to rise by an average of

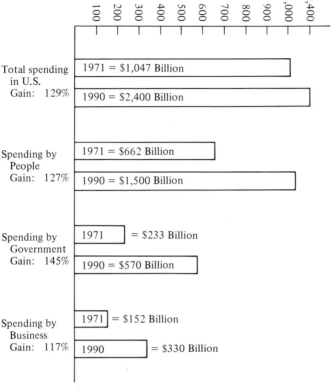

Billions of Dollars

| | 100 | 200 | 300 | 400 | 500 | 600 | 700 | 800 | 900 | 1,000 | 2,400 |

Total spending
in U.S.
Gain: 129%

1971 = $1,047 Billion

1990 = $2,400 Billion

Spending by
People
Gain: 127%

1971 = $662 Billion

1990 = $1,500 Billion

Spending by
Government
Gain: 145%

1971 = $233 Billion

1990 = $570 Billion

Spending by
Business
Gain: 117%

1971 = $152 Billion

1990 = $330 Billion

FIGURE 6–4. Measures of prosperity. (Projections by Conference Board, Non-profit Economic Research. Washington, DC: White House Conference on the Industrial World Ahead, 1979.)

The recreational vehicle business is particularly sensitive to such market variables as interest rates, inflation rate, and the general buying mood of middle class Americans. (John Bullaro)

211

129 percent. Considering that the inflation rate for 1983 was under 5 percent and considering the rapid growth of leisure expenditures during the past thirty years, we can conclude that the growth potential of the leisure market is indeed promising. It does not seem unreasonable to expect leisure revenues to reach $400 billion by 1991.

Yet this optimism should be mixed with caution. Not only is it difficult to fully grasp the size of the leisure market because of its diversity, it is also difficult to project future trends in the leisure market with reasonable accuracy. One reason for this is product and service instability. When a product or service rises and falls rapidly in terms of sales, we call it a fad.

A fad is a short-term market interest that appears and disappears rapidly. Hula hoops of the early 1960s, skate boards of the 1970s, and the roller skating retail shops of the 1980s are examples of fads that have suddenly appeared in the leisure market and then have rapidly declined. However, some fads disappear, but then reappear as stable products or services. The bicycle industry is an example of such a fad. Bicycles were replaced by the automobile, only to reappear during the health boom of the 1960s and remain a stable business.

Marketing versus Selling

Many people confuse "selling and promoting" with "marketing." These two concepts, in fact, involve two different orientations. In the sales and promotion orientation, a business and its salespeople assume that consumers will adjust their expectations to accommodate the product or service offered by the business. The marketing orientation, reverses this strategy. In the marketing orientation, the commercial leisure service business adjusts its products and services to meet the needs of consumers.

In the sales orientation, the focus is on the products or services that the business produces. In the marketing orientation, the focus is on meeting people's needs. For example, a travel agency "selling" a vacation tour to Hawaii would focus its efforts on encouraging consumers to buy plane tickets, hotel accommodations, and excursions. On the other hand, a travel agency "marketing" this same vacation tour to Hawaii would first focus its efforts on identifying consumer needs, such as desire for pleasure, desire for relaxation, desire for adventure, desire for economy, and desire for excitement, and then provide its services accordingly. These two concepts are illustrated in Figure 6-5.

From a broader perspective, businesses that focus on their products and services without adequate consideration of consumer needs are likely to be less successful than those that focus on consumer needs. It is important for a business to have a perspective beyond the products and services that it currently offers to consumers. In other words, it is important to remember that the interests, tastes, and behavior of consumers are constantly changing. In order to meet these changing needs, a service organization should be continually engaged in service evaluation, research, and promotion. If this is not done, even the most successful business can decline and become obsolete. If, for example, railroad companies had more broadly conceived of themselves as being in the "transportation business," rather than the "railroad business," they might have adapted their business to the own-

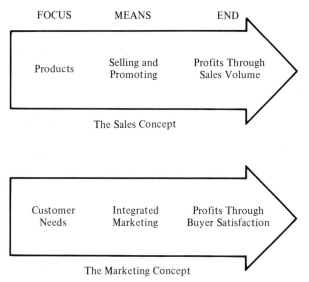

	FOCUS	MEANS	END
	Products	Selling and Promoting	Profits Through Sales Volume

The Sales Concept

	FOCUS	MEANS	END
	Customer Needs	Integrated Marketing	Profits Through Buyer Satisfaction

The Marketing Concept

FIGURE 6–5. The sales and marketing concepts contrasted. (Adapted from Philip Kotler, *Marketing Management*, 2nd ed. Englewood Cliffs, N.J: Prentice-Hall, Inc., 1972.)

ership of airlines, trucking companies, and automobile companies. An example of a company that has successfully identified its underlying purpose or mission is AT&T. This organization realized that it was in the "communications business" and not just the "telephone business." AT&T branched out into other forms of communication, such as computers. The decline of many public park and recreation systems may be because they view themselves as providers of parks, facilities, and equipment rather than providers of leisure experiences. Correspondingly, this may be the reason that commercial leisure service businesses have been so successful; they tend to focus on the marketing of an experience (i.e., the adventure and fantasy of Walt Disney World).

Market Research

Aspiring entrepreneurs frequently engage in seat-of-the-pants market research. That is, they "feel" that the market for a particular product or service exists and will experience significant growth based on media reports. All they need, so the logic goes, is a small share, say 19 percent of a $1 billion market, to generate a $10 million sales volume. Then they add, with some sense of assurance, that their projection is a conservative one.

Launching an enterprise based on hunches and feelings can be, at best, dangerous. Funding sources are reluctant to lend money to poorly researched ventures. The fact is, few entrepreneurs really do a lot of research, which accounts for the high number of new business failures.

Ironically, market research is easier than ever before. A business owner or manager can carry out some basic market research on his or her own or can hire a consulting firm to conduct market research. Computer technology has made professional market research affordable, primarily by the recent proliferation of specialized computer data banks. In addition, sophisticated Madison Avenue research techniques have become available to new start-ups through these data banks. The new entrepreneur has over 250 fee-based, data-based marketing services data banks to choose from. Research services may charge from $5 an hour for data banks to $100 an hour for research bureaus with large staffs.

Perhaps the greatest challenge new entrepreneurs face is evaluating a market that does not yet exist. New products and services lie outside existing market boundaries and cannot be validated with numbers (home computers and video games were in this stage a mere five years ago). In the case of these new offerings without a measurable market, the emphasis must shift from quantitative measure to qualitative research. This methodological shift involves one-on-one discussions with potential users and market experts. Thus, the entrepreneur gains a "feel" for the potential market.

To enhance chances of developing a marketable service, an attempt should be made to locate a gap in the existing market of a particular service and attempt to fill that gap. Richard M. White, Jr., author of *The Entrepreneur's Manual*, has an extensive chapter on market gap analysis that should be valuable reading for anyone needing to uncover "areas in the market in which demand far exceeds supply."[5] In his book, White lays out a ten-step program for locating hidden lucrative markets. Once a gap is discovered, an intense research program should be initiated to test the validity of the gap analysis.

What Is Market Research?

There are several specific types of research. *Pure research* aims at expanding the frontiers of knowledge and usually does not directly involve pragmatic problems. *Applied research,* on the other hand, is concerned with the solution of real-life problems that normally require someone to make a decision or implement policy. Market research is applied research and is directed toward helping owners and managers of businesses gain information regarding the market to which they want to sell their products and services. Market research is involved with such topics as the size of the market, consumer preferences (and changes in same), information about competition, price changes, conditions related to supply, and other economic or political variables that might affect a business's operations.

Market research can be carried out by an owner or manager through surveys of various types or through investigation of statistics. Typical questions that an owner or manager might want to answer are "Is there a market for my service or product?" "How can I identify this market?" and "Do I have a place in this market?"

The Research Process

In order to produce data that will result in solutions to the above marketing problems, the owner or manager of the leisure services organization should proceed with the research effort, which consists of four major stages:

1. Define the problem
2. Develop a research design
3. Collect the data
4. Analyze and interpret results

Defining the Problem

Defining the problem is essentially concerned with establishing the general boundaries of the inquiry. This is usually done by developing a list of questions related to the problem. The following checklist will provide questions to help define marketing problems.

Market Survey Checklist for a Commercial Leisure
Service Organization
  1. What economic levels of the population will patronize me the most?
  2. Is my service ethnic oriented?
  3. What is the sex of my prime customers?
  4. To what age group do my prime customers belong?
  5. What locations or areas are in harmony with 1 through 5 above?
  6. How far will the average buyer (user) travel for my service?
  7. What is the psychographic profile of the different market segments?
  8. What are the buying patterns of the various market segments?
  9. Who are my competitors?
 10. What are optimum customer densities for my service?
 11. What techniques are currently being used by competitors to attract users?
 12. What image should I project for each market segment?
 13. What additional profit centers are available to me that complement my services?
 14. How can I make my service interesting and enjoyable for my customers?

The above checklist should be modified to address the specific nature of an individual enterprise. Where possible, answers should be in quantifiable form.

After the questions are identified, the researcher must decide on the best method or methods for gathering data (see discussion on data collection).

Developing a Market Research Methodology

There are several research methodologies that can be used to conduct market research. These methodologies include face-to-face interviews, telephone interviews, direct mail questionnaires, combination mail–telephone surveys, library research, trade shows, and seminar raiding (see Figure 6-6). Most aspiring owners or managers of leisure service organizations will not have the funds available to conduct expensive market testing procedures. These methods are simple, effective, and inexpensive. Furthermore, they do not require extensive training as a market researcher.

Face-to-Face Interviews with Potential Customers. List several people you feel would subscribe to or buy your service. Plan a list of thought-provoking questions that will guide your interview. Mail the prospective interviewee a short note introducing yourself and explaining the purpose of your meeting. Make an appointment and be prompt. Allow the interview to stray from the planned questions and develop into a brainstorming session.

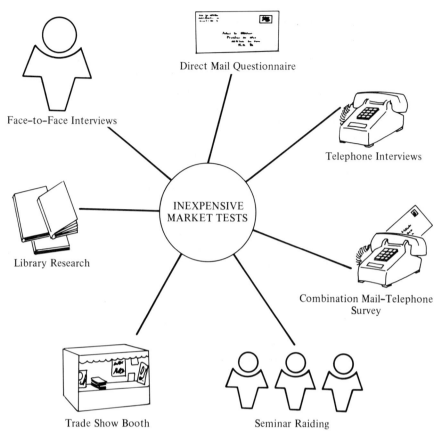

Face-to-Face Interviews

Direct Mail Questionnaire

Telephone Interviews

Library Research

INEXPENSIVE MARKET TESTS

Combination Mail–Telephone Survey

Trade Show Booth

Seminar Raiding

FIGURE 6–6. Market tests that can be employed by a small business.

Telephone Interviews. Have your opening statement and list of questions written out in detail before your calls. This will reduce the "phone jitters." The typical phone interview will last approximately eight minutes. Allow the interviewee to lead you so relevant information can be discovered.

Direct Mail Questionnaires. These can be sent to a sample of people to gain market information. Do not ask personal financial questions. Most respondents will not invest more than five minutes (approximately five simple questions) on your questionnaire.

Combination Mail–Telephone Surveys. We have had considerable success in overcoming the problems involved in both mail and telephone interviews by combining the two. By sending the interviewee a copy of the interview and following up with a phone call, the interviewee is less suspicious of the caller's intent. This strategy reduces the time necessary for explanation, and, in the case of long-distance calls, can save considerable phone charges.

Library Research. In using printed or published data sources the researcher is using secondary data, which is considered acceptable data by most funding sources. University and public libraries contain statistics on the industry that you are addressing. The Department of Commerce, the Small Business Administration, the larger stock brokers, investment bankers and commercial banks, all are valuable sources of secondary data.

Other sources of secondary data are marketing journals which include the *Journal of Advertising Research*, the *Journal of Consumer Research*, the *Journal of Marketing*, the *Journal of Marketing Research*, and the *Journal of Retailing*.

Trade Shows.   Rent a booth in a trade show and attempt to presell from preliminary sales literature. Information gathered from this source will be of extremely high quality. Professionals who visit your booth and answer your questions will save you years of personal interviews.

Seminar Raiding.   While questionable on ethical grounds, seminar raiding can be a valuable source of answers to marketing questions. In this strategy two or more people (a team) attend a seminar where experts are in attendance. One person of your team asks the speaker a question close to his subject, then another team member asks a question related to the first to keep the issue on the floor. Frequently, the session turns into a brainstorming session with the audience contributing to your research area. Team members should not be seated near one another.

Data Collection

Once a methodology has been identified the researcher must decide *who* will collect the data and *how* the questions will be worded and evaluated.

Who.   Asking the question "who will collect the data?" is essential in order to maintain proper perspective. An enthusiastic entrepreneur can frequently bias the data. Optimistic assumptions produce erroneous conclusions from raw data (answers to questions). Richard Buskirk, Director of the University of Southern California's Entrepreneur Program refers to this over optimistic syndrome as, "The Penny Myth," a name derived from the statement, "If we could just get a penny from everyone in the country . . . "

Hidden biases of the researcher can prejudice the way an interviewer asks questions and assesses the responses. To gain a realistic perspective, the researcher should consider having a neutral third party conduct the personal interviews.

How.   The wording of questions is an essential consideration in data collecting. First of all, where possible, every question should be quantifiable— that is, the answer is measurable. Further, the wording of questions will, in many cases, affect the response. Questions may be open-ended (allowing respondents to give individual answers), closed-ended (requiring respondents to choose a response), split-ballot (presenting two parallel versions of the same question), and forced choice (requiring respondents to choose between two statements).

For further discussion and clarification of interview techniques and questionnaire design, see *Finding Out: Conducting and Evaluating Social Research* by June Audrye True.[6] True's book is concise and easy to read and is suitable for the novice researcher.

Analysis and Interpretation

After the field work phase is complete, the data must be analyzed. If the researcher is unsophisticated in data analysis or wants to ensure against being overly optimistic, outside assistance is recommended.

The analysis of data requires organizing them into tables, charts, and graphs, manipulating them statistically, and relating the findings to the original market research boundary defined in step one of the research process.

The market research discussion identified two sources of data; primary data gathered by first hand experience, and secondary data gathered from published sources. We suggest reviewing secondary sources before collecting primary data or setting market research boundaries. Such a review will provide invaluable background for proceeding expeditiously with the market research process.

The Marketing Plan

Once the market research function has been completed, the leisure service organization must begin the market planning function. Figure 6-7 depicts this function. Developing objectives (philosophy statement) and marketing strategies are the two critical steps of the marketing plan. It should be noted that objective development and market strategy decisions are in a state of flux, i.e., changing as new information is received and experience dictates.

Objectives-Philosophy Statement

A marketing objective is the desired end-result we wish to achieve in terms of sales volume, number of customers, lines of credit, and so forth. It is not enough to state that the end-result is a profit. The result must be stated in actual dollar amounts measured annually.

Marketing objectives should always be specific, actionable, and achievable. Objectives that do not meet these three criteria provide little in the way of guidance for the marketing strategist and no basis at all for evaluating the effectiveness of the marketing program. At what level these quantifiable objectives should be set is essentially a judgment call on the part of the owner or manager and should be based upon consideration of the organization's resources (money, staff, facilities), the present market position, and the test of reasonableness.

Meta-Objectives.   While it is argued that objectives should be quantifiable, the leisure service organization should exhibit a high degree of community responsibility. Well thought out, identifiable, and written meta-objectives (such as benefits to the community) will enhance the organization's potential for long-term survival and generate a sense of pride in the owner or manager and employees.

Meta-objectives might include such statements as the client's safety is of paramount importance; the organization will take an active role in community affairs both as a participant and a contributor; employees are encouraged to take an active role in community organizations; the owner or manager and all professional level employees should take an active role in state and national recreation and leisure professional organizations.

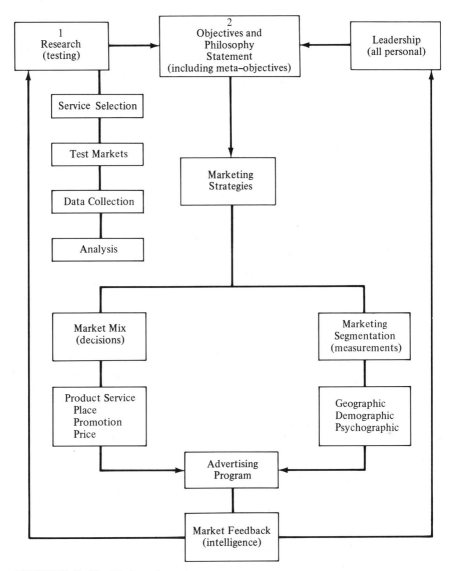

FIGURE 6–7. Market planning activities.

Meta-objectives are in effect a philosophical commitment to excellence of service and will form the foundation upon which marketing policy is set. In the long run, meta-objectives will provide a bedrock of strength to ensure the survival of the business during periods of difficulty.

Marketing Strategy

The development of a marketing plan and a marketing strategy is a test of leadership for the owner or manager. Developing marketing strategy requires an intimate familarity with the market, service offering, and the leisure industry in general. Implementing the marketing strategy is perhaps the ultimate test of leadership because of the temptation to disregard research data, to follow competition, and to listen to those less knowledgeable. Runyon states that "marketing strategy is the test that brings together understanding, imagination, vision, and decisiveness to give direction to the marketing effort."[7]

Marketing strategy is essentially a "clarification of the interrelationships" between advertising and sales promotion, between distributing and pricing, and the manner in which a service is presented to a customer.[8]

When developing a marketing strategy, it is best to formulate general statements. The specifics of pricing, media, and sales brochures should be left to specialists. Of course, a cash-light new entrepreneur may have to become the "expert" but specifics on the marketing mix come after the general marketing strategy is formulated. Following a general strategy is the specific plan of action. In determining a marketing strategy, two interrelated tasks are essential: selection of a target market, and developing the most appropriate mix for the target market.[9]

Selection of a Target Market

In discussing the target market selection process, Edginton and Williams define a target market as "a homogeneous group of consumers toward which an organization may direct its services."[10] To identify a target market is to define that market's boundaries. The boundaries can be described in various ways.

These boundary descriptions are also referred to as segmentation variables. These variables are descriptive tools for setting boundaries (who is included, who is excluded) to the group to which the organization will sell. These same variables can be used to describe the consumer or user (see section on market research above).

The use of variables to define a target market is termed *market segmentation*. Market segmentation, then, enables a business to select one or more "segments" of the market toward which it can tailor its promotional efforts. Such segments of the total market are composed of people with characteristics that are similar in terms of such factors as age, sex, location, income, and preferences, and who are potential consumers of the business's products or services. The reason that market segmentation is important to a business's marketing effort is that it enables the differentiation between those people in the market who would likely be interested in the business's products and services and those who probably would not. The business therefore can target its resources toward the people within the market most likely to respond to its efforts. In addition, a business may want to offer several lines of products or services to attract various segments of the market. It may have one promotional effort directed toward young singles, another directed toward established families, and a third directed toward youth. Each of these segments of a market would have different needs toward which a marketing campaign would have to respond in order to be successful. There are three basic market segmentation variables that are useful in the determination of a target market: geographic variables, demographic variables, and psychographic variables (see Figure 6-8).

Geographic Variables. A geographic market variable divides people according to a particular area in the world, nation, state, city, or neighborhood in which they reside. The geographic variable can be an essential boundary because such factors as mountains, lakes, oceans, bridges, and freeways

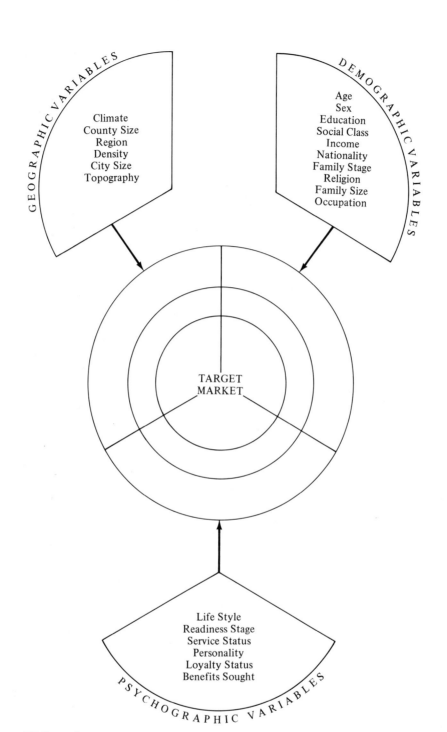

FIGURE 6–8. Segmentation variables to be considered in identifying a target market.

act as barriers to market access. For example, a bicycle shop owner, in the course of researching his or her market potential, might discover that a nearby freeway effectively limits potential customers from shopping at his or her shop because there are no cross-traffic thoroughfares reasonably close in either direction to allow patrons access to the bicycle shop. Thus, the shop owner may concentrate advertising efforts in areas not affected by this freeway barrier.

Demographic Variables. Kotler refers to demographic factors as being helpful in grouping large populations, independent of product interests or psychological characteristics.[11] Although demographic variables such as age, sex, income, and education have traditionally been the segmentation variables predominantly used in market research, recent practice has given equal importance to psychographic factors.

Psychographic Variables. Psychographic variables frequently account for the motivation of a user to purchase or not to purchase a service. It is possible and likely for people with common geographic and demographic characteristics to have entirely different reactions to a leisure service offering. Kotler explains this variance in reactions to psychographic variables. He lists six psychographic segmentation variables useful in establishing market boundaries and understanding user motivation: life-style, personality, benefits sought, service status, loyalty status, and readiness stage.[12]

1. *Life-style.* The life-style variable divides the population into such groups as "yuppies," "swingers," "family-oriented people," "jet-setters," "urbanites," "country persons," and "healthnics." Each of these groups has a unique orientation toward work, leisure, consumerism, politics, and environmental issues. They also display marked differences in their response to advertising.
2. *Personality.* The personality variable distinguishes between people who have a high degree of order, people who prefer flexibility in their lives, people who respond positively or negatively to spontaneous events and so forth. Some personality types may be best described as competitive, introverted, extroverted, passive, or aggressive.
3. *Benefits sought.* Individual service users, while consuming the same service, may be seeking totally different benefits. For example, backpackers may be seeking solitude, a test of their endurance, to live a simpler life for awhile, or perhaps just a change of scenery.
4. *Service status.* Service status is the familiarity of the user with the service. Thus, markets may be divided into, "nonusers," "potential users," "exusers," "first-time users," or "regular users." These groupings can be further refined to identify the frequency of service use.
5. *Loyalty status.* The loyalty variable describes the degree of attachment a user has to the product, service, or leisure service organization. In leisure service organizations, the owner or manager frequently determines the degree to which users display loyalty to the business entity.
6. *Readiness stage.* The "readiness" variable defines the buying states of the user. These states can be described as "ready to buy," "not ready to buy" (potential user), "no interest" (no potential), "negative" (no

potential and would dissuade others from buying), "unaware" (latent demand). The "ready," "not ready," and "unaware" groups are targets for advertising and promotional campaigns.

Keep in mind that during the market research process preliminary identification of a target market requires the application of segmentation variables. One outcome of market research is to verify the target market by analysis of the data.

Example of Segmentation Benefits.   A new leisure service organization offering river raft excursions might determine from secondary research sources that participants are between the ages of 25 and 50, mostly professional people, single, and live in urban areas. The boundaries of this market have been set geographically (urban dwellers), demographically (25 to 50 years of age), and psychographically (status). Further review of secondary data sources (journals, magazines, and so forth) might reveal that the raft excursion market (described above) can be further divided (segmented) by income level, regions of the country, and social class. Thus, the new raft excursion company has additional prospects for raft trips. Additional market opportunities are often discovered by applying only one new variable. By considering the senior citizen group, handicapped persons, or business executives (assuming the same geographic and demographic variables as the traditional market), it is possible to uncover a significant number of new target groups for sales. The management of the new raft excursion company has effectively applied additional segmentation variables to an established market and has identified new target markets to direct their promotional efforts.

The benefits of segmenting the market are readily apparent from the above discussion. The owner or manager of the leisure service organization knows who its customer is likely to be and where he or she is located. Other advantages of market segmentation are given below.

Advantages of Market Segmentation
1. It recognizes differences between groups
2. It brings greater clarity and precision to the defined market and its needs
3. The service provider is in a better position to direct and develop programs that will satisfy needs
4. An ongoing program of market analysis and segmentation leads to the identification of changing market demands
5. It directs resources to the most fertile segment
6. It facilitates the setting of pragmatic market objectives
7. It identifies future markets

When segmenting a market, three requirements must be satisfied: measurement, economic opportunity, and market access.

1. *Measurement.* It must be possible to identify and measure the characteristics and size of the market segment.
2. *Economic Opportunity.* The market segment must be large enough and have enough discretionary income to make it worthwhile; that is, the

consumers must have money to spend for whatever they want above their basic living expenses (or be motivated to find the money).

3. *Market Access.* The market segment must be reachable. Will the organization's location, service cost, and perceived benefits be attractive to the consumer?

Every market has segments, i.e., distinguishable groups defined by sets of variables with differing needs, styles, motives, limitations, and perceptions. In our raft excursion market example, we would expect teenage groups, middle-aged groups, and senior citizen groups to have different needs and motivational challenges. We should expect this uniqueness even though the only variation between the groups is age.

Market Mix

Marketing mix is an essential process in the market planning function. The process involves the manipulation of four controllable marketing variables: product, place or location, promotion, and price (see Figure 6-9). The object of the process is to arrange these variables so that the penetration (sales created) within the target market is maximized. The variables all influence one another. For example, if a business is attempting to market a poorly designed product or service, even the best advertising and sales people may be ineffective. In other words, the better the mix of these marketing variables, the greater the chance that the business will succeed in its sales efforts.

Product. Many leisure services and products begin as a result of an intuitive hunch, personal hobby, or personal experience. No matter how services and products come into existence, the management of the "product mix" is crucial to the success of a business. A business may have just one product or service, *a product item,* or it may have one or more *lines* of products or services. A product line is made up of similar product items. For example, a river raft excursion business might offer several different types of trips (each a service item). The sum total of product lines of a business is termed the *product mix.*

FIGURE 6–9. Components of the marketing mix.

There are various directions in which a business might want to move in the marketing of products and services. For example, the business might simply want to sell its current product or service to its current market. Or a business might want to sell its current product or service to a new market. In addition, a business might want to sell a new product or service to its current market or a new market. Finally, the business might want to sell a similar or modified version of a current product or service to a new or current market. Each of these different "product strategies" will require the use of different marketing techniques.

Products and services can be categorized in various ways to facilitate marketing efforts. One way that they can be categorized is in terms of consumer buying behavior. Using this method of categorization, products and services would fall under the following headings: convenience, shopping, specialty, and unsought. Marketing efforts may vary greatly, depending upon the category in which goods or services are found. These are described by McCarthy and Shapiro.

> *Convenience products and services* are those that customers want to buy immediately with minimum shopping effort, that is, where the busy customer feels he or she stands to gain little from making price and quality comparisons. In other words, this is routinized buying behavior.
>
> *Shopping products and services* are those items for which customers do shop, comparing the price and quality of various brands by visiting several stores, studying performance evaluations, and reading advertisements. Here we might see either limited or extended problem solving behavior.
>
> *Specialty products and services* are those that customers insist upon having and are willing to search for until they find them. Here the customer has already done extended problem solving and decided on a particular product as a solution. If the product's availability is unknown, the customer is willing to search for it. If only one place has it, as with some services, then he or she will only buy it there.
>
> *Unsought goods or services* are those items that potential customers do not want yet, or do not know they can buy, or are not looking for. Here the need has not yet arisen, or the consumer has not recognized that he or she has a problem, or that it can be solved with a particular good.[18]

As mentioned, marketing efforts should flex, depending upon various factors, including the type of product or service. When considering the marketing of *shopping* products and services, a business might want to stress the factors relevant to consumers, such as price or quality. Many leisure services and products are within the category of *specialty* items. Such specialty products are at an advantage in terms of consumer loyalty. Finally, *unsought* goods and services may require extensive marketing on the part of a business to encourage their acceptance by consumers. Often these types of services and products are new and consumers are as yet unfamiliar with them.

Many well-run commercial leisure service businesses produce a significant number of new users by referrals. That is, customers who during the reflection phase of the leisure experience perceive their experience to be positive will likely recommend the service or program to their friends. Private youth camps and river raft excursion outfitters are just two types of businesses that are often promoted by word-of-mouth. Once this self-generating customer flow becomes substantial, the organization may be wise in redirecting some of its promotional monies into improving further the quality of the service.

Any product or service should be tested for its appeal to consumers. The test market should be a small representative sample of its larger target market. Care should be taken not to choose a test market that might be distorted. The test market should be typical of the national or regional economy within which the business operates and be neither depressed nor booming as a result of purely local conditions unless the business will be operating only locally. It is prudent to carry out such tests on several test groups.

Depending upon the results of such market testing of products and services, a business may want to consider expanding, revising, altering, or otherwise changing its product to meet the preferences of test market consumers. It is important that a business's product, regardless of whether it is a convenience, supply, specialty, or unsought product or service, meet the expressed needs of consumers. Without a viable product, promotional efforts will be limited at best.

Some specific factors that should be considered when designing and marketing a product are the *product name* (brand), *packaging*, and possible *service* that will support the product. Both product name and packaging should support the image that the business wishes to convey and should attract the type of consumer (target market) to whom the business is attempting to sell the product or service. The name of the product or service should reflect the benefits of the product or service and should not be too long, should be easy to pronounce, and should be flexible enough to be applied to future new lines. Packaging should have a design and color that will appeal to the target market. Often a leisure service business will have a slogan or trademark that it uses regarding its product or service. Such slogans and trademarks should be simple, easily remembered, reflect the service ideal, and unique.

All products and services progress through developmental stages that are termed life cycles. Although organizations and industries also progress through life cycles, the term that is commonly used to describe this concept is the *product life cycle*. Knowledge of the product life cycle concept is very important in the management of any type of business, since the business will be affected by the stage of the product in its life cycle. Marketing efforts should attempt to correspond effectively and efficiently to each phase of the life cycle through which the product progresses. The four stages in the product life cycle are the introductory phase, the growth phase, the maturity phase, and the decline phase. The common curve of a product life cycle is presented in Figure 6-10. The vertical axis represents sales volume and profit and indicates the degree of market acceptance. The horizontal axis represents time and is divided into the four stages of the life cycle. The time dimension can represent days, weeks, months, or years, depending upon the knowledge desired by the business. Please note that the profitability curve does not parallel the sales volume curve but tends to peak earlier. Runyon argues that this phenomenon is, essentially, a function of pricing practices and increased competitive activity.[19]

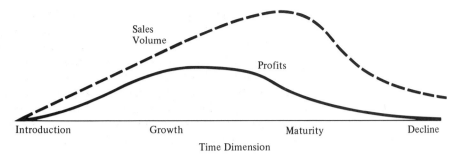

Sales Volume

Profits

Introduction   Growth   Maturity   Decline

Time Dimension

FIGURE 6–10. Typical four-stage product life-cycle.

- *The Introductory Phase.* This phase in the life of a leisure service or product is characterized by heavy promotional expense and slow growth. Growth is slow because of limited funds; service delivery problems that must be solved along with technical problems if a product is involved; difficulty in reaching a large representation of the market; and inertia on the part of consumers.
- *The Growth Phase.* During the growth phase, most of the factors that retard growth have been resolved. If the venture generates sufficient cash flow, more funds can be diverted to promotion.
- *The Maturity Phase.* Eventually the glow of a new service (or product) dims. As a result, the market diminishes. The reduction in growth rate exerts a downward pressure on prices and, ultimately, profits. Continued growth will require a service adjustment (renew interest) or an expansion of the market. The maturity phase lasts longer than any of the other phases and may be the incubation period during which destructive factors, such as incompetent employees, overextension of credit to customers, and service (or product) obsolescence are ignored in favor of other more "pressing" issues.
- *The Decline Phase.* This phase may be rapid, particularly in the case of a product that technology replaces with one that is functionally superior. The decline phase is frequently hidden until cash flow is insufficient (along with ready reserves) to meet current obligations.

Place. The place or location of a leisure service or product is an important component of the marketing mix. Providing the service or product at an appropriate time or location is vital in establishing a successful marketing strategy. Obviously, the physical location of a leisure service or product must take into consideration the desires of the target market for accessibility, convenience, and appropriateness of setting. For example, people wishing to purchase a pair of running shoes might be motivated to purchase them from an accessible and convenient retail outlet. On the other hand, a person desiring a high-risk adventure in a natural environment might be willing to forgo accessibility and convenience and travel to a location that is unique and suited to the activity.

Furthermore, the time at which services or products are made available is very important. This is also an aspect of "place." Products and services must be offered at times that are convenient for the target market.

The concept of "place" is also involved with channels of distribution.

Services and products are channeled through various means of distribution. As indicated in Chapter 1, a service can be produced and directly distributed by the business to the consumer. This is often the case with small leisure service organizations. Another channel of distribution is via a retailer to a consumer. Or products and services can be distributed first to a wholesaler who in turn distributes them to the retailer. The key factor in using channels of distribution in the marketing process is to choose the right channel or combination of channels of distribution in order to get the product or service to the consumer at the right time and the right place.

Promotion. Promotion is an approach used by a business to communicate with consumers. Promotional efforts attempt to convince consumers to purchase or recommend a product or service offered by a commercial leisure service business. In order to accomplish this objective, a business can use such communications tools as advertising, sales promotion, public relations, personal selling, and product publicity. Potential customers rely on promotional messages to learn of products and services and their benefits. Consequently, promotional style should attempt to conform to the expectations of the market the business is attempting to reach. These expectations can be roughly predicted by evaluating the market in terms of the variables presented in Figure 6-8. It is important to note that the expenditure of money alone will not guarantee the success of a promotional effort. The effort must be directed effectively in order to be successful. In market testing, promotion can be treated as a test variable and its effectiveness measured on the market sample.

The five components of promotion are advertising, sales promotion, public relations, personal selling and product publicity.

1. *Advertising.* Advertising can be defined as mass communication that is nonpersonal in nature, purchased by a sponsor such as a business. Advertising can be presented through various media, including television, newspapers, billboards, radio, and magazines.
2. *Sales Promotion.* Sales promotion is a phrase that describes marketing efforts designed to stimulate consumer activity, usually fairly quickly. Sales promotion activities include free materials, the use of coupons and contests, demonstrations, discount pricing, and door prizes.
3. *Personal Selling.* Personal selling requires a step-by-step strategy that involves person-to-person contact with prospective consumers in an attempt to convince them to purchase a business's product or service.
4. *Publicity.* Unlike advertising, publicity is not purchased by a business, but rather is nonpersonal communication about a business's product or service that is reported, i.e., in the newspaper, on television, and so forth. Businesses can initiate publicity through promotional efforts and via news releases in an attempt to ensure that they receive some positive publicity regarding their organization. Positive publicity can also be gained through involvement in community service projects.
5. *Public Relations.* Public relations can be thought of as a business's attempt to create a positive public image. A business's image is the total impression that it creates and the way it is viewed by its public. It is vital to its overall success. The image that a business projects to the public will

affect its ability to instill confidence in the quality of its services or products. Although "image" may be difficult to control completely, a business sends many messages through its daily operations that can be focused on the image that it desires to portray. According to Lee, the way that a business presents itself visually can be controlled. In particular, he encourages the development of an image that is consistent with the business's mandate via the following:[20]

- Company name
- Office appearance
- Design of logotype
- Signage
- Advertising
- Brochures
- Stationery, business forms, business cards
- Employees' appearance
- Building's appearance

He terms such image building as a "visual communications program," and suggests that a business review its marketing goals and plans for growth and development before planning such a program. Finally, he encourages businesses to evaluate their current communications in terms of the checklist on page 230. Other activities that can be used to build a business's public image are community service projects, public speaking, cash and manpower donations to worthy causes, and sponsorships of sports teams and clubs. A planning worksheet for a preliminary marketing communications budget is presented on page 231.

Price. Of all the areas of leisure service marketing requiring critical decisions, none is more crucial to market acceptance than pricing. Setting a realistic and effective price for leisure services (private camp tuition, health club memberships, leisure counseling fees, or theme park admission policy) requires that the market plan be carefully thought out, thoroughly researched, and meticulously tested. Pricing a product, on the other hand, begins with an assessment of the cost of development, research, and manufacturing. In the case of a service, there generally is no manufacturing cost (direct cost), thus we must consider pricing without a direct cost base.

Figure 6-11 presents three pricing methods without a direct cost base: going-rate pricing, demand-oriented pricing, and segmentation-differential. A fourth method, cost-oriented pricing, will also be discussed for comparison value.

1. Going-rate pricing is based on the assumption that the competition, if they are successful, have priced their service to provide an acceptable profit to the organization while their customers have accepted the price as fair. A disadvantage of this type of pricing is the fact that the leisure service organization using this method will be tied to providing a near duplicate service. Going-rate pricing also assumes that profitability is the result of charging a price sufficiently high to pay costs and provide a reasonable rate of return. Keep in mind that the competing business

A Checklist for Evaluating a Business's _____
Visual Communication

1. **What is your overall appearance?** Find out by gathering letterheads, envelopes, invoices, ads, brochures, direct mail pieces, signs, and all other forms that carry your identification. Look at them together. Do they project confusion or consistency?
2. **Do the materials have a look of quality?** Are they an appropriate expression of your image?
3. **Are your communications distinctive?** This is critical because no two firms are alike—and because competition is intense. Your image and message should be unique so that buyers and sellers remember them and do not confuse you with your competitors.
4. **Are you satisfied with your logotype—the design of your name on the letterhead, business forms, signs, and ads?** Is your name presented in a consistent style? Is it legible? Does it reproduce well in full color and in black and white? Is it appealing?
5. **Do you have a symbol?** If so, is it distinctive or is it a visual cliche? Does it add to or distract from your name? Do you use it consistently in all your communications?
6. **Are you identifying your company with a specific color?** For example, if you use blue on your signs, is blue on your letterhead? Remember, communication vehicles reinforce one another. Consistency is the key to building an identification system that buyers and sellers will recognize and remember.
7. **How do your employees dress?** While personal appearance is sometimes a delicate matter, more companies are establishing dress guidelines because they recognize that employees' appearance influences the overall image of the company. The same principle applies to the cars they drive, and the pride they have in their own image.
8. **Does your physical plant reflect your image?** Take a long, careful, and objective look around your offices. Are you making a statement of quality? If you were a buyer or seller would you want to do business there?

Source: Robert E. Lee, "Put Your Best Face Forward." *Real Estate Today,* September/October, 1981, p. 32.

---

may have an owner or manager who has created sufficient user loyalty to warrant the price level.

2. Demand-oriented pricing is based on the assumption that the various groups identified in the market research have a price of a service they find acceptable.[21] This pricing policy is frequently used by public and nonprofit human service agencies. Commercial leisure service organizations can make a similar determination of what user groups are willing to pay.
3. Segmentation-differential pricing is not recommended for commercial leisure service organizations. This strategy suggests that the organization charge a varying price based on the capacity of the individual user to pay. This policy runs the risk of producing a negative market response.

Planning Worksheet for a Preliminary Marketing Communications Budget

Project Activity	Your Staff Time* Low	Your Staff Time* High	Outside Services† Low	Outside Services† High	Buyouts‡ Low	Buyouts‡ High
	Estimates					
Marketing Communications Planning	___hrs.	___hrs.	$___	$___	$___	$___
Opinion Research	___hrs.	___hrs.	$___	$___	$___	$___
Graphic Identity						
Logo	___hrs.	___hrs.	$___	$___	$___	$___
Stationery package	___hrs.	___hrs.	$___	$___	$___	$___
Signs	___hrs.	___hrs.	$___	$___	$___	$___
Brochures						
Company brochure	___hrs.	___hrs.	$___	$___	$___	$___
Listing brochure	___hrs.	___hrs.	$___	$___	$___	$___
Other sales brochures	___hrs.	___hrs.	$___	$___	$___	$___
Special purpose brochure(s)	___hrs.	___hrs.	$___	$___	$___	$___
Publicity						
New releases	___hrs.	___hrs.	$___	$___	$___	$___
Feature stories	___hrs.	___hrs.	$___	$___	$___	$___
Advertising						
Planning and creating product	___hrs.	___hrs.	$___	$___	$___	$___
Periodic Publications						
Newsletter	___hrs.	___hrs.	$___	$___	$___	$___
Bulletins	___hrs.	___hrs.	$___	$___	$___	$___
Graphic Media (specify)						
_____	___hrs.	___hrs.	$___	$___	$___	$___
_____	___hrs.	___hrs.	$___	$___	$___	$___
Special Events (specify)						
_____	___hrs.	___hrs.	$___	$___	$___	$___
_____	___hrs.	___hrs.	$___	$___	$___	$___
Planning, Coordinating, Correspondence, and Expenses	___hrs.	___hrs.	$___	$___	$___	$___
Totals	___hrs.	___hrs.	$___	$___	$___	$___
Averages	___hrs.		$___	$___	$___	$___

Preliminary Marketing Communications Budget (total of averages) $_____

* Staff time will always be required, but hiring outside services will reduce these estimates.

† Disregard these columns if you use in-house staff.

‡ All expenses except your time or the services of an advertising agency or a public relations company. Includes paper, printing, photography, advertising space, sign construction, and special event expenses.

Source: Bob Clay, "Be the Wiz Who Plans to Win." *Real Estate Today,* Jan 1984, p. 37.

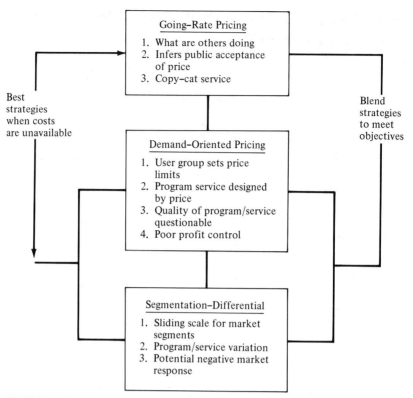

FIGURE 6–11. Pricing methods without a direct cost base.

4. Cost-oriented pricing takes into consideration the total cost of delivering the service. These costs include rent, advertising and promotion, telephone, transportation, utilities, recovery of investment capital, owner or manager's salary, and administrative expense. Variable costs must be accounted for, i.e., seasonal help, taxes, bad debts, and program supplies (in the case of an activity-based service). Cost-oriented pricing places equal weight on costs and market demand. The owner or manager pins the price to a unit cost (for example, the cost to keep one camper in camp for one day), and there are fewer adjustments needed as volume changes. Cost-oriented pricing adds a measure of safety to the market plan in that the manager is aware of costs and is reluctant to engage in price cutting to meet competition or to improve market share. Should one begin to lose price advantage or competitiveness in the market, the owner or manager might respond with a change in service or a change in promotional strategy.

It should be apparent from the foregoing discussion that manipulating the variables in the marketing mix is a crucial operation in market planning. Manipulating these variables is also an essential element in the ongoing duties of the owner or manager. The leisure market is in a constant state of flux and must be carefully monitored for changes. These changes, when relevant, should result in product, price, and promotion adaptation.

Advertising

Many small business owners consider advertising expense a necessary evil. Unlike expenditures for utilities, fuel, or postage, the dollars spent on advertising are considered by some entrepreneurs to be of questionable value. Yet advertising has come to be one of the most effective forces of American business.

Because we live in such a highly verbal atmosphere, many professionals do look on advertising as juggling words. They are under the misconception that they are manipulating consumers when they confront them with their slogans and themes. In actuality they are not manipulating anybody. Advertising is trying to communicate meaning to intelligent human beings; occasionally it fails in its purpose.

There are some basic assumptions about advertising that have biased our thinking:[22]

1. An overreliance on words. We have a belief that words persuade, they are the essence of meaning.
2. A belief in word magic. We believe that people are "stunned and miraculously transformed by a mere flick of words." Words such as "natural," "holistic," "back-to-nature," and "expert" will somehow change people's attitudes or move them to action.
3. As products and services become more alike, focusing on minute details is supposed to impress people.
4. Looking at the world from the eyes of the product or service, as if product or service has a life of its own that the consumer will learn to love.

The primary goal of any advertising program should be to *communicate* and *motivate*.

Communication in advertising programs has as its goal persuasion (motivation). Because of the persuasive power of the media on human behavior, psychologists have attempted to determine how communication functions in the formation of attitudes. There are four basic factors in the communication process: the communicator, the message, the audience, and the response of the audience (feedback).

Communication.

Figure 6-12 depicts a simple communications model. The communicator (leisure service organization) selects a message it wishes to direct towards its audience (target market). The owner or manager must first select a medium (radio, TV, newspaper, posters) to deliver the message. The choice of medium and the content of the message will, in a large measure, reflect the knowledge the owner or manager has about his or her target market. This knowledge will be in the form of the segmentation variables (see Figure 6-8).

The Communicator. The communicator is the person (or group) trying to bring about a change in attitude in the audience. Obviously, the most important trait a communicator can have is believability or credibility.

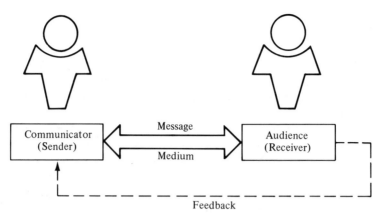

FIGURE 6–12. A simple communications model.

Credibility is influenced by people and organizations who are well-liked and trusted. People and organizations who are close to the audience in psychographic factors tend to be believed, and people (and perhaps organizations as well) with high status tend to be believed.

The Message. The message is the information that a communicator sends or transmits to an audience. The content of a message is obviously important, but the way in which a message is presented has been found to be an especially important factor in attitude change. The two most common ways of presenting a message are the "emotional" appeal and the "logical" appeal.

Emotionality, like credibility, helps the communicator get the attention of the audience. It must be noted, however, that emotional appeal serves to get the attention of the audience. Once this is achieved, the logical facts of the message can do their part in attitude change or formation.

The most successful advertising messages, therefore, are usually those that are constructed with the right amount of emotional content—enough to arouse audience attention but not enough to detract from the message itself.

The Audience. The potential service users are the ones whose attitudes are to be shaped (target market). This group (audience) has the psychographic, geographic, and demographic characteristics that determine the effect a message will have on attitudes. Knowledge about the target market (audience) is indispensible to the leisure service organization's owner or manager in fashioning a message that will fit his or her audience. This knowledge will come from market research and monitoring feedback during the course of operation.

The Feedback. Successful advertising campaigns require a link or feedback loop that constantly monitors audience response. If advertising campaigns are not meeting stated goals (measurable), the owner or manager knows to change the message or media or both.

Anatomy of an Ad

"The basic criteria of successful advertising are how creative is the presentation of product claims and to what extent the advertising helps the consumer in nontechnical ways."[24] Using Martineau's basic criteria and the preceeding communication model, let us review three ads for believability, type of appeal (logical or emotional), and creativity.

Comparing and contrasting Figures 6-13 and 6-14, we see examples of services appealing to readers of the travel section of the Sunday edition of the Los Angeles *Times*. The ad in Figure 6-13 is aimed at the potential traveler while that in Figure 6-14 targets the potential travel agent. There is believability about both messages. The bold face type of Figure 6-13 provides information. Any emotional appeal would come from reading the smaller print. In the smaller print one notices such emotionally charged words as "discover," "ruins," "sacred," "beautiful," and "magical."

The ad in Figure 6-14 is slightly more emotional in its headline, "Travel Careers in 4 Weeks." This message suggests that readers interested in entering the travel field can do so with speed and relative ease. There are no emotionally charged words, only the idea of a speedy entrance into the travel field. Neither ad is particularly creative, yet they should motivate interested readers to contact the respective business for cost information.

In the Sunday travel section the ad in Figure 6-13 is competing with eighty-seven other advertisements for travel packages—some half page and full page in size. The ad in Figure 6-14, on the other hand, is competing with one other travel school program, Figure 6-15. A review of this ad reveals a message with a stronger emotional appeal than the one in Figure 6-14, also one that is believable in that no unusual claims are made (such as immediate employment opportunities), yet emotionally appealing words and phrases such as "new," "introductory," "explore your potential," and "jobs to students who are trained" are placed throughout the advertisement.

SOUTHERN SOUTH AMERICA & EASTER ISLAND

22 DAYS * FULLY GUIDED TOUR
FEB. 10, 1984
Bolivia, Chile, Peru, Galapagos Islands
Discover colorful Bolivia with its Indian markets, gold museum, Tiahuanaco Ruins and sacred Lake Titicaca . . . beautiful Chilean Lakes area . . . 7 day cruise of Chilean Fjords to magical Laguna San Rafael Glacier . . . in depth visit of the Galapagos Islands' fauna and flora and much, much more . . .
HUNTER TRAVEL INTERNATIONAL INC.
500 Madison Ave., Ste 208, NY NY 10022
(212) 935-2000
COLLECT CALLS ACCEPTED

FIGURE 6–13. Advertisement directed toward potential travelers.

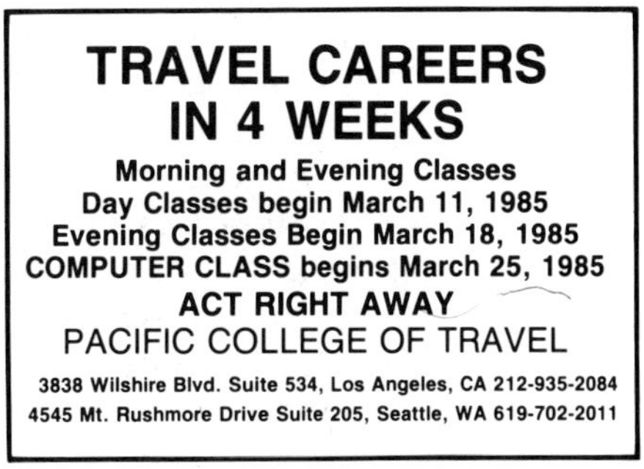

TRAVEL CAREERS IN 4 WEEKS
Morning and Evening Classes
Day Classes begin March 11, 1985
Evening Classes Begin March 18, 1985
COMPUTER CLASS begins March 25, 1985
ACT RIGHT AWAY
PACIFIC COLLEGE OF TRAVEL

3838 Wilshire Blvd. Suite 534, Los Angeles, CA 212-935-2084
4545 Mt. Rushmore Drive Suite 205, Seattle, WA 619-702-2011

FIGURE 6–14. Advertisement directed toward travel agents.

```
┌─────────────────────────────────────────┐
│                                           │
│  ┌──────────────────────────────────────┐ │
│  │  CAREERS IN TRAVEL                     │ │
│  └──────────────────────────────────────┘ │
│                                           │
│         BELFER INTERNATIONAL              │
│       JOBS GO TO THOSE WHO ARE TRAINED!   │
│                                           │
│                  NEW                      │
│         INTRODUCTORY 6 HOUR COURSE        │
│                                           │
│               LOS ANGELES                 │
│        TUE., MARCH 15TH 6:00 PM           │
│        WED., MARCH 16TH 6:00 PM           │
│                                           │
│           FULFILL YOUR POTENTIAL          │
│         IN THE CHALLENGING WORLD          │
│                 OF TRAVEL                 │
│                                           │
│           CALL FOR RESERVATIONS           │
│                                           │
│       TRAVEL TRAINING COURSES             │
│         1341 Lakeside Drive, Suite 504    │
│              Chicago, IL  30242           │
│            Telephone: 312 – 868-2000      │
│                                           │
└─────────────────────────────────────────┘
```

FIGURE 6–15. Alternative advertisement directed toward travel agents.

The ad in Figure 6-15 can be expected to produce more reader inquiries than the ad in Figure 6-14 because of its emotional appeal. What do you think and why?

Basic Points for Writing Advertising

Owners or managers of new commercial leisure service organizations will, in all likelihood, be required to write most of their own advertising copy. Once the organization is financially able, however, contracting with a professional advertising agency is recommended. In the meantime, there are some basic considerations to keep in mind when producing advertising copy.[25]

Check List[26]
1. Think before you write—refer to your marketing objectives and meta-objectives and review competitors' advertisements.
2. Have your facts at hand—data from marketing research should be reviewed.
3. Write the ad in its entirety—do not have a committee prepare the ad because this will break the continuity of the message.
4. Write a selling headline—refer to Figures 6-13, 14, and 15 and subsequent discussion.
5. Write adequate descriptive copy—give enough information to adequately describe your service and organization.
6. Make a layout that serves the reader—use pictures and phrases that are interesting yet authentic and believable.
7. Know how to calculate the space required by type—your local media representative can assist you here.
8. When using art, be clear about its message.

9. Read your own advertisements—be certain to read the ad when it is published and judge its effectiveness and impact in relation to other messages in the medium selected.
10. Be a prolific writer and reader of good literature—practice writing, take evening classes in advertising, and read well-written journals and books.

Advertising is directive communication. Its purpose is to persuade someone either to adopt a new habit or to continue some behavior. Such communication cannot be impersonal or dull. An advertisement must have high affective content. It must move people to act in your favor—if it does not direct behavior, it is not accomplishing anything.

An advertisement for a commercial leisure service should answer most or all of the following questions:

1. Who are you? The nature of your service.
2. What is your service trying to accomplish? Goals.
3. Who does business with you? Customer profile.
4. How long have you been in business and does your organization have a record of excellence? Contributions, milestones.
5. How will this service benefit the user? Expected outcomes.

These questions and others can be answered by using words, symbols, color, and sound. Communication includes all the ways by which people convey meaning to each other. Much human communication occurs through gesture, facial expression, voice modulation, symbols of identification, and expression such as clothing and hair style.

Media Selection

Marshall McLuhan, in *Understanding Media: The Extensions of Man*, proclaimed, "the medium is the message."[27] For the owner or manager of a commercial leisure service, selecting the right medium to reach his or her target market is indeed an integral part of the advertising message. Three factors influence the selection of media: target market boundaries, customer profile, and budget constraints.

Target Market Boundaries. Geographic factors will often determine media selection. If the organization's market is located within a small geographic area of a city or state, a national or state-wide advertising program would be wasteful. Local radio stations, neighborhood newspapers, and a direct mail campaign, on the other hand, would be more appropriate.

Customer Profile. If a travel agency determines from research that its customers live in an affluent area of the city, are married, are between the ages of 40 and 60 and are professional white collar workers, circulating hand-bills (advertisements placed on windshields of automobiles in parking lots) would not be very effective, because this market rarely selects professional services in this manner. Conversely, hand-bills might be an effective way to notify prospective customers about a local swap meet, a town meeting, or a sale at a local sporting goods store.

Budget Constraints. The dollar amount allocated to advertising affects media selection. A thirty-second local TV commercial could easily exceed the cost of running a small printed advertisement (see Figures 6-13, 6-14) for four consecutive Sundays in a large city newspaper.

Once guidelines for media selection are isolated from market research, the next question facing the leisure service owner or manager is the type of medium that will maximize the resources allocated to advertising. The following list represents some of the more traditional advertising media employed by small businesses. Keep in mind that most advertising organizations offering these media have research on marketing effectiveness, their own customer profiles, and cost per message.

1. *Direct mail.* Direct mail effectiveness depends upon the use of a mailing list with appropriate segmentation variables. Names on the list should reflect the customer profile of the business. Individual mailing packets are assembled and mailed by the advertising company. Each piece of mail sent out could cost as little as 75¢ per name or as much as $2.00 per name or more, depending on production costs of mailed material. The larger the mailing list, the lower the per unit cost.
2. *Radio and television.* Radio and television advertisement is expensive yet effective. The effectiveness of either medium depends on the medium's listening or viewing audience, the length of the message, the time of day the message is aired, and frequency of play of the message. Each station has an advertising manager who will furnish clients with the station's market research data.
3. *Magazine and newspapers.* These media serve national, regional, and local markets. It is also possible to select the magazine and newspaper medium based on reader interest. *Backpacker* magazine and the *Wall Street Journal* are two examples of special interest publications.
4. *Signs, posters, and flyers.* These media are especially effective for local markets. While some national products use outdoor billboard advertising, they do so by purchasing space in many major urban markets from national companies such as Foster & Kleiser Outdoor Advertising Company, Inc. Posters are useful in a limited way in that distribution and display areas are usually restricted for commercial enterprise. Flyers (handbills) are discussed in the preceding section.
5. *Novelty items.* Calendars, pencils, desk rulers, tee shirts and hats, Frisbees, cups, buttons, ash trays, and bumper stickers are a few examples of novelty advertising. These items can be costly and do not represent an effective way to penetrate a market. Novelty items are a good way to maintain visibility and create a positive public image.
6. *Community sponsorship.* Sponsorship of athletic teams, scout troops, and other community organizations is an effective way of meeting the organization's meta-objectives. Sponsorship of community activities, however, is more a public relations activity than an advertising strategy and, like novelty items, is not an effective way to penetrate a market. Yet such activity can help ensure the organization's control of its local market share by appealing to the community's loyalty.

7. *Other media.* Yellow pages advertising is effective for some retail operations. A review of local telephone company yellow pages listings under a given category will reveal if competitors are advertising in this medium. If they are, it may mean services are frequently selected in this manner. Realtors, plumbers, private schools, and printing services are a few examples of businesses that find yellow pages advertising essential to their advertising program. Business cards, brochures, holiday greeting cards, and retail store displays are other advertising strategies found to be effective in promoting and advertising commercial leisure services. Cable television is a new communication medium that promises to be an effective advertising vehicle. In particular, public access television allows persons and organizations to air personal messages (noncommercial) for a small fee. For example, Group W Cable TV in Santa Monica, California charges a reasonable fee for one half hour of air time. They provide the studio, technical staff, and video tape. A commercial leisure service organization might sponsor a show once a week, or once a month, on some facet of leisure services as a community service. The organization can mention its name as a sponsor at the beginning and end of the show. Check with local cable television channels for materials covering legal and production guidelines.

Of all the considerations used as guidelines for selecting advertising media, cost is perhaps the most common albeit not the most significant. Cost, too, is very objective. Table 6-1 is an example of a comparison of cost between two fictitious publications. It shows that the leisure magazine, while having a smaller monthly circulation and a higher absolute cost for running an ad, has a lower cost per potential customer. Since the circulation claim of every medium should be verifiable, the leisure service owner or manager should request such data before making a buying decision. Furthermore, advertising rates of most media are tied to the medium's circulation figure; the larger its circulation the higher the advertising rates.

TABLE 6-1. Comparison of Advertising Costs Between Two Publications

	Outdoor Magazine		Leisure Magazine	
Circulation/month	100,000		75,000	
Percentage of readership with user profile	20%		40%	
Potential reachable customers	20,000		30,000	
Cost of ad	$ 3,000		$ 3,500	
Cost of ad per potential reachable customer	$ 3,000 / 20,000	= .15	$ 3,500 / 30,000	= .12

Personal Selling

No discussion on market planning would be complete without reviewing the personal selling effort. No matter how good a service may be, how complete a business proposal is, or how ready customers are to buy, the commercial leisure service owner or manager will be engaged in some form of personal sales. He or she will be selling the business proposal to financiers, asking suppliers to extend credit to the organization, or selling the organization's service to a group or an individual customer. Within the umbrella of marketing, personal sales is perhaps the most immediate way to generate cash for a business.

A successful salesperson must be creative—not just an order taker. A creative salesperson takes the initiative by approaching the prospective customer, controlling the steps to the sale, closing the sale (asks for the order), and following through on after-sales service. In contrast, the order taker waits for the customer to seek him or her out, lets the customer decide what they need and when they are ready to buy. Order takers are not compensated very well. They can be observed in large department stores looking bored. Creative sales people are high-paid professionals who approach the customer (by phone, mail, in person), help the customer decide to buy (the service, product, or the business proposal), and demonstrate a genuine enthusiasm for the process. Creative salespeople can be the business owner, manager, a clerk in a store, a real estate salesperson, a camp counselor, or a bicycle mechanic. Order takers, by the way, can also be found in these same positions.

The typical adult purchaser of a bicycle will spend between $500 and $600 on the bicycle, equipment, and clothing. Some bicycles sell for as much as $3,500. Working in the bicycle industry today requires a great deal of knowledge in such areas as maintenance, manufacturing, economics, touring routes, and equipment design. (John Bullaro)

An example of an extremely creative salesperson is Walt Disney. Walt Disney had a dream. With money from a personal life insurance policy and a reputation for being a fair and honest person, Disney sold his dream to a group of investors and built the most successful theme park organization in the world, Disneyland. Disneyland, Disney World, and EPCOT (Experimental Prototype City of Tomorrow) would not exist had Disney not sold his ideas to financial backers, legislators, and the public. Nothing happens in the marketplace until someone (seller) sells something to someone else (buyer) for something of value (goods, services, or money).

Creative Sales Process

The creative selling process involves specific steps, each of which leads to a conclusion, such as a sale, call back promise, or future meeting. Occasionally, the step sequence varies, but each one must be a conscious effort.

Table 6-2 depicts the four steps of the creative sales process—approach, problem, solution, and close. These steps can be applied to door-to-door sales (excessively expensive strategy), advertising copy development, retail sales, group presentations, personal employment search, and raising capital. With a little creative imagination these steps are useful any time it is necessary to persuade someone to act.

A hypothetical case might best demonstrate how this four-step creative sales process works. We will take the case of Fred Miller.* Fred dreamed of owning his own outdoor recreation business. Fred had been an accounting major in college with a minor in recreation administration. Fred's first job was with a national computer company in their accounting department. After three years, Fred realized he wanted to work directly with people, wanted to live an outdoor life-style, and wanted to own his own business.

With the help of family, Fred raised $10,000. He planned on starting an outward-bound type leisure company that served the business community. His idea was to offer wilderness trip packages to individual entrepreneurs who in turn would give these trips to clients and customers as gifts. Fred made a list of people he felt might need and want such a service (prospects). The list included real estate brokers, insurance people, stock brokers, and attorneys—all persons who sold services and had a need to build good will among their clients and customers.

- *Step 1—Approach.* Fred sent letters announcing his wilderness company and how he visualized his services helping the prospect. Fred then called

* Based on an actual case history. Only the name and sequence of events have been altered to fit our scenerio.

TABLE 6-2. Creative Sales Process

Step	Process	Outcome
1. Approach	Contacting	Agreement to meet
2. Problem	Focusing	Agreement that need exists
3. Solution	Presenting	Agreement service is solution to step 2
4. Close	Increase tension	Decision to buy now

these prospects (owners of businesses) and asked for an appointment. Fred found three people willing to meet him in person.

- *Step 2—Problem.* Fred had researched the particular business before he met the prospect and discussed the persistent problem that the businessman had of holding onto good customers. The prospect agreed in principle with Fred's presentation on this problem and the fact that a solution was desirable. This agreement signalled to Fred it was time to offer the solution to the problem.
- *Step 3—Solution.* The discussion centered on the novelty of providing an all-expense-paid miniadventure to the customer for his loyalty and continued patronage. Fred argued successfully that even if the person could not accept the gift he would be flattered at the gesture. Fred offered to write the invitation on behalf of the prospect, giving the prospect review privileges of the letter's content before it was mailed. The prospect seemed excited about the concept. This enthusiasm from the prospect was a signal to Fred to begin Step 4.
- *Step 4—Close.* Pressure was increased by Fred on the prospect by reminding him the cost of the trip was tax deductible as an ordinary expense of business (promotion) and, furthermore, summer was approaching and the prospect's clients would need time to prepare for the trip. Fred pointed out that he could accommodate only a limited number of trips each season and his calendar was filling up. The prospect made out a check for $1,500 as a deposit on a four-day trip for ten persons. This single sale represented a $3,000 net profit for Fred's new business. In his first year of operation, Fred sold fifteen trips for a total before-tax profit of $40,000.

Personal selling expertise is particularly important to the commercial leisure service organization because of the abstract nature of the product (which is a service). Without a tangible product to take home, the service customer must rely on the integrity, believability, and enthusiasm of the sales person (owner or manager or his or her employee). Selling is essentially an organized communication process involving written, oral, and human relations skills. The successful commercial leisure service organization will make sales training an important part of the organization's marketing strategy.

Summary

No product or service, regardless of how well conceived and well planned, can have an impact on the buying public on its own. There must be a well conceived, thoroughly researched, and effectively implemented marketing plan. Marketing is a course of action that facilitates an exchange of something of value between two parties, i.e., money, goods, or services. Thus the objective of marketing is to ensure the survival (profitability) of the commercial leisure service organization.

Certain factors prove to be barriers to people spending in the leisure market. On the other hand, a'leisure imperative seems to be operating that sustains the national leisure economy through periods of high interest rates, inflation, and unemployment. This leisure imperative is the consumer's willingness to adjust personal budgets to accommodate leisure expenditures because of a shift in perspective from viewing leisure as a luxury to realizing it is essential to a person's well-being.

Leisure services have product life cycles. This cycle consists of an introduction phase, a growth phase, a maturity phase and a decline phase. Fads also go through this cycle but in shorter time periods, whereas stable services such as private camps, hospitality and tourism organizations reach the maturity phase and remain there for longer periods. Before entering a field it is important to know what phase of the product life cycle the service or industry is in.

The starting point for any marketing plan is market research. Market research is applied research in that data is useful to the organization for developing operational marketing strategy and establishing organizational policy. Market research consists of four major stages: defining the problem, developing a research design, collecting the data, and analyzing the data.

The marketing plan begins after the research data has been analyzed. The first step in market planning is to set objectives that are specific, actionable, and achievable. Marketing strategy is the step-by-step plan of action that results from the setting of objectives and market research.

The first step in the marketing plan is selecting a target market using the segmentation variables of geography, demography, and psychology. When segmenting a market (establishing a target market), three requirements must be satisfied: measurement, economic opportunity, and market access.

The marketing mix consists of product, place, promotion, and price. These variables must be manipulated to maximize market penetration. Once a marketing mix has been established, it is advisable to test market the service. Assuming that the test market data reveals a viable program is in place, an advertising program should be developed. The primary goal of advertising is to communicate and motivate. The communication model of sender—message—medium—receiver, feedback, should guide advertising decisions. It has been found that advertisements that have emotional appeal are more effective than ads based on logic. Ads, to be effective, must meet three criteria: believability, appeal, and creativity.

Selecting a medium for the message is an important decision in the development of an advertising program. Three factors influence the selection of a medium: target market boundaries, customer profile, and budget constraints. The one dominant factor in the media selection process, however, is budget. The percentage-of-sales method is the most frequently used. Using this method, a percentage of projected sales revenue to be devoted to advertising is predetermined. As a practical matter, the amount spent on advertising should be related to planned sales targets and the objectives for your advertising program.

Personal selling is the most immediate way to generate cash for a business. Personal face-to-face selling is an important skill for any owner or manager of a commercial leisure service and encompasses more than product sales. Personal selling is involved in raising capital, dealing with supplies, motivating employees, and representing the organization in the community. Creative selling involves four steps: approach, problem, so-

VISIT NEPAL

REACH NEW HEIGHTS

Trek through Nepal and realize a dream . . .
High adventure for those seeking the ultimate in
outdoor recreation. You'll hike in some of the
most spectacular and beautiful mountains in the
world, camp in the deep valleys, and visit many
interesting sights and towns along the way.

VISIT A BUDDHIST SHRINE

Travelling up a narrow mountain pass
you'll see a Buddhist temple nestled
under tall mountains, and it will be
like stepping into a time warp. A sense
of peace and serenity will engulf you.

EXPLORE KATMANDU

The capital city of Nepal is both exotic and
charming. You will walk among a population of
people that is as colorful as any in the world . . .
Newads, Bhotias (including Sherpas), and
Gurkhas. Hinduism and Buddhism coexist to
produce a rich cultural and religious environment.

Special Land Package for Three-Week Visit,
including meals, accommodations, and professional guide service:

$1500

Discounts for Students

Call All World Travel Services: 1-800-123-7654

FIGURE 6–16. Sample advertisement to be analyzed.

lution, and close. The commercial leisure service organization should make sales training an important part of its marketing strategy.

Study Questions

1. How do you define a leisure market?
2. Define and discuss the basic theory of marketing.
3. Discuss the life cycle of a leisure service using skate board parks as an example.
4. What factors would you use to segment a market for a private youth camp service?
5. Why is market research essential to raising capital for a new business?
6. List and define the four major stages of marketing research.
7. Why is it important to decide on the "who" and "how" in planning the data collection phase of marketing research?
8. What is the purpose of a marketing plan?
9. Why is segmentation-differential the least desirable way to price a commercial leisure service?
10. What are the four steps of the "creative sales process"? Discuss.

Experiential Exercise

Using the ad in Figure 6-16 as a model, answer the following questions. Discuss your answers with your colleagues.

1. In what ways does this ad appeal emotionally to the reader?
2. What logical appeal is present?
3. Is this ad believable? Why?
4. In what way(s) does the ad show creativity?

Assume you work for All World Travel Service. Your manager assigns you the task of developing an ad publicising an adventure type trip for college students. Select a country you feel would offer an exciting vacation package, gather some facts about the country, and write an ad similar to the one in Figure 6-16. Make changes you feel would improve the ad and be prepared to defend your ideas.

Scan local newspapers and magazines for examples of ads you feel lack integrity, taste, or any of the other criteria necessary for an effective ad.

Notes

1. C.R. Edginton, J.G. Williams, *Productive Management of Leisure Service Organizations*, New York: John Wiley & Sons, 1978, p. 255.
2. Philip Kotler, *Marketing for Nonprofit Organizations*, Englewood Cliffs, NJ: Prentice Hall, 1975, p. 22.
3. Kenneth E. Runyon, *The Practice of Marketing*, London: Charles E. Merrill, 1982, p. 54.
4. Ibid.
5. Richard M. White, Jr., *The Entrepreneur's Manual*, Radnor, PA: Chilton Books, 1977.

6. June Audrye True, *Finding Out: Conducting and Evaluating Social Research*, Belmont CA: Wadsworth Publishing, 1983.
7. Runyon, p. 88.
8. Ibid.
9. Edginton and Williams, p. 25.
10. Ibid., p. 257.
11. Kotler, p. 105.
12. Ibid., p. 110.
13. Ibid., p. 106.
14. Ibid.
15. Ibid.
16. Ibid., p. 107.
17. Ibid.
18. E. Jerome McCarthy, Stanley J. Shapiro, *Basic Marketing*, Georgetown, Ontario: Irwin Dorsey, Ltd., 1975, pp. 282–291.
19. Runyon, p. 294.
20. Robert E. Lee, "Put Your Best Face Forward," *Real Estate Today*, September/October, 1981, p. 32.
21. John L. Crompton, "Treating Equals Equally: Common Abuses in Pricing Public Services," *Parks and Recreation*, Vol. 9, No. 9, 1984, p. 2–3.
22. Pierre Martineau, *Motivation in Advertising*, New York: McGraw-Hill, 1971, pp. 2–3.
23. Ibid., p. 2–3.
24. Ibid., p. 88.
25. Ibid., p. 106.
26. Ibid., pp. 106–107.
27. Marshall McLuhan, *Understanding Media: The Extensions of Man*, New York: McGraw-Hill, 1965.

Close-up: Sportstown Athletics

Tom Cox is the owner of Sportstown Athletics, a retail outlet specializing in the sale of activewear goods. He currently operates three stores. Started as a family-run business, Sportstown Athletics continues to emphasize this image. According to Cox, "We like the family image. We like to be thought of as a family business. You can be large, but at the same time you can create an image of being 'small' and attentive to customer needs."

One of the things that he feels very strongly about in order to be successful in a small business is that you have to stay in touch with the books. "The person who does the buying also better be the person who is writing the checks," he notes. In addition, he feels that many small businesspeople attempt to run their businesses on their own without professional help. He found that as his business grew it became too complex to handle without the assistance of an accountant. The expense incurred through use of an accountant was balanced by savings to the business.

Another important dimension of Cox's business orientation is his involvement in the community. He makes an effort to become involved in community groups and organizations, such as youth sports teams. He is involved with such groups because, first, he enjoys working in the community. However, he acknowledges that it does make an impact upon people's perceptions of his business. He perceives himself as being very people oriented. Cox indicates that this is essential in the management of his business. "Our salespeople are also 'people-oriented;' they may or may not have a strong sports background, but they care about people. I look for active people who are goal-oriented and ambitious." In an effort to encourage productivity among his staff members, he attempts to structure their work schedules around their personal schedules. He feels that as a result of this approach, when his employees come to work, "they are ready to work."

Cox notes that his desire to spend more time with his family, as well as wanting to control his own time were major motivations for setting up his own business operation. When working for larger organizations, he felt that he was not able to achieve these goals. He tries to maintain a balance between his business and his need for personal and family time.

There are many challenges in running a small business, notes Cox. "A major challenge of owning a small business is that you are always training people; you have to develop plans and systems in order for the organization to run smoothly. This may be even more the case for small businesses than for large businesses," he says. In a small business, "*you* are the business! If someone makes a mistake it reflects on you."

Cox considers himself a conservative buyer. He looks to see what people in the area are wearing and attempts to identify trends. He attends large trade shows, but would rather buy from smaller companies who are able to respond quickly and personally to his needs. Cox sees continued growth in the health and fitness area, particularly in activewear for aerobics, triathalon, and jogging. He notes, however, that his business is constantly changing. There are new products on the market and new sports that capture the interests of people. In addition, there is always a new sports season approaching (i.e., baseball, football, soccer, basketball, and so on), which adds interest to his business and stimulates it. This factor was one of the things that attracted him to this type of business.

7

Financial Management and Accounting

The way that a commercial leisure service organization handles its finances is directly related to its success or failure. Many people think of financial management and accounting as a single concept. They may expect their accountant or bookkeeper to be in charge of "financial management." Or conversely, they may think that by engaging in accounting practices they are "managing their finances." Let us, from the start, distinguish between these two functions—financial management and accounting—that are so vital to the success of any commercial leisure service organization.

Accounting is primarily the gathering, recording, and reporting of the financial transactions of an organization for a specific period of time. It is concerned with providing information that accurately reflects the operations of a business. Financial management or planning, on the other hand, uses accounting and other information sources to determine how various management decisions or proposals will affect the organization's profitability. "Accounting deals with what has happened; financial management is concerned with what probably will happen. Accounting requires extreme accuracy with respect to money; financial management can be content with an approximation of future monetary activity. In other words, the two are involved with the same data base, but in entirely separate ways."[1]

In this chapter we will discuss the purposes of financial management, types of budgets, the accounting process and its uses, financial statements (including income statements, balance sheets), break even analysis, and working capital management. It is not possible to offer a thorough discussion of all of these topics in a single chapter. Our intent is to provide you with an introduction to these terms and concepts.

Why Financial Management?

Why is there a need to understand and employ financial management? Most decisions within an organization will affect its financial status and well-being. For example, a decision to employ a new training method in an organization may ultimately affect employee productivity and thus the organization's profitability. The acquisition of new technology, such as a computer, may involve retraining of employees, reorganization of work flow, and other activities that may also affect an organization's financial well-being. The decision to change a product, create a new promotional strategy, or expand the organization's service or product line all will affect the financial status of an organization as well. Since all of these types of decisions affect an organization's finances, it is important that they be managed in relationship to the broader financial goals of the organization.

As indicated in Chapter 1, people engage in business for a variety of reasons. A business, however, has as its primary objective providing a service or product at a profit. Therefore, the financial management of an organization should include the establishment of financial goals to ensure profitability. However, financial goals should not only be related to the organization's desire to make a profit, but should also be tied to its broad organizational concerns, such as a concern for quality of services, a desire to give customers fair value for their money, and a desire to be of service to the community. In fact, commercial leisure service organizations that have a broad, long-term perspective of their financial goals are usually more successful than those that focus on short-term financial gain.

There are other factors to take into consideration when engaging in financial management. For example, reinvesting the profit of an organization may ultimately result in greater value to the organization than dispersing the profit among the organization's managers, employees, or shareholders. Conversely, the decision to maximize individual wealth at the top of an organization will change the character and nature of the organization. For example, an organization may invest in high-risk projects that have the potential for greater immediate profit. Or the organization might trim the salaries and benefits of employees to increase immediate profits, although this might adversely affect employee turnover and productivity.

The financial management process and its related organizational goals take into account the business's ethical responsibilities. These responsibilities, as outlined in Chapter 1, include its human, social, community, and environmental responsibilities. Fulfillment or nonfulfillment of such responsibilities can affect an organization's long-term profitability. Taken into consideration should be the organization's responsibility to its consumers and employees, consumer groups, labor, and other relevant groups and individuals that interact with the organization and its operations. For example, consumers are very politically active today, and their demands for organizational responsiveness in the areas of safety, quality, durability, accessibility, cleanliness, and so on should be considered in the formula that produces the goals of an organization, including its financial goals. The type of relationship that an organization will establish with the community in which it operates will also affect its financial goals. Many businesses contribute directly to the welfare of a community by lending their human resources for special events, making direct subsidies and grants to voluntary and social welfare organizations, and contributing to public service projects. Last, environmental responsibilities are often mandated by government. Commercial leisure service organizations should weigh their actions in terms of both environmental costs and financial costs. For example, loss of public good will through pollution of a river or other environmental feature to maximize short-term financial gain might result in long-term financial loss.

The Purposes of Financial Management

There are a number of ways in which to view financial management as it relates to the operations of a commercial leisure service organization. In general, financial management is concerned with budgeting, raising funds, selecting and evaluating investment projects, and planning an organization's marketing and pricing strategies.[2] According to Gup, financial management can be classified into three categories: investment decisions, financing decisions, and analysis and planning.[3]

Investment Decisions. All organizations have assets. Some basic decisions must be made within the organization over how these assets are to be allocated. For example, decisions must be made about whether or not the funds of an organization should be invested in physical or financial assets. Physical assets refer to the inventory that the organization has on hand as well as its physical resources, such as equipment and buildings. Financial assets refer to an organization's cash on hand, money owed to the organization (receivables), and so on. The owner or manager of a commercial leisure service organization must make decisions regarding how the business will use its assets. These decisions will be based on its organizational and financial goals. These goals will guide the type of assets acquired and the type of investments made by the organization. Decisions regarding the utilization of assets should be re-evaluated continuously. An organization's needs can change rapidly and require that the way in which assets are used be restructured. In a small commercial leisure service business, there are many investment decisions that must be made. For example, owner of a restaurant might need to decide whether it is financially prudent to purchase additional equipment or retain and repair existing equipment.

Financing Decisions. Decisions about finance focus on ways in which funds can be acquired for the operation of a commercial leisure service organization. All organizations are faced with the question of how they will finance their operations. In order for organizations to expand, develop new service lines, or acquire new equipment, decisions must be made about the most appropriate way to finance them.

Financial decisions must be made, for example, about the balance of debt and equity that the business intends to maintain. A business that borrows heavily must pay interest on its loans, possibly adding to the financial risk of the company. The proportion of debt and equity of a business should reflect the degree of stability of the business and the amount of its expected earnings.

The decision to borrow funds should take into consideration the current cost of such funds. It might be wise to wait a few months, if possible, to borrow funds if interest rates are high but are predicted to decline. The prudent financial manager when considering the borrowing of funds will select the avenue most complementary to the needs of the business. Financing decisions must also be made regarding the amount of current income to be retained and the amount to be paid out.

Analysis and Planning.   In this chapter we will present a number of strategies that the owner or manager of a commercial leisure service organization can employ in analyzing the financial well-being of an organization. An ongoing analysis of the financial aspects of an organization can be extremely useful in monitoring the progress of the organization toward its financial goals. In addition, it is useful to compare the financial well-being of an organization on a year-to-year basis and also compare it with norms established by other similar organizations.

Financial planning is an activity that requires forethought, vision, and a sense of direction within a commercial leisure service organization. It requires that the owner or manager think through the financial goals of the organization, establish a profit plan, and then put this profit plan into operation. We often take planning for granted, assuming that a business will grow based on demand. However, when one plans for the future physical growth of an organization, one should also plan for its financial growth. Thus, financial planning should be linked to the long-term growth and development of an organization. This ensures that the organization has the necessary funds to carry out plans for growth. A particularly important aspect of financial planning is forecasting. Forecasting involves the use of various techniques to predict the financial future of an organization. By predicting the future financial status of an organization, an owner or manager can plan financing for the business. According to Scharl and Haley, financial forecasts serve the following functions:

1. Cash forecasts show when and how much new financing will be needed, given current operating and investment decisions.
2. The data obtained from forecasts provide a basis for decisions regarding cash management and investment.
3. Budgets prepared from forecasts provide a way to maintain control over a business's financial affairs and a signal of changing conditions that are reflected in the cash flow of the business.
4. Lenders, such as commercial banks are favorably impressed by careful financial planning, especially on the part of small businesses, where such planning is usually not done.[4]

Financial forecasts can be very specific or can be general. For example, some financial forecasts target one variable related to a business's finances (i.e., sales). Other forecasts are developed from the compilation of a number of such individual variables to offer a more comprehensive picture of the financial status of the business as a whole. The various accounts on a balance sheet can, for example, be forecast individually and then combined to form the whole balance sheet as a more complete forecast of the business's financial future.

Forecasts that focus on one variable of an organization's finances are usually based upon objective analysis of historical data regarding the business. Three commonly used forecast methods that are based upon this approach are trend forecasts, ratio forecasts, and statistical forecasts. Trend forecasts, as the name implies, rely on the analysis of previous financial trends to predict future financial trends. If, for example, sales have increased on the average of 12 percent per year for several years, then it might be forecast that sales will rise 12 percent in the coming year. Ratios can also be used in forecasting in various ways. One of the simpler ways in which ratios can be used in forecasting is by the comparison of historical data regarding ratios from year to year; that is, the determination of whether or not there is a consistent pattern in ratios over a period of years. Statistical methods of forecasting usually portray the relationship between two items, i.e., sales and inventory. This relationship can be depicted on a chart or graph and examined to determine whether or not the line or curve on the graph is suggestive of future financial activity. For example, an owner or manager could plot the relationship between inventory and sales to determine whether or not the business's inventory requirements will likely grow, decline, or remain constant.

The above information is related to the prediction of the future financial status of single variable within a business. In order to forecast more comprehensively the financial activity of a business, an owner or manager can use such tools as an income statement forecast, a balance sheet forecast, financial plans and budgets, or cash flow forecasts. Often these terms are preceded by the term *pro forma,* meaning that they are predicted or projected and not indicative of past or actual financial activity. The format for income statements and balance sheets can be used to record the actual financial activity that has occurred within a business for a certain period of time, or the same format can be used to predict the anticipated financial activity of a business for a certain period of time. Forecasting enables an owner or manager to engage in more effective financial management. By using forecasting techniques, the owner or manager can theoretically decrease some of the risk associated with financial decisions and in turn maximize profits.

What Is Accounting?

Accounting can be defined and described in numerous ways. For our purposes, accounting is the practice of gathering, recording, reporting, analyzing, and interpreting information regarding the business transactions of an organization. Accounting enables an organization to examine its profit or loss; to determine how this profit or loss occurred; and to determine the organization's assets, liabilities, and ownership for the accounting period specified. Such information ultimately assists the organization in its decision-making.

It should be noted that any accounting system, to be effective, must be designed to produce information that is useful yet reasonable and easily and quickly obtained. As depicted in Figure 7-1, accounting is a tool that should efficiently produce useful and relevant estimates of financial facts for use by such people as owners, managers, creditors, lenders, investors, and governmental agencies. Owners need access to such facts in order to determine the state of their investment. Managers use accounting information so that they can respond appropriately to the financial status of the organization. Lenders use accounting information when deciding whether or not to extend credit to an organization. Investors, of course, view such financial information when deciding whether or not to invest in a company. Finally, federal and state agencies use such information for tax purposes. An organization's accounting system should be able to produce financial information that is useful to all of these people.

The Accounting Process

The accounting process basically involves the transformation of evidence of business transactions into financial statements that can, in turn, be analyzed and interpreted. Archer has set forth five steps in the financial accounting process that are applicable to any organization:

1. Gathering evidence of business transactions through purchase invoices, sales slips, payroll records, and so on;
2. Recording the transactions as they occur in a journal;
3. Classifying the information recorded in the journal into special ledgers; for example, purchases on credit into an accounts payable register.
4. Summarizing and arranging the information contained in the various accounts in the form of monthly or annual financial statements.
5. Interpreting the information contained in the financial statements; for example, trends in earnings or relationships between assets and liabilities.[5]

Types of Accounts

As mentioned, information regarding an organization's transactions is at some point classified into accounts. Accounts are records that set forth the financial value of various aspects of an organization. Accounts may represent either positive or negative values. There are four principle types of

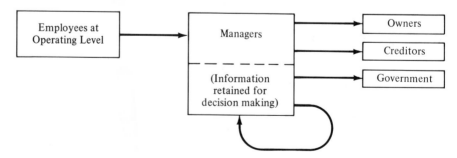

FIGURE 7–1. The flow of accounting information. (Adapted from John A. Reinecke and William F. Schoell, *Introduction to Business: A Contemporary View* 2nd ed. Copyright © 1977 by Allyn & Bacon. Used by permission.)

Commercial Leisure Services

accounts: expense accounts, revenue accounts, equity accounts, and asset accounts. Reinecke and Schoell have defined terms that are essential in working with these types of accounts.

- *Assets.* Assets are things that an organization owns and that have a positive dollar value. Their value is registered in asset accounts. Often, a large number of assets accounts are kept. Examples are land, cash, and accounts receivable (money owed by customers).
- *Equity.* An equity account is a register of claims or rights of different groups to a firm's assets. These include the claims of outsiders and the claims of owners.
- *Liability.* The claims of outsiders are called a firm's liabilities. An example of such an account is a notes payable account, which shows what is owed in the form of promises or orders to pay.
- *Owner's equity.* The claims of insiders or owners are kept in owner's equity or capital accounts. Examples of these are retained earnings or common stock outstanding accounts.
- *Revenue.* A revenue account is a register of gross earnings or inflows of value to a firm during a given time period. The most important revenue account is the sales account. It includes the total selling price of all goods or services sold during a given time period.
- *Expense.* Expense accounts are measures of the "using up" of the resources in the normal course of business in a time period. A typical example is a wages paid account.
- *Transaction.* The term transaction is used to describe any change in an asset or an equity. If we buy raw materials for cash, we must reduce the cash account balance and increase the raw material account balance.[6]

These different types of accounts can be related to one another and compared with one another to provide information about the business's financial status.

Cash Versus Accrual Accounting

The commercial leisure service owner or manager must make some decision about the way in which records will be kept in the business, that is, whether to employ the cash or accrual system of accounting.

Cash Accounting. The cash system of accounting recognizes revenues and expenses *only* when cash payment is actually received or made. If, for example, a customer purchased a product from the business via a charge, the sale would be formally acknowledged only when the cash payment was received from the customer at a future date. This approach to accounting does not always provide an accurate picture of profitability. It is not widely used in commercial leisure service businesses.

Accrual Accounting. In accrual accounting, the income and expenditures of a business are recorded when they occur, even though the cash received or paid out may be recorded at a later date. Because it involves the matching of associated revenues and expenses with one another, it is a much more widely used system of accounting than cash accounting. When a business using accrual accounting that makes a sale to a customer on credit, it records the sale immediately as profit. The business does not wait until the cash is received to record the transaction, as in cash accounting. This system offers a better measure of business's profitability.

Financial Statements

The keeping of accurate and comprehensive accounting records enables a commercial leisure service business to compile what is termed its *financial statements*. Perhaps the most important two financial statements are the balance sheet and the income statement.

Financial statements are essential to the effective management of an organization's finances for a number of reasons. They are necessary to procure capital from banks, financial companies, or venture capitalists. They are useful for income tax returns. They are used for auditing purposes and, in addition, provide information for shareholders where an enterprise has

TABLE 7-1. B and E Sporting Goods's Balance Sheet

Assets			Liabilities		
Current Assets			Current Liabilities		
Cash		$16,000	Accounts payable		$ 3,000
Accounts receivable	$7,000		Short-term notes		4,000
less allowance for doubtful			Current portion of		
accounts	$1,000		long-term notes	$_____	
Net realizable value		$ 6,000	Interest payable	$_____	
Inventory		$12,000	Taxes payable	$_____	
Temporary investments		$_____	Accrued payroll		$ 1,000
Prepaid expenses		$ 4,800	Total Current		
Total Current Assets		$38,800	Liabilities		$ 8,000
Long-Term Investments (detailed list)		$_____	Long-Term Liabilities		
Total investments		$_____	Notes payable		$ 20,000
Fixed Assets			Total Long-Term		
Land		$_____	Liabilities		$ 20,000
Building: $24,000 at cost, less			Total Liabilities		$ 28,000
accumulated depreciation of					
$4,800			Equity		
Net book value		$19,200			
Equipment: $6,000 at cost, less			J. Bullaro's investment		$ 10,000
accumulated depreciation of			Edginton's investment		10,000
$1,000			Plus: Net income after		$160,000
Net book value		$ 5,200	taxes		
Furniture/Fixtures:	$2,400		Less: Total deductions		
at cost, less accumulated			(withdrawals by		− 142,800
depreciation of	$400		owners)		
Net book value		$_____	Total Partner's Equity		$ 37,200
Autos/Trucks: $_____ at cost, less			*Total Liabilities and*		
accumulated depreciation of $___			*Equity*		$ 65,200
Net book value					
Total Net Fixed Assets		$26,400			
Total Assets		$65,200			

been organized as a corporation. For the purpose of explaining financial statements, we have created the hypothetical company B & E Sporting Goods (see Table 7-1).

The Balance Sheet

A balance sheet presents information about the assets, liabilities and owner's equity of the business for an accounting period. The assets of a business minus the business's liabilities will always be equal to the owner's equity. This is stated in the equation:

$$\text{Assets} = \text{Liabilities} + \text{Owner's Equity}$$

or (transposed)

$$\text{Assets} - \text{Liabilities} = \text{Owners Equity}$$

The balance sheet may be divided into two parts. On the left side of the example balance sheet the assets of B & E Sporting Goods are presented. On the right side of the balance sheet are its liabilities and the owner's equity. In this example, the business is a partnership.

In order to help you better understand the balance sheet, we will identify each of its components and describe what they mean.

Assets

- *Current Assets.* Current assets are cash and other assets that will be converted into cash within twelve months from the date of the balance sheet.
- *Cash.* Cash includes those funds that are actually in the cash register of the business or on deposit at a bank.
- *Accounts Receivable.* Accounts receivable is the amount of money due from customers that has not yet been paid. This figure should take into consideration allowances for that percentage of customers that may not pay their bills at all. In our example, we have calculated this "bad debt" allowance at $1,000.
- *Inventories.* Inventories are the raw materials, partially finished goods, or, in the case of B & E Sporting Goods, the finished goods that are available for resale to consumers. The value of inventory is calculated by determining either the cost or market value, whichever is lower.
- *Temporary Investments or Marketable Securities.* This item includes investments that the business has made, such as in stocks, bonds, or time deposit savings accounts, that will be converted into cash within a period of one year.
- *Prepaid Expenses.* Prepaid expenses are materials or services that an organization purchases or rents before they are needed. For example, a business might pay its rent in advance. These items, when added together, total B & E Sporting Goods total current assets. On the balance sheet the figure for the company's current assets is $38,800.
- *Long Term Investments.* Long term investments are investments that are made for a period of one year or longer. They can include stocks, bonds, or savings accounts.
- *Fixed Assets.* Fixed assets are property, furniture, buildings, or equipment acquired by an organization. Fixed assets are used in the operation of an organization and they are not intended to be sold but rather used to

produce the product or service of the business. In order to determine the value of fixed assets, the cost of each fixed asset minus its depreciation is calculated. Fixed assets, although not sold, may be leased to other businesses. In our example, B & E Sporting Goods has acquired fixed assets in three areas: buildings, equipment, and furniture. Fixed assets are depreciated on the balance sheet. Why is this done? Fixed assets will decline in useful value over time. It is important that this be reflected on the balance sheet. For example, a single piece of business equipment such as a cash register may be expected to last ten years. Thus, if the new cost of the cash register was $1,000, a *straight line* method of depreciation would have this item depreciated in value $100.00 per year. Therefore, after one year, the balance sheet would read: Cash Register (cost) $1,000, less accumulated depreciation of $100, equals net depreciated value of $900.00.

In order to calculate the "total assets" of B & E Sporting Goods, the "total current assets" of $38,800, "total investments" of 0, and the "total net fixed assets" of $26,400 are added together. This total would provide the sum of $65,200 or the total assets of the sporting goods store.

Liabilities

- *Current Liabilities.* Current liabilities are those debts that are owed by the organization and must be paid within the fiscal operating year of the organization. Because current liabilities must be paid from current assets, the relationship between these two items on the balance sheet is an important way of analyzing the financial well-being of the organization. This analysis is termed the *current ratio.*
- *Accounts Payable.* The accounts payable items are liabilities that the organization has incurred from goods or services that it has purchased on credit. Generally speaking, an organization has a fixed period of time, such as thirty days, to pay this type of account. Our example shows that the B & E Sporting Goods has $3,000 in the category of "Accounts Payable."
- *Short-Term Notes.* Short-term notes refers to the amount of principle that is due to pay off funds borrowed from a bank or other lending organization on a short term basis (twelve months or less).
- *Current Portion of Long-Term Notes.* Current portion of long-term notes refers to the amount due on long-term notes from banks or other lending organizations. Long-term notes are notes due in twelve months or more.
- *Interest Payable.* Interest payable refers to any interest that is due on either long term or short term loans.
- *Taxes Payable.* Taxes payable refers to the taxes that the business must pay if it is organized as a corporation. Businesses run as sole proprietorships or partnerships do not owe taxes on the business per se; rather, the owner or owners are taxed personally for business profits.
- *Accrued Payroll.* Accrued payroll refers to liabilities that must be paid in salaries or wages to a business's employees. The B & E Sporting Goods Company has $1,000 in this category.

These items, when added together, total B & E Sporting Goods' total current liabilities. On the example balance sheet provided, the business's total current liabilities are $8,000.

- *Long-Term Liabilities.* Long-term liabilities refers to debts that are not due during a business's current fiscal year. Long-term liabilities fall into two categories: intermediate and long term. Intermediate-term loans mature after two to five years, whereas long-term loans mature in from ten to twenty-five years. In our example, the B & E Sporting Goods has incurred $20,000 in long-term liabilities. The term *notes payable* refers to the amount due for money borrowed on a note. If money borrowed is used to purchase property, one type of liability might be a "mortgage payable."

Equity.   Equity is the amount that a business owes its owner or owners. In a sole proprietorship or partnership, the equity of the business is based on the owner's investment plus the income earned minus the withdrawals made by the owner. In our example, the owner's initial investment was $20,000. The net income of the business was $160,000 and the withdrawals made by the owner were $142,800. Thus, the total equity for the partnership was $37,200. In a corporation, the shareholders, that is, those who have invested capital, have the equity in the business.

Income Statement

The income statement (see Table 7-2) provides the owner or manager of a commercial leisure service business with information concerning the profit or loss made by the organization. It is the "bottom line" of the business. In our example of B & E Sporting Goods, we can see that the after-tax net profit for the business was $46,000. The income statement allows us to compare the cost of running the business with the sales generated by it.

Revenue

The first item that the income statement deals with is revenue. This is the amount of funds coming into the organization. In other words, the owner or manager, in determining revenue, determines the difference between gross sales and the cost of sales inventory.

- *Gross Sales.* Gross sales is the total dollar amount generated by the organization. In our example, the B & E Sporting Goods store generated $244,800 in sales. Gross sales are the actual cash transactions received from customers and other parties patronizing B & E's business.
- *Returns and Allowances.* Consumers may return items with which they are dissatisfied or when they change their minds about their purchase. In addition, businesses may incur costs associated with defective items or cash discounts to customers. In calculating sales, the owner or manager must consider that this occurs in a business. In the case of B & E Sporting Goods, customers returned $800 worth of purchases. This figure must be subtracted from gross sales on the income statement.
- *Net Sales.* Net sales results from subtracting returns and allowances from the gross sales of the organization. Again, following our illustration, B

TABLE 7-2. B and E Sporting Goods: Income Statement, 19XX

	Year to Date	
	Amount	% of Net Sales
Revenue		
Gross Sales	$244,800	102
Less sales returns and allowances	4,800	2
Net Sales	240,000	100
Cost of Sales		
Beginning Inventory	40,000	16.6
Plus purchases (retailer)	140,000	58.3
Total Goods Available	180,000	75
Less ending inventory	60,000	25
Total Cost of Goods Sold	120,000	50
Gross Profit (Gross Margin)	120,000	50
Operating Expenses		
Salaries and wages (selling and administration cost)	28,000	12
Commissions	4,000	1
Advertising	4,800	2
Insurance	4,200	1.7
Depreciation	2,000	.8
Miscellaneous	11,000	4.5
Total Operating Expenses	54,000	22
Total Operating Income	66,000	27.5
Pretax Income (after total financial revenue and expenses but before taxes and extraordinary items)	66,000	27.5
Taxes on income		
Income	66,000	27.5
Net Income (Net Profit)	66,000	27.5

& E Sporting Goods had total net sales of $240,000. Please note that the income statement has a column next to the dollar figures listed for each of the items presented. This column presents a percentage breakdown of the various items on the income statement as they relate to net sales. The net sales item always equals 100 percent. Reviewing the percentages found on the income statement provides useful information to the owner or manager in comparing various aspects of the organization's operation. For example, if the return of goods sold increased dramatically from one year to the next, he might want to investigate why this is occurring.

• *Cost of Sales.* The next several items on the income statement under the category of "Revenue" refer to the cost of goods or merchandise that have been or are to be sold. In the case of a business that manufactures a product, this item would refer to the cost of raw materials used in the creation of the product. In our example, B & E Sporting Goods would have purchased a variety of different types of goods to be sold, including sports clothing, equipment, shoes, and so on.

In order to calculate the total cost of goods sold, first the owner or manager must determine the beginning inventory of goods on hand. This dollar amount is added to the actual cost of purchasing additional goods in the period covered by the income statement. B & E Sporting Goods reported $40,000 in beginning inventory and $140,000 in additional purchases throughout the year. This figure represents the total amount of goods available to be sold by the business within the year represented by the income statement. In our example this figure is $180,000. In order to get an accurate picture of the total cost of goods sold, one final step must be taken. The year ending inventory must be subtracted from the total amount of goods available. Once this has been accomplished, the owner or manager will know the total cost of goods sold. As can be seen on our example income statement, the total cost of goods sold by B & E Sporting Goods was $120,000.

Operating Expenses
Operating expenses are the funds required to operate the business. There are numerous expenses with which the owner or manager must deal. In general, operating expenses can be generated into two categories: variable or fixed. Variable expenses refer to those expenses within the business, such as payroll, that vary depending upon the volume of sales and other factors. For example, the sales of many commercial leisure service organizations are seasonal; that is, their sales fluctuate greatly depending upon the time of the year. Ski resorts, for example, have their highest sales volume during the winter. Conversely, many water-based resorts where boating, sailing, fishing are offered have their highest sales volume during the warmer months of the year. Fixed expenses are those costs to a business related to long-term contractual agreements. For example, when a business contracts to rent space, it usually does this for an extended period of time. Thus, this expense is "fixed." Other examples of fixed expenses are insurance payments, utilities, interest on loans, licenses, and so on. In our example, we have not distinguished between variable and fixed operating expenses, rather we have listed both of them under the same heading.

- *Salaries and Wages.* Salaries and wages are the monies paid to persons to actually sell goods to customers. This may also include the salaries or wages of supervisory or administrative personnel. Note that B & E Sporting Goods spent $32,000 for salaries and wages. This is the highest operating expense that this business incurs. This is the case for most businesses and is especially the case for commercial leisure service organizations involved in the delivery of services. The "salary and wage" category may also include fringe benefits paid to employees.
- *Commissions.* Sales commissions are paid to persons based upon the volume of goods or services that they sell. Many organizations use the commission approach as a way of motivating employees to generate a higher volume of sales. Even in small retail stores, individual employees' sales can be recorded via computer cash registers.
- *Advertising.* Advertising expenses are the costs that are incurred in promoting a business. There are many different advertising expenses that a

business might have. For example, the cost of printing and mailing brochures, coupons, newspaper advertisements, flyers, and the cost of other promotional activities such as radio and television advertisements can all be recorded within this category.

- *Insurance.* In our example, B & E Sporting Goods spent $2,000 for insurance. This item was incurred to protect the business from theft, water, fire, lawsuits, and other undesirable consequences.
- *Depreciation.* As indicated previously, the fixed assets of an organization depreciate. This is a cost that can be calculated and recorded as an expense on the income statement.
- *Miscellaneous.* Any other expenses that do not fit into the categories indicated above can be itemized within the category of miscellaneous expenses. Miscellaneous expenses could include such things as the cost of leasing vehicles, supplies, and other materials necessary to run the business. B & E Sporting Goods spent $11,000 for items in this category, as reflected in the income statement.
- *Total Operating Expenses.* This item is the sum total of all operating expenses. The total operating expenses for B & E Sporting Goods was $54,000.
- *Total Operating Income.* The total operating income is calculated by subtracting the cost of total operating expenses from the gross profit earned by the business. This is done to provide the owner or manager with an understanding of what the business actually earned before taxes and before other special revenues (such as interest earned from investments) are calculated. Total operating income when added to interest earned provides the business with a calculation of its total pre-tax income.
- *Tax.* Our example income statement includes a category for income tax. A typical corporation will pay tax rates of more than 20 percent on the first $25,000 of income. On income greater than $25,000, the tax paid on profits is nearly 50 percent. In our example, B & E Sporting Goods pays no income tax, since it is a partnership and taxes on profits are paid by the partners on their personal income taxes.
- *Net Income or Profit.* The last item on the income statement is the "bottom line." It is arrived at by subtracting the gross profit from total operating income, taxes (where applicable), and funds earned on other items (such as interest). The B & E Sporting Goods business earned $66,000 profit during the fiscal year represented in our example. Their percentage of profit when compared with net sales was 27.5 percent.

Analyzing Financial Statements

An ongoing understanding of the financial position of a commercial leisure service organization is important to ensure profitability. The owner or manager must have a way of periodically determining the financial status of the organization. A balance sheet provides an owner with knowledge about the organization's assets and liabilities; an income statement provides an owner with knowledge about how much profit has been made. However, it is important for the manager to have other tools with which to analyze the organization's financial position. An owner or manager may be able to more accurately determine the financial status of the organization by analyzing financial statements in terms of various types of ratios or percentages.

Ratios and Percentages

Ratios and percentages allow an owner or manager to compare items on financial statements with one another. They are also useful in comparing items on financial statements from one year to the next. For example, if an organization has current assets of $50,000 and its current liabilities are $10,000, its financial solvency is obviously much greater than when its liabilities are $100,000. Such relationships can be shown via the use of ratios and percentages. It is important to remember that a ratio in and of itself measures one aspect of an organization's financial well-being. The effective owner or manager will use a number of ratios to provide an accurate picture of the financial well-being of the organization.

The use of ratios requires careful interpretation. Ratios can help point out trouble spots within the organization but do not necessarily reveal the causes or solutions of the problems. As indicated, some ratios can be used to compare current performance with past performance. They can also be used by individual commercial leisure service organizatons in comparison with standards that have been compiled on an industry-wide basis.

An owner or manager can obtain industry-wide ratios from a variety of sources.

1. Dun & Bradstreet
2. Accounting Corporation of America
3. Robert Morris Associates
4. Trade Associations
5. Trade magazine publishers
6. Specialized accounting firms
7. Industrial companies
8. Universities[7]

There are four major types of ratios or percentages that can provide useful information about an organization's financial position: liquidity ratios, leverage ratios, activity ratios, and profitability ratios.

Liquidity Ratios

This type of ratio helps the owner or manager determine whether or not the organization has the capacity to meet its short-term financial obligations. In other words, ratios dealing with liquidity help the manager assess the organization's capacity to meet its current obligations. We will discuss three types of liquidity ratios, current ratio, net working capital ratio, and acid test ratio.

Current Ratio. This ratio is calculated by dividing the organization's current assets by its current liabilities. A ratio of 2 to 1 is commonly thought of as an acceptable standard. The 2-to-1 ratio suggests that current assets should be twice the amount of current liabilities. In other words, for every $1 of current liability an organization should have $2 in current assets. An example of a current ratio, as well as the formula used to determine it is

$$\frac{\text{Current Assets}}{\text{Current Liabilities}} = \text{Current Ratio}$$

$$\frac{38,800}{8,000} = 4.85$$

$$\text{Current Assets} - \text{Current Liabilities} = \text{New Working Capital}$$

$$38,800 - 8,000 = 30,800$$

In the above example, this ratio would suggest that the organization has the ability to meet its short-term financial obligations. Lending organizations look favorably upon a current ratio of 2:1 or better.

Net Working Capital Ratio.   This financial indicator is calculated by determining the difference between current assets and current liabilities. It helps determine whether the organization has a financial buffer for creditor's loans. Creditors prefer that an organization have a large financial buffer so that their interests are protected, and they often evaluate this measure when determining the organization's liquidity. However, in evaluating net working capital, it should be noted that too much working capital can indicate that the organization is not effectively using its funds.

Acid-test or Quick Ratio.   Another ratio that can be used to determine liquidity is known as the acid or quick test ratio. This ratio is determined by dividing the total cash and accounts receivable by current liabilities. A commercial leisure service organization that has an acid test ratio of 1:1 is considered to be in a good position to pay its debts. The acid test ratio excludes the current assets that are the least liquid, such as inventories and prepaid items, since they are not as easily converted into cash. Therefore, it offers a more conservative estimate of an organization's liquidity.

$$\frac{\text{Total Cash} + \text{Accounts Receivable}}{\text{Current Liabilities}} = \text{Acid Test Ratio}$$

$$\frac{16,000 + 6,000}{8,000} = 2.75$$

In the above example, the commercial leisure service organization appears to be in a good cash position and should have no difficulty in meeting its current obligations.

Leverage Ratios

Leverage ratios are ratios related to an organization's debt position. In other words, they provide an indication of a business's ability to meet both its long-term and short-term debt obligations. The more stable an organization or business is, the more predictable are its rates of return on investment. For example, utilities have a very predictable rate of return and usually are in a position to carry more debt than other industries, where the rate of return on investment is less predictable. Certainly, the leisure service market in general is subject to large fluctuations in rate of return on investment because of the volatility and unpredictability of the leisure interests, tastes and behavior of people. There are three types of ratios that are useful in determining an organization's long-term and short-term debt obligation. They are the debt-to-total-assets ratio, the times interest earned ratio, and the fixed charges coverage ratio.

Debt-to-Total-Assets Ratio. This ratio measures the percentage of a business's total funds that has been provided by creditors. It is simply known as the debt ratio. The debt ratio can be obtained by dividing an organization's total debt by its total assets. Lending institutions prefer a business to have a low debt ratio; a high debt ratio indicates that a business may have to pay an interest rate that is higher when borrowing. A business with a very high debt ratio may not be able to borrow money at all. The debt can be reduced by paying off the long-term or short-term debts of the organization.

$$\frac{\text{Total Debt}}{\text{Total Assets}} = \text{Debt Ratio}$$

$$\frac{28,000}{66,000} = .4242 \text{ or } 42.42 \text{ percent}$$

The organization with the above debt ratio can be said to conform to conservative estimates of an acceptable debt-to-asset ratio. However, an organization should compare this figure with other similar clusters within the leisure market in order to determine what is an "acceptable" debt ratio.

Times Interest Earned Ratio. The times interest earned ratio measures the extent to which an organization's earnings can decline without affecting its ability to pay interest on its debts. This ratio can be calculated by adding earnings before taxes plus interest and dividing this total by interest charges. Again, this helps the commercial leisure service owner or manager determine whether the business can meet its interest payments on debt. A business with a times interest earned ratio that is at or above the average for the market will be in a stronger position to borrow money for development, expansion, or other needs.

$$\frac{\text{Earnings before taxes + Interest}}{\text{Interest Charges}} = \text{Times Interest Earned}$$

Fixed Charges Coverage Ratio. This ratio is calculated by determining the amount of income available for meeting fixed charges and dividing this sum by the fixed charges that the commercial leisure service organization has incurred. A fixed charge is a charge that an organization has incurred because it has entered into a contractual obligation. Fixed charges may include such things as rent, depreciation of equipment and buildings, and salaries. Regardless of the sales volume of a commercial leisure service organization, fixed costs remain constant and their amount is predictable.

This ratio is valuable because it offers the owner or manager an indication of whether or not there are sufficient funds to cover all fixed charges.

$$\frac{\text{Income Available for Meeting Fixed Charges}}{\text{Fixed Charges}}$$
$$= \text{Fixed Charges Coverage Ratio}$$

Activity Ratios

Activity ratios are also known as efficiency ratios. They help the manager or owner understand how efficiently and effectively the commercial leisure service organization is using its assets in the creation and distribution of services. Or in other words, how effectively is the business using its resources in relation to its sales.

Activity ratios are important in that they offer the owner or manager information regarding the degree to which resources are being used to their fullest. Sometimes an organization's assets are disproportionate to its market needs. For example, a commercial leisure service organization might find itself with an inventory of goods lower than the demand. As a result the consumer may not be served in a satisfactory way. On the other hand, an organization might find itself with more of its assets tied up in a non-productive manner than is necessary. Empty office space, too much idle equipment, or too much inventory are all examples of inefficient use of the assets of a commercial leisure service organization. There are four types of activity or efficiency ratios that compare sales to investments in assets: inventory turnover, average collection period, fixed assets turnover, total assets turnover, and liability turnover ratio.

Inventory Turnover Ratio.   The inventory turnover ratio helps the commercial leisure service owner or manager determine whether or not the business is carrying too much inventory. This determination is especially important for the leisure organization selling a product. The data for calculation of the inventory turnover ratio are obtained from the income statement and balance sheet. It provides the owner or manager with an understanding of the relationship between sales and the inventory maintained by the business. This ratio is determined by calculating the costs of goods sold by the business and dividing it by the business's average inventory on hand. The inventory turnover ratio of a commercial leisure service business can be compared with industry-wide standards to gain perspective on whether the amount of inventory on hand is appropriate. Average inventory is determined by adding together the beginning and ending inventories for the year and dividing this total figure by two.

$$\frac{\text{Cost of Goods Sold}}{\text{Average Inventory}} = \text{Inventory Turnover}$$

(Beginning and ending inventory for the year divided by 2)

Again, it is important to remember that a large inventory can tie up an organization's resources in an unproductive way. By calculating the inventory ratio, an owner or manager is better able to use the resources of the business productively.

Average Collection Period Ratio. This ratio provides information to the owner or manager of a commercial leisure service business on the amount of time it takes to receive cash from the consumer from the time that a sale is made. Again, this figure should be compared with an average for the industry as a whole. If the average collection period is fifteen days and the industry-wide average is twenty-five days, then the business is operating efficiently in this regard. On the other hand, if the business's average collection period extends to thirty days, this may signal problems and should be investigated by the owner or manager. The average collection period of a business involves two steps. First, the business's average sales per day are calculated. This is done by determining the total sales per year and dividing this figure by 360. The next step in the process is to divide this "average sales per day" amount into year end accounts receivable or average accounts receivable for the year.

$$\frac{\text{Annual Sales}}{360} = \text{Average Sales per Day}$$

$$\frac{244,800}{360} = 680$$

$$\frac{\text{Accounts Receivable}}{\text{Average Sales per Day}} = \text{Average Collection Period}$$

$$\frac{\$6,000}{680} = 8.8 \text{ or } 9 \text{ days}$$

The average collection period offers an indication to the owner or manager of the business's effectiveness and efficiency in collecting on sales. Because many organizations today give credit, this ratio is also a reflection of an organization's policy toward credit.

Fixed Assets Turnover Ratio. This ratio indicates how efficiently the fixed assets of a business are being used. In other words, this ratio helps the owner or manager understand whether or not the fixed assets of the organization (physical buildings and equipment) are being used in the most productive way possible. A business may make a large investment in fixed assets (for example, equipment) with a low return on this investment. In this case, it would be better for the business to liquidate some of its fixed assets and reinvest the funds in a more productive manner. The fixed asset turnover ratio is calculated by dividing net sales by fixed assets.

$$\frac{\text{Net Sales}}{\text{Fixed Assets}} = \text{Fixed-Asset Turnover}$$

$$\frac{240,000}{26,400} = 9.0$$

Total Assets Turnover Ratio. This ratio assesses how effectively the total assets of a commercial leisure service business are being used. It is calculated by dividing net sales by total assets. If the ratio is low when compared with industry averages, one could surmise that the business should liquidate some of its assets in order to decrease its current liabilities or increase its current assets.

$$\frac{\text{Net Sales}}{\text{Total Assets}} = \text{Total Assets Turnover}$$

$$\frac{240,000}{65,200} = 3.6$$

Liability Turnover Ratio. In addition to managing an organization's assets, it is important to also effectively manage its liabilities. A business's liabilities can include such things as interest due, accounts payable, income tax, salaries, and wages. This ratio is calculated by dividing net sales by total liabilities.

$$\frac{\text{Net Sales}}{\text{Total Liabilities}} = \text{Liability Turnover Ratio}$$

$$\frac{240,000}{28,000} = 8.5$$

Profitability Ratios

Profit is a primary concern of any commercial leisure service organization. As such, ratios that provide the manager or owner with an indication of profitability are key indicators in measuring the organization's success or failure. There are three ratios that are useful in providing information to small commercial leisure service businesses. They are net operating margin, profit margin on sales, and return on total assets. These ratios are all expressed as percentages.

Net Operating Margin Ratio. The net operating margin ratio helps an owner or manager determine a business percentage return on sales or investments. Taxes and interest payments are excluded from this calculation. Basically, this ratio is calculated by subtracting both the cost of the services or goods sold and the expenses necessary to operate the business from the sales made by the business.

$$\frac{\begin{array}{c}\text{Operating Income}\\ \text{(Sales } - \text{ Cost of Services}\\ \text{or Goods and Expenses)}\end{array}}{\text{Sales}} = \text{Net Operating}$$

$$\frac{240,000 - 120,000 - 54,000}{240,000} = 8.3 \text{ percent}$$

Again, the percentage obtained from this ratio should be compared with ratios of previous years, desired financial goals, and industry-wide standards. This ratio provides an indication of the extent to which a business is effective in its generation of profits from sales before taxes and interest are subtracted.

Profit Margin on Sales Ratio. The profit margin on sales ratio provides an owner or manager with information regarding the business's profit on sales, per dollar. This ratio is calculated by dividing the organization's net profit by its sales.

$$\frac{\text{Net Profit}}{\text{Sales}} = \text{Net Profit on Sales}$$

$$\frac{66,000}{240,000} = .275$$

Return on Total Assets Ratio. This ratio is useful in helping an owner or manager of a business determine what the rate of return on investment is for investors. Investors might include the owner, shareholders, or other investors in the business venture. This ratio is determined by calculating net profit earned after taxes plus interest on debt and dividing by the total assets of the organization.

$$\frac{\text{Net Profit After Taxes} + \text{Interest on Debt}}{\text{Total Assets}}$$
$$= \text{Return on Total Assets}$$

Ensuring Financial Solvency

Perhaps the most important task that a commercial leisure service business must accomplish is the management of its funds to ensure its financial solvency. An organization must carefully monitor and manage the rate at which its funds come into and go out of the business. The most devastating thing that can happen to a business is to be in a position in which it cannot meet its financial obligations and as a result is no longer able to continue in business.

Working Capital

In order to understand the concept of working capital, we first must understand how funds are used in a business. Using the example of B & E Sporting Goods, it can be seen that each of the partners in this business made a decision to invest a certain amount of money in the business. Some of these funds were initially used to purchase fixed assets that were necessary to start up the business and continue its operation over an extended period of time. Some of these fixed assets included a cash register, furniture and display cases, and so on. The rest of the funds formed an initial pool of working capital.

In order to understand the concept of working capital, it is best to go back to the balance sheet. Working capital is the difference between current assets and current liabilities. In other words, the working capital of a business consists of cash, accounts receivable, and inventory minus the accounts payable.

How much working capital should a commercial leisure service organization keep on hand? This is an important decision that must be made in any business. First, the amount of working capital a business should have will vary from business to business. Some businesses require a large amount of working capital to function effectively and efficiently and others may require very little. If a business has too much working capital, more than it needs, it ties up money that could be used more productively for other purposes, such as investments. Conversely, a situation could arise where a commercial leisure service organization does not have enough money on hand to pay its debts. Because many commercial leisure service organizations provide services that are seasonal in nature, careful attention to the management of working capital is important. For example, there is a greater demand for working capital in ski resorts in the winter months than there is during the summer. Such a business might even have to take out a loan to be repaid later, to increase its working capital in the winter months.

The flow of working capital within a business is cyclical in nature. Funds are used to purchase inventory, which is in turn sold, and to pay employees' salaries. The money received from sales flows back into the organization and, in turn, is used to purchase additional inventory, pay debts, pay employees' salaries, and so on. Working capital management essentially involves the management, then, of cash, inventory, accounts receivable, and accounts payable.

Cash Management

As mentioned, it is important to maintain a balance of cash on hand that reflects the specific needs of a business at any given time. In order to accomplish this, careful planning must take place to ensure that cash is not tied up unnecessarily when it is needed. The cycle of cash progresses from the input of cash from sales, investments, and so forth to the output of cash for purchases, repayment of loans or debts, operating expenses, and the like. Cash comes into and flows out of a business in a cycle.

There are three motives for holding cash in a commercial leisure service organization. The primary motive for holding cash is to enable the business to conduct its day-to-day transactions. Every business is involved in making purchases and selling services or merchandise. During certain periods of time, there may be a greater need for a business to have more cash on hand to be able to purchase inventory that will meet demand. Furthermore, in commercial leisure service organizations where the service delivered is dependent upon trained personnel, there will be a need for cash to be made available in order to pay for these services. In other words, as the business is engaged in transactions that affect its affairs, it needs cash available to operate effectively.

There are also instances in which an organization will desire to increase its cash pool in order to take advantage of investment opportunities that are particularly profitable. Although most organizations invest their idle cash, others accumulate cash on hand for speculative purposes. Finally, an organization may hold cash as a precautionary measure for use in an emergency. Organizations that have a very predictable flow of cash may hold only a small amount of cash for emergencies. However, organizations with a very unpredictable flow of cash may need to hold larger sums of cash ready for emergencies.

Inventory Management

Inventory management is especially important in commercial leisure retail businesses. However, all businesses carry inventories of various materials and supplies to assist in their operations. In general, there are three types of inventories that most businesses purchase: raw materials, work-in-process, and finished goods. Raw materials are goods that are used in the creation of a product or service. For example, cloth used to manufacture tents is a raw material. Inventory under the heading of work-in-process consists of partially completed items that are used in the creation of other products and services. Last, finished goods are those that can be sold directly by the business to a consumer. All of these types of inventories require careful management to ensure that appropriate portions of them are on hand at any given time.

In a successful commercial leisure service business, inventory should be constantly moving. That is, materials or goods purchased by the business should be used or sold within a reasonable period of time in order for the business to succeed. Knowledge of the rate at which inventory is being used or sold is essential. One of the most frustrating things that can happen in a business—especially a retail business—is for the demand for products or services to outstrip the supply of inventory. Consider our example of B & E Sporting Goods. What if this business were unable to meet the consumers' demand for running shoes? This would represent lost sales to the business. Conversely, if B & E Sporting Goods made a decision to stock too much inventory, they would incur holding or storage costs, and money spent on this idle inventory could be used elsewhere to more advantage.

Accounts Receivable Management

In certain business transactions credit is extended to the consumer. In accounting terms, payments due a business by its customers and other parties resulting from the extension of credit are called "accounts receivable." Credit can be extended to customers for specific periods of time. It is most common to extend credit on a 30-day to 120-day basis. It is important for the owner or manager in a commercial leisure service business to manage accounts receivable and understand how they can influence the cash flow of the organization.

Businesses may establish a format for aging accounts receivable. This means that they categorize accounts receivable in terms of how long they have been outstanding. This enables a business to take appropriate collective action that complements the age of the various accounts outstanding. Such a system also enables a business, over a period of time, to predict how long it will take to convert accounts receivable into cash and what percentage of accounts receivable will likely be unpaid. It is important for the owner or manager to realize that it can take a great deal of time to convert accounts receivable into cash. The billing card collection cycle should be analyzed and evaluated to ensure that accounts receivable are converted to cash as quickly as planned.

Managing Accounts Payable

As is the case with other businesses, a business will purchase items on credit. In other words, a business may make an arrangement to receive goods or services on credit from another business. In accounting terms, payments due to other businesses are "accounts payable." Often the terms for payment for credit extended to a business carry incentives for prompt payment. Furthermore, because carrying an amount due on credit often involves the payment of interest by a business, early payment can result in savings. Conversely, sometimes it may be more advantageous for a business to pay an account payable as late as possible in order to maintain its cash pool for other transactions of higher priority. A business should *always* pay its debts within the negotiated time limit; however, within this time limit accounts payable can be managed to best serve the interests of the commercial leisure service business.

Budgeting

A budget is a mechanism for both planning and controlling within commercial leisure service organizations. Using a budget as a plan provides a mechanism for forecasting future costs as well as revenues. It is a method for translating ideas for services into a financial statement that can provide a foundation upon which to base decisions regarding the number of people necessary to operate a business, the type and quantity of supplies and equipment needed, the facilities needed, and so on. A budget as a control mechanism provides a standard against which the manager or owner can compare actual expenditures. If a certain amount of money has been budgeted for an item and actual expenditures exceed this amount, a budget sends up a red flag prompting closer examination of the expenditure. An organization can budget so that the end result is a certain amount of profit. In fact, it is desirable to establish financial goals that specifically target desired return in order to produce profit. Thus, a budget is a very important instrument in the financial management of any commercial leisure service organization.

There are numerous advantages to the development of a budget, no matter how small the operation. A budget is the cornerstone of good financial planning. Edginton and Griffith state that there are four major advantages to budgeting:

1. The budget translates programs and other services into financial terms.
2. The budget provides a mechanism for appraising staff, officials, and other interested parties in the financial operations of the organization.
3. Budgeting provides a means for systematically identifying and evaluating procedures, programs, and other services.
4. The budget provides a record of the financial transactions that take place within the organization itself and with other persons and organizations.[8]

Often larger commercial leisure service organizations will develop programs of financial compensation based on the ability of the individual manager to generate and sustain a level of profit. In this type of situation, the budget is invaluable in helping the manager share in the profits of the organization through careful financial planning and control.

Operating and Capital Budgets

There are two types of budgets that are used in commercial leisure service organizations: operating budgets and capital budgets. An operating budget is also referred to as a profit plan. Establishment of an operating budget provides a statement that can be used to project revenues, estimate expenditures, and determine the projected profit desired within a given period of time. Operating budgets can be prepared quarterly, semi-annually, or annually, depending upon the stability of the market within which the organization operates and the stability of the organization itself. The less stable the situation, the more frequently an organization might want to carry out a review of its financial status.

The first step in an operating budget is the projection or forecasting of sales. In other words, the manager or owner will first want to determine as specifically as possible what future revenues will be. This is an extremely critical part of the budgeting process and in part is based on past experience as well as on the owner's or manager's knowledge of present market and other conditions. This forecast of sales provides a base upon which the owner or manager can determine estimates for future expenditures. The determination of estimates for future costs is the second step in an operating budget. Often, the preparation of a budget is carried out with the assistance of other persons within the organization in both superior and subordinate roles. For example, in a large commercial leisure service organization such as a restaurant, an owner might collaborate with his restaurant manager as well as his area sales manager in order to develop the budget. Obviously, it is important to consider all of the factors that may be affecting the organization as a whole when establishing a budget for a particular unit within an organization.

All of the units within a given commercial leisure service organization can combine their budgets to provide an overall organizational budget. Participation in the budget process is something that should be encouraged. It helps persons who are committed to the overall philosophy of a commercial leisure service organization to understand in realistic and practical terms how its goals are to be attained. We feel that this orientation can be especially useful in businesses that emphasize profit as a way of contributing to the growth of the organization. In larger commercial leisure service businesses that are organized as corporations, a budget will be approved by its board of directors.

The second major type of budget used in commercial leisure service businesses is known as a capital budget. It assists an organization in its plans to finance the acquisition of large pieces of equipment, new facilities, or long-term research projects. A capital budget provides funding for the more permanent and long-term needs of the organization. Capital budgets are usually drawn up over a longer period of time than operational budgets. For example, it is not unusual for a business in projecting its long-term needs to set forth a five-year or ten-year expansion program requiring a separate capital budget. Often, an organization will set up a depreciation reserve as a part of its capital budget to offset the cost of depreciation of equipment. The assumption in doing this is that the equipment will ulti-mately have to be replaced and a reserve fund will be available to do this. Funds for capital projects primarily come from two sources. First, they can be retained from the earnings of the organization. Money retained from earnings may be invested yet ear-marked for capital improvements and used when needed. The second source for capital projects is money from outside sources. In the case of a corporation, this may involve issuing stock. It may also involve a decision to borrow funds for capital improvements. In this latter case, the owner's or manager's ability to accurately determine the potential future earnings of the organization is essential.

Developing a Profit Plan

Often people look at budgeting from a negative viewpoint. However, budgeting is a key factor in both long-term and short-term financial sol-vency. Budgeting is a way of planning for profit. Hence, the term *profit plan* can be substituted for the term *budget*. It is important to remember that business is sometimes at a high volume and at other times it is sub-stantially lower. For example, as mentioned previously, some resorts will take in more cash during particular times of the year and less during other times of the year. Likewise, their expenditures may fluctuate and be tied to peak periods of business during the year. These changes should be an-ticipated, and planning for them should take place ahead of time to ensure that the organization earns a profit.

The formulation of a profit plan first begins with the establishment of sales and cost estimates. One source of information that can be used to aid the owner or manager in the estimation of budget items is the records of previous years. However, no business is static from one year to the next. Therefore, estimating potential sales and costs (expenditures) requires that the owner or manager take into consideration a variety of factors when estimating the profit plan. Some of these factors are the effects of inflation on the costs of products and services, changing market conditions, con-sumer preferences, the influence of governmental regulations (federal, state, and local), the cost of more highly skilled labor if mandated, and so on. In addition, estimates regarding profitability, liquidity, and leverage ob-tained from trade associations, financial institutions, and other organizations can be used in developing estimates for items on the budget. For example, trade associations often present information concerning the industry norms for profit margins on sales. Such information can be used as a guide to help plan a business's profit plan. The end result of this process is the development by the owner or manager a "best guess" as to the sales and expenses of the business.

Most budgets or profit plans are established on a yearly basis. However, for the process to be truly effective, the profit plan must be broken down into smaller units. The majority of businesses establish monthly projections that enable them to carefully analyze their sales, costs, and gains or losses for each month. The format of the profit plan is similar to the income state-ment. Using our income statement from B & E Sporting Goods, we have developed a profit plan that sets forth, on a month-to-month basis, the sales and costs of the business (see Table 7-3).

As can be seen from viewing the monthly projections for the profit

TABLE 7-3. B and E Sporting Goods Monthly Projections for Profit Plan

	January	February	March	April	May	June	July	August	September	October	November	December	Total
Sales	$9,800	$7,650	$10,800	$7,580	$9,075	$10,500	$25,300	$19,800	$25,000	$30,125	$40,370	$43,500	$240,000
Less cost of sales	7,140	2,045	4,050	4,125	5,825	7,025	10,390	13,600	14,300	16,500	18,000	17,000	120,000
Gross Profit (Gross margin)	$2,660	$5,605	$6,750	$3,455	$3,250	$3,475	$14,910	$6,200	$11,200	$13,625	$22,370	$26,500	$120,000
Less Operating Expenses													
Salaries and wages	$1,500	$1,500	$1,500	$2,000	$2,000	$2,000	$2,500	$2,500	$2,500	$3,330	$3,330	$3,340	$28,000
Commissions	100	100	100	100	100	100	250	250	400	500	500	500	4,000
Advertising					1,000	1,000	400	1,000	400	1,000	1,000		4,800
Depreciation	350	350	350	350	350	350	350	350	350	350	350	350	4,200
Insurance	160	160	160	160	160	160	160	160	160	160	200	200	2,000
Rent	500	500	500	500	500	500	500	500	500	500	500	500	6,000
Telephone	100	100	100	100	100	100	100	100	100	100	100	100	1,200
Other	300	300	300	300	300	300	300	300	300	300	400	400	3,800
Total	$3,010	$3,010	$3,010	$3,510	$4,510	$4,510	$4,560	$5,160	$4,710	$6,240	$6,880	$5,880	$54,000

plan or budget, various items on the income statement are represented. For example, the sales are represented for each month as well as the cost of the sales for inventory. Thus, in each month, the gross profit can be determined. One will note that the gross profit is larger in some months than in others. As one would expect, sales were high in the months of November and December, traditional strong sales months for retail businesses. Table 7-3 also presents operating expenses of the business. They vary from month to month, depending upon the volume of sales. It is evident that some expenses remain constant whereas others vary. This is especially the case with salaries and wages, where the owner or manager might want to forecast the greater need for additional sales help during months in which sales volume is greater.

This profit plan presents a healthy financial forecast for B & E Sporting Goods. Note that we have not tried to estimate to the nearest cent, but have rounded figures to the nearest dollar. The sales forecast for B & E is for $240,000. The cost of sales is $120,000. This leaves a gross profit of $120,000. B & E's operating expenses are $54,000. When the operating expenses are subtracted from the gross profit, this leaves the business with a pretax income of $66,000, or about 27.5 percent of sales. This is an excellent return.

When starting a new business, the development of a profit plan is the owner's or manager's prediction of what he or she thinks is likely to occur. Financially, however, as a business operates from year to year, historical information can be established to more accurately predict or forecast sales and expenses. Furthermore, when tied to the larger economic picture, the owner or manager should be able to predict quite accurately the financial future of the organization. An owner or manager with a long-term perspective of an organization's finances can begin to determine more accurately the influence of, for example, increased advertising on sales. With the use of microcomputers, information can be stored, retrieved, and updated very rapidly so that the profit plan can be periodically revised to reflect the current financial status of the organization.

Cash Flow Forecast Statement

Establishing a profit plan helps a commercial leisure service business understand one of the most important factors in ensuring the financial solvency of the business. If we look back at Table 7-3, it can be seen that in certain months B & E Sporting Goods is producing a surplus of funds, whereas in others it has a deficit. Table 7-4 presents the surplus or deficits for the months of January through July. As can be seen, B & E Sporting Goods has a deficit in the months of January, April and June. In the months of February, March, May, and July it has a surplus of funds.

In order for B & E Sporting Goods to remain solvent, it must be able to meet its financial obligations twelve months of the year, even though in some months it may operate with a deficit. This necessitates that the business secure additional funds for the months in which it has a deficit. In order to determine the exact amount of funds needed from month to month, a cash flow forecast can be used. For the purposes of this example, we have assumed that the business is starting with no cash pools, cash on hand (although this is usually not the case). In Table 7-4, we can see that

TABLE 7-4. B and E Sporting Goods Cash Flow Analysis

	January	February	March	April	May	June	July
A. Sales	$9,800	$7,650	$10,800	$7,580	$9,075	$10,500	$25,300
Less cost of sales	7,140	2,045	4,050	4,125	5,825	7,025	10,390
Gross Profit (Gross Margin)	$2,660	$5,605	$ 6,750	$3,455	$3,250	$ 3,475	$14,910
B. Less Operating expenses:							
Salaries and wages	$1,500	$1,500	$ 1,500	$2,000	$2,000	$ 2,000	$ 2,500
Commissions	100	100	100	100	100	100	250
Advertising					1,000	1,000	400
Depreciation	350	350	350	350	350	350	350
Insurance	160	160	160	160	160	160	160
Rent	500	500	500	500	500	500	500
Telephone	100	100	100	100	100	100	100
Other	300	300	300	300	300	300	300
Total	$3,010	$3,010	$ 3,010	$3,510	$4,510	$ 4,510	$ 4,560
C. Cash Flow from Operations							
Surplus (or deficit) (C = A − B)	($350)	$2,595	$ 3,740	($55)	$1,260	($1,035)	$10,410
D. Cash Balance:							
Cash at Start	0	$ 150	$ 2,745	$ 6,485	$6,430	$ 7,690	$ 6,655
Cash Flow from Operations	($350)	2,595	3,740	(55)	1,260	(1,035)	10,410
Bank (L) or Repayment (R)	500L						(500)R
E. Cash at End	$ 150	$2,745	$ 6,485	$6,430	$7,690	$ 6,655	$16,565

during the month of January the business had a month's-end deficit of $350. In order to ensure that the business had sufficient cash to cover this deficit, a $500 loan was obtained. This provided a $150 cash balance for the beginning of the month of February. We also were able to generate $2,595 from the operation. The addition of these two figures provides us with the cash balance for the beginning of the next month, March. Working through the same process for each of the twelve months of the year, in addition to repaying the $500 loan for the month of July, provides us with an accurate analysis of our business needs.

Cash flow forecasting is useful from several standpoints. First and most obviously it helps an owner or manager understand how much cash is needed to run a business in such a way that it remains solvent from week to week and month to month. If its cash flow is not sufficient during certain periods, the business must borrow funds or accelerate its collection of accounts receivable. Furthermore, cash flow forecasting can be useful in helping the owner or manager of a busiess plan short-term investments. For example, during months where the business has a surplus of funds, it would be prudent to invest them on a short-term basis.

Break Even Analysis

A useful analytical tool that is available to commercial leisure service organizations is the break even analysis. Break even analysis can help an owner or manager calculate the point at which the revenues generated from sales of a given product or service meet the expenses that the business has incurred. In other words, it provides information regarding the point at which the organization will start to make a profit. Basically, break even analysis provides an owner or manager with a statistical tool that helps him or her understand the relationship between the organization's fixed costs, variable costs, and profits.

As portrayed in Figure 7-2, a break even analysis presents the costs (fixed and variable) expended by the organization and the income earned by the organization. Fixed costs can include salaries paid to administrative staff, depreciation on buildings and equipment, rentals, interest charges on debts, and others. Fixed costs mean that these costs do not vary depending upon the volume of sales or the number of the products produced. Variable costs or costs sometimes referred to as direct costs include the cost of labor and materials that increase or decrease with the volume of sales made by the organization. As you will recall in our discussion of the Happy Hills Day Camp in Chapter 4, the owners of this business wanted to know how many campers they needed to make a profit and to reach their magic break even point. By calculating the variable and fixed costs and by determining the price of the program, it was determined that thirty-eight campers a month were needed to begin to make a profit.

Our break even analysis presents the income and costs of the business on the vertical axis and the volume produced on the horizontal axis. Fixed costs of $20,000 are depicted by a horizontal line. As mentioned, fixed costs remain constant regardless of the number of units (volume) produced. Variable costs in this break even analysis are projected to be $.60 per unit. Therefore, the business's total costs will increase by $.60 (variable costs)

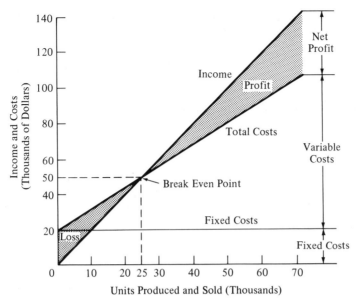

FIGURE 7–2. Break-even chart. (Adapted from J. Fred Weston and Eugene F. Brigham, *Managerial Finance*, 6th ed. Hinsdale, IL: The Dryden Press, 1978, p. 72.)

for each unit produced. The products or services sold are projected to be sold at $1.00 per unit; therefore, total income of the business will be a straight line on the vertical axis that will rise as production rises. The total income line represented in the break even analysis will always represent a greater amount (i.e., steeper) than the total cost line, since the business will earn $1.00 income for each $.60 that is paid out for its variable costs, such as labor and materials.

The actual break even point can be found at the intersection of the total income and total cost lines. The business will suffer a loss up to the break even point. However, after reaching the break even point the firm will make a profit. Our example shows a break even point at a production level of 25,000 units and at a cost and sales level of $50,000.

Financial Control

All commercial leisure service organizations should institute procedures to assure tight financial control and prevent financial mismanagement by employees. In larger organizations, the handling of financial transactions is usually worked out so that procedures are established that prevent errors and fraud and ensures that the organization collects its accounts receivable and disperses its accounts payable.

There are a number of safeguards that any commercial leisure service organization can take to tighten its internal financial control and thus minimize the possibility of employees' mismanagement of funds. Gray has suggested that the most important factor in ensuring financial control is to make sure that there is a subdivision of duties so that no one person handles a transaction ". . . from beginning to end." He notes that in larger organizations the grouping of duties by administrative function (i.e., finance, sales, production), prevents one person from handling and processing an entire transaction. However, he goes on to note that in smaller organizations this is often not the case. According to Gray, there are ten steps that an organization can take to increase internal financial control in a small business:

1. Assign someone other than the bookkeeper to receive bank statements directly from the bank and reconcile them.
2. The person responsible for the recording of disbursements should not be authorized to sign checks. Furthermore, two signatures should be required.
3. The person signing the checks should review, approve, and cancel invoices and other documents supporting disbursements.
4. All disbursements should be made by serially numbered checks with the exception of small disbursements from petty cash.
5. Someone other than the bookkeeper should open the mail and prepare a list of all remittances.
6. The persons opening mail should restrictively endorse all checks upon receipt.
7. Someone other than the bookkeeper should authorize write-offs of accounts receivable.
8. Detailed fixed asset records should be maintained, and periodic physical inventories of those assets should be taken.
9. Fidelity insurance to insure against loss from embezzlement should be carried.
10. Monthly financial statements should be prepared in significant detail to disclose significant variances from the prior year or the budget.[9]

Each of these procedures provides a commercial leisure service organization with a way of cross-checking financial transactions within the organization. The prudent businessperson will establish such procedures as a way of reducing the possibility that errors or fraud will slip by unnoticed and adversely affect the financial well-being of the organization.

Summary

This chapter has discussed the topics of financial management and accounting. Financial management is primarily concerned with the financial decisions that an owner or manager makes that affect his or her business's profitability. Accounting is the process of gathering, recording, analyzing, and interpreting financial transactions that go on within a business. Accounting deals with what *has* happened, whereas financial management is concerned with projecting what *will* happen.

Two of the most important types of financial statements within a business are the income statement and the balance sheet. The balance sheet provides an owner or manager with information concerning a business's assets, liabilities, and equity. The balance sheet is determined at the end of an accounting period, usually the fiscal year. The income statement provides information concerning the profit or loss made by an organization. Basically, the income statement enables one to compare the expenses that are necessary to operate the business with the sales generated by it.

There are a number of tools that are available to help the owner or manager analyze a commercial leisure service business's financial position. Using the balance sheet and the income statement, there are a number of ratios and percentages that can be calculated to help the owner or manager more accurately determine the organization's financial status. There are four major types of ratios or percentages: liquidity ratios, leverage ratios, activity ratios, and profitability ratios. Liquidity ratios help the owner or manager determine whether the organization has the capacity to meet its short-term financial obligations. Leverage ratios help the owner or manager understand the commercial leisure service business's debt position. Activity ratios help the owner or manager understand how effectively and efficiently the organization is using its assets in the creation and distribution of services. Finally, profitability ratios help the owner or manager measure the actual profit made by the business.

One of the most important aspects of management of a commercial leisure service organization is ensuring its financial solvency. Basically, a manager must be certain that his or her organization has sufficient funds (working capital) to meet its financial obligations as they occur. The amount of working capital that a business will need will vary from organization to organization. Working capital includes an organization's cash, inventory, accounts payable, and accounts receivable.

In this chapter we have referred to budgeting as the process of developing a profit plan. A budget, or profit plan, is a way of translating ideas for services or products into a financial statement. There are two types of budgets: operating and capital. Operating budgets are concerned with the projection or forecasting of both sales and expenses. The capital budget is concerned with the financial plan necessary to acquire large pieces of equipment, land, or new facilities. Once a budget has been developed, an organization may find it useful to develop a cash flow forecast based upon the budget. This tool can help the manager understand how much cash is needed to run the business month by month, throughout the year, so that it remains solvent.

We have also presented a discussion of break even analysis. This financial analysis tool is especially useful in small businesses. It can help the owner or manager determine the point at which revenues generated from sales of a given product or service meet the fixed and variable expenses associated with them. The break even point, then, is the point at which an organization begins to make a profit.

Study Questions

1. Why is financial management important in a commercial leisure service organization? What types of financial decisions does the owner or manager of a commercial leisure service organization make?
2. What is accounting?
3. Describe the accounting process. What types of accounts might a commercial leisure service organization have?
4. What is the difference between financial management and accounting?
5. Describe a balance sheet.
6. Describe an income statement.
7. Identify four types of financial ratios and discuss their purposes.

8. What is working capital? Why is it important in an organization?
9. What is budgeting? What is a profit plan?
10. What is break even analysis? Diagram a hypothetical break even analysis for a business that you would like to start.

Experiential Exercise

During the past several months B & E Sporting Goods has been considering expanding their operations. Recently, another sporting goods store has approached the owners of B & E and asked them if they would be interested in purchasing their business. Your job is to analyze this business in terms of its financial performance, specifically the following considerations:

1. Its ability to meet its financial obligations.
2. The riskiness of the business from the lender's point of view.
3. The business' overall management effectiveness.

To assist with your analysis, you should calculate the following ratios and provide an explanation of why each of these ratios is useful in understanding the financial condition of the business. Specifically, you want to be able to explain, in your own words, what type of information each of the ratios provides and why it will be useful in analyzing the financial condition of the business.

Ratio	Your Calculation	Industry Norms
a. Current	_____	1.7
b. Net Profit	_____	10%
c. Debt Ratio	_____	36%
d. Net Working Capital	_____	NA
e. Total Assets Turnover	_____	NA

To calculate this information, a balance sheet and an income statement are provided. After you have completed your analysis, what decision do you think B & E Sporting Goods should make concerning the acquisition of this business? Do you think this business has a solid financial basis or are there problems? *Note:* You may calculate other ratios if you think it will help you in your analysis.

Balance Sheet

Assets		Liabilities	
Current Assets			
Cash		*Current Liabilities*	
Accounts receivable	$ 20,000	Accounts Payable	$150,000
less allowance for doubtful	10,000	Short-term notes	$6,000
accounts		Current portion of long-term	
Net realizable value	2,000	notes	
Inventory	8,000	Interest payable	600
Temporary investments	150,000	Taxes payable	2,000
Prepaid expenses	0	Total Current Liabilities	158,600
Total Current Assets	178,000		
		Long-Term Liabilities	64,900
Long-Term Investments		Notes payable	
(detailed list)	—	Total Long-Term Liabilities	64,900
Total investments	—	*Total Liabilities*	$223,500
Fixed Assets			
Land			
Building: $50,000 at cost, less accumulated depreciation of $16,000	40,000		
Net book value			
Equipment: $5,000 at cost, less accumulated depreciation of $1,000			
Net book value	3,000		
Furniture/Fixtures: $3,000 at cost, less accumulated depreciation of $500			
Net book value	2,500		
Autos/Trucks: $_____ at cost, less accumulated depreciation of $_____			
Net book value			
Total Net Fixed Assets			
Total Assets	$223,500		

Income Statement, 19XX

	Year to Date	
	Amount	**% of Net Sales**
Revenue		
Gross Sales	$171,360	104%
Less sales returns and allowances	6,260	4%
Net Sales	164,000	100%
Cost of Sales		
Beginning Inventory		
Plus purchases (retailer)	60,000	36.5%
Total Goods Available	160,000	97.5%
Less ending inventory	220,000	134%
Total Cost of Goods Sold	50,000	91%
Gross Profit (Gross Margin)	14,100	8.5%
Operating Expenses		
Salaries and wages (selling and administration cost)	53,000	32%
Commission	5,000	3%
Advertising	5,300	3%
Insurance		0%
Depreciation	1,000	6%
Miscellaneous	2,000	1.2%
Total Operating Expenses	66,300	40.4%
Total Operating Income	(52,200)	(31.8%)
Pretax Income (after total financial revenue and expenses but before taxes and extraordinary items)	0	
Taxes on Income	0	
Net Income (Net Profit)	($52,200)	(31.8%)

Notes

1. Edward N. Rausch, *Financial Keys to Small Business Profitability*, New York: AMA-COM, 1982, p. 6.
2. Benton E. Gup, *Principles of Financial Management*, New York: John Wiley & Sons, 1983, p. 8.
3. Ibid.
4. Lawrence D. Scharl, Charles W. Haley. *Introduction to Financial Management*, New York: McGraw-Hill, 1977, p. 468.
5. Maurice Archer, *Introduction to Canadian Business*, 2nd ed., Toronto: McGraw-Hill Ryerson Ltd., 1974, p. 356.
6. John A. Reinecke, William F. Schoell, *Introduction to Business: A Contemporary View*, 2nd ed., Boston: Allyn & Bacon, 1977, p. 248.
7. Richard Rubin, Philip Goldberg, *The Small Business Guide to Borrowing Money*. New York: McGraw-Hill, 1980, p. 36.
8. Christopher R. Edginton, Charles Griffith, *The Recreation and Leisure Service Delivery System*, Philadelphia: Saunders College Publishing, 1983, pp. 195–196.
9. Robert N. Gray. "How to Prevent Fraud in A Small Association."

Close-up: Great Pacific Iron Works

Yvon Chouinard's name has long been synonymous with the sport of mountain climbing. A resident of Moose, Wyoming, Chouinard has climbed mountains in Europe, New England, California, Alaska, South America, Nepal, and China and is, according to *Outside* Magazine "one of the best all-around climbers in America. . . ."

Before 1960, most climbing hardware was manufactured in Europe. Around 1957, Chouinard taught himself the art of blacksmithing and began making his own pitons (spike-like objects driven into cracks in rocks to which climbing ropes are attached for safety) of chrome-molybdenum steel. This innovation made the Chouinard pitons stronger and lighter than their European counterparts. Soon Chouinard was making most of his own climbing hardware. He would sell this hardware from the trunk of his car to other climbers at the end of the day's climb. Chouinard is also credited with redesigning the ice axe by curving the pick end of the axe to correspond to the arc a climber's arm makes while swinging the axe. This change allowed the climber to swing the axe over his or her head into an ice wall and be able to hang on for support. Thus, safety in ice climbing was improved.

In addition to his light and safe climbing hardware, Chouinard is known for his development of a climbing technique known as "clean climbing." *Outside* Magazine describes clean climbing as a technique "that calls for replacing hammered pitons and drilled bolts with metal stoppers, which wedge into the cracks and do little damage to the rocks."† The scarring of the rock surface from the climbing technique of that period was becoming a serious problem because the sport, in the 1960s, was attracting many new practitioners.

In 1965, Chouinard teamed up with Tom Frost, an engineer and climbing friend, to form the Great Pacific Iron Works. Chouinard's reputation as a climber, his knowledge of the sport of climbing, his concern for the safety of his customers, and a commitment to excellence in all aspects of his business assured the success of Great Pacific Iron Works.

In 1972 Chouinard began manufacturing and selling outdoor clothing. His Patagonia label ultimately became a success. As a result of this new product line, the business grew rapidly. Selling in a highly competitive market, engaging in corporate planning and manufacturing problem-solving, and dealing with personnel complexities created many challenges for the mountain-climber-turned-entrepreneur.

Chouinard is careful of product image. Most of his advertising is done in catalogs with aesthetically appealing formats, professional art work, and well-written text. Success came comparatively rapidly and the Chouinard management team was challenged with controlling growth.

According to *Outside* magazine, sales projections for Chouinard's business will grow from $18 million to $100 million in the next five years. Started in a back yard shed, the company has grown into its own 16,000-

---

* Craig Vetter, "Lucky Yvon" *Outside*, March, 1984, p. 40.
† Ibid., p. 44.

square-foot building. There are six separate business entities owned by Chouinard: Patagonia, Patagonia Mail Order, Chouinard Equipment, Rencon Machine, and Cheap Store.*

The Chouinard management style reflects an intense personal commitment to creative solutions to problems. He believes that all employees should be kept informed on relevant company matters and that giving employees responsibility and authority will keep a rigid hierarchy from developing.

Chouinard surrounds himself with a variety of experts who, hopefully, will catch design flaws and quality problems before the product reaches the consumer. Chouinard wants employees to enjoy their work, but they must be dedicated to the concept of quality.

In preparing this close-up, the authors interviewed several well-known mountaineers and owners of mountaineering retail shops and concluded that the *Outside* magazine interview with Yvon Chouinard was indeed accurate in its portrayal of a man who has built a commercial leisure business that deserves the mark of excellence for the products it sells to climbers and the service it renders to its customers.

* Ibid., p. 77.

8

The Commercial Leisure Service Organization and the Law

This chapter presents the more salient legal issues likely to confront the owners and managers of commercial leisure service organizations. One chapter on law can only attempt to identify and briefly explore these issues.* For the sake of clarity we have omitted specific case citations and long discussions of case development, the appeals process, and formal legal decisions. Readers who desire indepth case discussions are directed to the references in the back of this chapter.

The purpose of this chapter is to assist the leisure service owner or manager to so structure his or her affairs as to avoid or at least minimize legal entanglements. To this end the following topics and issues are discussed: historical development of the American legal system including a discussion of the local and federal court system; legal liability and relevant legal issues germane to the operation of a commercial leisure service organization; contract law, including the elements that make up a contract and a discussion of the uniform commercial code and the statute of frauds; risk management, including strategies for risk identification and risk handling; laws relating to employment practices; and finally, steps to finding a competent lawyer.

---

* Those readers desiring a more complete discussion of the law and leisure services should consult Arthur N. Frakt and Janna S. Rankin, *The Law of Parks, Recreation Resources, and Leisure Services.* Salt Lake City, Utah: Brighton Publishing Company, 1982.

Historical Development and Classification of the Legal System in America

Laws are rules laid down by society to provide understanding and reasonable certainty for its citizens. Writers on the subject substantially agree about the general purpose of law—the ensuring of an orderliness in all human activity; their definitions of the term vary considerably, however. Consider, for example, the following:

> We have been told by Plato that law is a form of social control, an instrument of the good life, the way to the discovery of reality, the true reality of the social structure; by Aristotle that it is a rule of conduct, a contract, an ideal of reason, a rule of decision, a form of order; by Cicero that it is the agreement of reason and nature, the distinction between the just and the unjust, a command or prohibition; by Aquinas that it is an ordinance of reason for the common good . . ., by Bacon that certainty is the prime necessity of law; by Hobbes that law is the command of the sovereign; by Spinoza that it is a plan of life; . . . by Hume that it is a body of precepts; by Kant that it is a harmonizing of wills by means of universal rules in the interest of freedom . . ., by Hegel that it is an unfolding or realizing of the idea of right.[1]

The principle of the rule of law, with its emphasis on broad considerations of fairness and the orderly settling of disputes, is generally felt to be so superior to the alternatives (economic coercion, vigilante groups, physical force) that today it is the concept upon which the governments of all civilized nations are based. However, the laws of modern society are hard pressed to keep up with the social concerns emerging as a result of technology. Cloning, genetic engineering, sperm banks, space migration, home video taping, and other social innovations such as euthanasia (mercy killing) have placed challenges and pressures on legal scholars never contemplated by the framers of the Constitution or classical legal thinkers who gave us our basis of law.

Add to all this the proliferation of laws dealing with employment practices, environmental issues, consumer and product safety, and taxation (which are written in an almost occult language), and we begin to understand the sense of bewilderment and frustration that is growing on the part of business owners and managers. As the law grows more complex and legal language more baffling and ambiguous, we find ourselves with a growing dependence on professionals (lawyers) to gain understanding of the law and access to the legal system. While the system contains the notion of entitlement to representation by those brought before the bar on criminal matters, it does not address the problem of how this representation is to be paid for. Nor does it address the problem of adequate representation in civil matters. Contrary to opinions of some legal scholars, those able to employ the most able counsel will fair better than those with limited resources.

Given the above concerns it is important that the new leisure service organization owner or manager become a "student" of the law and issues that affect his or her business. With scarce financial resources and the drive for efficiency and economy, the new business owner or manager can easily

TABLE 8-1. Common Classifications of Law

Administrative Law	Evidence
Agency	Maritime Law
Commercial Paper	Partnerships
Constitutional Law	Patent Law
Contracts	Personal Property
Corporation Law	Real Property
Criminal Law	Sales
Domestic Relations	Taxation
Emigration Law	Torts
	Wills and Estates

Source: F. A. Howell, J. R. Allison, G. A. Jentz, *Business Law*. Hinsdale, Ill.: The Dryden Press, 1978, p. 12.

stumble into legal problems with their corresponding expensive solution; this can spell economic disaster. While we do not recommend being one's own lawyer (thus having a fool for a client), we do suggest, as a prerequisite to successful management, a solid grounding in business law as a means of avoiding costly litigation.

A simplified way of categorizing the classification of law, depicted in Table 8-1, is by governmental unit: federal law or state law. The great bulk of our law is state (or "local") law.[2] All of the classifications in Table 8-1 are within the jurisdiction of the individual states.

How Law Is Made

Classifying American law by its source results in these divisions:[3]

1. Constitutions—both federal and state
2. Statutes—federal, state, county, and local
3. Judicial decisions by the courts
4. Common law

Constitution. The Constitution of the United States defines the powers of government and defines the limits of this power. In turn, each state has a constitution of its own, conferring powers of government appropriate to the state level and at the same time providing safeguards for the rights of the individual citizen.

Constitutions confer two types of powers on the governments that they control. These have been described by Howell, Allison and Jentz.

1. Expressed Powers. These are specifically stated; for example, the right to raise an army, to tax the citizens, and to create courts of law.
2. Implied Powers. These are the powers which the courts have found in the constitution through interpretation and implication of the expressed powers. An example would be the right of Congress to create agencies for the probing of outer space, something not even imagined by Thomas Jefferson and others who drew up the Federal constitution.[4]

The federal and state constitutions can be amended. Amendments to the Federal Constitution require ratification by three-fourths of the states.

Statutes.   Any law passed by Congress or by the state legislatures, acting within their constitutional powers, is known as a statute. These laws, together with the federal constitution and the state constitution, are known as the written law.

Judicial Decisions.   In the adversarial process, each side to an issue has its own interpretation of the law governing the case in question. It then becomes the duty of the courts to weigh and interpret the words of the law in question. The courts' interpretations, expressed in decisions, are then accepted as the law. The process is called judicial, or court, decision.

Common Law.   The common law is the framework of law that originated in England and served as the foundation for the legal system of our early colonies. It includes the decisions of the old English courts and is what colonial governors followed in meting out justice in the courts of this country. This type of law is often referred to as judge-made law or case law. The common law is frequently changed or expanded by the enactment of state statutes that alter, add to, or eliminate the common law entirely in specific areas. This constant revision of law, whether by legislative action, constitutional amendments, or judicial decisions, makes the legal system a dynamic and often bewildering institution.

Civil and Criminal Law

Civil Law.   Civil law regulates the rights and duties between persons. For example, if one person refuses to live up to the terms of a binding contract or agreement, the other party, under the law of contracts, has the right to recover damages—a sum of money equivalent to the loss sustained as a result of the breach of contract. The majority of laws fall within this category and will be a major concern of the commercial leisure service organization owner or manager.

Criminal Law.   This is a category of law composed of those statutes by which a governmental body prohibits specified kinds of activities and that provide for the imposition of fines or imprisonment upon persons convicted of violating them.

For our discussion purposes we only need to be aware of the two basic divisions of criminal law: felonies and misdemeanors. While the definition of felony differs from state to state, it is usually defined as a crime where the punishment is either death or imprisonment. Examples of felonies are murder, kidnapping, or arson. Misdemeanors, on the other hand, are crimes carrying lesser penalties. An example of a misdemeanor is a speeding ticket.

To sum up, civil judgments usually impose monetary settlements while criminal law imposes fines or imprisonment. However, some actions can be tried as criminal cases and later as civil cases. Civil rights violations are an example of such a situation.

Court Systems

In spite of the complexity of American life today, justice appears to result in an unusually high percentage of cases brought to court. In order to create a system where justice is likely to prevail, it is essential that legal issues settled by a court in a particular jurisdiction (state courts for instance) be applied throughout all the courts in the jurisdiction. At times throughout history, the United States Supreme Court, responding to current social and political pressures and philosophical ideologies of current justice, has changed a long-established line of decisions to establish a new law. Its decisions are binding on all other courts. The issues of abortion and school prayer are examples of traditional principles that have been changed as a result of rulings by the U.S. Supreme Court.

State Court System. Figure 8-1 illustrates a typical state court system.[5] In states with small populations, the appeals court often acts as the Supreme Court and hears constitutional issues. The Courts of Limited Jurisdiction deal with minor issues (as noted) and as such will not concern us further. It is worth noting, however, that in California the small claims court prohibits representation by lawyers, limits claims to under $4,000, and is a quick and inexpensive vehicle for the person seeking judicial relief. Usually, only the defendant may appeal a judgment made in a small claims court.

The most important cases involving state law take place in the General Trials Court. Judgments made in the General Trial Courts can be appealed to the State Courts of Appeal, which has three judges.

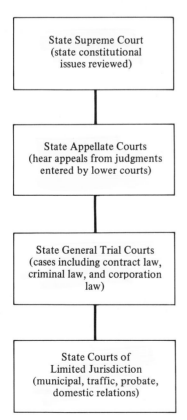

FIGURE 8–1. Typical state court system.

The Federal Court System. Figure 8-2 depicts the relationship between the Federal and state court systems. These two court systems interface only at the level of U.S. Supreme Court, which is the ultimate appeals court in the country.

Trial courts in both jurisdictions settle questions of both fact and law while appellate courts rule on questions of law only. In other words, once a case and its facts are presented (trial court level), the appeal by the losing party (the appellant) is made to the appeals court only on the issue that the law was not properly applied. The facts in the case stand.

Cases tried in state courts stay in that system until the highest state court has spoken. Only if the appellant can raise a federal question, such as the taking of property "without due process of law," will a U.S. District Court or the U.S. Supreme Court agree to hear the case. Violations of federal laws, such as civil rights cases and certain employment practices, are dealt with in federal courts.

As mentioned earlier, the legal process in this country can be expensive to employ. Few small entrepreneurs will have the financial resources to utilize the entire appeals process when a judgment is deemed unjust.

Only cases heard at the appellate court level or higher result in the writing of a formal opinion. These opinions are reported, and access to them is available to anyone wishing to research the rulings of law involved. These documented opinions can be found in a "Regional Reporter" published by West Publishing Company, called the National Reporter System. These publications are available to the public in most county and city law libraries. A brief orientation to the cataloging system in such libraries should suffice to facilitate personal research on an issue. Also, computer software companies, such as Compuserve, are currently offering legal research programs for sale. It should not be too long before these programs are available in public libraries.

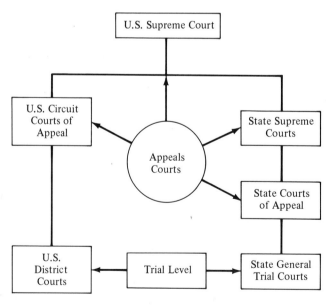

FIGURE 8–2. Federal court system and typical state court system.

Legal Liability of Commercial Leisure
Service Organizations

Not many professions have more potential for liability suits than leisure businesses. Those engaged in the business of providing leisure products or services to the public for a profit are finding litigation expense a growing budgetary item. Several factors contribute to the increased incidences of lawsuits against commercial leisure organizations.

1. More people are engaging in high risk activities that invite injuries, i.e., mountain climbing, SCUBA diving, off-road vehicle racing, hang-gliding, and so on.
2. Large settlements by juries in personal injury cases have received wide coverage in the press.
3. More commercial leisure organizations are entering the lucrative leisure market and many are poorly trained in programming skills necessary to ensure adequate safety of the participant.
4. There is a large number of new lawyers graduating from law school each year. Because of competition for cases and the removal by the American Bar Association of the prohibition against advertising by lawyers, people are more "suit conscious" and some lawyers are accepting more and more marginal cases.

The end result of such factors is a rash of lawsuits that ultimately increase the cost of doing business.

Torts

Historically, a tort was an act recognized as a "wrong." If this act caused injury to another, even if the injury was unintentional, the person committing the act was liable. Over the years this broad approach to torts was narrowed to embrace the concept of "fault." In this approach, conduct was considered legally wrongful when it violated the moral standards of a community. For example, the courts imposed liability upon persons who knowingly used property of others without the owners' consent and upon those who maligned the reputations of innocent persons and upon those who cause physical injury to another through an intentional act. As society grew more complex, the relationships between individuals created conditions that broadened the application of tort law to an ever-growing range of human conduct. Because of this broadening of application of tort law, a tort is defined as "any wrong excluding crimes and breaches of contract" or "any civil wrong committed upon the person or property of another, independent of contract." The discussion of torts by Howell, Allison, and Jentz identified:

> . . . one common thread to all torts: the breach of a legal duty owed by the defendant to the plantiff. If no such duty is found to exist, or if the defendant's conduct has met the duty imposed by law, the essential element of a tort is lacking.[6]

Negligence

Negligence is a branch of the law of torts. "Negligent acts" is a classification of behavior that needs to be understood by the leisure service professional as it relates to the conduct of his or her duties. A negligent act is a careless or reckless act rather than an intentional harm. It is the omission of a duty that should have been performed or the performance of an act that should not have been done. A person is negligent when he or she fails to use the care that a reasonable person would use in the same circumstances. The criterion is: how would a reasonable person act?

Elements of Negligence.   Van Der Smissen lists the following four elements, all of which must be proved to recover damages from the negligent party:[7]

1. A duty, or obligation, recognized by the law, requiring the actor to conform to a certain standard of conduct, for the protection of others against unreasonable risks.
2. A failure on his part to conform to the standard required.
3. A reasonably close causal connection between the conduct and the resulting injury.
4. Actual loss or damage resulting to the interests of another.

Duty.   The subject of "duty owed" is complicated by the wide range of legal relationships that exist between people. We will limit our discussion to care owed a person who is a participant in a recreation program or service.

Every recreation leader, administrator, or manager has a duty to provide a safe environment for the participant. In this case, the "duty owed" is imposed by the circumstance of leader and participant. Duty may be imposed by statute, as in the case of a fireman being required to perform the duties of a firefighter, or by voluntary assumption. In the latter case, a person may observe another person in peril. The observer, we will postulate, is a passer-by and therefore does not have any type of relationship that could be judged to be an obligation. If, however, the:

> observer voluntarily enters the activity or embarks on a course of action to save the individuals (sic) life, he, then, is said to have created a relationship which gives rise to a duty to employ care.[8]

"Duty owed" can be divided into two primary categories: (1) relationships between leader and participant, and (2) relationships established as a result of facilities offered for use by a customer. In the case of the first category, we find a doctrine of loco parentis. Here the recreation leader stands in place of the parent. This involves general discipline and close supervision. Standard of care is high, i.e., as a reasonable and prudent parent would act. Children left at a private resident camp, for example, would be required to have this standard of care. Lesser care is required of those who are subject to general supervision. Here the recreation professional whether conducting an activity, teaching, coaching, or leading an activity owes a standard of care that "a reasonable and prudent professional or trained person in that field" would be expected to deliver.[9] This standard of care applies to teenager leaders. Frakt and Rankin caution that those leisure service organizations utilizing teenagers as camp staff, for example, may be expected to hold these young persons to an adult standard of care in the performance of their duties.[10] It is essential that the leisure service owner or manager employing young persons select, train, and supervise them with great care.

In the second category, the responsibility of the recreation professional will vary, depending upon whether the persons on the premises are invitees (licensees) or trespassers.

An invitee is one who is on the premises by invitation (a customer or nonpaying visitor) for his or her own purposes. The operator of the premises must not only exercise reasonable care to protect these people but must warn them of unsafe conditions. To this end the owner must periodically inspect the premises to discover hazards. Innkeepers and other travel service providers are held to a very high duty of care to their customers.

A licensee is a person who enters upon the land with the owner's consent. The owner must warn the licensee of dangerous conditions but is not required to render the grounds safe, as in the case of the invitee. The licensee is not invited onto the premises as is the invitee, but does have the consent of the owner. For example, if a person is a customer of a campground owner, he or she is an invitee. However, if this person wanders into an adjacent area, also owned by the same campground owner, and is injured by slipping on old wooden steps made slippery by a recent rain, the courts would likely not hold the campground owner liable. The reason for this position is that the customer became a licensee when he left the area from which he was a customer for a specific purpose (camping) and was injured in an area he was not specifically invited to use. Frakt and Rankin point out that the law is beginning to demonstrate a "tendency to blur the distinction between invitees and licensees . . . a number of courts have placed social guests into the invitees category.[11]

When there is no consent given to use the property, the user becomes a trespasser. Trespassers are on the premises without the consent of the owner. The owner owes no duty to keep the premises safe. However, highly dangerous conditions, such as the use of firearms, or the presence of mine shafts must be identified. This is especially important in those cases where it is known that trespassers enter the property and if there are some "attractions" that could prove harmful to children (swimming pools, construction equipment).

The underlying legal concept to the issue of duty and breach of duty is: given that there is a relationship between the leisure service organization owner and customer or client, then the standard of care exhibited must be that of a reasonably prudent person given the same circumstances. Rankin states that the courts have held that the reasonable person concept:

> does not make the professional recreation programmer or agency the absolute insurer of the safety of the participants, nor does it relieve the participant of the responsibility to exercise reasonable care and to be observant.[12]

What is important to understand is that recreation activity has certain risks and that the leader or the organization sponsoring an activity cannot ensure an accident-free experience. In the Rankin article, Chief Justice Benjamin Cardoza of the New York Court of Appeals, speaking of the need for risk in the recreation experience (1929) denied legal recovery to a plantiff injured in a fall from a Coney Island ride, made the following remarks in his opinion: "there would have been no point to the whole thing, no adventure about it, if the risk had not been there;" and ". . . one who takes part in such a sport accepts the dangers . . .; and "the timorous may stay at home."[13]

Causal Link (Proximate Cause). In addition to establishing a duty and a breach of duty in a negligence suit, the plantiff must show a direct causal connection between the defendant's misconduct and the injury that the plantiff sustained. It must be acknowledged that a particularly wrongful act may set off a chain of events so unforeseeable, and resulting in an ultimate injury so remotely related to the wrongful act itself, that common sense suggests the defendant should not be held liable for it. For example: person A drives his recreational vehicle into person B's campground. After registering at the office person A proceeds to his assigned space. While backing his RV into the assigned space, person A knocks over a tree, which falls on person C's car. Person C drives his car to an auto body shop to get estimates for repairs. While enroute, person C's car is hit by a car running a light at an intersection. The driver hitting person C's car has no insurance. Person C sues person A to recover total damages, arguing that had not person A knocked over the tree, person C would not have been at the intersection where the accident occurred. In this suit the proximate cause was the driver running the signal, not the negligent act of person A. While it is true the damage to person C's car would not have been as great had not the collision at the intersection occurred, it was such an unforeseeable and unusual consequence of person A's wrong that person A has no liability for it.

On the other hand, person A is liable for damage to person C's car by virtue of person A's knocking down the tree while attempting to park. Of course, person A might retain a good lawyer to try and shift the blame to person B for having the tree in a poor location. (It is an interesting game.)

Establishing Loss or Injury. In our discussion dealing with recreation services as the product of a commercial leisure service organization, establishing loss or injury is not a complex issue. "When it is a question, it is one of fact (e.g., 'was he or wasn't he really hurt?') and as such becomes a matter for the jury to decide."[14] Loss can also mean a monetary one, e.g., loss of job, money, or real or personal property. It can also involve loss of use of a limb, or loss of a loved one where death of a spouse denies a child the companionship of a father or mother and subsequent loss of earning for the worker(s) and/or replacement of domestic services.

Acts

The law generally classifies acts into four categories:

1. Intentional acts to harm.
2. Acts that unintentionally harm.

3. Unavoidable accidents.
4. Recklessness.

Intentional acts are those behaviors in which the consequences were known and intended. Examples of intentional acts to harm include trespass, holding a person against his or her will (false imprisonment), and assault and battery. These intentional acts "have no place in negligence, for negligence implies lack of intent."[15]

Acts that unintentionally harm are the basis of negligence suits. Here the plaintiff (person being sued) will try to show that a reasonable person (here is that standard to measure your behavior) would have forseen the consequences of this unintentional act and because of bad judgment, excitement, inattention, lack of experience (here is where appropriate training is essential, especially in high risk recreation), ignorance, or forgetfulness caused harm. It is immaterial that the defendant (person accused of the act) was acting in good faith.

If a person is judged to have been negligent, the courts will establish just how negligent he or she was. If the act was one of ordinary negligence, then we might assume the person was careless but did not disregard the rights of others. This is, in a manner of speaking, the mildest or least offensive form of negligence. An example of ordinary negligence would be a camp counselor failing to stop rough-house play in a cabin and consequently one of the participants is injured.

Gross negligence, by contrast, is a different story. In these cases the courts look at the negligent act as almost one of recklessness. Recklessness is conduct "which falls below the standard established by the law for the protection of others against unreasonable risk of harm."[16] In the case of reckless conduct, the court considers this behavior as bordering on intent. (See intentional acts to harm, above.)

Keep in mind that negligent conduct may result from what one does (an act of commission) or what one fails to do (an act of omission). The owner of a recreation enterprise who offers a service to the public (camping facilities, packing services into the mountains, off-road vehicle parks) has a duty to conduct the enterprise with due care for the rights of others. Failure to do so, says Van der Smissen, is an act of omission or an act of commission: you either did not do what was necessary or acted improperly and became vulnerable to a judgment of negligence.[17] Of course, all this discussion assumes lawful acts that are judged negligent.

Please keep in mind that the four elements of negligence must be proved for negligence to be an issue. For example, suppose a person trained in first aid witnesses a fall by a hiker from a trail onto a ledge thirty feet down the side of a canyon. At this point, there is no legal relationship between the observer and the victim; therefore the observer may legally remain inactive, although a moral argument might be made for him or her to act to save a life. However, our trained observer, feeling the pull of moral responsibility, attempts to rescue the victim. At this point, common law imposes a duty on the rescuer to use reasonable care in the attempt at rescue.

For those who enjoy legalese, what we have been discussing can be classified as misfeasance (an act of commission) or nonfeasance (an act of omission). There is another classification of acts that should be mentioned: malfeasance. Malfeasance refers to an illegal act that should not have been performed. Using our camp counselor example, the fight between camper A and camper B that resulted in injury to one is over. The counselor on hearing of the fight proceeds to inflict excessive physical punishment on camper A causing injury. The counselor could be held liable for malfeasance. It is illegal to inflict physical punishment on another. This is not to say that a counselor or other recreation professional cannot restrain an aggressor but restraint must be the objective, not punishment or turning the tide of battle. A fine line, albeit a blurred one, exists between human nature and legal procedure.

The Standard of Care

When a legal relationship exists between the parties at law (plaintiff and defendant in the case of negligence), whether one is negligent depends upon how one acted. Determining how one should act is not an easy matter. The test for whether or not a person has violated his or her duty is did this person act in the way a reasonable and prudent recreation professional (either activity leader or business owner) would have acted in the same or similar circumstances. The test, while not complicated on its face, is open to a great deal of ambiguity on the part of the courts.

Defenses to Liability

Contributory Negligence. Contributory negligence is a common defense against a negligence suit. In this case, the defendant is saying that even if he is guilty of negligence, "the plaintiff should nevertheless be denied judgment for the reason that he, too, is guilty of an act of carelessness that contributed to his injury."[18] Until recently courts in the states that recognized the defense of contributory negligence applied the common law rule. This position, sometimes called "assumption of risk," will defeat a recovery in a negligence action. The rule of contributory negligence has been criticized for its harshness, for it may absolutely bar recovery for damage against the person most to blame.

Comparative Negligence. In most states the courts apply the rule of comparative negligence in suits brought before the bar. In applying comparative negligence, an injured person is not barred from recovering damages when he or she is guilty of failure to use the care that a reasonable person would have used to avoid danger that resulted from his or her voluntarily exposing himself or herself to danger (contributory negligence). In this case, a judgment for a plaintiff who is guilty of contributory negligence is reduced by a percentage the court feels is attributable to his or her own negligence. For example, Mr. Jones is injured at the Happy Mountain Ski Resort. The case is tried in Utah, which has the rule of comparative negligence. The jury finds that the Happy Mountain Ski Resort was negligent, that the amount of damages suffered by Jones was $10,000, and that Jones's own negligence contributed to his injury in the proportion of 25 percent. Therefore, judgment is rendered in favor of Jones against the Happy Mountain Ski Resort for 75 percent of the total injury, or $7,500.

Doctrine of Last Clear Chance. A person who has negligently exposed himself to injury may nevertheless recover from a negligent wrongdoer if the latter was aware of the claimant's helplessness and could have, had he chosen to, avoided injuring him. This doctrine of last clear chance is based on the principle that even when the plaintiff is negligent, the defendant should be charged with liability if by exercising care he might have avoided the consequences of the plaintiff's negligence. For example, Mr. Jones is driving his automobile down Main Street in a legal manner. Mr. Smith, meanwhile, is backing his vehicle down his driveway and fails to stop and look for cross traffic. Jones, admitting he saw Smith's car moving down the driveway and into the street, stated he thought Jones would stop, because he, Jones had the right-of-way. Smith did not see Jones. A collision occurred. Based on Jones's own admission that he saw the negligent act of Smith, he failed to use reasonable caution in stopping before he hit Smith's automobile. Smith may recover damages against Jones under the doctrine of last clear chance.

Voluntary Assumption of Risk (v.a.r.). Essentially, the voluntary assumption of risk argument posits that the participant in certain sports accepts the dangers inherent in it. Thus, a piton that breaks away from the rock and causes a climber to fall is an inherent risk to the sport, one that, as Judge Cardozo wrote in another case, was foreseen as one of the risks of the adventure. Without certain risks, there would be no adventure at all in some adventures.

Yet the defense of v.a.r. is clouded at best and is subjected to many nuances and legal subtleties. For example, wilderness trips into undeveloped country may impose the v.a.r. doctrine on all participants. However, injuries occurring in more developed areas such as barbeque areas or baseball games at a private camp might result in the court rejecting the v.a.r. defense.

Standard of Care: Being Reasonable and Prudent

Any discussion about negligence in leisure service delivery organizations must include the topic of supervision. Supervision should be discussed and should be measured in terms of professionalism. As professionals, recreation specialists must strive for a standard of care that is reflective of conscientiousness; that is, knowing and doing what is right, showing care, and being painstaking in performance of one's duty. Being a reasonable and prudent person in legal issues is a matter for the courts to decide; however, performing in a professional manner at all times reduces the likelihood a court will find leadership performance negligent.

When dealing with the public, the commercial recreation professional must perform in a manner that places public safety above all other considerations—including profit. As a patient expects conscientious behavior from a surgeon, so does the client on a river raft trip expect like behavior from the person in charge of the trip. If this behavior is present in all staff members, then the commercial leisure service manager can operate with relative confidence that accidents will be avoided.

When the recreation supervisor is managing, directing, and overseeing his or her charges, the likelihood of an accident or injury is greatly reduced. Regardless of how conscientious the supervision is, however, accidents and injuries occur. It is just a matter of time, and every organization providing recreation services (particularly high risk activities) will be asked to account for its behavior. "The majority of the cases involving the nature of supervision are concerned with stopping of dangerous activities."[19] Some activities are high risk and as such require a more intense level of supervision than others. For example, swimming, horseback riding, handling of firearms, mountain climbing, SCUBA diving, to name only a few, require close supervision and specialized training on the part of the supervisor.

Measures of Performance

Supervisors must prevent the use of defective equipment, warn participants (or parents in the case of minor children) of dangers inherent in the activity, and see to it that participants with physical or emotional disabilities are not placed in jeopardy. A supervisor does not just "look on," he or she must be conscious of what is going on, be able to anticipate the likelihood of problems developing, and be knowledgeable of sound programming guidelines. Van der Smissen has listed several problematic situations that give rise to lawsuits:[20]

1. Competency of supervision
2. Adequate number of supervisors
3. Implementation of program
4. Size, age, and skill of participants
5. Adequacy of instruction
6. Warning of danger of activity
7. Safety devices
8. Rules and regulations
9. Medical considerations
10. Spectators
11. Equipment
12. Facilities and areas
13. Bleachers and grandstands
14. Construction and design
15. Layout of areas
16. Barriers
17. Steps and stairways
18. Walks, paths and streets
19. General maintenance
20. Transportation

Many of these areas have been discussed earlier. Others do not concern us here. We will briefly comment about some of the potential trouble zones that are of a general interest.

Levels of Supervision. While supervision is important to the safe implementation of recreation services, the law recognizes different levels of supervision. As we said, especially dangerous activities require "specific supervision," which is in contrast to "general supervision" that is generally in effect in a special event such as a Halloween party or dance at a camp. The absence of a supervisor often encourages a suit. There are times when a supervisor is justified in leaving his or her location, but if a problem seems imminent this abandonment of duty could prove detrimental to a defense in a lawsuit. For example, the action of a lifeguard leaving a crowded swimming pool to use the rest room. If an injury occurs, then the question of agency policy and procedures might come under scrutiny. Perhaps a supervisory guard should have been notified to replace the vacating guard. Or suppose the lifeguard was hired without a thorough check of his or her credentials by a superior. In this case the administrator charged with hiring a qualified instructor is negligent should an injury occur under the supervision of the unqualified lifeguard.

Then, again, having an adequate number of supervisors is crucial for supervision in certain circumstances. Risk activities and large crowds usually require "adequate" numbers of supervisors. In the case of private camps, the American Camping Association recommends one counselor for eight campers as an adequate ratio of supervisors to campers. Yet, in the interest of cost efficiency many camp owners include maintenance personnel and camp cooks in their camper supervisory pool to comply with the ACA requirement.

Program Design.   When planning activities, the leisure operator must plan activities based on size, age, skill, and condition of the participant. A 195-pound player running into a 105-pound player can do considerable damage. Persons of the same age can have wide weight disparities, and the programmer must consider this in his or her scheduling. Of course, noncontact sports need not consider weight as much as the skill level of the participants. Baseball games are an example of an activity where skill matching is more appropriate than weight differences.

Adequate Instruction.   Frequently, the commercial leisure service manager must be concerned with teaching effectiveness. Sometimes an activity becomes inappropriate and injury occurs because the participants have not had adequate instruction. Activities such as horseback riding, SCUBA and skydiving, fencing, and mountain climbing, just to name a few, require adequate instruction to ensure safety. This point is illustrated in the following case: a participant brought a friend along on a backpacking trip with the permission of the leader. The class project for this particular trip was to learn proper form in arresting a fall on a mountain slope using an ice axe. The participant assured the instructor his friend had sufficient experience in winter hiking to participate without posing a liability to the class. The drill required that the student, belayed (secured) on a climbing rope, "slip" off the trail and follow the procedure for using the ice axe to stop the slide. While the guest was executing this maneuver his hand slid off the ice axe shaft and he was cut above the left eye by the pick portion of the ice axe. The guest avoided possible blindness by less than one half inch. As it was, the cut required evacuation to a hospital where six stitches were required to close the wound. The guest sued the store owner for negligence claiming he had no prior knowledge of the nature of the activity, nor did he receive adequate instruction in this dangerous maneuver. The suit was settled out of court by the store owner paying all medical expenses.

The point of this story is that in our litigious-intensive society, in the case of personal injury there is a tendency for the injured persons to blame some external set of factors or some other person for the injury. Thus, the best preventative measure that a supervisor can take is to establish program policy to guide the actions of staff members, particularly when dealing in high risk recreation services.

Warning of Dangers. As the preceeding story illustrates, besides adequate instruction the participant must be aware of the nature of the activity, so that he or she will be fully knowledgeable about the program and can decide if he or she wishes to assume part of the risk. It is a good practice, one that is followed by most successful commercial organizations offering these "risk activities," to clearly spell out the nature of the program in their printed literature. In addition, where feasible, an orientation meeting should be duled where risk factors and safety suggestions are covered in a group. Trip agendas, equipment lists, and brochure descriptions are not only statements of the organization's programs and suggested procedures, but they also could demonstrate to a court the professionalism of the management and its leaders.

While release forms prepared and signed by a client do not relieve those in charge of exercising responsible leadership, such a document signed by the adult participants or parents of minor participants may reduce the incidence of so-called nuisance suits. In the case of adults signing such a release, these documents are regarded as contracts of adhesion. That is, the participant can either adhere and agree or forego the activity. Parents, on the other hand, cannot contract away the rights of children.

Figure 8-3 is a suggested Participant Notification Agreement that may prevent litigation on several issues. It suggests that each participant seek medical advice (assuming, of course, a medical examination is not mandatory, in which case the wording would reflect that position). The participant is informed about the nature of the trip and the fact that the en-

---

PARTICIPANT NOTIFICATION AGREEMENT

Great American Outdoor Adventures suggests that each expedition member seek the counsel of his/her personal physician regarding the advisability of participating in the current expedition. Participants should be aware that high altitudes and/or hostile environment can exacerbate the effects of medication and cause diseases not encountered in more temperate surroundings, mountain sickness being the prime example.

I have read the literature provided by Great American Outdoor Adventures and understand the risk involved. Further, I agree to follow the safety measures required by the expedition leadership.

_____   _____
Signed   Date

FIGURE 8–3. Sample participant notification agreement.

vironment is hostile and could alter the effects of prescription medication. The participant is acknowledging that specific rules governing conduct are in effect and that the trip leaders are the authority. This latter issue is important especially if the trip is an adult activity, because independent-minded persons occasionally delight in challenging leadership. If, for example, a participant takes it upon himself or herself to leave the group early, against the advice of the trip leader, and gets lost or injured, the thought of a lawsuit could be cooled by the presence of this signed "friendly agreement."

When dealing with minors, especially teenagers, it is a good idea to include a statement prohibiting the use of alcohol or recreational drugs. Again, this only serves to discourage suits where a participant is injured and may have been using alcohol or drugs without the knowledge of the leader.

Waivers.   Waivers used for field trips for minors are of little value except that the parent has the knowledge of the child's whereabouts and sanctions his or her presence there.[21]

Participation in leisure activities has risen dramatically in the past two decades. This increase in participation has been accompanied by an increase in law suits against owners or managers of commercial leisure service organizations. Damage awards have grown accordingly, and large awards are not the exception today but more likely the rule. The court has made it clear that not every injury that is sustained will result in an unfavorable decision to the recreation practitioners. The court generally holds for the practitioner who acts in good faith and uses sound judgment. It will not tolerate grossly negligent conduct by practitioners. Those in the commercial leisure service field must exercise extra care for the persons who place trust in their ability to deliver a safe and sound program.

Contracts

It is possible to conduct a successful leisure business without having to deal with the complexities of a negligence suit. It is virtually impossible, however, to engage in an enterprise without dealing with contract law. Taking a partner, leasing a vehicle, borrowing money, hiring an employee, buying a coffee pot, selling a product, contracting to perform a service— all these events and most other commercial transactions will involve the conditions inherent in contract law. Therefore, the commercial recreation student who enters the marketplace as an entrepreneur (or a consumer for that matter) is advised to become familiar with the area under the Common Classification of Law (Figure 8-4) labeled "types of contracts."

Definition

A contract is a promise that creates a legal obligation. It is an agreement between two competent parties based on legal consideration to do or to refrain from doing some particular thing that is neither illegal nor impossible. The agreement results in an obligation enforceable by law.[22]

The intent of this section is to familiarize you with the significance of

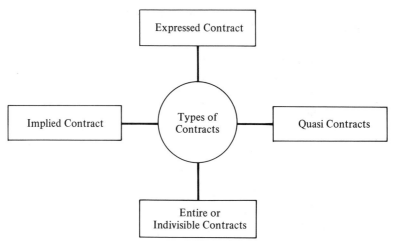

FIGURE 8–4. Types of contracts.

many routine actions and their relationship to contract law. Howell, Allison, and Jentz said it succinctly:

> . . . a substantial number of cases involving contract law do have to be settled by courts every year, and these cases most clearly bring into focus the principles of contract law. It is one thing to get a general idea about a principle that is stated in the abstract; it is quite another to see the practical results of its application to a concrete situation. It is the latter stage that a principle or theory takes on real life; . . .[23]

To breathe life into the abstract contract definition presented above, we will intersperse our discussion with some abbreviated legal cases. Case citation will not be included. You are directed to the chapter reference notes should more specificity be required. It is our experience that discussion intended to convey general knowledge tends to get obscured by a deluge of detail. However, examples that are easy to follow do the greatest service to the cause of general knowledge.

Types of Contracts

As we stated above, a contract is a promise that creates a legal obligation. However, not all contracts take the same form; indeed the substance is often different. All contracts, however, contain four essential elements: offer-acceptance, consideration, capacity, and legality. A comprehensive definition cannot be presented until all four of these elements are examined in some detail. Generally, and with specific exceptions to be noted, the law does not require contracts to be in writing.

Contracts can be either expressed or implied (see Figure 8-4).

Expressed Contract. An expressed contract is one in which the terms are specifically stated by the parties. The intentions of the parties are stated fully and in explicit terms, either orally or in writing. Leasing an apartment or a vehicle are examples of expressed contracts. Expressed contracts are frequently in writing and of considerable length, but this is not necessarily so. For example, Mr. Smith offers to sell his stereo set to Mr. Jones for $400 cash, and Jones answers "I accept." Thus, an expressed contract has been formed. Although extremely brief, it is sufficient to obligate each of the parties to perform.

Implied Contract.   An implied contract is one in which terms are not expressly stated but are inferred by law from the acts of the parties and the surrounding circumstances.[24] For example, a bottled water delivery person leaves bottled water at your home (we'll assume he was at the wrong address). You use the water and place the empty bottle on the porch. This is repeated each week for a month. At the end of the month the bottled water company sends you a bill for the water delivered. The action and conduct of both parties implies that the delivery of the water is acceptable and creates an obligation on your part to pay for the water.

Silence may also result in an enforceable implied contract. Watching another who mistakenly performs services that benefit you creates a burden upon you to point out the mistake to the one making it. For example, a work crew of three persons enters the property you own. They begin repairing the pot holes in your private roadway. You watch them work, perhaps knowing they were supposed to be repairing your neighbor's driveway. If you have no reason to believe that the work is being done gratuitously, you have an obligation to pay reasonable value for the service and materials.

Quasi Contracts.   Sometimes the court will impose contract obligations on a person who neither knew of nor sought the services of another. For example, an unconscious man was found in the park by a passerby, who transported the man to a hospital for medical attention. When the injured man regained consciousness, he denied any obligation to pay for the treatment on the ground that he had never entered into an agreement with the hospital.

In this example, the court may rule that an obligation exists through a quasi contract. A quasi contract, although not actually a contract, results from circumstances wherein a court concludes that one party is being unjustly benefitted at the expense of another whose services were given in an emergency. Howell, Allison, and Jentz argue that while it is perfectly obvious that the man did not contract for services (neither expressly nor by implication), services were rendered and "to permit him to escape liability entirely on the grounds that a contract was not formed would be to let him get something for nothing—a result the law generally abhors."[25] It should be noted that quasi contracts are not true contracts as defined above, but a fictitious construct conceived of by the courts to serve a just end to a particular litigation.

Entire, or Indivisible, Contracts.   Under certain conditions it is advisable to construct a contract that requires each part of the contract to be completed (executed) or the contract will not be considered performed. For example, a couple purchase a small sail boat, to be delivered to their home. A few days later the dealer's delivery service appears at the couple's home to deliver the hull, the mast, and one of two sails. Was the couple obligated to accept the shipment, since the dealer was acting in good faith? Or might they have refused to be bound at all?

The failure of the dealer to deliver the entire purchased item, even if the missing sail would be delivered at some future date, resulted in a complete cancellation of the agreement. The Uniform Commercial Code (U.C.C.) states:

> Unless otherwise agreed, all goods called for by a contract for sale must be rendered in a single delivery and payment is due only on such tender, but where the circumstances give either party the right to make or demand delivery in lots, the price if it can be apportioned may be determined for each lot.[26]

In this example the couple could have set aside the contract and not accepted the shipment. Had the couple accepted the shipment knowing the one sail was to be delivered at a later date their action would be an acceptance of the new terms of the contract. Or they might have offered to pay the charge minus the cost of the missing sail. If the merchant agreed to this proposal, then a divisible contract would have been created. In a divisible contract, demand for payment may be made for completed parts even though other parts have not been completed. Partial performance is permissible.[27]

Status of Contracts

At any given moment, contracts may be completed, partially completed, or awaiting initial action.

- *Executory contracts.* Contracts that have not yet been fully performed by the parties are called executory contracts. They may be completely executory, in which case nothing has been done, or they may be partly executory, in which case the contract is partially complete as in the divisible contract created by the couple buying the boat above.[28]
- *Executed contracts.* These are contracts the terms of which have been completely and satisfactorily carried out by both parties. Such contracts are no longer active agreements and are valuable only in the event of later dispute about the agreement.

Enforceability of Contracts

In the case where a contract is contested in the courts, its status is classified as being either valid, void, or voidable. A valid contract is one that meets all legal requirements for the type of agreement involved. Such a contract is fully enforceable by either party.

A void contract is one that is not enforceable from the very beginning. Selling property to another when one does not own or have legal title renders the sales agreement void.

Voidable contracts are not as straight forward in terms of enforceability as are valid and void contracts. The law provides for contracts that contain contestable features but that are otherwise legal in subject matter and operation. Contracts in this category are considered valid until the injured party declares them to be otherwise. Contracts in which fraud is present fall within this category as are contracts with minors.[29] For example, a minor enters into an agreement to purchase your car. You are aware of the minor's age and proceed to execute the sale. Upon discussing the transaction with a friend, the minor discovers he could purchase a similar vehicle at a cheaper price. The following day the minor returns the vehicle in the same condition as it was at time of purchase. The law would permit the minor to void the original agreement and insist on the return of his purchase price. This contract is deemed voidable.

Painting a slightly different scenario with a minor, we can illustrate how assisting a minor in a "life-threatening" situation could result in recoverable claims by an adult providing the service. For example, a minor wanders into your resort showing signs of exposure and neglect. You furnish food and clothing until the minor's parents can be contacted. You could collect reasonable charges for the food, clothing, and lodging because they were provided as a benefit to the minor and a necessity for life. This quasi-contract arrangement would be enforceable in the courts even though you were dealing with a minor.

Another type of contract is referred to as being "unenforceable." While all the conditions for a valid contract exist at the time it was made, the contract was rendered unenforceable because of a special rule of law. For example, under current bankruptcy law, bankruptcy proceedings distribute the debtor's nonkept assets among creditors. This prevents a creditor who was not paid in full from bringing legal action to recover any balance owed.

Elements of a Valid Contract

Should any contractual questions arise, legal counsel should be sought. One of the first steps usually taken by legal counsel is to determine if a valid contract actually existed. As stated above, a contract need not be in writing to be binding. Only certain types of contracts must be in writing (see Uniform Commercial Code below). For an oral or written contract to exist, however, these elements must be present:

1. *An offer* and then acceptance of the offer.
2. In some states there must be *consideration*, something given in return for a promise.
3. Parties must have the *capacity to contract*.
4. The *purpose* of the contract must be *legal*.

Some states consider a promise to do something, marry, take care of someone, and so forth, as sufficient "consideration." There must be at least two parties to the contract.

A contract should be complete; it should cover all the important acts to be performed by each party, and nothing should be left for future understanding or agreement. There should be a definite understanding of who is to do what and when and where and how. There is a legal axiom that an agreement to agree is no agreement.

Offer. An offer is a promise that something will or will not happen.[30] An expression of an intention is not an offer. For example, "I plan to sell my house for $50,000," writes Mr. Smith to Mr. Jones. Jones promptly writes back an answering letter and says, "I will buy your house at the price stated in your letter." There is no contract, because Smith simply expressed a plan or intention.

An offer must be so definite in its terms that the parties can be certain about what is intended. In case of a dispute concerning the terms, thus casting doubt on the existence of a valid contract, the court will frequently emphasize the principle that the intention of the parties is controlling. If the court finds that their intentions were the same (a "meeting of the minds"), then there is a contract.

An offer may be withdrawn at any time before it is accepted. Withdrawal of the offer must be definite and positive.

Under certain conditions an offer is deemed terminated. Rejection by offeree, lapse of time, occurrence of some specific condition stated in the offer, death of the offeror, destruction of subject matter, and revocation by the offeror are all conditions that may terminate an offer.

Generally the courts have held that advertisements are preliminary negotiations, even though goods are described and a price set. Howell, Allison, and Jentz note:

> Under typical 'false and misleading advertising' statutes, for example, an advertiser is guilty of a misdemeanor and subject to a fine if it is proven that he or she did not intend to sell at the advertised price at the time the advertisement was placed.[31]

An act of assenting (agreeing) by word or by conduct to the offer is acceptance. We have seen how conduct constituted acceptance in the example above of the bottled water transaction. Generally, an acceptance is effective when it is communicated to the offeror or his or her agent. If an offer contains conditions for acceptance such as the acceptance must be made in person or by a specific time, then the conditions must ordinarily be met.

Silence does not usually constitute an acceptance. This is true even when the offer states, "if you do not reply within ten days, I shall conclude that you have accepted." Acceptance, states Howell, Allison and Jentz, "must be reasonably definite and unequivocal and must be manifested by some overt word or act."[32] Please keep in mind that as with the offer, the need for definiteness is equally mandatory in the acceptance. For example, Mr. Jones makes a specific offer to sell his car for $5,000. The offer, run in a classified ad, attracts Mr. Smith, who examines the car and states, "I am interested, and will return in an hour with the money." In the meantime, Jones sells the car to Mr. Brown. Smith's expression of interest and promise to return does not constitute acceptance within the guidelines discussed, thus has no standing in a lawsuit for a breach of contract.

Consideration. Generally a contract must be supported by consideration. Consideration need not always take the form of money. Any exchange of values is sufficient to constitute an enforceable agreement.

Consideration is defined as doing, or promising to do, a legal act or service that yields pleasure or benefit to the other party, when one is under no legal obligation to do this act. For example, a college student agrees to work at a ski resort three hours per day in exchange for free lift tickets. His work constituted valid consideration. Or it can be defined as refraining, or promising to refrain, from doing something that one is otherwise free to do and has a legal right to do. For example, an uncle wrote a letter to his niece promising he would give her $10,000 if she did not marry until she finished college. Mary graduated in June and was married in July. The uncle refused to pay the money claiming that a contract did not exist because he, the uncle, had not received any benefit from Mary's waiting to marry. He claimed he was doing her a favor by encouraging her to finish her education. The court ruled in favor of the niece. It was held that it is not necessary that the person making the promise be benefitted by the consideration.

The benefits agreed upon in a contract need not accrue to the contracting parties themselves. If the benefits are bestowed upon others at the request of either party, the consideration is valid. For example, your parents make a contract with an automobile sales agency for the purchase of a new vehicle, which is to be registered in your name and delivered to you on your graduation day at your residence. Your parents have reserved no rights in the vehicle. Delivery of the car to you at your residence will be consideration to your parents for their promise to pay the dealer. The dealer's sacrifice was his obligation to carry out a promise made to your parents.

Capacity to Contract.   Contractual capacity refers to the "ability" of contracting parties to enter into binding agreements. Those not having this "ability" (capacity) include those declared insane by a court, those with diminished capacity, convicted felons while imprisoned, and minors who are "so young that their minds have not yet matured sufficiently to understand the meaning and obligation of an agreement."[33]

You will recall that the discussion under voidable contracts emphasized the notion that under certain conditions the incompetent party may set aside an otherwise valid contract. The exception was contracts made by minors for merchandise and services considered necessary to their health, education, and welfare. Practitioners in the commercial leisure field should be especially cognizant of this feature of contract law because a large segment of the leisure market is composed of minors.

Persons suffering from mental disease but not declared insane are generally permitted to make contracts for necessities—other contracts usually are void.

Contracts of intoxicated persons are usually voidable by the person with "diminished capacity" to reason and understand. For example, Jim was attending a fraternity party. During the course of the party, and while intoxicated, Jim sold his expensive watch to Bob, a fraternity brother, for $10. The next day Jim demanded the return of his watch when he realized what he had done. Since Jim did not comprehend the meaning of his acts when he sold the watch, he could legally demand that his property be returned upon his tender of the $10 he received.

There are some circumstances in which a person can escape contractual liability by proving duress or excessive influence. Examples of duress include physically disabled persons who become dependent and thus are easily influenced by a younger caretaker, buyers of goods persuaded to contract by the high-pressure selling tactics of the other party, and employers who pressure employees into a contractual arrangement upon the threat of losing their jobs.

A necessary element of duress is fear—a genuine and reasonable fear on the part of the victim that he or she will be subjected to an injurious, unlawful act by not acceding to the other party's demands.

Legal Purpose.   The fourth element required of an enforceable contract is valid subject matter, or having a legal purpose. A party to an illegal contract cannot ask the court to enforce the terms of the contract. While on the surface this proviso appears self-evident, it is one that, like the voidable contract concept, is easy to misunderstand and thus can inadvertently cause a problem of enforcement, especially with contracts involving a civil wrong which is contrary to public policy or public morals.

Legality of subject matter refers to the legality of the goods or services covered by the agreement and the purpose of it. Both goods and services and manner and purpose of execution of the contract must be acceptable under the law if the contract is to be enforceable.

There are three general types of acts that render contracts void because of illegality of subject matter. These are:

1. Acts contrary to the common law.
2. Acts contrary to statutes and local ordinances.
3. Acts opposed to the welfare and security of the public at large. These are known as "acts against public policy and good morals." Example: The sale of stolen goods would represent all three types.

It should be understood that, while a person's intent to contract may be legal, it is possible to inadvertently engage in contractual arrangements that are in fact illegal or violate any or all of the above three categories. For these and other reasons, it is advisable to have all contracts that involve substantial sums of money or bind one to significant performance, such as employment, to be reviewed by legal counsel.

The Uniform Commercial Code

In 1952, the first draft of the Uniform Commercial Code (U.C.C.) was completed under the joint auspices of the American Law Institute and the National Conference of Commissioners on Uniform State Laws. It was revised several times, with slightly different versions being enacted by all states except Louisiana between 1957 and 1967.

The Uniform Commercial Code contains nine articles. Article 1 contains general provisions applicable to all transactions governed by the code. Article 2 governs the sale of goods; Article 3 covers commercial payer (checks drawn on bank accounts, promissory notes, and bank drafts); Article 4 pertains to bank deposits and collections; Article 5 governs letters of credit; Article 6 covers bulk transfers (the buying and selling of businesses); Article 7 pertains to warehouse documents of title; Article 8 covers investment securities; Article 9 governs secured transactions, sales of accounts receivable, and chattel (personal property) paper.

The U.C.C. regulates most aspects of business transactions, thus it should be familiar to the serious student. For our purposes, i.e., the discussion of contract law, Article 2 and Article 9 deal with the assignment (transfer) of some contract rights.

The Statute of Frauds

The parties to a contract may decide for themselves whether their agreements shall be written, oral, or merely implied. The Statute of Frauds, however, specifies that certain agreements, to be enforceable, require written contracts.

While there are some minor differences in the interpretation of the statute in the several states, uniformity does exist in its most important phases. The statute specifically outlines six types of contracts that must be written if they are to be enforceable.[34]

1. Agreements by an executor or administrator to pay debts out of his own personal estate. Thus, brother Jim is executor for brother Tom's estate. A creditor demands a payment of $1500 owed by the deceased. To protect Tom's wife from creditors' claims and harrassment, Jim promises to pay the bill himself. This promise is not enforceable by the creditor unless it was put into a written agreement.
2. A promise to pay another's bill or to settle for any of his wrongful acts is an obligation that must be in writing if it is to be valid and enforceable.
3. Agreements that cannot possibly be completed within one year from the date on which the agreement is made. For example, a recreation agency promised to hire a student in a full-time capacity after graduation, which is eighteen months away. The agency agrees to pay the student a minimum wage for part-time employment until graduation, which is accepted. Upon graduation from college the student learns the position was filled by another. Any action against the agency would fail in that the contract could not be completed within one year and there had been no written agreement.
4. Agreements made in consideration of marriage. This does not relate to the marriage contract, which in almost all cases is oral. It refers to those promises made by parties before marriage in which they accept additional obligations not ordinarily included in the implied obligations of marriage itself. These obligations (and conditions) become more prevalent in second and subsequent marriages, where personal property is affected. Such promises, obligations, or conditions are enforceable only if they are in writing and are agreed upon before the marriage.
5. Agreements for sale of any interest in real property. All contracts for the transfer of any interests in real property must be in writing. A lease for the renting of another's real property must be in writing unless it is for a period of less than one year.
6. Agreements for sale of personal property, the price of which exceeds the amount set by statute. This requirement is basically the same as Section 2-201 of the U.C.C., which provides in part: Except as otherwise provided in this section, a contract for the sale of goods for the price of $50 or more is not enforceable unless there is a written agreement.

When a transaction is required to be in writing, the terms of a written agreement cannot be altered or added to by the use of parol (oral) evidence.

The statute requires only that the agreement be in writing—nothing more. A pen, a pencil, a typewriter, computer printout, or any other mechanical device comes within this definition. The writing should be legible; it may be written on any surface sufficiently suitable for the purpose of recording the intent of the parties.

To be complete, the written agreement, or memorandum as it is often called, should contain the following information:

1. Terms of the agreement
2. Identification of subject matter
3. Statement of consideration promised
4. Names and identities of the persons to be obligated
5. Signatures of the parties to the contract

Harold Havighurst wrote in *The Nature of Private Contracts* that contracts help people organize their lives:

> . . . with technological advance and a greater division of labor, groups become larger, intercourse with other groups more extensive, and human objectives more individualized and complex, contract comes to have a larger place in establishing the relationships and making the adjustments whereby men live together and get their work done.[35]

Risk Management Planning

Managers and owners of commercial leisure service organizations are faced with a multitude of legal issues. These issues range from managing the financial integrity of the business to the selection and training of competent personnel. One strategy that grows with ever increasing relevancy is risk management planning.

Risk management planning is concerned with minimizing physical loss of assets (theft, fire, vandalism); liability loss; personnel loss (key employees leaving for other employment or because of illness or injury); or interruption of personal income from market loss or personal illness or injury. One outcome of risk management planning is identifying a potential loss and transferring as much of that potential loss as possible, for example by purchasing a specialized form of insurance. This chapter will consider this and other strategies for managing risk.

Objective of Risk Management

The commercial leisure service manager must be concerned with "the effective planning of resources needed to recover financial balance and operating effectiveness after a fortuitous loss, thus obtaining a short-term cost of risk stability and long-term risk minimization."[36] To Greene and Serbein's objective, the commercial recreator must add Van der Smissen's thoughts on risk management, which hold that "risk management . . . must minimize the likelihood of client (sic) injury, and hence being sued."[37]

In the event one is sued, a well-defined risk management policy and plan can assist greatly in the defense.

Risk Identification and Classification

One of the most important duties of the leisure service manager is the identification and analysis of possible sources of loss to the organization. Normally, one thinks of loss in relationship to falling revenues from market exigencies. However, many events can have an impact on the profitability of the organization that have very little to do with loss of market position. Fire, windstorm, flood, and similar natural phenomena may bring serious damage and destruction to buildings and their contents. Commercial recreation organizations such as camps, marinas, resorts, campgrounds, and the like are particularly vulnerable to these types of losses. Employee theft, liability suits, changing market conditions, and economic recession add to the list of potential losses that can spell disaster for the small enterprise struggling to survive the particularly perilous early years of existence.

There is no ideal procedure for risk identification, but logic seems to suggest several steps:

1. Confer with knowledgeable professionals such as an insurance agent, a lawyer, and an accountant.
2. Contact the Small Business Administration and seek counsel from their volunteer program known as the Service Corps of Retired Executives (SCORE).
3. Review journals and publications from professional organizations in the field and business journals dealing with the subject of risk management. These can be found in libraries at local colleges and universities. Several references are listed at the end of this chapter.

Methods of Handling Risk

Once the risk analysis is complete, there are a variety of techniques available for handling the consequences of chance events. These techniques can be classified into four categories (see Figure 8-5): avoidance, prevention (control), assumption (retention), and transfer.[38]

Avoidance. By risk avoidance is meant deliberately refraining from engaging in those activities that are known to be risky. Resident camps, after

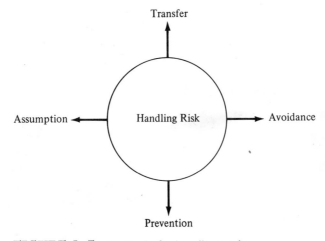

FIGURE 8–5. Methods for handling risk.

careful risk review, may decide not to offer horseback riding or ocean sports for the reason that they are regarded as high risk activities. On the other hand, competition from other established organizations may force the new enterprise to offer high risk programs in order to capture market share.

Prevention (Control).   Here the manager wishes to lower the probability that a given event will occur. Van der Smissen offers several excellent strategies.

1. A procedure for accident emergencies.
2. Hiring only competent personnel with verified appropriate certification and an on-going leadership training program.
3. Well-established safety rules that are enforced.
4. In-service education dealing with first aid procedures, safety awareness, and safety procedures for activities.
5. Regular inspection of facilities with timely repairs being made and an effective general maintenance program.

Risk Assumption.   Financial losses caused by chance events are met through the financial resources of the firm. Emergency or contingency funds might be set aside to pay for large insurance deductibles or for meeting other losses that have limits that are defined. Risk assumption is usually used as a strategy only when the risks are low and the costs associated with the risks are also very low.

Risk Transfer.   Here the organization shifts the risk to a firm who agrees to accept the risk of others. Perhaps the best known transfer procedure is insurance companies. Bonding companies and hold-harmless agreements are two other ways of transferring risks. Under certain conditions the type of business ownership (i.e., corporations and limited partnerships) can protect the business owner(s) from liability exposure.

Public Relations

Once a sound risk prevention program is in place, it is wise to boast of these practices and to be certain a public relations program follows up by educating the public. Sending news items to the local media on in-service training, for example, is one way to get your leisure service organization known as practicing high standards of care. In this way lawsuits brought against the firm will be easier to defend against and the organization's staff will be more inclined to provide a high quality of service.

Laws Relating to Employment Practices

Although there is diversity and uniqueness among commercial leisure services organizations, all of these enterprises share some common concerns. Chief among these common concerns are laws relating to employment practices. These laws can be divided into laws relating to taxation of small business, equal opportunity and affirmative action legislation, and employee safety.

Taxation-Payroll. Every commercial leisure service organization owner or manager has an obligation concerning the following taxes:

1. Income taxes. Each employee signs a withholding exemption certificate that specifies the number of allowable exemptions he or she decides to take. These funds must be passed on to the government (Internal Revenue Service) periodically.
2. Social Security taxes. The federal law requires a business that pays more than $50 in quarterly wages to contribute to the social security fund. This amount is a percentage of wages paid to the employee. This percentage and wage base has risen consistently over the years. The employer's contribution and employee's social security taxes withheld must also be passed on periodically to the government by the employer.
3. Sales taxes. Many state and local governments impose a sales tax on goods sold. A business firm is obligated to collect the required tax and pass it along to the appropriate governmental agency. (Sales tax obviously is not an employee related tax, but it is included to remind the reader of another tax, where applicable, which must be remitted periodically.)
4. Unemployment taxes. Firms that have four or more employees must pay both federal and state unemployment taxes on salaries and wages. The rate is related to previous unemployment experience. At the state level, workers laid off without cause who are willing but unable to find appropriate work are paid weekly benefits for a prescribed period of time from this tax fund.

Workers who are covered under the wage and hour law are also covered under several federal employment acts. These acts include the Civil Rights Act, Title VII; and the Age Discrimination in Employment Act. Title VII of the Civil Rights Act (Bureau of National Affairs, 1983).[39]

Equal Opportunity and Affirmative Action Legislation

Title VII. Title VII of the Civil Rights Act of 1964, as amended by the Equal Opportunity Act of 1972 and the Pregnancy Discrimination Act of 1978, is the most significant federal law dealing with civil rights and employment. It is the purpose of this act to ensure that all job applicants and employees are treated fairly and equally, regardless of race, color, religion, sex, age, or ethnic origin.

To further strengthen the impact of the Civil Rights Act, Title VII, Congress passed the Age Discrimination in Employment Act. As in the Civil Rights Act, Title VII Guidelines, affected organizations are any "employers" engaged in an industry affecting commerce who have "twenty or more employees for each working day in each of twenty or more calendar weeks in the current or preceding calendar year" (Fair Employment Practices Manual, 1983). Note the absence of the $500,000 revenue guideline that is in place for the Federal Wage and Hour Law.

Age Discrimination in Employment Act. The text of the age Discrimination in Employment Act of 1967, P.L. 90-202, effective June 12, 1968 states:

> Statement of Findings and Purpose
> The Congress hereby finds and declares that—
> 1. in the face of rising productivity and affluence, older workers find themselves disadvantaged in their efforts to retain employment, and especially to regain employment when displaced from jobs;
> 2. the setting of arbitrary age limits regardless of potential for job performance has become a common practice, and certain otherwise desirable practices may work to the disadvantage of older persons;
> 3. the incidence of unemployment, especially long-term unemployment with resultant deterioration of skill, morale, and employer acceptability is, relative to the younger ages, high among older workers; their numbers are great and growing; and their employment problems grave;
> 4. the existence in industries affecting commerce of arbitrary discrimination in employment because of age burdens commerce and the free flow of goods in commerce.
> 5. It is therefore the purpose of this Act to promote employment of older persons based on their ability rather than age; to prohibit arbitrary age discrimination in employment; to help employers and workers find ways of meeting problems arising from the impact of age on employment.

On September 25, 1978 the Uniform Guidelines on Employee Selection Procedures went into effect. This legislation attempts to deal with the effect of written employment tests used by some employers without evidence that the tests were related to success on the job.

The fundamental principle underlying the guidelines is that employer policies or practices that have an adverse impact on employment opportunities of any race, sex, or ethnic group are illegal under Title VI and the Executive Order (signed by President Carter in 1977) unless justified by business necessity. "Business necessity" is carefully defined and reference should be made to the text of the guidelines for specific discussion of this point.

Commercial leisure service business managers or owners should seek professional guidance to make sure they honor all legal obligations. Federal, state, and local requirements change constantly.

Occupational Safety and Health Act (OSHA). This law requires all businesses to make sure their operations are free of hazards to workers. This act has come under heavy attack by the National Federation of Independent Business as being oppressive to small business.[40] You should be aware that this act exists and should be certain that the business conforms to current OSHA guidelines.

Selecting an Attorney

The foregoing discussion has demonstrated that engaging in business is both challenging and confusing. There are a myriad of legal considerations that require the services of a competent attorney. Selecting a legal advisor can be a difficult task. Following are some guidelines for selecting an attorney.[41]

1. Begin by asking friends or others you trust for a recommendation.
2. Check with the state bar association. They will provide a list but no evaluation.
3. Legal clinics offer lower fees and are useful in preparing a simple will and reviewing real-estate closing procedures.
4. For taxes, trusts, criminal matters, or other specialities, be sure the lawyer is experienced or specializes in these areas.
5. Interview a lawyer before you need his or her services (if possible) or be prepared to interview several before you find one with whom you can feel comfortable.
6. Check the Martindale-Hubbell Law Directory at the public library, which lists lawyer's abilities and key clients.
7. Check the state lawyer's discipline agency to determine whether the lawyer has had an ethics violation.
8. Be clear about fees. Fee structure should be in writing. Usually there will be an hourly charge in the office, a separate fee for court appearances, and percentage of your recovery in a damage suit.

There are 610,000 lawyers in the United States.[42] Fees can range from $70 to $500 for each hour of consultation. Competence is not always a reflection of the fee charged, so be thorough and particular in your search and selection of this most important member of your management team.

Summary

This chapter has presented the structure of our legal system and some of the laws and regulations that specifically relate to the operation of commercial leisure service organizations. The overriding theme of the chapter has been the prevention and avoidance of legal entanglements. On this point Judge Learned Hand expressed the following opinion sixty years ago: "As a litigant, I should dread a lawsuit beyond almost anything short of sickness and death."[43] Yet, in spite of careful program planning and impeccable risk management practices, recreation business owners can anticipate being a litigant in a lawsuit. *U.S. News & World Report* stated:

> The flood of lawsuits has swelled to a tidal wave in recent decades—more than 12 million suits now are brought each year. Awards in big personal-injury cases are scraping the sky—they jumped almost 25 percent in dollar volume in a recent 12 month period.[44]

Perhaps one final note is in order. While we have focused on the many problems that can confront the leisure service manager, it must be stressed that the leisure profession has served the public with distinction. Leisure professionals are engaged in the occupation of bringing happiness and fulfillment to the public. This is a special opportunity to earn an often-time excellent income, not at the expense of another's trials and tribulations but in the service of improving the quality of life of the service users. It makes sense to so organize the affairs of business that these varied services are delivered in as professional a manner as possible.

Study Questions

1. In what ways are laws made?
2. What is a "tort"? Give an example.
3. What are the elements that must be proved to recover damages from a negligent party?
4. List five problematic situations that may give rise to lawsuits and give an example of each.
5. What is a contract and what elements must be present to have a valid contract?
6. What is the Statute of Frauds and how can it protect the consumer?
7. What is Risk Management?
8. What are the methods of handling risk?
9. What is the most significant federal act that protects the civil rights of employees? Discuss.
10. What steps should you follow to secure competent legal services?

Experiental Exercise

One segment of our legal system that can be helpful to the owner or manager of a commercial leisure service organization is the Small Claims (People's) Court. In the Small Claims Court, litigants cannot be represented by attorneys—they must present their case to the judge in their own words. This court is inexpensive and cases are heard in a relatively short time from the filing date. The plaintiff usually seeks financial recovery for some loss (a modest sum of money, between $500 and $2,000 depending on the local jurisdiction).

In order to acquaint yourself with the operation of this court, you should visit the county court house for the following purposes:

1. Determine the financial recovery limit of the local small claims court.
2. Secure copies of the necessary documents for filing an action.
3. Determine the fees connected with filing an action.
4. Visit a Small Claims Court while it is in session and take note of at least five cases, citing the nature of the issues, the remedies (amount of reward if any) awarded, and, where possible, the evidence presented by the litigants to make their point.

Sharing these findings in a discussion group will multiply the experience and help make the Small Claims Court a useful tool for the business owner.

Notes

1. Huntington Cairns, *Legal Philosophy from Plato to Hegel*, Baltimore: Johns Hopkins University Press, 1949, p. 20.
2. F.A. Howell, J.R. Allison, G.A. Jentz, *Business Law, Text and Changes*, Hinsdale, IL: The Dryden Press, 1978, p. 12.

3. R. Robert Rosenberg, William G. Ott, *College Business Law*, 3rd ed., New York: McGraw-Hill, 1966, pp. 4–6.
4. Howell et al., p. 2.
5. George Gordon Coughlin, *Your Introduction to Law*, New York: Barnes & Noble, 1975, pp. 16–19.
6. Howell et al., p. 140.
7. B. Van Der Smissen, *Legal Liability of Cities and Schools for Injuries in Recreation and Parks*, Cincinnati: W.H. Anderson, 1973, pp. 51–52.
8. Ibid., p. 53.
9. Ibid., p. 55.
10. Atthur N. Frakt, Janna S. Rankin, *The Law of Parks, Recreation Resources, and Leisure Services*, Salt Lake City: Brighton Publishing Co., 1982, p. 116.
11. Ibid., pp. 134–135.
12. Janna S. Rankin, "Legal Risks and Bold Programming," *Parks and Recreation*, Vol. 12, No. 7, 1977, p. 48.
13. Chief Justice Benjamin Cardozo, quoted in Frakt and Rankin, p. 129.
14. Rankin, "Legal Risks and Bold Programming," p. 48.
15. Van Der Smissen, p. 75.
16. Ibid., p. 78.
17. Ibid., pp. 78, 79.
18. Howell et al., p. 134.
19. Van Der Smissen, p. 194.
20. Ibid., pp. 196–235.
21. Albert M. Farina, "Accident Liability—What is Your Legal Responsibility?" *Parks and Recreation*, March, 1979, p. 51.
22. Rosenberg and Ott, p. 36.
23. Howell et al., p. 159.
24. Coughlin, p. 41.
25. Howell et al., p. 165.
26. *Uniform Commercial Code*, Section 2-307.
27. Rosenberg and Ott, p. 40.
28. Ibid., p. 41.
29. Ibid., p. 42.
30. Ibid.
31. Howell et al., pp. 180–181.
32. Ibid., p. 198.
33. Ibid., p. 230.
34. Rosenberg and Ott, pp. 105–106.
35. Harold Havinghurst, *The Nature of Private Contract*, Evanston, IL: Northwestern University Press, 1961, p. 13.
36. M.R. Greene, Oscar N. Serbein, *Risk Management: Text and Changes*, Reston, VA: Reston Publishing Co., 1978, p. 5.
37. Van Der Smissen, p. 208.
38. Green and Serbein, p. 15.
39. Bureau of National Affairs, Labor Relations Reporter, *Fair Employment Practices Manual*, Washington, D.C.: Bureau of National Affairs, 1983.
40. *U.S. News & World Report*, Nov. 24, 1975, p. 70.
41. "The Pervasive Influence of Lawyers," *U.S. News & World Report*, Nov. 1, 1982, p. 55.
42. Ibid.
43. Judge Learned Hand.
44. The Trauma and Tedium of a Lawsuit," *U.S. News & World Report*, Nov. 1, 1982, p. 51.

Suggested Additional Reading

John D. Calamari, *The Law of Contracts*, St. Paul, MN: West Publishing, 1977.

Richard D. Gatti, Daniel J. Gatti, *Encyclopedic Dictionary of School Law*, West Nyack, NY: Parker Publishing Co., 1975.

A.E. Pfaffle, *Fundamentals of Risk Management: An AMA Management Briefing*, New York: AMACOM, 1976.

Close-up: Gymboree Corporation

One of the most innovative entrepreneurial-based leisure services to emerge in the past decade has been the Gymboree Corporation. Organized to provide play, exercise, and movement experiences for children three months to four years of age, the Gymboree Corporation has grown from a small business to one with projected revenues in the millions. Established by Joan Barnes, who previously worked as a dance and recreation instructor, the major sources of income of the Gymboree Corporation are franchise fees, royalties, and fees derived from company-owned centers.

The Gymboree concept is built on the idea that youngsters can benefit from developing body awareness, balance, and motor control at an early age.* Basically, the program involves both a parent and a child in a once-a-week program where children are put through special play and exercises using a variety of specially designed pieces of gym equipment. The 45-minute activity period itself is led by trained leaders. Activities are designed to be fun.

Use of the computer in several of the franchise centers of the Gymboree Corporation was recently discussed in an issue of *inCider: The Apple Journal.* The article was devoted to the topic of how entrepreneurs were using their ingenuity and initiative to employ the computer to more productively manage their business.† According to Sharon Silverman, co-owner of Illinois Playtime, Inc. (a franchise of the Gymboree Corporation), their computer system has "whipped their business record-keeping into shape."‡ Accounting tasks that previously took two hours or more to complete now can be done in a matter of minutes. Information about participants can be retrieved rapidly to assist in the formulation of groups for instruction and monitoring the progress of students.

Specifically, Illinois Playtime, Inc. uses software programs for their basic accounting functions. Each month they prepare financial statements that present their organization's financial status, including its profitability. They are able to present information about income, expenditures, and withholding taxes. Their program also allows them to maintain quarterly financial reports that are required by the Gymboree Corporation.

In addition, their computer allows them to store and retrieve vital information about their clients. They are able, for example, to set up a file that includes each child's name, birthday, parents' names, address, how they heard about Gymboree (this is obviously important for marketing purposes), and the amount they paid for participation in various activities. From this information alphabetical lists of relevant information are established for each class. In addition, they are able to use their computer to generate mailing lists and mailing labels for use in advertising their services. The company uses generic mailing lists, which they purchase, but by using the computer they are also able to sort their advertising mailings by Zip code so that they can direct their advertisements to children in Zip code areas that are near their location.

* John Levine, "Close Up," *Venture*, December, 1982, p. 92.
† Sharon Silverman, "Keeping My Gymboree Franchise in Shape," *inCider: The Apple Journal.* March, 1985, p. 41.
‡ *Ibid.*

9

The Application of the Computer in Commercial Leisure Service Organizations

Commercial leisure service businesses without computer support are likely to find themselves increasingly at a competitive disadvantage. The purpose of this chapter is to discuss computer applications in commercial leisure service businesses and to provide insights into how these applications may be used to advantage by an owner or manager. Having a background or understanding of the computer or being computer literate is absolutely essential in today's business world. In this chapter, we will discuss the growth of electronic culture, types of computers, the computer system, benefits of the computer, business uses of the computer, and methods and procedures used in selecting a computer system. "A Brief Dictionary of Computerese" presenting a list of terms that can be used for reference regarding computers can be found in the Appendix at the end of this chapter.

The Growth of Electronic Culture

Society is undergoing a dramatic transformation. This transformation will affect the ability of people and organizations to process and use information rapidly. We are literally being transformed by the creation and evolution of computers. We have evolved from a culture solely dependent upon written and oral communication to one in which communication is achieved more and more through the electronic media. Discussing the evolution of electronic culture, Gotlieb has written:

To a great extent, our consciousness is determined by our use of word and number. Our use of these two fundamental building blocks was transformed during the first millenium BC, when we largely evolved from an oral culture to a written culture. Now, in the last moments of the second millenium AD, we are experiencing a second such transformation: the transition from written to electronic culture. Simply put, we are seeing the first steps toward a quantum leap in the volume, speed, and versatility of the average person's use of information (word and number).[1]

When considering the advances and developments made as a result of the advent of writing, it is obvious that the computer has far reaching implications for the development and expansion of our ideas. Commercial leisure service organizations certainly can benefit from the use of computers in their operations. Although initially the use of computers in small business might focus on storing and retrieving information, the possibility for more creative uses is on the horizon. "We are now in the same relative position to the electronic media that we were 3000 years ago in relation to writing. Initially, writing was used for record keeping and the preservation and adaptation of works . . ."[2] Only later did we develop more creative uses of the written word. The same could be said about the use of the computer.

The Historical Development of Computers

The historical development of computers is an interesting topic. The first computer was built at the University of Pennsylvania in 1943. Known as ENIAC (Electronic Numerical Integration and Computer), this computer was initially developed to calculate missile trajectories and predict the weather. ENIAC was massive when compared with today's microcomputers. It had over 18,000 tubes, 70,000 resistors, and 10,000 capacitors. Weighing 30 tons, it occupied 3,000 cubic feet of space and used 140,000 watts of power. Today's microcomputers, by contrast, weigh about 4 pounds and are much much faster and more powerful than this early model.

The important factor in the development of computers was the invention of the transistor. The transistor replaced the vacuum tube in computers. It made the electronic computer possible. The transistor was invented in 1947 by John Bardeen, Walter H. Brattain, and William Shockley. The transistor was very small in size, very dependable, and required less power.

By 1954, IBM introduced two computers, the 704 scientific computer and the 705 data processing computer. In 1959, IBM introduced two transistorized computers, the 1401, used for data processing, and the 1620, used for scientific calculations.

Following the initial development of transistors came the invention of integrated circuits. During the 1960s a process was developed whereby many transistors, resistors, and capacitors could be placed on a single piece of semiconductor material. By the 1970s, large scale integrated circuits had been developed. Large scale integrated circuits allowed for the development of the electronic calculator. They generally involved the use of one piece of material, usually silicon, upon which a number of different layers of other types of material were laid. The pattern of these layers "creates the effect of transistors, resistors, and capacitors without the necessity of manufacturing individual components and then installing them in a circuit."[3]

This development was followed by the invention of the *microprocessor chip.* Microprocessor chips were first introduced by the Intel Corporation in 1971. The development of the eight-bit processor by Intel in 1974 provided the basis for the development of microcomputers. The first commercially successful microcomputer—the Altair 8800—was introduced in 1975. The first personal computers were introduced in 1977—the Apple II, Radio Shack's TRS-80, and Commodore's PET.

Computer hardware, as discussed above, is only half of today's computer system. To make use of a computer you must be able to program it, that is, provide it with a set of instructions. Computer programming in its early stages was seen as being a highly specialized task done by extensively trained people. The use of computers was hampered by this fact. Not only were computers large, costly to purchase, and costly to maintain, but they also required the talents of highly trained people to program them. In 1963, a simple computer language that could be easily learned was develolped. Called BASIC, (Beginners All-purpose Symbolic Instruction Code), this important step forward in the historical development of computers was invented by two men at Dartmouth College—John Kemeny and Thomas Kurtz.

The creation of BASIC enabled people to interact directly with computers by using simple English-like computer language. The computer could "ask" questions to which the user could respond by typing the answers into it manually. This eliminated the need for computer cards and keypunch machines, which were used previously to program computers. It is interesting to note that BASIC was popularized as a result of its use in the creation of recreational computer games. Interest in personal computers was also spread initially and very rapidly because of its leisure uses. Some other languages that have been developed are Pascal, PILOT, FORTRAN, COBOL, and RP6, although BASIC is the computer language built into the majority of the microcomputers.

The latest significant development related to the computer was the creation of canned software. Canned software programs are prepackaged and easily used. Since canned software programs are mass produced, they are considerably lower in cost than the custom programs often tailored to an individual situation. In other words, with the current advances in the state of the art, it is no longer necessary to learn to instruct a computer. Rather, most persons or businesses can purchase a computer and appropriate canned software to suit their purposes. There is a large amount of software available.

What does the future hold for computers? It is predicted that by the 1990s engineers will be able to place over ten million transistors on a single chip. That is compared with the approximately 30,000 transistors currently on a single chip. Within the decade, people will have at their disposal pocket computers that are as powerful as today's large main frame computers. In fact, it is possible even today to purchase a pocket-sized computer at a very low cost that is equivalent to the ENIAC computer of the 1940s. It is also predicted that hardware costs will continue to decline and that great emphasis will be placed on the development of new and innovative software packages by computer companies. Without question, the microcomputer will have an increasingly important role in commercial leisure service businesses.

Types of Computers

Computers can be classified into five categories: micro, mini, small, medium, and large. These categories of computers are based on their cost, size, memory size, input/output speed, and access time. For example, a micro-computer is a computer that is used by one person at a time. A minicomputer is a computer that is accessible to more than one individual at a time and has the capacity to process more information than a microcomputer. Most small commercial leisure service businesses would be interested in acquiring a micro- or minicomputer. Generally speaking, these types of computers could meet the functional needs of such organizaions at a reasonable cost. Much of our discussion will focus on mini or microcomputers.

The Computer System

There are very few people in the United States and Canada whose lives have not been touched by computer systems. Most people pay income taxes, shop at grocery stores, attend schools, and carry out other daily life functions that are based upon use of the computer. Many tasks, from turning the lights on in a home to managing our personal finances, can be assisted by a computer in the home. Computer-based instructional programs are helping students to learn in a very personalized manner. The computer provides leisure opportunities in the form of games and can be used to control audio and video systems. Today, it is possible to program a computer system for almost any imaginable function.

What is a computer system? A computer system consists of several components: input devices, a central processing unit and memory, and output devices. Input devices allow the user to introduce words or numbers into the computer itself. The central processing unit and the memory section of a computer system are its brains. Output devices provide a way to obtain information from the computer. There are several ways to enter information into a computer. Today the keyboard is the most widely used device for entering information into the computer by small businesses. There are also numerous ways to get information out of the computer: printers, television screens, or cathode ray tubes (CRTs). All of these components are interconnected to make up the computer system.

The Central Processing Unit and Memory

The central processing unit, or CPU, is the heart of the computer system. The CPU in a mini or microcomputer is made up of a collection of silicon chips containing many miniature circuits where actual data manipulation and processing occurs. The CPU interprets information received from input devices and, in turn, issues commands to other parts of the computer system. The circuits within the CPU allow it to respond to instructions that have been placed into the unit. A CPU will respond to those instructions that it has been designed to accommodate. It may perform analytic calculations, logical decision-making functions, process data, display information on a monitor, or communicate with disk storage devices.

The next important part of the computer system is its memory. The memory is the place where information is stored. It is directly controlled by the CPU. The memory is composed of electronic circuits on boards that can be plugged into the computer. In this way, the memory of the computer can be expanded. Each of the memory circuit boards contains information that can be used in performing tasks by the central processing unit. The memory of a computer is measured in bits (bit is an acronym for BInary digiT). A bit is an electronic impulse and refers to the amount of information that the computer can manipulate at one specific time. Eight bits make up what is called a "byte." A byte can represent a single numeric value or a letter of the alphabet, a punctuation mark, or some other code. The memory of a computer is calculated in terms of bytes. One thousand bytes are a kilobyte or "K." For example, a computer may have a 64K memory. The term "M" is also used; "1M" memory represents 1 million bytes.

A computer generally has two types of memory: Random Access Memory (RAM) and Read Only Memory (ROM). RAM is the working memory of the computer. If the computer is turned off and there is no short-term back-up power system, the information in RAM will be lost. It is the area of the computer where information is read or written. Before any processing can take place, data and a program must be in RAM. ROM, Read Only Memory, stores basic instructions regarding the computer's functions. It is termed "system" memory. ROM can be reviewed, but it cannot be changed and will not be lost when power is turned off. The memory size of a microcomputer is expressed in terms of the Random Access Memory. As mentioned, this memory is measured in terms of bytes or kilobytes (K). To give you an idea of the memory needed for a common computer function, a typewritten page of fifty lines requires approximately 4K of RAM or 4,000 bytes of storage. The memory size of a computer, it should be noted, reflects the computer's RAM size only, that is, the total amount of information that can be stored *in the computer* at any moment. With the use of auxiliary devices, such as floppy disks, almost unlimited amounts of information can be stored easily and compactly and used in conjunction with the computer when needed.

Input and Output Devices

Input and output devices, along with the CPU and the memory, make up a complete computer system. Input and output devices, as previously indicated, get words, numbers, and other coded information into and out of the computer. Presently the most commonly used input and output devices are the cathode ray tube (CRT) combined with a typewriter keyboard and a printer. Using these tools, a user can type information into the computer; view information already in the computer on the CRT video display screen, and print that information on paper with the printer. Furthermore, there are two types of devices that can be used to store large amounts of information that cannot be held in the working memory of the computer: magnetic disks and tapes.

Disk Storage. It is important to remember that the working memory of the computer (RAM) is only capable of holding a certain number of bytes at one time. Furthermore, when the computer is turned off, information in the working memory of the computer is lost, unless there is some back-up power capability. Disk devices provide a way of storing information so that it can be used at a later time. Disk devices also provide a way of entering programs (software) into the computer.

There are two types of disk storage: the floppy disk and the hard disk. The floppy disk, so named because it resembles a floppy record, is available in two sizes: 5¼ inch and 8 inch. The floppy disk is made of flexible plastic that has been coated with a magnetic material similar to that found on recording tape. These circular disks can be "written on" by the user or can store information that can be viewed by the user. Blank floppy disks are inexpensive, and a single density 5¼ inch disk can hold up to 100,000 bytes, whereas an 8 inch disk will hold up to 500,000 characters. This roughly translates into 80 pages of typewritten material. Double density disks or quad density disks can hold much more information. For ease in handling, floppy disks are encased in a protective sleeve. Floppy disks are by far the most commonly used disk storage devices today.

The second type of disk storage is the hard disk. A hard disk can store more information than a floppy disk. There are two types of hard disks: removable and fixed. The fixed hard disk remains encased in the computer; the removable hard disk can be taken out like the floppy disk. Hard disks are used when there is a need to store very large amounts of information.

Audio Tape Recorders. Another way of storing information is by using magnetic tape. Both cassette and reel-to-reel tape recorders can be used as input/output devices to help the user process information in a computer. Cassettes are more commonly used than reel-to-reel tapes, although disks are used more often than either of these options. Again, like the disk, magnetic tape storage devices provide a means whereby information can be stored until it is needed by the user.

The Keyboard. The keyboard is probably the most common method used to enter information into the computer. A computer keyboard is very similar to the keyboard of a typewriter, although it may have special keys that allow the user to enter commands. It may also have a calculator-like numerical keyboard to one side, which allows the user to enter numerical information as well.

Printing Devices. A printer receives information from the computer and prints it on paper. A printing device is essential where there is a need to produce written or graphic materials, such as letters, financial statements, charts, forecasts, mailing lists, and so on. A standard typed page contains approximately 80 characters per line. Although printers can handle over 130 characters per line, most are designed to conform to the standard-sized page. Printers are usually equipped to handle perforated paper that can be continuously fed into the mechanism for high speed production of printed material. The printers that are the most effective are ones that have upper and lower case letters; proportional spacing; both friction (for single page printing) and adjustable tractor feed mechanisms (for continuous form printing); multiple type fonts; expanded and compressed type; print on various paper widths; and print on preprinted forms, labels, and envelopes.[4]

There are three types of printers commonly found in use with mini or microcomputers. These are thermal dot matrix printers, impact dot matrix printers, and letter quality impact printers. Two other less common printers are the electrostatic printer and the ink jet printer.

- *Thermal Dot Matrix Printers.* This process involves the use of heat applied to special "heat sensitive" paper. The heat turns the paper a different color, creating numeric or alphabetical characters where the heat has been applied. This is a very inexpensive and simple method of printing. It does not, however, produce letter quality printed material. It is useful in drafting documents.
- *Impact Dot Matrix Printers.* This process creates letters and numbers that are composed of closely spaced dots. Dot matrix copy looks almost like letter quality copy. The characters are produced on paper using a ribbon that is struck by a matrix of tiny wires. This type of printer is the fatest of the three types of devices. The quality of the copy of the dot matrix printer is better than the thermal dot matrix printer, but not quite as good as the letter quality impact printer.
- *Letter-quality Impact Printers.* Letter quality printers are the most expensive and complex of the three types of printers. Most printers of this type use what is known as the daisy wheel printing device, although there are printers that use the thimble printing device that is found on most IBM typewriters. The quality of copy produced by these printing devices is very high. Better than the average typewriter, letter quality printers are used when appearance is important; for example, for letters, reports, financial statements, and so on.
- *Electrostatic Printers.* Another type of printer is the electrostatic printer. This printing device uses electrical charges to make dots on paper that has been electrically sensitized. It is similar to the other dot matrix printers in that it can be used to print graphics, charts, or other types of designs.
- *Ink Jet Printer.* Still another type of printer is the ink-jet printer. This printer actually squirts tiny drops of ink at paper; thus, the name ink jet. Ink jet printers are just starting to make their way into use in businesses.

When selecting a printer, there are a number of different questions that should be asked by the owner or manager. The two most important questions are "What is the print quality desired?" and "What is the speed at which printed material is needed?" The type of printer, as well as the price will vary according to these two factors. For example, there are high-speed printers, such as laser printers, that could print this entire book in one minute. However, the cost of such printers usually runs into six figures and would not be practical for most small businesses. A further consideration is whether or not a business needs to produce graphic materials. If so, plotters that can produce graphs can be purchased and used in conjunction with the computer.

CRT Terminals

The CRT (Cathode Ray Tube) terminal in combination with a keyboard is perhaps the most widely used mechanism for entering information into a computer. The CRT is like a television screen, although the picture is much clearer than on an ordinary television screen. CRT terminals are either monochrome or color. A color terminal requires the proper color processing circuitry on the computer's "board" (a color card) and software designed to "drive" it. Some terminals come with full color screens. In most businesses a monochrome terminal is sufficient.

The number of characters that can be displayed on a screen determines the "size" of the CRT screen. This formatting varies, although the standard size used in business is 80 characters per line by 24 lines. Two important factors must be investigated when selecting a CRT terminal. The first is known as the *baud rate*. The baud rate refers to the speed at which the computer receives and transmits data. Generally speaking, most computers receive and send information at between 300 and 1200 baud. (Interestingly, the baud rate also affects the speed at which printers receive information— the higher the baud rate, the more quickly information can be printed, with the only limitation being the speed at which the printer can print, i.e., characters per second. The second factor to be considered when selecting a CRT terminal is whether or not the system will operate at *"full duplex"*. Some computers require that certain functions remain idle while others operate. When the computer can process and receive information at the same time, it is said to be operating at full duplex. When the system is operating at half duplex, it can only send or receive information at one time.

The real beauty of using a CRT terminal is that it allows the user to display information before it has been printed. In this way, the user can move information around on the screen or add or delete information as desired before printing it. Material can be proofread, spelling and grammatical errors can be caught, information can be formatted in a different way, or material can be added or substracted. This book was prepared using a computer. It enabled the authors, who live in different locations, to make changes in the original manuscript inexpensively and rapidly. There is no question that the production of books such as this one is assisted greatly by the use of computer systems.

Although less effective than the CRT terminal, a television can be adapted for use with the computer to display information. Televisions are less clear in terms of focus, and the number of characters that can be displayed on a television screen are usually less than on a CRT terminal. When the television is used with a keyboard, it can perform functions equivalent to the CRT terminal.

Modem

The term *modem* is derived from the words MOdulator/DEModulator. The modem is basically a telephone hook-up. It converts the tones it hears into electrical signals that can enable one computer to "talk" to another computer and gain information from it. It may be desirable in certain situations to obtain data or perform calculations that cannot be done with a minicomputer by communicating with a larger computer. These larger computers can be accessed with the use of a modem. Modems vary in terms of the speed with which they can transmit electrical signals, or baud rate. Their cost will largely be determined by this factor—the faster their speed of transmission, the more expensive they are.

Figure 9-1 depicts the relationship of a computer system's components to one another. As you can see, the keyboard is connected to the CPU and

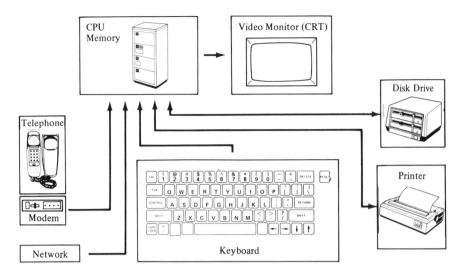

FIGURE 9–1. Components of a computer system.

memory. In turn, the CPU and memory are connected to the disk drives, printer, CRT terminal, and modem. The CPU and memory unit take direction from the user, resulting in the transmittal of information to or through the other devices. For example, a person might place information in the CPU and memory unit, which commands the unit to elicit information from materials stored on a disk in the disk drive. This material in turn is displayed on the terminal. Information entered into the central processing unit and memory and displayed on the terminal may be printed with the use of the printer. The modem can be used to communicate with another computer.

Benefits of the Computer

It is predicted that nearly 75 percent of all jobs will require some knowledge of computers within the next fifteen years. The question becomes not whether your commercial leisure service business will have a computer, but rather to what extent your organization will use a computer system to assist with the operation of the organization. The advantages of the computer far outweight the disadvantages. Not only can the computer assist the organization as a whole, but it also can assist each member of the organization. Some of the specific advantages of the computer are (see Figure 9-2):

- *Storing, Processing and Transmitting Information.* Because a computer provides a way of storing, processing, and transmitting information quickly and in great volume, it can increase the efficiency and hence the productivity of an organization significantly. It can plan work schedules, assist in analyzing, assist in making sales, and so forth.
- *Reduction of Repetitive Tasks.* A major benefit of a computer system is that it reduces the need for repetitive tasks. Such items as mailing lists, correspondence, and so on can be handled easily in a computer. This elim-

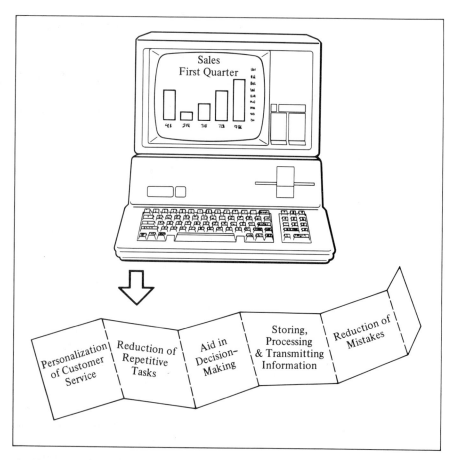

FIGURE 9–2. Benefits of the computer in small businesses.

inates the costly clerical time needed to reproduce such items. Also, it is possible to add or subtract from inventory lists, mailing lists, and so on, without having to redo the entire list. The new information can simply be inserted or deleted where appropriate within the existing list or text.

- *Reduction of Mistakes.* A major problem in any organization is the mistakes made by employees in carrying out their work assignments. The computer can be helpful in reducing or correcting human error. For example, a person typing a letter on a computer system can review the letter for spelling, content, accuracy, and so forth before it is printed. The computer also reduces human error by making accurate calculations.

- *An Aid in Decision Making.* The presence of a computer in an organization can also greatly assist the decision-making process. Modeling and forecasting programs provide information upon which decisions can be made that affect current and future resource allocations. Without such information, shifting organizational resources to meet changing market conditions may be difficult if not impossible. The computer can also help the organization in its day-to-day decision making. For example, the computer can inform the user when supplies and materials need to be reordered, at what rate they are being used, and when they will likely need to be reordered again.

- *Personalized Customer Service.* The computer allows the organization to personalize its communications with its consumers at a relatively low cost. Personalized letters, catalogues, contest forms, and custom-designed services are all made easier through the use of a computer system. Although a large number of customers can be sent personalized letters through usual secretarial methods, the cost can quickly become prohibitive; the computer can accomplish the task quickly and cheaply.

It is obvious that the computer can be of great assistance to a commercial leisure service organization. If meeting consumer needs with high quality services at great value is the goal of the organization, the margin between success and failure in a rapidly changing market may be the utilization of a computer system.

Business Use of the Computer

As we progress into the computer age, the uses of computers in businesses will expand. Considering the fact that electronic computers have been in existence only since the late 1940s and microcomputers have only been in existence since the late 1970s, growth in the application of computers in business is staggering. We often think of the computers used in business as carrying out such tasks as processing payrolls, maintaining inventories, maintaining mailing lists, and performing other record-keeping functions. However, it is clear that the uses of the computers in businesses are expanding at a rapid rate. Not only are hardware and software packages increasing dramatically in terms of variety, but they are becoming more accessible to larger numbers of people as their costs decline and they become more "user friendly." For example, Apple Computer, Inc. provides businesses with a variety of functions. In their excellent buyer's guide, entitled *Personal Computers in Business* by Barbara Gibson, it is noted that the personal computer can improve the work of a business by performing a ". . . wide range of tasks with extraordinary speed and accuracy."[5] Some of the applications suggested in this document include modeling and forecasting, graphic illustrations, word processing, data base management, accounting, training, and communications (see Figure 9-3).

- *Modeling and Forecasting.* The speed with which the personal computer can perform complex calculations makes it a valuable tool for managers, planners, and analysts involved in financial modeling and forecasting—examining the corporate past and predicting the corporate future. As an electronic worksheet, the computer replaces the laborious spreadsheet-and-calculator method of planning (or costly timeshare-system planning). It offers managers a better means of exploring the "what-ifs" of different business situations. It also allows them to develop more accurate business plans, sales and cash-flow forecasts, department budgets, product and marketing strategies, and material and labor estimates. Sophisticated mathematical formulas are built into the better modeling programs, so the computer does all the calculating and recalculating work when different assumptions are tested.

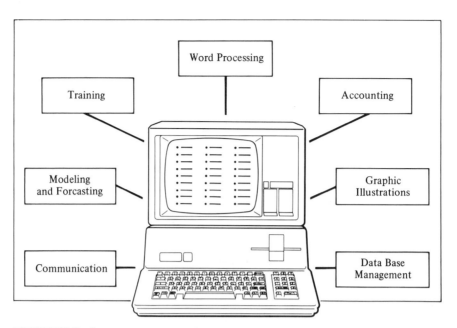

FIGURE 9–3. Potential uses of the computer in small businesses.

- *Graphic Illustrations.* Computer-generated graphs, charts, and maps have become valuable decision-making tools for managers who otherwise would have to digest and interpret truckloads of statistics generated by computer printouts. Easy to produce and easy to understand, graphs and charts prove particularly useful in monitoring performance, spotting trends, and evaluating business opportunities. They also serve as valuable communication tools. Graphics programs designed for business use can convert virtually any numerical information—profit and loss, gross margin forecast, sales, budget, cash flow—into presentation-quality bar, pie, line, and scatter graphs.
- *Word Processing.* What the electronic calculator did for the number, the word processing computer has done for the written word. It has shortened, practically exponentially, the time it takes to produce and edit memos, personalized form letters, reports, even book-length manuscripts. It is possible to edit a document—add sentences, delete or move paragraphs, correct spelling errors, and search for and replace words—in a single operation before text is committed to paper. The computer can also store written information so it can be edited and updated whenever necessary. The text stored by the computer is as easy to update as it is to edit. And the writer can product letter-perfect copies of each updated text.
- *Data Base Management.* In computer jargon, filing information electronically is termed data base management. Data base management systems keep records (of personnel, sales, statistics, marketing survey abstracts) that can be easily updated and manipulated in various ways. If you own a small business and maintain a computer list of several hundred customers, you might use it to generate mailing labels for a special promotion, review purchase activities for the fourth quarter, or send a letter just to customers with certain zip codes.

- *Accounting.* Accounting by computer streamlines the five most basic business functions: general ledger, accounts receivable, accounts payable, sales invoicing/inventory control, and payroll. Besides cutting the time that it takes to do the same work by hand, computerized accounting offers businesses an opportunity to improve cash flow management, boost the collection rate of receivables, plan payments to take advantage of vendor discounts, and maintain inventory levels that minimize cash investment and improve customer service. Who stands to benefit most from personal computer accounting systems? The small business owner or bookkeeper who ordinarily handles the books, or whose books go to an accountant or bookkeeping service bureau each month or quarter.
- *Training.* A personal computer is a masterful training tool. Programs are available that make it easy to develop dynamic instructional materials. These, in turn, open the door to new, more creative approaches toward improving employee performance and productivity. The personal computer is the teacher. Sales, management, and service employees learn in a one-to-one, self-paced environment in which the computer actively prompts, monitors, and tests for understanding. And the teacher is quite talented—it can be a text with sound, graphics, color, simulations, and video technology. Besides increasing learning retention, computer-assisted instruction (CAI) and computer-assisted training (CAT) programs make better use of meeting time, fit more readily into demanding executive schedules, and travel to branch offices more economically than do training personnel.
- *Communication.* To extend the potential of the personal computer, many business people link it, usually by telephone, to an interoffice "network" of other personal computers, to data bases stored in large main frame computers, and to information services provided by commercial computer networks. These communication links allow managers to share data bases and models used in business planning, to speed delivery of correspondence by electronic mail, and to draw on information found in large, complex data bases. It's unlikely, of course, that you will use a personal computer for all of these functions. As a manager, you might rely on a personal computer to help you develop business models and budgets, or you might use it to produce graphs that compare actual sales against forecasts, or expenditures against budgets. As a small business owner, you may depend on a personal computer to automate your accounting procedures or to generate letters and mailing labels for direct mail advertising.[6]

The potential uses of the computer in an area such as accounting are amazing. When considering the speed at which information can be obtained and processed and the volume of information that can be processed, there is no question that the computer can positively affect the effectiveness and efficiency, and hence the profitability, of small commercial leisure service businesses. For example, in discussing the application of personal computers to the area of accounting, Gibson has identified numerous functions that can be performed by the computer. With regard to the five basic accounting functions—general ledger, accounts receivable, accounts payable, inventory control, and payroll—Gibson specifies their uses to businesses as follows:

- *General Ledgers.* Most general ledger programs keep a master chart of accounts (with user definable account number) that maintains basic information about each; maintain a general ledger that records and summarizes financial information for each account; print financial reports and summaries; and generate audit details through transaction listings.[7]
- *Accounts Receivable.* Most accounts receivable programs generate accurate monthly customer statements (on either ordinary paper or preprinted forms); automatically post receipts to each account and to the general ledger; automatically "age" accounts into 30-, 60-, 90-, and 120-day time periods; calculate and post charges on past due accounts and provide up-to-date information on account activity and status.[8]
- *Accounts Payable.* Most accounts payable programs give you a choice of different payment methods (all outstanding invoices, pay by due date, partial payments, selected invoices); provide audit trails; flag and/or automatically pay invoices that offer discounts; and automatically generate checks and mailing labels or envelopes.[9]
- *Inventory Control.* Most inventory control programs maintain a master record of each item in stock (including product number, name or description, quantity on hand, unit cost, unit price, retail price, and total cost); identify stock by weight, volume, or liquid or dry measure; work with several costing methods, such as LIFO (last in, first out), FIFO (first in, first out), and averaging, call up any item on record to find out quantity in stock, on order or on back order; delete or update any item on record; automatically record sales, receipts, and adjustments (such as returns, shrinkage, or overages) and transfer information to the general ledger and accounts receivable; tag products with several prices (normal, retail, discount, and bulk order); identify reorder levels, which the computer can watch for and flag (even calculate and suggest reorder quantities based on sales); learn, within a few seconds, the total value of your inventory by product or department; and sort, search, and arrange information into summaries and reports by merchandising category, department, location, vendor, or periods (commonly month-to-date and year-to-date).[10,11]

This list of services that can be provided to businesses by computer accounting programs is impressive to say the least. One can see there are many, many uses for which the computer can be used in small businesses. It is important to remember that all of these programs are readily available, and most can be purchased reasonably. Furthermore, today's mini or microcomputer is affordable for most small businesses. No longer does the small business have to purchase "computer time" from outside sources; rather, each business can if it so desires have its own in-house computer for which it can buy programs or create custom programs to facilitate its operation.

Methods and Procedures Used in Selecting a Computer System

Selecting the right computer system is not an easy task. It takes time and effort to determine exactly what you want a computer system to accomplish within your organization. Furthermore, there is a large amount of hardware from which to choose and many, many software packages. There are three basic areas that must be investigated in order to purchase a computer system that will complement and enhance the organization's operations: functional needs, software needs, and hardware needs.

Determining Functional Needs

The first step in selecting a computer system to meet your organization's needs is to determine specifically what you want the system to do. A good place to start would be to ask yourself and others within your organization such questions as: Can we use the computer to provide better, more efficient service to our consumers? Can we use the computer to provide information to help in our decision making? Can we eliminate some of the routine manual work within our organization by using the computer? Can the computer help us accomplish our work more quickly? Can the computer help us with inventory control? Can the computer help us with our scheduling of activities, meetings, and events? Can it help us in scheduling the activities or work schedules of personnel? Can it help us with our correspondence?

Most business people can readily identify many needs within their organization with which a computer can be of assistance. Many business applications of the computer are very standard, such as payroll, word processing, inventory, client mailing lists, and so on. However, business people may not be aware of *all* of the various services that a computer can perform within their organization. They may think that they know their needs and can select a computer to meet them, but they will do themselves a disservice if they do not consider using a computer consultant to help them analyze their business operations. When working with a computer consultant, the businessperson must compile up-to-date and comprehensive information regarding the business, so that the consultant's choice of a computer is based on the actual needs of the organization. Murphy has compiled a list of suggestions for compiling information to assist a computer consultant:[12]

1. List the various volumes of your work by type and category on a monthly basis for the most recent twelve-month period. If actual figures are not available, informed estimates will suffice.
2. Describe your present procedures and staff. Make your descriptions clear, leaving no room for misinterpretations.
3. Explain in unambiguous language the standards of performance that you require.
4. Clearly define your special requirements. For example, if you have complicated receipts, disbursements, and so forth, these should be explained.
5. Spell out your expectations for the (commercial leisure service business's) future growth in addition to the nature and requirements of anticipated future programs. This can affect both system design and cost.

Once a consultant and the owner or manager have reviewed the operations of a commercial leisure business, a decision can be made between the alternatives in terms of computer use. Basically, there are three alternatives available to the commercial leisure service organization. First, the organization can contract with a computer service company to provide necessary services. For example, it is not unusual to purchase mailing labels used in the distribution of advertisements from such a company. A second approach is to pay for a time-sharing service. Time sharing allows several organizations to use a computer at one time. Generally speaking, time sharing applies to the use of large computer systems where cost is a great consideration. The third alternative is to purchase an in-house computer system. Our discourse from this point will focus on the establishment of an in-house computer system for small businesses. More specifically, we will primarily discuss the use of microcomputers in small commercial leisure service businesses.

Software Selection

If the decision is made to set up an in-house computer system, the next major decision for the owner or manager is that of determining the types of software that should be purchased to meet the organization's needs. It is important to recognize that a computer must have a set of instructions to follow. These instructions are provided by computer software. There are two types of software—systems software and applications software. *Systems* software programs are those sets of instructions that enable the efficient use of the hardware by controlling the execution of other programs. Systems software provides general operational instructions. *Applications* software programs are designed to help the user perform specific tasks, such as financial ratios, accounting, inventory, assessment, and so on. To reiterate, systems software instructs the microcomputer in its general operation, and applications software instructs the microcomputer to perform more specific tasks related to the needs of the commercial leisure service business.

There are three different types of application software: packaged (canned) programs: modified packaged programs; and custom programs.

1. *Packaged or Canned Software.* Packaged or canned software programs are readily available, relatively inexpensive, and easily serviced. These types of programs have already been written and can be applied in many different types of businesses. There are numerous off-the-shelf software programs that are distributed through retail computer stores.
2. *Modified Packaged Software.* Modified packaged software is a combination of canned software and custom software. This type of software uses as its base a canned program, which is then modified slightly to conform to the specific needs of a particular business. For example, small adjustments can be made to canned software at a relatively low cost to change business forms slightly or to incorporate the logo of an organization in printed materials.
3. *Custom Software.* Custom software programs are written specifically to accommodate the individual business needs of an organization. Custom programs are usually very expensive if written by an outside expert and are impractical for the small commercial leisure service business in most cases. Such programs are written by consulting programmers or software companies that offer this service. They may also be written by an owner or manager of a business who has had programming instruction. This may consume a great deal of time and effort, however.

What are the advantages and disadvantages of packaged, modified, and custom software? Packaged programs have several clear advantages. First, and perhaps most importantly, canned or packaged programs are readily available. In addition, the cost of this type of software is less expensive than custom software. Also, because most canned software programs have already been on the market, they are relatively error free; most of their "bugs" have been identified and corrected. The major disadvantage of canned software is that it is not flexible. The organization must tailor its operations to the packaged software program.

Custom software programs also have advantages and disadvantages. Their greatest advantage is that the program is specifically designed for the operations of an individual organization. The disadvantages of custom software are the greater cost involved in having a special program created and the time required to write it, test it, and refine it. Another disadvantage of the custom software program is that it has not been used extensively and may have more "bugs" than packaged software programs.

Modified packaged software programs combine the advantages of both the packaged and custom programs. They are far less expensive than custom programs, yet they allow the organization some flexibility in the format of the programs used. The disadvantage of modified packaged software programs is that costs for modifying programs can become prohibitive if not watched carefully. Major changes in packaged programs that modify them to meet an organization's needs can cost as much as or more than a custom program.

The following advice can be considered as a general rule of thumb to be used by the small commercial businessperson when selecting software:

1. Decide how much main memory will be required.
2. Determine how many and what kind of storage devices will be needed.
3. Determine whether or not the package is flexible to accommodate changing business requirements.
4. Determine whether or not the system can be modified or upgraded, and what the cost of this would be.
5. Determine whether or not the package can be installed and operated easily.
6. Find out whether or not the software vendor will furnish any training assistance and, if so, whether or not there will be a charge.
7. Talk to other users to find out whether or not the program has worked successfully for them in their business venture. Find out whether or not the package has been used widely and has a proven reputation.
8. Peruse the vendor contract. Does it provide enough protection and support for the user? If not, can this be negotiated?
9. Calculate the costs and benefits of the package with respect to other available packages.[13]
10. Operate the software without the salesperson's help before purchasing. Do not be sold by a salesperson's demonstration.
11. Buy "user friendly" software—software that is interactive. You should be able to enter questions in everyday language, and, if entered incorrectly, the computer should tell you how to do it correctly.

12. Review the software manual carefully before purchasing the software. However, buy software designed for the decision-maker (owner or manager) not the computer expert.

13. Determine the software vendor's policies for updating the software.

14. Do not develop your own software if packages are available; it is too expensive and time consuming.

15. Shop for microcomputer programmers. Rates for programmers vary greatly. Quality and speed have little relationship to the rate. Try to find a programmer who understands your business; the savings can be substantial. And be sure the programmer has experience on the hardware for which the software is being developed; otherwise you pay for an education.

16. Shop for discount prices on nationally marketed software. Purchase mass user programs, such as bookkeeping, accounts payable and receivable, word processing, and automated spreadsheets.

17. Find out if hands-on or on-site training is available with the software. Last, carefully consider the expense of creating large data banks that require data collection and input from primary sources.[14]

Again, it is important to remember that a computer can only do what it is told to do. In other words, it needs a set of instructions or a program. It is the software that enables the computer to process information, make calculations, and transfer information.

Hardware Selection

Now that software selection has been discussed, let us move to a discussion of what is known as hardware. Hardware is the actual physical machinery of the computer system. A computer system's hardware will consist of at least one input device, such as a keyboard, the computer itself, and some way of obtaining information from the computer, such as a printer and video display terminal. Furthermore, a computer system will require other types of physical equipment such as disk drives through which to load instructions or software (see Figure 9-4).

The basic computer itself should be selected so that it provides the amount of memory needed to carry out both present and projected future functions of the organization. Furthermore, it should provide the desired input and output capabilities. Obviously, it is important that the computer's potential for expanding, both in terms of memory and input and output capabilities, be explored before selection. Many microcomputers are designed in such a way that additional memory or input/output cards can be added at a low cost. Thus, as new computer applications are desired such systems can be modified.

Another important variable to consider when selecting hardware is whether or not the system is open to more than one user at a time. This is known as multiuser capacity. In many businesses there will be a need for more than one person to have access to a computer at one time. For example several secretaries might be involved in word processing and an accountant might be involved in record keeping and bookkeeping functions. Therefore, hardware selection should consider actual as well as future user needs.

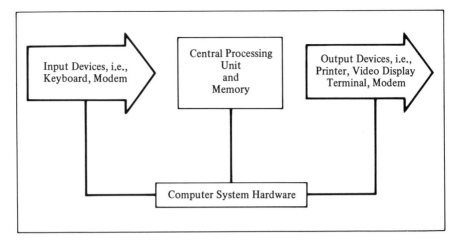

FIGURE 9–4. A computer's hardware system.

Another factor to consider when selecting hardware is its storage system. The computer storage system employed by small commercial businesses, usually a disk system, should have at least two disk drives. With two disk drives, the user can make copies of diskettes, providing greater safety for records. It can cost a great deal of both time and money to replace information that is accidentally destroyed.

A factor that should also be considered when selecting hardware is the ability of the system to interface with other computer systems and available software packages. For example, some computers currently on the market are compatible with a very large number of canned software programs, others are not. The small commercial business should select a computer that will accommodate the number and variety of canned software programs currently needed and potentially needed to avoid the costly alternative of having to design custom programs.

When selecting hardware, the organization should also determine whether or not it is "friendly" to use. This can include such factors as the layout of the keyboard, the "friendliness" of error signals, and so on. The user should feel very comfortable with the hardware and find it easy and pleasant to use. In order to make hardware "user friendly," an on-site training program is helpful. Most companies selling computers will provide personnel to train an organization's staff in the use of its computers. The character and extent of such training should be thoroughly investigated before the purchase of hardware.

The last factor that should be considered when selecting hardware is the availability of a service contract. Although most computer manufacturers offer a warranty covering their product for a limited period of time, it is important to determine whether or not repairs and parts are readily available and their cost. Before the expiration of the initial warranty that usually comes with a computer, the organization may want to extend the service contract to cover any future repairs or parts. The manager or owner should carefully analyze such service contracts to determine the likely cost to his or her organization of any repairs that may be needed. Because of the reliability of microcomputers, many small businesses do not feel the need to have a service contract on their computers. Repair service is quickly available from most computer companies, and the costs involved in repairs are *usually* less than the cost of a service contract. This decision is, of course, up to the discretion of each owner or manager.

Here are some specific recommendations for the selection of hardware that will meet the needs of a small commercial leisure service business:

1. Consider hardware and software needs together. Is software now available for the hardware? What software will be available for your system in the future?
2. Find out how many additional vendors are supplying additional support equipment for the computer.
3. Learn some of the basic terms and definitions before conversing with sales people and consultants.
4. Consider whether or not hard disk storage will be needed. If so, how much? Also, decide whether multi-user or multi-tasking capabilities are needed.
5. Consider the purchase price of the computer. The real cost of the computer is in making it do what you want it to (the software and interface equipment), not the purchase price of the hardware system. Most hardware and software prices can be negotiated.
6. Compare and contrast systems before making decisions. Read magazines and other literature that provide information and cost comparisons.
7. Do and do not listen to computer salespeople, computer consultants, software vendors, and experienced users. The decision is yours to make. Use the same good business sense you use in making other decisions. Get several opinions on the same question. Write down your questions and expand your list of questions as you learn more. Also jot down each advisor's opinion and evaluate each one carefully.
8. Ascertain the servicing available, especially during the initial ninety days after the sale. Problems usually occur during the first month or two as the equipment is "burned in."
9. Do not worry about hardware becoming obsolete. Most hardware is obsolete before it reaches the market. Be more concerned with its adaptability to new hardware as it becomes available. Remember, an obsolete computer three years from now will still perform the original tasks for which it is purchased.
10. Purchase the microcomputer system with the most memory for the money but be sure that any computer you purchase has a wide range of reasonable software that can be used with it. Sometimes support systems lag behind the hardware technology and the latest microcomputer with the most memory will not always have a support system adequate for your needs.[15]

These practical suggestions can be used by commercial leisure service business wishing to purchase a computer system. Because of the potential of computers and their benefits, the owner of any commercial leisure service business should attempt to gain knowledge about them.

Computer System Cost Analysis

The following form, "Computer System Cost Analysis," presents a computer system cost analysis profile sheet. The first section of the cost analysis details the cost of installing a new computer system. Some of the costs include site preparation, training, conversion, and software. The second section in the cost analysis involves projection of estimated annual operating costs. Here, the physical machinery is costed out, as are maintenance costs, software rental, staff, supplies, and utilities. This cost analysis profile sheet can be a useful tool to an owner or manager in determining accurately those costs that would be involved in establishing a computer system within a small commercial leisure service business.

Computer System Cost Analysis Profile Sheet

I. Estimated Cost of New Computer System
   A. Cost of site preparation $_____
   B. Training costs   _____
   C. Conversion costs (converting present records to new system) _____
   D. Costs of software   _____
   E. Miscellaneous costs (security, forms, communications, consulting _____

                                      Total one-time costs $_____

II. Estimated Annual Operating Costs
   A. Equipment rental or amortization $_____
   B. Maintenance costs   _____
   C. Software rental or amortization or license fee   _____
   D. Professional staff   _____
   E. Supplies   _____
   F. Utilities (extra costs for housing other than physical costs) _____

                                      Total recurring costs $_____
                                      Total System Costs $_____

Source: William C. Weaver, "The Ideal System—A Reference Point," *Real Estate Today*, May, 1980, p. 22.

The next page offers a checklist for vendor evaluation. Because the number of computer vendors (both hardware and software) is so large, careful consideration should be given by the owner or manager to the reliability, reputation, and continuity of such organizations. The checklist identifies six areas from which evaluations of computer vendors can be made. Some of the areas of evaluation include the organization's time in business, its profitability, its support network, as well as the nature of its contractual arrangements and obligations. At present, there are many, many small companies involved in the production of both hardware and software and there will inevitably be rapid shifts in the status of such companies. Competition is great and some companies will not survive. It is imperative, therefore, that the manager or owner purchasing a computer deal with a computer vendor that is solid and likely to remain so.

Check List for Vendor Evaluation _____

I. Historical
    A. Time in business (when actually started delivering systems)
    B. Profitability (see annual report)
    C. Type of ownership (public company, private?)
    D. Other businesses (provide only hardware, software and/or other services?)
    E. Number of systems actually installed and their location

II. Expertise
    A. Type of customer base—especially for type of equipment in which you are interested
    B. Customer list for references
    C. Degree of commitment in your area
    D. Ability to offer meaningful demonstrations

III. Financial Status
    A. Dun & Bradstreet
    B. Local Better Business Bureau
    C. Chamber of Commerce
    D. Balance sheet (often difficult to get)

IV. Size of Firm
    A. Location
    B. Number of officers
    C. Number of employees
    D. Number of repair/maintenance staff
    E. Yearly gross sales and trends

V. Local Support and Size
    A. Cost and location of local maintenance staff
    B. Response time for hardware and software problems
    C. Provision of full-line products, e.g., printers, CRTs, etc.

VI. Contractual Obligations
    A. Flexibility of contract
    B. Performance guarantees
    C. Ownership of resulting software
    D. Percent of system provided by vendor
        1. equipment
        2. software
        3. training
        4. maintenance
        5. installations
        6. systems support

Source: William C. Weaver, "The Ideal System—A Reference Point," *Real Estate Today*, May, 1980, p. 23.

Some Concerns Regarding the Implementation of a Computer System

The use of computers within businesses is not without its problems or disadvantages. Obviously, there is a need to make a financial investment, perhaps a substantial one, to introduce a computer system into a business. Furthermore, work patterns may need to be rearranged and this may result in some job dislocation and create a need for retraining of employees. It is also a major undertaking to convert "paper" files into electronic files. This can require a great deal of effort and, again, will change the way that the business's information is obtained and stored. The business's processes or procedures will usually need to be re-examined and revamped as well. Some businesses will not have the skills or expertise to operate a computer system without the aid of specialized computer personnel. This may require still more expense on the part of the business.

Computers are not immune to human error and deceit. Either of these factors can be a serious disadvantage if not controlled by a business owner or manager. The computer does not "think" by itself, it does what it is told to do. Therefore, if misinformation, inaccurate financial reports, or other misrepresentations of actual business procedures are introduced to the computer, it can potentially result in inaccurate information, faulty statements, and inaccurate reports. What comes out of a computer is only as good as what goes into it. Although a business owner or manager can attempt to train employees to avoid human error in their computer inter-actions, there is always the possibility of an employee intentionally entering erroneous information into the computer to cheat the business. The National Center for Computer Crime Data has identified seven basic computer crimes that can be perpetrated within a business or organization that a manager or owner should guard against. They are:

1. False or illegitimate invoices submitted to computerized accounts payable systems.
2. Unauthorized transfer of funds by computer from a company account to a personal account.
3. Falsification of inventory levels maintained by computer, allowing inventory thefts to go undiscovered.
4. Computer output malfunction resulting in double payment to a supplier or employee.
5. Unauthorized sale of computerized information, such as client lists or even the program itself.
6. Employee manipulation of computerized company records for payment from company outsiders.
7. Computer system sabotage by dissatisfied operations employees.[16]

These concerns can be overcome if a proper control system is established. A computer consultant can help the business owner or manager design a program to assist in the establishment of adequate control procedures.

Summary

In this chapter we have discussed the application of computers in commercial leisure service organizations. The growth of electronic culture is viewed by many as being similar in impact to the transformation that took place as we moved from an oral to a written culture. The speed and volume with which the information can be transmitted today is simply staggering.

Computers were first developed after World War II. The invention of the transistor made the electronic computer possible. It was followed by the invention of integrated circuits. This led to the development of micro-processors, which led to the commercial development of mini- and micro-computers. Not only has computer hardware (physical machinery) developed rapidly in the past several decades, but also there has been a tremendous growth in computer software. The creation of BASIC provided an important step in the use of computers by incorporating simple English-like language into the computer–user interaction.

A computer system has several components. These can be defined in broad terms as input devices, the central processing unit and memory, and output devices. The central processing unit is where actual data manipulation and processing occurs. Some of the input/output devices commonly associated with the use of computers include disk storage devices, audio tape recorders, computer keyboards, printers, CRT terminals, and modems. The disk storage systems and audio tape recorders are devices that enable information to be stored for use in the computer. A keyboard is a way of entering information into the computer, and a printer is a way of producing written or graphic materials. The CRT terminal, used in conjunction with a keyboard can be used to display information in such a way that it can be read and manipulated by the user. A modem is a device used to connect the computer with another computer via telephone lines.

There are numerous benefits of the computer. Some of these are storing, processing, and transmitting information; reducing repetitive work tasks; reducing mistakes; aiding in decision making; and personalizing the organization's consumer services. Some of the business uses of the computer include modeling and forecasting, graphic illustrations, word processing, data base management, accounting, training, and communication.

In order to select a computer system that will complement a business's needs, several areas must be reviewed. First, the business manager should determine the functional needs of the organization. This means that it should be determined what it is the computer is to do. Second, consideration must be given to the type of software desired. There are three types of software: packaged or canned software, modified packaged software, and custom software. Last, consideration must be given to the hardware or physical machinery needed. Consideration of hardware and software should be done in conjunction with one another.

Study Questions

1. Discuss the implications of the growth of electronic culture in society.
2. List five key events in the historical development of computers.
3. Identify five types of computers. What type of computer do you think will be found in small commercial leisure service organizations.
4. What is a computer system? Discuss the functions of the (1) central processing unit and memory, (2) disk storage, (3) audio tape recorders, (4) keyboard, (5) printing devices, (6) CRT terminal, and (7) modem.
5. Identify and define five benefits of computer applications in commercial leisure service organizations.
6. Identify and discuss seven applications of computers in commercial leisure service organizations.
7. What areas need to be investigated before buying a computer system?

8. List and describe three types of software. What are the advantages and disadvantages of each in your opinion?
9. What does the term "user friendly" mean?
10. What are some areas that require good managerial control when working with computers?

Experiential Exercise

Instructions: Pick any leisure service business of your choice and determine the potential uses of the computer in its operation. Be specific, investigating the operations of the business carefully in terms of such things as communication, training, accounting, data base management, graphic illustrations, word processing, and modeling and forecasting.

Communication _____

_____
_____
_____

Training _____

_____
_____
_____

Accounting _____

_____
_____
_____

Data Base Management _____

_____
_____
_____

Graphic Illustration _____

_____
_____
_____

Word Processing _____

_____
_____
_____

Modeling and Forecasting _____

_____
_____
_____

Notes

1. James Gotlieb, "The Evolution of Electronic Culture," *Journal of Real Estate Education*, Spring, 1983, p. 5.
2. Ibid.
3. Jerry Willis, Merl Miller, *Computers for Everybody*, 2nd ed. Beaverton, Oregon: Dilithium Press, 1983, p. 8.
4. Barbara Gibson, *Personal Computers in Business*, Cupertino, Calif.: Apple Computer, Inc., 1982, p. 41.
5. Ibid., p. 7.
6. Ibid., p. 7–9.
7. Ibid., p. 26.
8. Ibid., p. 27.
9. Ibid., p. 28.
10. Ibid.
11. Ibid., p. 29.
12. Gerald S. Murphy, "Computer Service Bureaus: Learn to be Selective," *Association Management*, November, 1982, p. 81.
13. T. Harold Jambers, Jr., "Comprehending Your Computer," *Journal of Real Estate Education*, Spring, 1983, p. 22.
14. Joseph M. Davis, "Microcomputers: An Invitation to the Future," *Journal of Real Estate Education*, Spring, 1983, p. 29.
15. Ibid.
16. The National Center for Computer Crime Data as cited in Jerome Dasso, James D. Vernon, "Computer Applications in Real Estate Brokerage," *Real Estate Today*, May, 1980, p. 17.

Appendix
A Brief Dictionary of Computerese

No doubt Webster would incandesce over the number of new words born to the world through computers. The speedy evolution of so many new terms, in fact, has virtually produced a new English dialect—computerese. You will find that the technology itself is responsible for terms like "bit" and "CPU"; others, like "input" and "documentation," give new meaning to the familiar.

Acoustic Coupler. A mechanical device that allows a telephone hand set to be connected to a modem; also used to refer to the entire modem. See Modem.

Address. A number that identifies the specific location in the computer memory where a piece of information is stored.

Alphanumeric. Characters consisting of letters and numbers, as opposed to special characters. See Special Characters.

Application Software. Software designed to accomplish a specific task such as accounting, financial modeling, or word processing. See Software.

ASCII. American Standard Code for Information Interchange; computers use binary numbers (combinations of ones and zeros) to represent letters, numbers, and special characters; the ASCII code specifies which binary number will stand for each character and provides a standard that allows computers from different manufacturers to "talk" to each other.

Assembly Language. A means programmers use to communicate with a computer; assembly language is a type of "low-level" computer language that lies between "high-level" languages such as BASIC and Pascal, and machine language (the fundamental codes of the computer). See Language.

Backup. An extra copy of information stored on a disk. If the program or other data stored on the first disk is damaged, it is still available on the backup copy.

BASIC. Beginners All-purpose Symbolic Instruction Code; the most popular language for personal computers. See Language.

Baud. A measure of the speed at which computer information travels (normally between a computer and a peripheral or between two computers). A baud is about equal to one bit per second.

Binary. A word used to describe a number system that uses only ones and zeros; an efficient way of storing information in a computer since the microscopic switches in a computer can only be ON (1) or OFF (0).

Bit. BInary digiT; the smallest piece of information (either a one or a zero) that the computer can handle at one time; eight bits constitute one byte.

Boot. To start the computer.

Bug. An error; a hardware bug is a malfunction or design error in the computer or its peripherals; a software bug is a programming error.

Bus. The means used to transfer information from one part of a computer to another.

Byte. The basic unit of measure of a computer's memory, representing a single alphanumeric character (A, B, C, 1, 2, ?, &, etc.); the equivalent of eight bits.

CAI/CAT. Computer-assisted instruction/Computer-assisted training; education or training that involves the use of the computer to instruct and monitor student performance.

Central Processing Unit. See CPU.

Character. A single letter, number, or other symbol; in a small computer, a character is normally eight bits or one byte.

COBOL. COmmon Business-Oriented Language; a computer language developed specifically for business use. See Language.

Command. A word or character that causes a computer to perform a specific task.

Computer. Any device that can receive, store, and act on a set of instructions in a predetermined sequence, and that permits both the instructions and the data upon which the instructions act to be changed. The distinction between a computer and a programmable calculator is that the computer can manipulate text as well as numbers, whereas the calculator can only handle numbers.

Computer Program. A series of commands, instructions, or statements put together in a way that tells a computer to perform a specific task or series of tasks.

CP/M. Control Program for Microprocessors; the name of a specific operating system. See Operating System.

CPU. Central processing unit; the part of the computer that collects, decodes, and executes instructions; often made up of a microprocessor and associated circuitry.

CRT. Cathode ray tube; the television-like tube that displays information used in a program; also called monitor or video monitor.

Cursor. A flashing or nonflashing square or arrow that appears on the computer's monitor to indicate where the next character of text or data will appear.

Custom Software. A computer program that is custom-designed to meet a particular user's specific need.

Data. All information, including facts, numbers, letters, and symbols, which can be acted on or produced by the computer.

Data Base. A collection of related information, such as found on a mailing list, that can be stored in the computer and retrieved in several ways.

Debug. To go through a program or hardware device to correct mistakes.

Disk. A flat, circular device that resembles a phonograph record and is used to store information and programs for the computer. Two types of disks are used with personal computers: floppy disks (or diskettes) and hard disks. See Floppy Disk, Hard Disk.

Disk Drive. The machinery that operates either a floppy or hard disk, rotating it at high speeds to read information stored on the disk or to write new information on it.

Documentation. Instructional materials that describe the operations of an individual computer program or a piece of system hardware.

Dot Matrix Printer. A type of printer that forms characters of multiple dots. See Printer.

Downtime. Any period of time when the computer is not available or not working.

Electronic Mail. Sending and receiving information by computer.

Floppy Disk. A flexible plastic disk, enclosed in a cardboard jacket, that stores information generated by the computer; in small computers, usually either 5¼ inch or 8 inch in diameter.

Format. As a noun, the physical form in which information appears; as a verb, to specify parameters of a form or to write address codes on a blank disk in preparation for using it to store data or programs.

FORTRAN. FORmula TRANslation, a high-level computer language used primarily for mathematical computations; though FORTRAN is available for some small computers, it is mainly used with large computer systems. See Language.

Hard Copy. Printed information generated by a computer. See Printer.

Hard Disk. A magnetically coated metal disk, usually permanently mounted within a disk drive; capable of storing 30 to 150 times more information than can a floppy disk; also called Winchester disk.

Hardware. The physical components of a computer system, particularly the CPU, disk drive, video monitor, and keyboard.

High-Level Language. A programming language that allows a person to give instructions to a computer in English rather than in the numerical (binary) code of ones and zeros; BASIC, COBOL, and Pascal are examples of high-level languages. See Language.

Impact Printer. See Printer.

Input. Information entered into the computer by means of a keyboard, graphic tablet, or other mechanism.

Input/Output (I/O). Software or hardware that exchanges data with the outside world.

Interactive. Describes a computer system in which a two-way conversation occurs between the user and the computer.

Interface. A piece of hardware or software used to connect two devices (usually the computer and a peripheral) that cannot be directly hooked together.

Language. A code that the computer understands; low-level languages resemble the fundamental codes of the computer; high-level languages (such as BASIC and COBOL) resemble English.

Letter-quality Printer. A printer, usually an impact printer, that generates documents of typewriter quality. See Printer.

Line Printer. A type of high-speed computer printer that prints an entire line at a time, rather than one character at a time.

Machine Language. The "native language" of a computer; the fundamental symbols, usually ones and zeros, that the computer is capable of recognizing and to which it can respond.

Memory. The part of the computer that stores program instructions and data; memory size is measured by the number of characters (bytes) it can store, in terms of "K" (1024) or "M"; 64K = 65,536 bytes, 1M = 1,048,576 bytes. Also called "user memory." See RAM, ROM.

Menu. A list of operations or commands available in a computer program, usually displayed on the computer screen when the program begins.

Microcomputer. A computer based on a microprocessor. See Microprocessor.

Microprocessor. Core of the central processing unit of a computer; it holds all the essential elements for manipulating data and performing arithmetic calculations.

Modem. MOdulator-DEModulator, a device that converts a computer's electrical signals into audible sounds (modulation) for transmission over the telephone, and back again (demodulation) for reception via telephone; used to link one computer to another.

Monitor. See CRT.

Network. A structure capable of linking two or more computers by wire, telephone lines, or radio links.

Operating System. A group of programs that act as intermediaries between the computer and the applications software; the operating system takes a program's commands and passes them down to the central processing unit in a language that the CPU understands; application programs must be written for a specific operating system such as DOS, SOS, CP/M, and others.

Output. Information the computer transmits; this is done by means of a video monitor, printer, or other mechanism.

Packaged Software. Computer programs that are available commercially through retail stores.

Parallel. Two or more computer operations happening at the same time; a parallel interface is one that receives and sends out a number of bits at the same time. See Serial.

Pascal. A high-level programming language with a larger, more sophisticated vocabulary than BASIC, used for complex applications in business, science, and education; named after the 17th-century French mathematician.

Peripheral. Hardware, such as a printer or modem, attached to the computer in order to perform a specific function.

Plotter. A printing mechanism capable of drawing lines rapidly and accurately for graphic representation.

Printer. A mechanism that reproduces, in printed form, the information entered into or generated by the computer; impact printers make impressions by physically striking a ribbon and paper, thermal printers make impressions by applying heat to heat-sensitive paper; some printers can produce graphs as well.

Printout. A printed copy of information produced by the computer. See Hard Copy.

Program. A sequence of instructions that the computer can understand and execute.

RAM. Random Access Memory; the part of the computer's memory that allows both reading and writing, as opposed to ROM (Read Only Memory). See Memory, ROM.

RF Modulator. A device that lets a personal computer use any ordinary television set for a monitor; also called a modulator.

ROM. Read Only Memory; the part of the computer's memory that allows just reading and is used to hold information that never changes, such as a computer language.

Save. To store a program on a disk or somewhere other than in the computer's memory.

Serial. Computer operations occurring in sequence; a serial interface is one that receives and sends out one piece of information at a time. See Parallel.

Software. Instructions that operate the computer hardware; system software is used for the computer's general tasks or functions (such as operating a printer or understanding BASIC); application software is used to accomplish a specific task, such as financial modeling or word processing.

Special Characters. Characters that can be displayed by the computer, but that are neither letters nor numbers, such as &*$()<>+©,.

System. An organized collection of hardware, software, and peripheral equipment that works together.

Telecommunication. Transmission of information between two computers in different locations, usually over telephone lines.

Terminal. A piece of equipment used to communicate with a computer, such as a keyboard for input, or a video monitor or printer for output.

Thermal Printer. See Printer.

Timesharing. A process whereby the facilities of a single (usually large) computer are shared by a number of users.

User Group. An association of people who meet to exchange information about a particular computer or group of computers.

Video Monitor. The computer picture screen; also called monitor, CRT.

Window. A portion of the computer's video display that is dedicated to a special purpose.

Word Processing. The entry, manipulation, editing, and storage of text using a computer.

Source: Barbar Gibson, *Personal Computers in Business,* Cupertino, CA: Apple Computer, Inc., 1982, p. 41.

Index

Segmentation variables, market, 220–223

Selengut, Stanley, 74

Self-development activities, 9–10

Self employment, 89, 96

Self-employment tax, 142

Self-improvement activities, 9–10

Sentry Insurance Company, 79

Service to people, 4–5

Services, why consumers buy, 207–209

7–S System of Management, 171–172

Shamu Stadium, 65

Shapiro, Albert, 102

Shapiro, Stanley J., 225

Shares of stock
  common, 164
  preferred, 164–165

Sheehy, Gail, 102

Sherburne Corporation, 46

Shockley, William, 324

Short-term notes, 258

Silver River, 42

Silverman, Sharon, 321

Six Flags Corporation, 64

Six Flags over Texas, 29

Ski resorts, 68

Small Business Administration, 217, 313

Small Business Reporter, 100

Smart, Neil C., 82

Smith, Adam, 22

Software, advantages and disadvantages of, 339

Software, computer, 338

Software selection, computer, 338–340

Sole proprietorship, 155–160

Sole proprietorship, advantages of, 157–158
  ease of dissolution, 158
  freedom to act, 158
  high personal incentives, 157
  less expensive to establish, 158
  privacy in financial statements, 158
  tax savings, 158

Sole proprietorship, disadvantages of, 159–160
  lack of continuity, 159
  limited capital, 159
  limited talent, 159
  possible heavier taxation, 159–160
  unlimited personal liability, 159

South America, 285

Spectator sports, 9

Spinoza, 288

Spirit of Enterprise, The, 21

Sportstown Athletics, 247

Sri Lanka, 45

St. John's River, 42

Staff functions, 183

Staff, hiring, 190–199
  compensating and training, 190–201

Staff, working with, 185–186

Stallone, Sylvester, 121

Standard of care, 298, 299–300

Stars Hall of Fame, 64

Starting a Leisure Service Business, 123–152

Statements, financial, 255–261

Statler, Ellsworth M., 47–49

Statute of Frauds, 311–312

Statutes, 290

Staying Alive, 121

Steinfeld, Jake, 78

Stevens Point, Wisconsin, 79

Store outlets, 76–77
  department store, 76
  factory outlet, 77
  flea market, 77
  full-line discount store, 77
  off-price chain, 77
  retail-catalog showroom, 77
  specialty store, 76
  variety store, 76

Strong Vocational Interest Blank, 91

Study of Values, 91

Success, characteristics of, 97–98

Super 8 Motels, Inc., 49

Tannenbaum and Schmidt Leadership Continuum, 179

Target market, 209
  selection of, 220

Tax, operating expenses, 262

Taxation payroll, 315

Technological electronic entertainment, 10

Temporary investments, 257

Terminal, computer, 329–330

Texas, 46

Texas Instruments Corporation, 187

Theme parks, 60–66
  the Disney model, 60
  foreign investments, 65
  historical perspective, 62–54
  job opportunities, 65–66
  prospects for growth, 66

Thermal dot-matrix printer, 329